Confessions
of an
Unknown Congressman

Confessions
of an
Unknown Congressman

Mahesh Manzar

Published by
Renu Kaul Verma
Vitasta Publishing Pvt Ltd
4348/4C, Ansari Road, Daryaganj
New Delhi-110 002
info@vitastapublishing.com

ISBN 978-81-19670-47-5
© Mahesh Manzar
First Edition 2025

MRP ₹ 695

All Rights Reserved.
No part of this publication may be reproduced, stored in a retrieval system, or transmitted in any form, or by any means—electronic, mechanical, photocopying, recording or otherwise—without the prior permission of the publisher. Opinions expressed in this book are the author's own. The publisher is in no way responsible for these.

In this autobiographical work, some names have been changed to protect identity.

Edited by Team Vitasta
Layout & Cover Design by Rohit Gautam
Printed by Vikas Computer and Printers, New Delhi

Contents

Dedication
Acknowledgement

First Decade: First Flashbacks	**12-43**
1. My Baby Brother is Born	13
2. My First Seven Years	17
3. The Pull of Politics	24
4. Love Infinite	30
5. A Poet is Born	39
Second Decade: Audacious Ascendancy	**44-87**
1. New Beginnings	45
2. The Power of Words	53
3. The Rise of Indira Gandhi	61
4. Awakenings	63
5. Growing Up, Almost Overnight	72
6. Discovering the Poet's Voice	80
Third Decade: Youthful Yearnings	**88-153**
1. Proximity to Power	89
2. Joining the Youth Congress	93

3.	A High-Flying Flag Idea	98
4.	The Excesses of Emergency	100
5.	A Nation in Turmoil	103
6.	Trouble at the Personal Front	107
7.	A Poetry Mentor	113
8.	Distress in Person and in Politics	123
9.	A Corrupt Congress Creeps Back	129
10.	A Momentous Blow	135

Fourth Decade: Thriving Thirties — 154-223

1.	A Harmless Poet in a Political Scenario	155
2.	Arguments and Misunderstandings	173
3.	Lessons from Mr Clean	178
4.	A New Home and New Alliances	185
5.	You Win Some, You Lose Some	192
6.	A Change in Fortunes	199
7.	A Poetic Tribute to Rajiv Gandhi	205
8.	Unseen Battles, Unspoken Wounds	211
9.	Scams, Corruption, and Some Priceless Moments	217

Fifth Decade: Exuberant Evolution — 224-384

1.	A Time of Liberalisation	225
2.	Politics and Family Matters	231
3.	The Dark Side of Politics	236
4.	The Decline of the Congress Party	240
5.	Upwardly Mobile on the Personal Front	257
6.	Kingmaker and Right Hand of Sheila Dikshit	261
7.	My Growing Spiritual Leanings	272
8.	Radharani's Blessings for Me	274
9.	Trouble on Several Fronts	288
10.	Shayar-e-Azeem	294
11.	Of Politicians, Brokers and Kalals	299
12.	Keeping the Faith	302

13. The Politics of Relationships	308
14. Merchant of Love	314
15. Admissions Saga	320
16. *Manzar Dar Manzar* Takes Shape	324
17. Politics Without Patriotism	330
18. *Ek Shaam Mahesh Manzar Ke Naam*	335
19. Outcast at Home, but Popular Outside	347
20. More Trouble at Home and Outside	355
21. Making Modi Retreat	365
22. A Dinner Party	372

Sixth Decade: Wins & Woes — 385-467

1. So Near and Yet So Far	386
2. *Man ka ho ya na ho, sab achhchha*	397
3. Family Matters	408
4. In Search of Enlightenment	424
5. Wedding Bells	432
6. Dark Depths of Depression	437
7. Climbing Back	451
8. Life Around IIC	461

Seventh Decade: Spiritual Sixties — 468-524

1. High on Translations	469
2. IIC Diplomacy Vs Home Wars	476
3. Blessed at Mt Kailash	484
4. A Spiritual High and a New Low	489
5. Domestic Upheaval and an MOU	493
6. The Pandemic Years	504
7. Stuck in the Status Quo	512
8. A Journey of Love Infinite	519

Aum Sai Ram

In the Memory of
Shri Bhagwat Prasad

My Beloved Father
Gurudev, Friend, Companion,
Inspiration
and to the
Best Man Ever in My Life

Mahesh Manzar
98100 78500, 98100 78509
011 41 827 827

The author paying floral tributes at Hz Nizamuddin Aulia Mazar, with late Rajesh Khanna (Film Actor, contesting June 1992 by-election from New Delhi) & Mr Salman Khurshid, (Union Foreign Affairs Minister); before starting the campaign.

The author with Late Rajesh Khanna (MP) during a political programme in New Delhi, August 1993.

The author being blessed by Parents: Sh Bhagwat Prasad & Smt Shanti Devi at his engagement ceremony at Taj Mansingh Hotel, New Delhi on 3 Feb 1980.

The author and wife on their wedding day (7 Feb 1980) at Convention Hall, Ashoka Hotel, New Delhi.

The author with Poetry Guru Sh Shankar Dutt "Kumar Pashi" (Left) at his First All India Mushaira & Kavi Sammean at Gwalior on 14 January 1980.

The author with Hon'ble Congress President Sonia Gandhi at a political function in New Delhi, July 1999.

The author with Hon'ble Prime Minister of India, Rajiv Gandhi at PM House on 10 May 1989.

The author with Hon'ble Congress President, Sonia Gandhi at a political function in New Delhi, July 1999.

At the launch of ***Manzar Dar Manzar*** in Hindi & Urdu at IHC in New Delhi on 20 Jan 2002. (From Right: The Author, Prof G C Narang, Kamleshwar, Sibety Razi, Prof K K Tiwari, Vasant Sathe, Sheila Dikshit (CM, Delhi, speaking), Mani Shankar Aiyar (Presiding), Dr Balram Jakhar, Deepchand Bandu, J P Agarwal, Kanhaiya Lal Poswal and Makhmoor Sayeedi.)

Dancer Padma Shri Geeta Chandran, dancing on my ghazals sung by Sudeep Banerjee at the launch ceremony on 20 Jan 2002.

(Left) The author with Vasant Sathe & (Right) Dr Balram Jakhar at the launch on 20 Jan 2002.

(Left) Prof Gopi Chand Narang releasing Urdu Version & (Right) Kamleshwar, Hindi version of my poetry on 20 Jan 2002.

Sajjan Kumar (MP) felicitated the Poet with a Shawl at the launch ceremony on 20 Jan 2002. Also seen in the picture Dr B N Singh. (Right) The poet addressing the gathering.

Suneet Aiyar felicitated her husband Mani Shankar Aiyar who presided over the function on 20 Jan 2002, with the artists, poet & his wife.

Hon'ble Vice President of India M Hamid Ansari releasing the English translations of my poetry ***The Essence of My Spirit*** in the presence of my Family, my Mentor Mani Shankar Aiyar & translator, Meenu Minocha on 9 June 2014, New Delhi.

Hon'ble President of India Pranab Mukherjee releasing the French translations of my poetry ***A La Recherche De Moi-Même; In Search of The Self*** (English) at Rashtrapati Bhavan in the presence of my mentor Mani Shankar Aiyar & my wife, on 29 March 2017.

Acknowledgements

I would like to record here my profound debt of gratitude to my Sadguru Sai Baba, Shirdi, with whose Divine Grace, this book has come into existence.

I express my deepest gratitude to my mentor Mani Shankar Aiyar who helped me enormously right from approving the idea of penning down the story of my life but also in bringing my autobiography to a satisfactory conclusion.

I thank with all my heart, my four gracious goddesses named Dr Kavita Sharma, Prof Anamika, Meenu Minocha, and Madeena Mir, who from time to time during these five long years helped me mainly, suggesting what not to be included in my story—a bit complex, complicated and contradictory, thus, reducing my 3 lakh words to 2.12 lakh. So, I can say what comes in my book is half of my story.

Things have a way of working themselves out, with the divine grace of god almighty. Else, it was truly a herculean task for me.

However, I not only enjoyed this wonderful journey, but re-lived as well, the main events of my life.

A life lived twice.

Finally, I would also like to thank my esteemed publisher, Renu Kaul Verma and competent editor Reena Singh for accepting and editing 2.12 lakh words to approximately 1.5 lakh of my autobiography.

Mahesh Manzar

New Delhi
10 Feb, 2025

FIRST DECADE
FIRST FLASHBACKS

Chapter 1

My Baby Brother is Born

'A TINY BABY boy has come into the family!'

My Bua's voice echoed around the small courtyard of the house in Chandni Chowk, Old Delhi, on that night of 18 August 1956, where I lay asleep with my father, two sisters and two brothers. Snatched from the arms of Morpheus, I groggily sat up, unable to grasp the sudden excitement pervading the atmosphere. My father hastily dashed towards a bundle my aunt was holding up, not unlike a victory stance! My father brought the bundle close to my face and said, 'Oh Mahesh, see your new playmate…a brother!'

The new addition, lovingly called Babloo, was jubilantly welcomed into the family and soon became everyone's heartbeat. Ours was a joyful family, loving each other, eating together, sometimes even from the same plate. We used to have our share of fights as well, but they only added a spicy depth to our bonding. As he grew up, Babloo exhibited a deeply spiritual bent of mind. Even as a tiny child, he loved to distribute prasad that our mother used to bring from the temple every Tuesday. He was an intelligent and happy child, spreading cheer wherever he went. Whenever my elder sister and I happened to be fighting, which we did quite often, he would pick up a stick and threaten us. We would run helter-skelter from him and would have to invariably hide to escape his energetic fury.

That indeed was a sad day when this precious bundle succumbed to diphtheria soon after his second birthday. The whole family was plunged into grief as even in that short span of time, he had created a deep space in our hearts!

***

In 1937, at the age of thirteen, my father came to Delhi and got a job as an assistant accountant at a wholesale dry fruit and spice merchant for a salary of Rs 12, a princely amount for his age. That was the first step in his journey to prosperity and in proving himself to be a self-made man.

He has been a true role model to me; hardworking and dedicated. In my life I have regarded only a handful of people as my role models, my father, my mentor Shankar Dutt Kumar Pashi and Rajiv Gandhi, but my father's influence has always been tremendous. I could even go as far as to say that I have not met a man better than my father till today! I had a marvelous relationship with him right from the beginning, allowing us to work closely together at our clothes shop till the day he left this world. We could talk for hours and often people would mistake us for friends rather than father and son. Even today, I begin my day first by bowing to the Divine and then greeting Father, asking his forgiveness if I had ever hurt him in any way and feeling deep gratitude to him for being a special component in my journey of life.

Soon after his marriage, he shifted to a rented accommodation in Chandni Chowk and in 1963, managed to buy a very good house in Sitaram Bazaar that had once belonged to one of the family members of the Delhi Cloth Mills. Singlehandedly, he had rose from a salary of twelve rupees at the age of thirteen to buying his own house before he turned forty. His was of a thrifty nature, an inherent characteristic of his clan, and it was this that stood him in good grace throughout his life. There are only two things that matter to our clan—to have a good house and to marry daughters off in a royal manner and for both these events, they love to save a lot. Thankfully, I too display traits of our clan and have managed to live a prosperous life through my inherited thrifty nature.

***

In the summer of 1962, my father took us to Kashmir for a month-long holiday. Kashmir is famous for its delicious apples and mangoes and I remember an incident where my father once brought two kg of mangoes and my elder sister Simran and I started fighting over them.

'Give them to me,' I yelled excitedly. 'I want to have them first!'

'No!' was Simran's instant response, 'I will have them first!' A scuffle ensued as the two of us began to pull at the basket of mangoes.

This infuriated our father. 'Hey, stop that, the two of you! I am fed up with your quarrels! Once and for all, it has to end!' He placed the basket on one side and made both of us sit next to it, ordering us to eat as many as we could. My sister joyfully attacked the beneficence but I somehow felt degraded, as if we had been animals to fight so and succumbed to tears. It wasn't as if we were not getting enough to eat. We were provided with so many different things to eat, yet we were fighting on the size of mangoes! That incident made me realise the importance of camaraderie and never after that did I fight with my siblings! My longing for mangoes and all other kinds of fruits too, seemed to have got satiated! This incident proved to be a turning point in my life, for my attitude towards food changed. I became mindful about my eating habits, having only the essential, that too only when I felt hungry. It all proved to be a blessing in disguise as it has helped me maintain my slim built comfortably.

I was truly awestruck by the beauty of the Kashmir Valley. Snowcapped mountains, meadows, the vibrant surroundings of lush green, the flora, the fauna, everything appealed to the sense of beauty in me, touching the core of my being. I was spellbound by nature and the God-made beauty that surrounded us.

The icing on the cake of that holiday was the presence of two superstars, Raj Kapoor and Pran, who happened to be shooting at Pahalgahm, near Srinagar. Meeting such renowned personalities in person was nothing less than a magical experience. I felt as if I had experienced ultimate beauty in all aspects—of handsome men, beautiful Kashmiri women, magnificent mountains, wonderful sceneries, bonding with family and most of all, a deep love for everything in and around me!

We spent a month in Srinagar visiting nearby places and temples. I was fascinated at how people worshipped the Goddess, with the temple priest pricking a devotee's thumb and pinching out blood to anoint the Goddess. It was a most astounding act of devotion that I had ever seen! However, later, thinking deep on this act of religious belief, I understood why someone would go to this extreme extent just to please the Goddess. The following lines said by a poet exemplify the justification for sheer devotion:

Tu dil me toh aata hai samajh me nahi aata,
mai jaan gaya bus teri pehchaan yahi hai

And yet, it is the nature of the Divine to remain beyond comprehension. Another well-known poet has worded it precisely.

Jo samajh me aa gaya
Woh Khuda kyun ker hua

(If fathomed clearly
How can God remain Godly)

Chapter 2

My First Seven Years

IT IS SAID that the first seven years lay the foundation of a person's whole life. Circumstances and events have always played a major role in the shaping of my character and destiny. The very circumstance of me being born practically at the doorstep of the great Mirza Ghalib must have had something to do with igniting the spark of poetry in my being. I was always either humming or singing at the top of my voice.

When I was four, one of my uncles had come to visit us. Watching me enthusiastically rendering ditties, he playfully asked, 'Oh Majnu, where is your Laila?'

I seemed to have become more energetic at his question and dashed around the verandah chanting, 'Laila O my Laila!' Not only did I run around, but also dashed my chest against the wall at times, perhaps to show the intensity the words had roused in me.

I think I must have been a precocious child, for I was already aware of deep emotions that simmer beneath the surface. I used to sleep next to my mother and occasionally would become aware of my father's presence, sharing the same quilt. The muted whispers and strange scufflings somehow left a deep imprint on me, rousing a part of my mind much ahead of its time. It laid the groundwork of my passionate nature, at the same time, stirring a deep sense of empathy for the people of those times, who were deprived of the privacy they needed for their intimate moments. I was relieved of my embarrassing situation only about four years later, when I was considered old enough to sleep separately. But there can be no denying the fact that my father was my first Love Guru!

That ignited yet dormant passion would emerge in the performances demanded by my elders, for watching me perform my Laila act became a form of entertainment for them. Everyone would revel in teasing me into looking for my Laila. It would trigger me and off, I would go in a wild search for a non-existent Laila, banging my chest against the walls like an ardent lover!

Time changed the question from 'Where is your Laila' to 'What kind of bride will you have?'

And I would cheerfully announce 'One that will make you all stare, open-mouthed!'

It almost became a self-fulfilling prophecy when I got married to a comely beauty. There can thus be no denying the actuality that I was in every way, Divinely guided and was ever receiving messages in my subconscious, which would often come out of my mouth unbeknownst, giving credence to the fact that the Divine does speak through us. Not forgetting that even the act of the frenzied lover or the Majnu which I used to display, has become my fate, for even after attaining the age of seventy years, I continue to live an unfulfilled life, devoid of an absolute love that could fulfill me emotionally, physically and spiritually. Who knew that which I had displayed so innocently at the age of four was actually expressing the Divine Act of Premonition at that time!

In about 1960, a Punjabi family from Lahore moved next to us in our Chandni Chowk area. It was a big family of five children, all sons, the eldest being Dev. The lady of the house, Mohini, must have been forty years old, yet seemed truly fascinating to my six-year-old heart. She was fair and beautiful, with an aristocratic look, totally unlike her husband, who was tanned and did nothing other than lie around the whole day. We developed family-like relationships with them and Mohiniji or Behenji as everyone called her, would often invite me to play in her home while she remained engrossed in her chores. 'Kaku come and play here; I like to see you gamboling around.' Her personality, her unique charisma and her figure made her a perfect beauty, making me feel a kind of pull towards her.

It became a norm for me to be constantly at their place, a part of their daily life and a silent observer of how other people lived! I think my mother was also pretty happy with this arrangement for there was no denying the fact that I was quite a handful! I was equally happy. No one checked my exuberance there and I was always given a lot of goodies to eat. What more could I ask for!

Her husband would be at home, just silently sitting or lying in the small internal courtyard. Behenji was always deeply involved in her chores, and would keep serving him something or the other every little while, revolving around him as if to be near him and would often stoop to place her cheek against his lips. My young heart felt he was no match for her personality. I never understood their kind of love, where one was just an endless giver of affection with the other receiving as if by right and yet both seemed to find a loving delight in each other's presence. My immature mind would try to grapple with the question as to how could a lady like her love someone who was totally opposite to her own personality? Shah ji, her husband, though had a friendly mien. He would regard me indulgently and would often entertain himself by asking me to pinch him.

'Come, little man! Show me your strength!' I would oblige by trying to squeeze the flesh of his abdomen between my puny fingers.

He would give a roaring laugh, 'Is that the best you can

do? Come on try harder...and harder! That seems to be a brush of butterfly wings!'

Strange man with strange tastes, yet with a luck running deep as he possessed the most beautiful lady as his wife who also loved him to the core, and five devoted sons, always standing at attention for him.

One such time when I was in their house an incident happened which wrenched my very heart and made me take a lifelong resolution. The houses we lived in were very old, with rafters and small congested storerooms that would inevitably be a home for mice. While I was playing, Behenji suddenly began screaming and jumping, and I could not understand why. She had been cleaning out the store room when it so happened that a small mouse got into her lower garment—salwar. She jumped around the courtyard, trying to get rid of it! I stood there, stupefied, my young brain unable to cope with the dire situation being enacted in front of my eyes. She called out my name, 'Kaku! Kaku!' but I gazed stupidly, powerless in my bewilderment. No one else was at home that day and thankfully my mother heard her screams and hastily ran over to see what had happened. Behenji was running round and round the courtyard, while I was looking on in stupefaction, on the verge of bursting into tears! I hated myself for not being able to do anything about it, yet since that day something within me changed. My valiant heart made a resolve that whenever I came across a damsel in distress, I would do my utmost to help her in any way required, at any given hour, even if I had to go out of my way. I have always had a soft corner for the fair sex in my heart and never hesitate to be of service to them.

My mother immediately took charge and catching hold of Bhenji's arm, guided her into the nearest room. The culprit must have been found and released for peace descended back on the house!

Behenji's eldest son was a strapping lad of twenty-two summers and my hero. My childish heart adored him and I would try to mimic his actions and style. The water closet used to be on the roof and whenever Dev went to use it, he would sing Hindi songs loudly. I would copy them exactly, much to the amusement of my siblings!

It so happened that Dev fell in love with a young girl Rama, who lived a few houses down our street. Those were very strict times and casual interaction between the opposite sexes was not encouraged. Oh, the joy of discovering each other through coy glances is indeed a lost art today! Slowly those glances became more intense and a point came when a closer interaction was longed for. Dev zeroed in on me, deciding to put my devotion to the test.

'Will you do something for me?'

'Of course, whatever you say!' I heard myself say.

'Go and give this letter to Rama,' he handed a missive to me.

How could have I been immune to the charms of the lady with whom my hero was so smitten? I joyfully seized the opportunity to have a closer look at my heart throb.

Checking if the coast was clear, I scooted up the narrow stairs leading to Rama's house and knocked on her door. It had not occurred to me what I would say to whoever opened the door, but by God's Grace, she herself did so! I tentatively proffered the letter saying, 'Dev Bhai has sent this for you.'

My heart almost stopped when I found myself suddenly engulfed in soft fragrant arms and a gentle kiss was deposited on my flaming cheek.

'Oh, thank you so much! Wait here, I will be back.'

I looked around the neat courtyard as she disappeared into the nearest room. Obviously, no one was at home, else I definitely wouldn't have got such a passionate welcome!

Within minutes, she was back and handed me a paper. 'Please give this to Dev and tell him I will wait for his response.'

Carrying my trophy, the one in my heart as well, I hurried back to Dev to tell him of my successful foray, the first of many. And oh glory of glories, I would inevitably be rewarded with a sweet and sometimes with a hug or a kiss too, a secret delight which of course I never shared with Dev, and I am sure he must have wondered at my willingness to act as his messenger boy!

No one is immune to the pivotal charms of love and passion, and throughout my childhood, I was aware of the stirrings of a deep passion, wherein I could appreciate the profound beauty within a woman and admire it from my core. It fascinated my subconscious being, whether it was a woman as mature as forty years of age or as young as a svelte twenty-year-old, and despite my being just a child of six years, their innate graciousness would enthrall me and make mellow movements in my heart that were difficult to express or show in any manner.

Little did anyone know that I too felt the throb of passion in my heart for it would race madly the moment Rama showed how grateful she was to me. The way she expressed her affection, had me pining for love from that time onwards and therein began a deep longing for my own perfect mate who would similarly fulfil me and match the vibes that I experienced when I received the utmost affection from the one who had captured my heart at that time. The exchange of letters and the hugs were my first experiences about how beautiful it felt to be at the centre of a loving attention. It was not only making a romantic out of me but also a poet. Feeling the flow of love like oceanic surges gave my soul a high, quite like riding a wave of a love odyssey!

Even though Rama was fourteen years my senior, the way she made me feel was an unforgettable experience, rousing in me my first impulse of love! It was just not her, Dev too, would pour his feelings of gratitude, both for being the link between and also a recipient of his deep feelings of passion, into my tender, hungry soul. Not that I much understood the sentiments involved, but the intensity of his emotions did seep into my being, fueling the already simmering fire of passion there. They once decided to reward me with the most memorable experience ever, taking me to a restaurant in Kamla Nagar to treat me royally to a cup of tea. Almost like a celebration of love, the incident got etched in my mind and there and then I decided that whenever I felt the stirrings of love for a girl, I too would add that touch of intrigue to my romance through written missives. Perhaps, due to this incident I began to consider writing and became a conduit of love.

Chapter 3

The Pull of Politics

BY THE TIME I was eight, I had decided on which political party I wanted to be a part of. Though my father also supported the same Congress party, I pride myself on having chosen it on my own, or rather the party chose me! My father had always been a big admirer of Pandit Jawaharlal Nehru and Indira Gandhi. My brothers, who were four and six years older to me, would always segregate me as being too young, while they hung around together. At that time, they had joined RSS and had begun attending their camps. I was fascinated by the way they were addressed with respect as the members had a habit of adding 'ji' to every name.

After the elections in 1962, there was a victory procession for Lala Shamnathji, who had won the seat in our area. The procession happened to pass down our street. My father went out into the street to congratulate and garland him and I tagged along. I started dancing in a carefree, spontaneous manner to the beats of the drums. The heavily garlanded MP took me up in his arms, and carried me along with him for quite a distance. In between, he would put me down and I would immediately break into an enthusiastic dance, much to everyone's amusement. That was my first experience of a political celebration, setting the trend for many more to come, for I have always celebrated others' victories, never having got a chance to celebrate my own! I have not just celebrated, but even stood by them till they attained ultimate victory. The incident with Lala Shamnathji however, served as a way of showing my solidarity with the ruling party. I was now very happy that I had my own party to support, different from my brothers' organisation. It really satiated me to a great extent, for now I didn't feel the need of going with my brothers. I felt I belonged.

That same year, when I was not yet nine, I became a witness to the Indo-China war. Our country was in a state of crisis and each family was ready to send their sons to the army to fight for the country against the Chinese. The worst hit was the economic condition of our country. It was, at this time, that I faced another life changing incident that really filled me with wonder at the patriotic feelings of my countrymen. A huge procession, led by a very dynamic, tall man, was going through Chandni Chowk. He was holding one end of a long cloth, a bedsheet perhaps, while the other corners were being held by three other people. The procession was moving forward with patriotic slogans filling the air, with many participating emotionally. To my astonishment, I saw ladies taking off their jewellery and tossing them into the sheet. Even from the balconies and roofs of the houses around, people were tossing gold and money into that sheet. It moved me to the core to see how even after not being in a good financial situation themselves, people from all strata of life were willingly giving away their savings for the noble cause of soldiers fighting the war for our country. This overwhelmed me and I too joined the procession, intermittently clutching the edge of the sheet, while my tears continued to flow. I walked with them for quite a distance, adding my voice to theirs. The participants also noticed me and here, too, I was much feted and appreciated, that despite being so young, I was able to understand the gravity of the matter. That gave me my first taste of social activism in a political scenario and a glimpse into the fact that a cause could spark off a strong patriotic fervour in our countrymen.

My heart has always ached to see how some selfish politicians could wage a war against another country for resolving their own selfish motives, without giving a thought to the fact of so many innocents, who have nothing to do with it, suffer directly or indirectly. The soldiers, who come from different backgrounds or status, are wasted away fighting a war they never started and would rather avoid. They are forced to leave their homes and families behind, as they fight far away from home. There is nothing to be gained out of war, only loss of lives on both sides, something totally meaningless. The vagaries of war hold no meaning for bureaucrats who initiate it as they continue to live their luxurious lives, not at all affected by the sacrifices of the soldiers fighting at the front. I saw how it affected each individual on a personal level, especially the families who lose a loved one, sometimes the only breadwinner of the family. War is indeed absolutely useless, no matter what the reason.

***

Time went by, and I remained engrossed in studies and books. I was not the kind to be loitering around with other lads of my age, for I never felt the urge to mingle or play with my peers. Rarely if ever was I to be found in their company as I considered them to be wasting their energy in illogical activities. I think I was mature much beyond my years and felt happier in the company of older people, feeling intensely piqued by the intricacies of relationships, a trait that only deepened with age.

My heart always lingered in the memory of the one who had captivated it the first time. Her fragrance as she had engulfed me the very first day always inundated my senses. Her delicate softness inspired a yearning in my vulnerable mind, making me weave beautiful stories in my head. Definitely the foundation of both my romantic nature and love for poetry was laid back then!

It was thus no surprise that I manifested a love of my very own when I was all of nine years old. Neera, a wheatish beauty, perhaps a couple of years older, with beautiful lustrous hair, a contagious smile and kissable skin was the one to mesmerise me at first sight. She was a friend of my elder sister, and lived right next door. She would often be at our place playing with my sister and myself. Those were wonderful balmy afternoons when all of us would dress up in my mother's sarees and dance to tuneful songs.

Slowly she began to gain a stronger hold on my tender heart and it became so that just her thoughts were enough to rouse ripples of a delightful sensation in every cell of my immature body. Wallowing in these new found feelings, I felt a need to pour them out and recalled my resolve to do so through a letter, whenever I experienced love. Thus giving in to the compulsive urge to let her know that she vibrated within my heart, I composed my very first love letter. Budding sensations of love have the power to create an extraordinary world within but it gains relevance only when the other is there. Hence an urgency to deliver the painstakingly composed letter at the earliest was very much present!

The air of that February of 1963 was redolent with the colors of Holi, the much-loved Spring festival, and a fledgling love. Intrigue and passion laced the atmosphere with a naughtiness that allowed the youngsters a certain laxity, which would have been frowned upon at other times. Finding an opportunity, I slipped my missive into Neera's hand. Surprised, she looked at me and seemed to catch the import of my expression. Withdrawing a little aside, she quickly opened the letter and began to go through it. My heart was in my mouth and butterflies were having a field day in my stomach as anxiously I focused on her face. Reaching the end, she slowly raised her eyes to look at me, blushing beautifully. Was that a positive sign? My heartbeat accelerated with suspense, but suddenly, to my great shock, she tore my letter to bits!

Throwing caution to the winds, I burst out, 'Oh, why did you do that?'

There was a strict maturity in her response, 'Do you know what will happen to us if someone was to read this letter of yours? What nonsense are you writing!'

It was as if a jolt went through me! I stared at her openmouthed, all those dreams in my head crashing around me like ninepins. Those were growing years where my manly dignity was still in its nascent stage and certainly not up to receiving such a hard blow! I felt really angry at the rejection and thereafter refused to even look at her. Somewhere her own action of rejection was also irking her, for she was bothered by my indifference. One day, she really got after me.

'Come on, Kaku, let's play.'

'No, I will not play with you.'

'Oh Kaku, stop being angry; let's be friends again.'

I was on my high horse. 'I don't want to be friends with you.'

'Okay tell me what should I do to make you give up your anger? Shall I bring a gift for you?'

'I don't want a gift.'

'Oh ho! Should I dance for you, then!'

A devilish streak in me surfaced and I said, 'Yes, dance!'

Caught in her own trap, she had no option but to comply. Singing a popular song, she started to dance to its rhythm. After a few steps, she said, 'Is that enough?'

The devil was still at work, so I roared, 'No, no, keep on dancing! Your punishment is still not over!'

She really wanted to win me over so continued to dance in front of me and finally, we both collapsed laughing on the floor, back to our earlier footing!

Years later, visions of this scene came to mind, a sort of déjà vu feeling, when a movie of that time had a similar incident, where the heroine is forced to dance by villains in front of a captive hero. It was as if the idea had been stolen from my mind.

Chapter 4

Love Infinite

I MUST HAVE been a little over four years old when my mother began sending me out on small errands.

'Here Kaku, go and get a gourd from the vegetable vendor. Tell him to give the lower portion.'

Those were the days when even daily vendors used to get involved with the families they catered to, exchanging family backgrounds and keeping track of members.

Feeling very important, I took the proffered money and bag and skipped outside.

'Dada, please give half of the gourd. Lower half.' I lisped enthusiastically, handing the money to him.

'Oh, you have become very big! Buying vegetables!' he laughed at my tininess as he handed the gourd to me.

I ran back into the house, proudly handing my trophy to my mother.

'Oh no! I told you to bring the lower half! This is the upper one! You didn't tell him to give the lower one?'

'I did! I did!' I jumped up and down to prove my point.

'I am sure you didn't!' was her unjustified accusation. 'Go back and tell him to change it.'

Snatching the bag from my mother, I raced back outside seething at being wrongly accused.

A little tornado then confronted the laughing vendor, demanding an exchange.

'Yes, yes, I know I gave you the wrong part. I was just teasing you! Calm down, big man and take this!'

Still fuming, I took the bag back inside and handed it to my mother.

'Yes, now it is fine! Always check what you get.'

That was one of the many life lessons that gained importance in my life. Every incident, every interaction happens as a process of learning, laying the foundation of one's nature.

Each moment that we live and breathe, it is essential for us to focus on what is happening here and now or else we miss out on the present.

As I say it 'It's called present, a gift from God, given to us humans so it should be utilised in the best possible manner and it should be treated with utmost attention to every detail.'

Everyone, who is always looking into the future for their fulfillment and any happiness, needs to understand this thought. It is essential to live in the here and now to be able to comprehend that the present moment is where one should actually be living. Awareness should be given to the moment that we are in, as each moment that we are living and breathing is where we are one with the Almighty, and that is when we are walking in awareness. The incident that occurred at that tender age left an everlasting imprint on my mind, something that I recall even in my advanced age, as an important life lesson for me, teaching me a lot. I realise now that even then I was very much aware of my surroundings and my environment, for they were helping me grow as an individual. I developed a knack for being someone who would observe things that a majority of people brush off as normal or don't comprehend the extraordinariness in any event.

***

Life has always been kind to me and I have ever been blessed with more than what I could contemplate or desire for, making me constantly thank God for everything given to me. Gratitude has been a part of my learning process since childhood. Another thing that makes me feel really blessed is the boundless love that I have received in innumerable forms from most of the people with whom I interacted regularly. Never did I ever feel not cared for or left out. Yet it is essential that love should not be looked upon as something that comes only from a beloved; it can come in various ways, like the first source of love is the family. I had been surrounded by a lot of love right from childhood and that proved to be nurturing for me. It is said: *Only a cup full can give another.* So, that is what I have been, a cup full of overflowing, infinite love. And it is this love that has facilitated all spheres of my life!

But no manner of love can compare to the love received from grandparents, and I have received oodles of it. My father's parents lived in Pilkuwa, so every holiday, until I was about ten years, found us making our way there. My mother would make about 15 kg of *laddoos and mathris,* filling a big tin with them, to take there. Sometimes, only my elder sister and I would go with her, while the other three remained at home with my father. Those holidays would be pure enjoyment, feted by the grandparents. In the afternoons, my grandmother would love to treat us with a kind of local ice cream, more like ice lollies. But she would never buy for herself, preferring to spend only on us children. But we all shared with her and she usually ended up having the lion's share!

My maternal grandparents were equally caring and would treat us royally when we visited them at Baghola, near Ballabgarh. My grandfather ran a shop which offered an innumerable variety of stuff ranging from fresh vegetables, fruits, sweets to even stationery and cloth! It was as if we could get whatever we wanted from that one shop itself, whether fruits, sweets or pencils. One of my uncles was a tailor and he occupied a corner of that unique departmental store and would often get orders from the customers who came to the shop to purchase cloth. This uncle of mine was a pretty grounded person, mellow by nature. Later on, we worked together on a prestigious and profitable project.

What I realised early in life was that my father was at a better position in society and that demands respect, even within the family. We always would get VIP treatment from not only them but also the neighbours! It is a fallacy that all children are equal for parents, for the one who does better usually has a better place in their heart.

My mother regarded me as being the most spiritual in my family, for according to her, when she was carrying me, she would read the scriptures, particularly *Bhagavad Gita* daily and said I was blessed with wisdom while I was still in the womb. In actual fact, about that time, she had known Guru Maharaj Paramhansji of Uttarakhand, and he had encouraged her to read the *Gita*. He had taught her how to meditate, a practice she continued throughout her life. Maybe, this helped me connect more deeply with the *Gita*, for reading it later in life helped me to uplift myself from depression.

I recall an unfortunate incident when I was about ten. The maternal side of the family was not as close-knit as the paternal side. Despite being blessed with a big family comprising two daughters and seven sons, three of whom were in government posts while the other sons had been set up in business enterprises, my maternal grandparents were not at the receiving end of the love and care that they deserved in their geriatric phase. Seeing them tormented by her own brothers, my mother would often try to persuade my grandparents to live with us. However, irrational rules laid down by society ostracized parents living in a married daughter's home, so they would refuse to come, despite my father's entreaties, as well.

At that time, it was rare for children to abandon their parents, now a common feature of our so-called modern society, where parents are often treated as discarded furniture, to be done away with as soon as children wish to break out of the close-knit bond that once existed.

This attitude has given rise to the concept of old-age homes where children can dump their parents without guilt as they feel by paying for their upkeep, they are doing their duty towards them! But it was not so in those times, when living with the family was the norm and large families living under the same roof was customary. Nuclear families were a rare phenomenon, unlike today. It pains my heart to see that old parents are nowadays considered to be superfluous and breaking ties with them has become an easy task. This collapsing of the family structure has brought nothing but torment and loss of essential *sanskaars* or traditional values within each family, for children are now being brought up bereft of them.

Maybe my maternal family was a trendsetter for they showed these traits of modern times, then itself. I had seven maternal uncles, yet none of them wanted to take care of their parents. Three meals a day was all that they required for they had no medical expenses and even did all their household work themselves. Each uncle was bound to keep them for only a month, yet that too would prove to be burdensome, making him leave them at the next brother's place a day earlier, saying his thirty days were up. It was no wonder then that my grandfather went into deep depression and one day, fed up of his life, left home without informing anyone. No last rites were ever done for him, for no trace could be found of him although searches were initiated. My grandmother kept hoping for his return for a year or so and then she too moved on into the other world, brokenhearted. The lack of blessings is evident in all of my uncles' lives, for hurting parents is the biggest sin.

This incident made me understand the stark reality of the real world where parents work their whole life to set up their children in a good way, yet those very children don't feel it incumbent on themselves to take care of the parents once they are old. The logic of holding onto their money and property till the very end and then distributing that through the offices of a will thus seems much more sensible. It is indeed harsh, but the fact is one cannot trust even one's own children and should definitely take steps to ensure their own security.

***

Going down the memory lane back to my school days, one of my maternal uncles who worked as a teacher, at my father's instigation, got me admitted to the prestigious Delhi Public School, the first co-educational school in our city. It was a turning point in my life, where I was awestruck with the humongous premises of the school and the large playground. To the uncouth lad from Old Delhi, it all appeared magical. Our class teacher, Jennifer, a Christian lady of poise, grace and a charming demeanor had a bobcut hairstyle, which fascinated me. Even at the tender age of four years, the inherent ability in every male made me notice her oversized bust and peculiar gait that drew attention to her proportions. She is still the most beautiful thing in the entire school memory that I often recall, which brings a smile to my face, even today. It was the first time I had seen any lady wear skirts and high heels and it added to the charm of the school.

My mother used to daily pack me a lunch of *parantha* and lemon pickle and sometimes, during lunch time, my teacher would share her lunch of sandwiches with me, helping herself to mine. That was another first, for till then, I had never eaten a sandwich! It was almost like trading of our pure love for each other! I was mesmerised with her completely and my subconscious mind was filled with fondness for her, forging a special bond. Her persona left a deep impact on my tender heart!

My life at that school was shortlived due to the commute that was cumbersome for me as well as my mother. Living in Chandni Chowk, my school bus picked me up from Ghanta Ghar every morning and dropped me off at 3 pm; my mother had to pick me up in a rickshaw. One such fateful day, we had an accident when our rickshaw overturned on being hit by another vehicle. My mother hurt her back while I sustained an injury on my head. That was the end of my school life at DPS. I was transferred to another school in our vicinity.

Anglo Sanskrit Victoria Jubilee Higher Secondary School was a prestigious and popular school in Daryaganj. It was quite old, presented a mix of western and Indian education, and was for boys only. I was given admission in the first standard as my father enhanced my age to five years, so that I could continue my education without missing out on anything.

In retrospect, looking at my school years, I have formulated a theory, one which I am sure many psychologists concur with and that is 'Appreciatively encouraging a child goes a long way in developing the personality of the child.'

A child feels nurtured and cared for in every way by the teachers during the formative years of his life, and that becomes the foundation of building a character that can withstand life's storms. I believe that it is essential that teachers who are responsible for the personality development of a child should be aware of the impact of their actions and words on the psyche of the child they interact with during school time. I was fortunate to be a favourite of all my teachers for I was quite sharp. They gave me the requisite encouragement that helped me outgrow my own inadequacy of not being agile enough like my classmates. I was a bit shorter than the average kids of my age, weighing me down with a complex that would not allow me to participate in anything that involved physical activity.

Yet, though I was short, I was so full of energy that I never could sit in one place even while the class was in progress. I recall a rather funny incident, when I was in the fourth class, when the teacher, Mr Kaul, a Kashmiri, annoyed at my fidgety nature and my trotting around in class, gave me the sobriquet of *Chuhaa*, meaning a mouse.

'Why do you keep jumping around the room like a *Chuhaa*?' was his anguished demand, much to the amusement of the other students, who roared with laughter at my new name.

My classmates snapped it up and I was bombarded by this name from all sides, a fact that made my teacher feel somewhat guilty, for though he used it only once, it stuck with me for a long time. I felt very conscious, attributing the name to my stature, which was probably the outcome of my non-existent diet as I barely used to have half a chapatti at mealtimes and was not the athletic kind, either. It was sometime later that I realised that it was no reflection on my height, but rather on my restlessness. I would be jumping all over the room, refusing to sit at my assigned place, always chatting with classmates or playing the fool in class. The appellation remained with me, carrying over to the next class as well, becoming synonymous with my personality, confining my real name to only the school attendance register!

The extent of the influence of those formative school years can still be seen in my nature. The moniker endowed on me somehow made me develop a chip on my shoulder as my shortness has ever been a sore point. Later incidents only strengthened that chip, traces of which can be observed even today.

At the time of competitive dramatics at the primary level, I was given the part of a clerk, while another boy who was rather tall and fair, played the lead role of Principal. That was a big jolt to my self-esteem as I felt it was again a reflection on my short lanky stature, for I was definitely brighter than the other in studies, always scoring more than him. It motivated me to give my best, and much to our delight, we won the third prize.

That day when the picture with our school principal was being clicked, I was sitting right next to him dressed in formals, with a tie that made me look smart, my arm resting on the Principal's chair. That was my first brush with a powerful and influential personality and it made me feel really buoyant. That feeling became so addictive that it became an integral part of my life in the coming years. I have always been drawn to powerful people like a magnet, prodding me to forge numerous relationships with the powerful, both in social circles and in political scenarios. I believe that the foundation was laid at the very moment when I felt drawn towards the personality and power of our school principal.

One incident from my childhood that has always haunted me involved Daya, a young and beautiful woman who was overcome by episodes of hysteria. She used to shiver and tremble as if she was possessed by a demonic spirit. Unable to understand her affliction, her husband, Tejram, and his brother used to beat her mercilessly.

One day, I saw them beating Daya and ran to tell my mother about it. She admonished Tejram for his deeds and brought Daya to our home so that she could tend to her wounds.

Chapter 5

A Poet is Born

IT IS INDEED strange but the foundation of my life as a poet reading out compositions actually got laid out in wedding ceremonies. It began with my maternal uncle's wedding back in 1961, when I was only seven years old. The wedding procession had to proceed to a village Poonahana near Agra and at that time, only the men folk and children used to go for the festivities while the womenfolk stayed back to welcome the bride when she came home. The festivities went off smoothly, with the usual fun and frolic. In those days, the groom's party was always feted and were housed in the best of places, served with the most delicious food and given special treatment. A barber, a *dhobi* and even a cobbler was especially appointed to cater to the wedding guests. The bride's family was bound to indulge them for two whole days.

Reading a poem called *Sehra*, praising the bride, the groom and the new relations, is an integral part of our weddings. It is usually read by the groom's sister's husband, but at this wedding, my father encouraged me to do so. Pitaji was an Urdu scholar and he made me practice the diction well before I read it. He was my first Urdu Guru and was very insistent on a precise pronunciation. I felt really important at being entrusted with the task and read the whole page very melodiously. I started by announcing 'Today's latest news' thrice to attract everyone's attention.

Aaj ki taaza khabar
Aaj ki taaza khabar
Aaj ki taaza khabar!

Everyone loved my recitation, overwhelming me with accolades! I was wearing a traditional sherwani and a few opined that I looked like a junior Rajinder Kumar, a venerated actor, much to my delight.

That was my first ever attempt at public speaking and its success gave my morale a tremendous boost! I was already evincing signs of being a studious child, not much inclined towards outdoor activities, unlike my brothers, who loved physical ventures along with studies. Destiny had started to shape my taste for literary pursuits from that early age, carrying on to another such memorable wedding event, a few years later.

***

It was my paternal uncle's wedding in 1963 where I was given the honour of being the groom's special companion or *sarbala* as he is called. I was dressed like him in a sherwani and turban and looked dashing. Below where we lived, were the enterprises of some cloth merchants and I was pretty friendly with their accountants. When they saw me all dressed up, they naturally wanted to know why I was dressed so nattily.

With great importance, I informed them, 'It's my uncle's wedding and I am his *sarbala!*'

'Oh, but do you know you will be asked to recite a couplet?'

'A couplet? What's that?'

'That's a ritual! All his new sisters-in-law will demand that the groom recite a couplet for them.'

Another said, 'No, not for them! For the bride!'

'Really? But they won't ask me, will they?'

'But you also have to speak there. Come on little man, demand to speak there! Remember you are the *sarbala*, demand importance.'

Puffing up, I acquiesced readily and asked, 'What will I say?'

All those accountants were out to have some mischievous fun, so one of them said, 'We will teach you. When you are asked to speak, say:

> *Chacha chachi se keh dena*
> *bhatija tum pe marta hai,*
> *agar thodi si dilvaa do*
> *tumhara kya bigadta hai!'*

> *(Uncle says to aunt*
> *I am her admirer,*
> *won't be a loss to you if you ask her*
> *to share with me some).*

Well-coached by my mentors, I made my presence felt at the wedding and when my uncle spoke his lines, I demanded to be allowed to say mine. Everyone was much amused at my forwardness and went into ecstasies when I delivered my well-prepared volley of words. Such couplets are usually called *Chhand* and are spoken in an exclusive all-women gathering, where after the formal ceremonies are over, the womenfolk of the family gather to tease the new couple, especially the groom. At those tantalising words, the women couldn't hug and kiss me enough and when the men folk heard about it, they found it rollicking fun. Suddenly, I became the most feted person around, as nobody had expected such an impish couplet from a babe's mouth. In fact, the next day, I was called to the market place as to who was the child who had rendered such an interesting couplet! I was treated very royally by them all, as a real prodigy.

That incident left a mark on my subconscious that if by speaking two lines, I could gain so much popularity, was it not worth exploring? Either the thought had a lot of power or the form had! Actually, both have power—how you express your thought, the words and the form, both combine to create poetry. I thus became a poet at the age of nine and poetry began to seep into my psyche.

***

Reminiscences of my childhood would be incomplete without mentioning my eldest sister, Shobha Jiji, eight years my senior and my favourite. My earliest memory is of her carrying me to the rooftop, where all of us siblings would love to play in the evenings. As a two and half year old, I would revel in that dusk time togetherness, giving free vent to my joyous energy by racing around. Shobha Jiji loved carrying me around, even after I was quite grown up, much to my mother's despair, who would scold her for spoiling me. Through my growing years, my closeness to Shobha Jiji deepened and she became quite adept at handling me. We shared a special bond which we did not have with the other siblings. It was an indubitable fact that, leaving aside Shobha Jiji, we brothers and sisters were of a difficult nature, me more than the others.

As I grew up, I would often accompany Shobha Jiji whenever she had to go out. It was another trait of those times that a girl could not go out unaccompanied. But the company of even a six-year-old brother was regarded as enough chaperonage. She too used to feel secure in my company while I felt really grown up going out with her as a guardian. Our love for each other got enhanced over the years. Immediately after her marriage, she took me with her to her new home, where I stayed for well over a week. Over the years, I would visit and stay with her quite often and was pretty upset when her health began to fail her in the latter part of her life. Her demise in 2012 left a yawning gap in my life.

Many incidents come to my mind of my childhood days, the fun, the pranks, the travails, and the victories. One sporting antic really stands out in my mind till today. Planning with a friend, I would somehow manage to smuggle us both into the Gandhi grounds for the annual Ramleela, entrance for which was based on passes. We would dress ourselves in our best clothes and each of us would slip in with any of the better-looking families going in. No one ever stopped or caught us, though a sinking doubt would always be there in our hearts. But we never allowed that to stop us from having fun! Once inside, we would sit in the front row, for I have always liked to be in the forefront of things. Once I even managed to go right up to the stage and had a conversation with the presenter! As a consequence, I even gained entry into the green room, made immediately beneath the stage where the characters awaited their turn to appear on stage. With wide-eyed curiosity I took in everything, and even noted the fact that the characters playing roles supporting Ram were of a sober nature while those supporting Ravana seemed to be of a rowdy kind!

When I look back over the years, I realise that being enterprising has ever been an inherent part of my nature. I have always been able to find a way of venturing into areas where no one thought it possible to enter. My natural curiosity and eagerness to know about things is at the bottom of it, as well as a craving to know what makes people tick. I love to delve deeply into people's psyche, to understand their mindset, their personal life, sometimes even enquiring about their resources and earnings, which often offends them! There is no harmful intent in my inquisitiveness, just an insatiable interest in human nature. The later years of my life are a witness to the enterprising nature of my character.

SECOND DECADE
AUDACIOUS ASCENDANCY

Chapter 1

New Beginnings

WE HAD SHIFTED to our new house in May 1964 and it was as if we had come from a pond into the ocean! It was a huge mansion spread over 900 square yards, a colossal after the puny 100 square yards we had lived in earlier. Pitaji had been lucky to have got it for about Rs One lakh, which was actually a fortune in those times. There were eight rooms on the ground floor, six on the first, and a biggish room at the top of the house along with a vast roof. The house was an old construction, with the walls being almost three feet thick, as it was a trend to build alcoves in olden days. It had garages with rooms above it. What fascinated us most were the spacious gardens with fruit trees in front of the house, along with a cemented centre. My father had thrown a grand party for all his relatives, friends and business associates. Almost 500 people attended that gala event! My father was really popular and all had been eager to celebrate his good fortune in buying a lavish house.

Friends and neighbours would often request to hold their functions in our extensive grounds and Pitaji never refused them.

We were blessed to have such a beautiful house, famous in the Sitaram Bazaar area as the *'Bageeche wali Kothi'*—the bungalow with a garden, with fruit trees and all! Our area was a pretty affluent one, and one of its claims for being famous was that it was the locality to which Pandit Jawaharlal Nehru's wedding procession had come to. Kamla Nehru's family had lived in the area after migrating from Kashmir, their homeland. The businessman from whom we had bought the house, Ishwar Chand, was one of three brothers and they had other properties in the area. One of the brothers had converted his property into a Dharamshala, in memory of his father.

***

In the same month that we shifted to our new house, tragedy struck the country in the demise of our beloved Prime Minister Jawaharlal Nehru, a great leader and statesman, revered not only in India, but the world over. His charismatic personality had made him a force to be reckoned with and his passing created a deep void in the country. Nobody can deny his contributions, both pre- and post-Independence, for he laid a solid foundation for modern India, with strong industrial and scientific parameters. However, dissenters don't hesitate to pick on the fact that despite being in power for seventeen years, he was unable to resolve the real issues of poverty, hunger and unemployment. They argue that Sardar Patel would have been a better head for the country. If Gandhiji had not supported Nehru, Sardar Patel would surely have become the Prime Minister.

India was basically an agro-based nation, with 85 per cent of its population living in villages, yet we couldn't produce enough to feed our whole country and had to import wheat from the USA. One reason for Nehru's lack in this regard may have been the fact that he had never seen poverty, coming from an affluent family, and as he had studied and lived abroad, hadn't had much opportunity to interact with the masses. The other prominent leaders of those times, Sardar Patel and

Subhash Chandra Bose, were connected to the grassroots and understood the country and the basic issues of the common people better. They had a more practical approach unlike Pandit Nehru, who was more of a dreamer.

Osho opines that politicians and religious leaders have done more harm than good to the world in general and to our country, in particular. However, it is my conviction that Nehru did less harm and more of good for our country and if someone was to impartially make a true balance sheet for him, it would be proved so, despite our ignominious defeat in the Indo-China war in 1962! It was not for nothing that he was given the epithet of 'Philosopher King of India' by an American journalist.

My father had always revered Jawaharlal Nehru, following his precepts closely, and was encouraged by his appeals to the people to educate their children as doctors and engineers, for there was a paucity of these professions in the country. And so he had decided to send his two elder sons to engineering and medical colleges. Unfortunately, Nehru had not made any provisions for a third son, and consequently, my father remained at a loss for a vision for me, his third son! But then he did need someone to manage his own business setup, so things worked out well for me!

Anguish filled my father's heart when he heard the news of Nehruji's passing away on the radio. He heard that the funeral procession was heading for Shantivan, adjacent to Rajghat and was to pass near Turkman Gate, about a km away from our home. This was the very point where once I had had the good fortune to see our Prime Minister in person, as his cavalcade passed that way. I had been impressed by his magnetic personality as he had stood in an open vehicle, waving to the crowds. My father got the information that the procession was about to reach Turkman Gate and without a moment's hesitation, he began to run in that direction! I immediately raced after him. That indeed must have been a sight to see, Lala Bhagat Prasad, the President of the Mohalla Sudhaar Samiti racing distractedly in his sparkling silk kurta, with his ten-year-old son chasing after him! Dodging through the rickshaws, tongas and people, unmindful even of his kurta getting ripped, he swiftly continued on his course, bent on obtaining a last glimpse of his ideal. We reached panting at Turkman Gate and joined the mammoth sea of mourners in the wake of the procession. My father could see the huge vehicle on which the body of Pandit Nehru was being transported on his last journey and swiftly began to cut a path through the crowd, focused only on reaching his target. In that moment, his one-pointed intensity was at its peak, his burning desire to fulfill his wish of a final glimpse! We caught up with the slow-moving cavalcade at Delhi Gate and gained a front row view.

It was a poignant moment as I looked at the grand tableau in front of me, touching the very core of my heart, rousing a deep sense of patriotism within me, a passion which I wasn't aware I possessed. So intense was the moment that I felt that it was more of a personal loss rather than the nation's, and a wave of despair overcame me, akin to what my father must have been experiencing! That instant somehow helped me to forge a bond with my roots, as it gave rise to a sense of belonging, a sense that automatically set a course for me towards politics in my later life!

***

A home environment is considered to be the safest place to raise children, but if predators exist therein, what safety can be guaranteed? Innumerable cases have come to light of child molestation in the home itself by members of close or extended family, shattering all trustworthy parameters. Even age is not a deterrent, for babies too are not secure, going by recent incidents. And it is not only girls who are vulnerable, boys can also be victimised. I, too, faced such molestations at two points in my life. The first was when I was seven years old. I was quite a winsome child, and people would be affectionate towards me. One of the accountants living below us was a bit of a homo, but fortunately he only fondled me a little. The second time, I was almost ten years old when I faced similar misbehaviour at the hands of a close relative. It is a tragedy of life that such occurrences take place within the confines of a family structure, which should actually be a completely safe haven! It was an unfortunate incident, but again I got off lightly. But I truly sympathise with those who are not so lucky, for indeed it is highly traumatic and can cause an aberration in a person's growth, either creating a terror of physicality or of becoming overindulgent, invariably leaving them scarred for life.

***

With a change of residence, a change of school happened again. I moved to the Marwari Higher Secondary School near our new house in Sitaram Bazaar, and I would walk to school with our servant, Heera carrying my bag for me. I was the only student to have such a service and this enhanced my image in the eyes of the other students. Faced with their adulation, I began to regard myself as a VIP!

I remember my PT instructor very clearly, Taneja Sir, for he was quite a jovial personality. Once he roped me in to participate in a dance programme, the kind schools have on annual day functions.

I cannot dance at all and till date am unable to do so! But Taneja Sir would not accept it and pushed me again and again to make me do the steps correctly. I even received thwacks from his scale to motivate me. But to no avail! I finally had to appeal to his better sense to let me drop out.

However, I was able to redeem myself in his eyes a few days later. During a class activity, he was encouraging students to sing and focused on me.

'Come on Mahesh! Let's hear you sing! Can you do that or not?' he said, taking a mild jibe at my earlier disastrous attempts at dancing. I looked at him like a trapped rabbit, but suddenly my mind took me back to the times when my hero, Dev, used to sing gustily on the roof, proclaiming his love for his beloved! I took inspiration from that memory, as I remembered that I used to copy him, much to my siblings' enjoyment! When one is pushed to the wall, a latent talent can surface to rescue you!

Full of bravado, I took up the challenge and sang a popular love song from the film *Sangam*, with a lot of style.

'Oh! so this is where your talent lies! You are a born singer, not a dancer,' Taneja Sir exclaimed in delight, much to my own astonishment as well, for I didn't know I had a singer hidden within me! I realised another thing in that moment—that I was actually a romantic at heart! The lyrics that I had sung, *O Mehbooba* had sprung from deep within, and it was not as if I had consciously memorised them. It just shows that my subconscious was steeped in romance, perhaps the influence of the love between Rama and Dev that used to fascinate me as a child!

From that day, I gained popularity among my friends and teachers for my newly found singing abilities. So much so that I was even selected to sing a patriotic song at the Independence Day celebrations in our school on 15 August, before the whole assembly. I was asked to sing a very famous song, *A Mere Watan ke Logon* By the age of ten, I had thus seen shifts in my interests from being a clerk in a drama to a singer-artist, a journey leading to the eventual politico-poet that I finally became!

My favourite song back then was a very popular one sung by Mukesh, picturised on Raj Kapoor in *Anari* and whose philosophy I loved to apply to life. I would fall in love with someone's smile or would attempt to alleviate another's pain and always felt my heart to be overflowing with love!

> *Kissi ki muskarahato pe ho nissaar*
> *kissi ka dard mil sake toh le udhaar*
> *kissi ke vaaste ho tere dil me pyaar*
> *jeena issi ka naam hai*

During my school time, what impacted me a lot was the morning Aarti to Goddess Saraswati during assembly performed by a group of senior students. All the children participated and it sort of inculcated a deep sense of religiosity in our hearts.

At home, my parents daily read from our Holy Scriptures, father from the *Ramayana* and mother from *Bhagavad Gita*, before starting the routine of their day, and this sowed the seeds of spirituality in me. My father would get so intensely involved in his reading that he would be unaware even of the tears rolling down his cheeks! This is the highest kind of devotion, where the devotee gets completely lost in his ardour, and his piety flows unchecked from deep within. Till date, I do not start the day without paying my reverence to the Divine and sitting in communion with Him for a while. I also daily reverentially bow to my parents and my Gurus even before getting out of bed in the morning, filling myself with gratitude for their manifold blessings. My bedroom is no less than a temple-cum-art gallery, what with the portraits of my sixteen Gurus, supported by pictures of Sai Baba, Shiva, Surya, Goddess Saraswati, Hanumanji and images of my parents, Indira Gandhi and Rajiv Gandhi!

***

When I was in the sixth class, we were taken on a five-day school trip to Mathura, Vrindavan and Agra. My father gave me Rs 5 for my personal expenditure, and on my return, I handed Rs 4.5 back to him.

'You did not spend anything?' was his astonished exclamation.
'I did! I bought a small Taj Mahal when we went to visit it.'
'Only that?'
'Yes.'
'But didn't you feel like eating anything?'
'No, we got all meals from there itself.'
'No sweets? Nothing?' he said, shaking his head in wonder at my judicious nature. 'You'll certainly become a very good businessman!'

I never spent unnecessarily and never snacked in-between meals. Everything else had been paid for by the school, so where was the need to spend any more money! My father could only marvel at the thrifty nature of his son, regarding him as a true scion of his clan. The Baniyas are considered to be prudent in their expenditure.

Chapter 2

The Power of Words

MOVING TO THE seventh class brought about a change in my school once again, for I was moved back to my earlier school, Anglo Sanskrit, to its senior branch. It was a daunting new environment, and a huge complex. My elder brother, Devender, was in the same school in the eleventh class, so it was easy for me to accompany him. My father bought me a medium-sized bicycle and I was thrilled to the core! My elder brother used to ride to school and now since I had to go with him, I needed a cycle. I would enjoy riding through the bylanes of Jama Masjid to our school in Daryaganj. It also allowed me a little more freedom and I would go on cycling expeditions with my friends. Once we had an exhilarating ride on the slopes of Raisina Hills leading to Rashtrapati Bhawan. Another time, we managed to venture as far as Bengali Market and enjoyed the delicacies it was famous for. That was the first time I tasted the famous south Indian dosa and really relished it!

In this school, however, I maintained a low profile, which was not to my liking, as I had got used to being feted! But again, the teachers were very good and encouraging, especially my English teacher, Ram Nathji. He was quite a contrary personality for though he spoke fluent English, he wore a pristine white dhoti and kurta, along with a white cap! He encouraged us all to read English newspapers daily and to keep a dictionary handy to check difficult words and so improve our vocabulary. I inculcated the habits he suggested. My father had started a sort of open library at the Welfare Association's office nearby, and it became a routine with me to devour the newspapers and magazines available there. It is thanks to my teacher that I still receive compliments on my hold on the language!

Painting and PT classes were, however, the bane of my life as both did not interest me at all! With my drawing abilities I could only contrive to make a flag and maybe that was a portent for the future, for I made innumerable flags for election purposes later in my life—that is what helped me to make a fortune!

My period of low profile continued in the eighth class but I remained centred in my studies. During that year, both my brothers left for college, the eldest for engineering in Roorkee and the other for medical college in Varanasi. It sort of elevated my position at home, as all focus shifted to me, especially my father's. We had always shared a very close bond since the beginning, and it deepened even further.

It was my father who had shown me my first picture *Purnima* in Shiela theatre in 1964, a totally new experience for me, sitting in the darkness and watching a movie. He often took me along wherever he went, whether to a social meeting, or a function, as I was very restrained and mature as a child, and showed a deep interest in events. On returning from work in the evenings, he would fondly call out to me to have dinner with him. I used to study on the ground floor while he would be on the first floor and would call loudly from the balcony, 'Mahesh, *aao*!' All the neighbours, especially the ones across the lane, would also hear the daily call and marvel at our bonding! Somehow, as I connected deeply to my father, my relations with my mother got subtly distanced, much to my regret.

Sigmund Freud has said that daughters have a natural inclination towards fathers while sons gravitate towards their mothers. But in my family, I noticed an opposite effect, for as I began to bond with my father, my mother and sister drew close to each other.

In our society, the persona of a father matters a lot and he should display a number of inspiring qualities like open-mindedness, maturity, authenticity and honesty. He should be capable of supporting and protecting his family. I felt I was really fortunate that my father was an epitome of all these qualities, along with depth of intensity. I have always looked up to him for inspiration, and venerated him as my role model. But unfortunately, I could not generate the same reverence for my mother, who brought us up in a very disciplined manner. Though she preferred to stay in the background, it was her will power that kept our household running smoothly. My father revered her and would often tell me that I should listen more to my mother as she was invariably always correct! He would quote a well-known Urdu verse which sums up the importance of both parents:

Maa ke paun ke neeche Jannat hoti hai
Jannat ke darwaze ki chabi Pita ke haath me hoti hai

(Paradise exists beneath the feet of a mother
The key to the door of Paradise is in the father's hands)

It was not that my mother did not cherish or care for me. She always made sure to serve me hot meals and would take me along with her to visit relatives or go to religious meets, and often took me to the park when I was small. However, in the delight of being feted by my father and experiencing the larger aspects of life, I overlooked that mothers, too, play an important role and deserve real respect, love and attention.

It has weighed much on my mind over the years, and I still feel guilty about it, suffering emotionally for not valuing her presence as much as I should have.

Life, however, paid me back in my own coin! After my marriage, I experienced firsthand the loneliness and alienation that she must have had to face, for I received a similar kind of indifference from my wife when I needed her emotionally. Things really do turn around and we perforce have to pay for what we do to others. Even though I did not consciously ignore my mother, circumstances somehow allowed her to be distanced, while my father became everything to me.

It needed an astrologer to make me aware of the turning wheel of Destiny, of how what we give, comes back to us. 'Your wife is now giving you back all that you did to your mother at that time; you have to face the same indifference multifold towards your very existence, as you meted out to your mother.' His analysis really shook me up, making me realise the bitter truth that when we ignore our near and dear ones, particularly the one who brought us into this world, we have to experience a similar or an even more intense kind of suffering, sooner or later in our own lives! Karma has a long reach and has a tendency to catch up, paying us back for our deeds. Even though a mother would never ask her progeny to give her anything, we are beholden to cater to her and treat her with respect and love. Just because we may not need her the way we did when we were children, doesn't mean that she too doesn't need us. I know what I did was wrong especially now when she is just a memory. In my senior years, I understood how she must have been hurt by my careless attitude towards her, especially after my brothers had left to pursue their studies.

***

My father supported Nehru's Non-Alignment ideology, and

had always been a staunch Congressman. However, when he became the President of the Welfare Society, he would proclaim that he neither supported the Congress nor the Jan Sangh, as BJP was called back then. Instead, he said he was there for everyone. He would say that when someone is elected, they represent everyone and so should distance themselves from their own self-concerns. Just before the 1967 elections, he had given rooms on the ground floor of our house to both the opposing parties, warning them not to create any disagreements within his compound. It was indeed unique that two contesting parties were operating from adjacent rooms! And they did so peacefully, respecting my father's authority, for his persona was indeed a towering one while his helpful nature and ability to resolve things enhanced his charisma even more.

In 1965, war broke out and there used to be a lot of blackouts which were quite scary. After the debacle of the 1962 war, the country's morale was at its lowest ebb. Defeat had not been expected in 1962, and people were apprehensive about a repeat. Patriotic thoughts were announced daily in school and Master Gulshan Kanwal, one of our senior teachers, would compose poems to inspire a nationalistic zeal and recite them during assembly. He later became the principal. After the 1962 Indo-China war, a renaissance had happened in me towards my country, and this intensified during the 1965 Indo-Pak war. The atmosphere in school was truly patriotic, so much so that when Shastriji passed away in January 1966, I felt the devastation deeply along with my parents. His body was brought back from Tashkent and kept in state before the funeral. Whenever a great leader passes away, an all-party condolence meet happens at the Ramlila Grounds. I decided to get a last glimpse of the proceedings. Neither my father nor my brothers were able to go, and I went alone to pay my last respects.

An immense crowd had gathered there to pay homage to a truly outstanding leader. A short tenure of only eighteen months had showed that performance could easily score over personality, and revealed his straightforward and down-to-earth leadership qualities. He had tried to secure the nation and make provisions for her self-sufficiency. It was under his competent authority that our country gloriously won the 1965 Indo-Pak war! His slogan *Jai Jawan Jai Kissan* showcased his ideology precisely, for he realised that the first task of a government was to provide food and security to the country. He was very connected with the masses, having risen from amongst them, and so was entirely focused on their basic needs. As a child, he had to swim across the river to attend his school as he didn't have enough money for the ferry crossing!

It was a mesmerisingly overpowering sight of how people paid their homage. I somehow managed to make my way right to the forefront of the crowd, to have a closeup view of the whole scenario. Politicians were laying floral tributes at Shastriji's portrait placed there, bowing to pay their condolences. One thing that really had an impact on me were the few lines spoken by the opposition leader, Atal Bihari Vajpayee. In his speech, he simply said that Mother India's lap had become derelict, not her womb!

Bharat Ma ki goud sooni hui hai, kokh nahi

No applause happens at such gatherings, yet at his words, a large part of the crowd stood up in inexpressible appreciation. I didn't understand what was said but felt it was laudable, as it seemed poetic to me. Later, I told my father what had been said and when he explained its meaning, I was really impressed and realised the power of words. I think that laid the foundation of my literary inclinations, for I understood the importance of presenting deep thoughts in simple words and molding prose into poetry. I had a very inquisitive mind and loved to ask questions and when the mind is enquiring, destiny creates circumstances.

***

Along with all other things, my father was also my political guru, and was always ready to satiate my curiosity. It was his patience and willingness that spurred my growth and evolvement from quite an early age. When I look back to those times, I feel a sense of deep pride at having had the opportunity to watch history in the making. Right from Gandhiji to the later politicians, all somehow touched my life through the views of my father. I felt really attracted to the personality of Subhash Chandra Bose, the phenomenal leader who had shown his mettle even against the British. The reminiscences of my father of the immense contribution of Subhash Chandra Bose, fondly called Netaji, to the Indian Nationalistic movement was the inspirational stuff of my childhood. He was a great admirer of Netaji, who singlehandedly raised an army for his country, and was much above the politics of those times. His slogan had roused people's patriotism to a fever pitch.

> *Tum mujhe Khoon do, mai tumhe Aazaadi dunga*
> *Countrymen, give me your blood; I will give you freedom!*

Controversy also shrouded him as there were many who didn't concur with him, even describing his army as a suicidal squad. However, his call had power; thousands came forward to be a part of it, despite him giving the call from exile. After being arrested in Bengal, he had managed to escape to Afghanistan, and from there, he made his way to Germany in November 1941, where he received unexpected support from Adolf Hitler. Later, Japan too offered help, enabling him to set up his 'Azad Hind Fauz' or 'Indian National Army' with the aim of securing Independence from British rule. Charismatic and driven, Bose had displayed an unflagging zeal for the cause of liberating India, which, affected the British morale much more than the show of strength involved in raising the army! It cannot be denied that the formulation of the army worked as a catalyst, giving an impetus to Gandhi's freedom movement, for it gave the Britishers a psychological jolt and showed that battles first have to be won in the mind before victory can be achieved on the field!

When Bose had won the Congress presidential election over Gandhiji's preferred candidate, Pattabhi Sitaramyya, Gandhiji had not appreciated the win and publicly stated that Sitaramyya's defeat was his own. When Subhash Chandra Bose came to know about it through the papers, he summoned a press conference and announced therein that if Sitaramayya's defeat makes Gandhiji feel belittled, then 'I resign from my post immediately. He is my senior and I revere him a lot and I cannot accept that Gandhiji should feel so and, therefore, prefer to step down!' That was the stature of my hero, embodying a dedicated and intense persona! Destiny unfortunately did not support him, else he would definitely have taken India to a different level altogether. It was the country's loss that it didn't happen. Well-known writer and a good friend, Bhuvan Lall aptly summed him up when he titled his book, *The Man India Missed the Most*! He said, 'Subhash Chandra Bose was indeed a man of extraordinary will, never hesitating to embark on death-defying journeys for his Motherland's freedom, even though he was pursued by assassins and the spectre of death. Faced with impossible odds, he was determined to triumph over an undefined future with courage, dignity and honour, becoming a legend in his own lifetime.'

Chapter 3

The Rise of Indira Gandhi

AFTER LAL BAHADUR Shastri's untimely death, Indira Priyadarshini Gandhi became the Prime Minister of our country in early 1966. She had been accompanying her father on numerous foreign trips and had generally been assisting him before being elected as the President of the Indian National Congress in 1959. Indira Priyadarshini married a long-standing friend, Feroze Ghandy, son of Jehangir Ghandy, a Parsi, in 1942, who later changed the spelling of his name to Gandhi, for he was deeply inspired by Mahatma Gandhi. They were blessed with two sons, Rajiv and Sanjay. As both Indira and Feroze were active participants in the political scenario of the country, their domestic life did not prosper much.

After her father's death, Indira became a member of the Rajya Sabha and, later, a minister in Shastriji's cabinet and consequent to his death, she stepped into his shoes. Thus, at the young age of forty-nine, she became the first and only woman Prime Minister in the world! Two things helped her to gain this distinction—first that she was Nehru's daughter, and second, some senior political leaders of that time gave her their support for they felt that as she was a woman, she could be molded and would remain a puppet in their hands! Initially, she was mocked with comments like *Goongi Gudiya* (a dumb doll) and just a beautiful face to decorate the first page of the newspaper! But time showed her mettle and soon she shattered all perceptions of docility, emerging as a strong leader with an iron will, thus earning the epithet of Iron Lady. After a rocky start, she evolved magnificently, even having the gumption to split the Congress into two factions and gloriously defeat Pakistan in 1971, thus giving birth to a separate country, Bangladesh. She was not only a powerful and dominating figure in India's political scenario, but also a popular and charismatic leader. Accolades poured in with even the opposition leader, A B Vajpayee calling her Durga in Parliament and the Congress president, D K Barooah proclaiming, 'India is Indira and Indira is India.'

Chapter 4

Awakenings

MY FATHER ONCE took me to watch a wrestling match between two known wrestlers at Feroz Shah Kotla stadium. It was a mesmerising experience, so much so that I began to seek opportunities to attend similar shows. About that time, my father had given two big rooms on the ground floor on lease to an industrialist as office space. I became friendly with the manager, who often went to the Feroz Shah Kotla stadium, as he knew someone there, and would take me along. Besides getting to see innumerable sport activities, I loved the promotional handouts that advertisers distributed there, like hot bournvita and so on. One time, during a football tournament, I jumped onto the field when the winning team had been announced, to enthusiastically congratulate them. The captain appreciated my exuberance and hugged me lovingly!

After that, I made sure to somehow get a memento at the events I attended! Some dignitary, like a CM or governor or some renowned personality, would present the awards to the winners, and I would invariably manage to get my picture clicked at the momentous moment of presentation, along with the VIP! We had visited Nainital in the summer of 1967, where a hockey match had been scheduled and I managed to get myself photographed with the team. I thus had a huge collection of these photographs displayed in our drawing room for many years, attracting the attention of visitors, turning the conversation towards my enterprising nature in getting such pictures! I loved to be at the centre of events and make my presence felt. I was always dressed impeccably, a trait which later earned me the sobriquet of 'Dandy' from one of my teachers in school, Dr Gulshan Kanwal, who later became the Principal.

***

Another event etched in my mind is my sister's wedding in May 1966. My father had got a telephone installed, its installation giving us children an exciting high, with Simran and myself rushing to answer whenever it occasionally rang. My father was worried about my sister's nuptials as, even though she was very good-natured, she was a little dusky. But his fears were unfounded, for she got a good-looking, educated match from a prosperous and illustrious family, the grandson of great freedom fighter, Lala Desh Bandhu Gupta, whose statue stands at Ajmeri Gate even today. They had been charmed by my father's personality and were sure his daughter would suit them, as they were looking for a simple, homely girl, who would take care of their family, for the lady of the house had passed away just six months previously. The prospective groom shared that he had done CA, LLB, MBA, a string of degrees really remarkable for those times. Once they had left, Shobha jiji asked our father,

'What does CA mean?'

'I have no idea!' our father replied.

'Must be a very high degree!' was my elder brother's contribution.

'Never mind!' Shobha jiji had said, 'I am BA, so definitely CA is something better than that!'

My father delightedly accepted her explanation and we

didn't delve more deeply into the matter. The whole family had been aristocratic in their demeanour and when acceptance came from them that night, we all were ecstatic. Within a month, the marriage took place and even though father was still at a low stand after buying the house, he spent lavishly on her wedding, flooding the new couple with gifts such as a refrigerator and a television, not commonly given then. In those times, all such gifts or dowry as they are called, were displayed in style for a couple of days in the bride's house for the guests to see. Neighbours would help in setting up things artistically and even the sellers themselves would come to do so!

That was soon after the Indo-Pak war and a Guest Control Act was enforced, limiting them to fifty. However, 500 guests were expected from the groom's side, which we requested to reduce to 300, while ours numbered about 200. The whole locality would pitch in to help, considering themselves a part of the family. The guests were easily accommodated in neighbouring houses, as well as the Dharamshala. Everyone was all praise for the arrangements. We three brothers guided the guests to different houses, where preparations had been done on the rooftops for the wedding repast.

Sometimes the best of plans get sabotaged by unexpected hitches! When the groom's procession reached our gate, the electricity failed. A wave of anguish swept us all, and we didn't know how to deal with the contingency. My father fainted in that moment. Mercifully, the lights came on soon enough, and my grandfather and uncles were able to revive my father and the rest of the celebrations passed off smoothly. But that one incident was enough to make my father vow that he would subsequently hold all his children's weddings in big hotels.

Being the youngest in the family, a lightweight suit was indulgently stitched for me, complete with a tie and I was really looking forward to wearing it, for even my brothers did not possess such a one! But disaster happened! On the day of the wedding, the suit couldn't be found.

'Where are my clothes?' I wailed.

My mother was completely hassled, trying to get last minute tasks done.

'Go and ask your sister. I have work to do.'

Tugging at her saree, I kept creating a ruckus, 'She is also not helping me. Says she has to get ready herself. You find my clothes!'

She did try, but a wedding household is usually in a state of utter chaos, and the suit couldn't be found. Much to my disappointment, I had to wear an older outfit and that made me really morose.

The next day it was found and such was my desire for wearing it that I wore it immediately, as my sister and her husband were coming home for their first visit, which is celebrated as a big event. The extended family also gathers and my father had even summoned a photographer. Everyone made me a butt of their jokes, but I complacently accepted their humour, for I was feeling supremely happy at being able to wear my new suit, tie and all! I treasure the photographs clicked at that time!

I was pretty attached to my sister, so she took me back with her to her new home. Till now I had never experienced how other people lived. Theirs was a small family, but unfortunately, as the mother had expired, my sister's father-in-law was handling all the responsibilities. I was fascinated by their standard of living; at mealtimes, a whole repast was laid out, making me marvel at the number of dishes. The family would sit and watch television together, also discussing the day's activities. A very close friend of one of the sisters used to be around and often when we were watching television, she would come and sit next to me. In those days, it was the norm to switch off lights while watching television. Taking advantage of the darkness, she would hold my hand and sometimes touch and caress me. It made me feel quite good and became an allurement to visit my sister more often. Those soft moments helped to develop a sensuality in me and made me aware of this aspect of life more deeply.

How closely this sensual aspect of life is woven into its fabric became evident more clearly as time went on. Pitaji had allowed a Jain family, comprising of two brothers and their wives, with a child each, to stay on rent in the rooms on our terrace. They belonged to a struggling family of Meerut and had come to the city to set up a factory. Both the wives were quite attractive, with a unique small-town charm. The husbands would take turns in going out of town for business and consequently, that wife would be alone. She would then request my mother to send me upstairs for some time to play cards with her and so alleviate her loneliness. I had a good relationship with both and used to enjoy our cozy evenings together. I would feel a strong pull towards them which seemed to be reciprocated as well, for often a more intimate atmosphere would get created. Those were feelings I couldn't understand, and I only knew that they made me feel buoyant. Maybe something more than playing cards was needed from me but it was only in later years that that thought arose in my mind. At that time, it was just some kind of a rousing excitement that lent a charm of its own to my interactions with them!

I became an admirer of beauty from those days itself, for the women I was surrounded with were the ones who inspired my daydreams, and my creative pursuits carry an impression of some of these women who had influenced my childish mind!

But somehow, I have perpetually felt disgruntled, for mine has been the classic case of what S T Coleridge depicted in his famous lines, '*Water, water, everywhere, nor any drop to drink!*' I have always lived surrounded by a sea of women from all walks of life, yet to date, I feel unfulfilled, for I have yet to meet the one who was made exclusively for me, a match for my temperament!

***

When I moved to the ninth standard, my father wanted me to take up science, but I wanted to opt for commerce. Even at that age, I understood that more than science, commerce was of value. What use were scientific formulae in our day-to-day life? I felt that as we were a business family, I should opt for commerce, but my father was adamant. In those days, people thought that taking up science subjects was for the very intelligent; studying the commerce stream was for the slightly less intelligent and those doing arts, were the least intelligent! It is so very wrong of parents not to accept a child's bent of mind and to force their own onto them. I argued that one brother has become a doctor and the other an engineer, so it would be good for me to be a pure business person, but my father refused and I had to study science in higher secondary. That is why when I got a chance in college, I immediately took up commerce.

One of my cherished memories of that time is of the way father would wake me up in the mornings. He would invite me to snuggle into bed with him and would hold and caress me till I woke up fully. Those tender moments roused a longing in me to have such awakenings later in life as well, but unfortunately, it was never to be so, and it has ever remained a grouse in my heart. The close bonding of a family really matters for love should be an integral part of life!

***

My height has always been the bane of my life. I did not gain inches after my tenth class! Of course, hereditary traits play a very important role, but I also attribute it to another incident in my life. I had once called a tall, gangly looking classmate, an 'ostrich', which appealed to the other children and we all would tease him, much to his discomfiture. Once he lashed back, literally cursing me that I would not grow an inch beyond my current height. In hindsight, I realise that we should never point out shortcomings, especially physical ones in others, for that amounts to a criticism of our maker Himself and may somehow rebound back, as it did for me!

Another thing that impacted me was a pre-recorded interview of Jawaharlal Nehru, which I watched on television. The BBC interviewer had asked Nehru, 'Mr Prime Minister, you are supposed to be the philosopher king of India. What according to you is the purpose of life?'

Without an instant's hesitation, Nehru had replied, 'Living with a purpose!' the interviewer was stunned by his repartee and so was I! Even at fourteen, Nehru's response struck me as being something phenomenal and it had a deep impact on my own thought process, to such an extent that I decided to make it my own life's philosophy.

My values had become quite strong at even that age, as I would often go with either my mother or father to religious discourses and once had even stayed at an ashram. What I understood from all the knowledge I thus gained was that we need to do four things in life, which came under the categories of *Dharma, Arth, Kaam* and *Moksha*. *Dharma* was more about fulfilling our duties rather than just being religious. *Arth* was connected to our earning capacity. Kaam was connected to our desires and how we enjoyed all the pleasures under the sun. When everything had been enjoyed, we needed to turn towards *Moksha* or salvation.

***

I never had a technical bent of mind and would get stumped

by even the simple act of changing a fused bulb. I also found my subjects in high school pretty dry, as they did not appeal to my creative nature. So, I took up biology instead of mechanical drawing, as that felt a little more interesting. I was deeply interested in dissections of frogs as my brother also did them, and I did become quite good at them. In this class too, I became my English teacher, Gulshan Kanwal's favourite, as my hold on the language was pretty good right from the beginning. He was happy with me, my work and the way I dressed immaculately. He was the one to call me 'Dandy'! The next year, I changed my style a little by growing a short beard, so he endowed me with the epithet, 'Yogi' for he felt that I had begun to resemble the popular proponent of Transcendental Meditation, Maharishi Mahesh Yogi! Besides, according to him, I remained in a state of contemplation, absorbed in my own world, not unlike a yogi!

I'm still in touch with Kanwal Sir; he attended my sons' weddings and was present at the most momentous time of my life, the simultaneous launch of my poetry books in Hindi and Urdu! Indeed, it were his nationalistic poems which had first inspired me!

In 2019 on Vasant Panchami, my alma mater, A S V J, celebrated its 150th anniversary and several prominent principals and students were invited as guests. I met Mr Kanwal there and he met me on the stage. I was overwhelmed and touched his feet, while he lovingly embraced me.

Ever since, he has been showering daily blessings on me on Whatsapp in the mornings and we are even connected on Facebook. I reciprocate by symbolically bowing to him.

***

In 1969 I had gone to see a national level wrestling match between Master Chandgi Ram and Mehardeen at Feroz Shah

Kotla Stadium. The next day, the newspapers carried a picture of me standing next to Chandgi Ram and the LG of Delhi, much to everyone's astonishment! My enterprising nature had once again helped in highlighting my love for the limelight!

Chapter 5

Growing Up, Almost Overnight

CHRISTMAS DAY IN 1969, when I was in the eleventh standard, brought a turning point in my life. My elder brother was at home from college and we all had slept, when the phone rang. My father picked up the phone. Calls in the middle of the night are ominous. This was no exception.

My father froze and the phone slipped from his hand. He seemed to be in total shock. Amma quickly grabbed the phone and at once, recognised the voice of our Munshiji.

'Fire! Very bad fire! Come quickly to the shop!'

Within minutes we were out of the house and swiftly reached Sadar Bazaar on my brother's scooter, my father and myself riding pillion.

Our whole shop was enveloped in fire and there was total chaos. Four fire engines were already on the scene, but the inferno was completely out of control.

We just stood there stupefied, as we watched our means of earning dissipate completely in front of us! Goods worth thousands of rupees were going up in smoke, for we were wholesalers and kept our shop stocked. Never had I felt so helpless as in that moment, especially as I saw the ashen face of my father. The whole night passed like a nightmare as the fire brigade struggled to douse the flames. Two more engines had to be called before the situation could be brought under control. Fortunately, a small section somehow escaped the ferociousness of the fire and we were able to salvage some of the goods. Another fortunate thing was that the peak season for selling our stuff was at its tail end, consequently we had already fulfilled a number of orders, so we were saved from heavy losses!

With the help of neighbouring shopkeepers, we shifted the recovered stock to my elder sister's house.

The shock was too much for my father and the next morning, he collapsed, falling into a semi-conscious state, in which he remained for the next few days. All three of us had been standing in the cold, the whole night, even in water, and my elder brother too, went down with a bout of pneumonia.

Now I was left to hold the fort all by myself, for though relatives constantly swamped my mother with their presence, none came forward to stand by me. When my father regained consciousness, he was completely shattered, wondering how to handle everything. Somehow, I got the strength to assure him not to worry and took charge of the situation, and the way I coped proved beyond doubt that God endows you with a superhuman strength when it is needed! I began to go daily to the shop, sometimes working nonstop for sixteen hours, not allowing my father to go at all. I even took the decision to drop out of school, telling my father that he was more important to me than my studies. Maybe I felt that it was now time for me to repay all that my parents had done for me, and such was my desire that it gave me a phenomenal capability to accomplish everything—recovering goods, getting the shop renovated, dealing with customers and suppliers, arranging transportation of stuff, tallying accounts! I still marvel as to how I managed to get the fortitude to do all this!

Pitaji wanted to summon both my brothers back from their colleges, saying that he definitely couldn't afford their education. I persuaded him not to do so. It had been my father's dream to make one son a doctor and the second an engineer, as was the trend in those days. My elder brother had been at home during the incident, but had fallen ill at that crucial moment. He was so overwhelmed with the whole situation that he would at times cry bitterly and he even began to doubt his own competency in pursuing the medical profession! But we somehow convinced him and sent him back to finish his studies.

One thing stood us in good stead. My father had always supported his customers, even selling 90 per cent of his goods on credit. At this time, they pitched in to help us out and all those who owed us money, paid up. His goodwill was so strong that our suppliers were willing to send us stock on credit. Just as the shop recovered, my father's health also began to recover. So, within a month, our business limped back to some semblance of normalcy, for I had managed to get the shop renovated in that time as well, staying there till 1 am in the morning at times, setting up everything as it was earlier.

My father was impressed with my energetic initiatives and after a month or so, he took the reins back into his hands. The whole situation had also shown me my potential, how much I could achieve and even people used to comment to my father that this one son was equal to all three, much to my delight! Definitely I couldn't have done all that without the backing of my sister's husband and her father-in-law, who was really fond of me. This turning point in my life was of such tremendous impact that I gained maturity, literally overnight. Next year, we had earned enough to buy a car!

***

Rejoining school at the end of February 1970, plunged me into a whirlwind of activities. I needed to assist my father in the shop, and at the same time, do justice to my studies.

I joined coaching classes at night and also made it a point to visit the temple daily to appeal to the Divine to help me clear my exams! Unfortunately, I fell ill, perhaps because of the immense pressure I had put on myself. Consequently, I had to drop my exams that year. In retrospect, those few months were the most profitable for me in terms of enhancing my knowledge. I got ample time to pursue my own interest in reading and even began journaling daily. I had read an article by Gandhiji in which he had said that 'Diary writing is the first literary exercise.' That inspired me to maintain a diary of my daily activities and thoughts. I would pour all my feelings onto those blank pages and I think it helped me to a great extent to become articulate, which later reflected in my expressiveness and opened the way for me to venture into the world of writing.

I had a lot of time on my hands, and I decided to catch up with my reading of Urdu shayari, which I found alluring. I, got a number of poetry books by Ghalib, Iqbal and others translated into Hindi, as my hold on the Urdu language was not quite strong at that time. I had a deeply creative streak and once my father and brothers had even been astonished at the way I was adding lines to a qawwali being sung on television, though I had not heard it earlier and was just fifteen at that time. The singer was presenting his song:

Dil diya
Woh mere pyaar ki hadd thi
Jaan dee
Woh mere aitbaar ki hadd thi
Merne ke baad bhi
Aankhen khuli rahin meri

(I gave my heart
That was the limit of my love

> *I gave my life*
> *That was the limit of my trust*
> *Even after I died*
> *My eyes remained open)*

And I spontaneously continued:
> *Woh mere intezar ki hadd thi*
> *(That was the limit of my patience)*

Another important influence which inclined my mind towards Urdu poetry was our chemistry teacher, V K Sehgal. He was very well read and loved to share his knowledge on different topics with us. One day, he encouraged us to write a couplet by a well-known poet, Allama Iqbal,
> *Khudi ko kr buland itna ki har taqdir se pehle*
> *Khuda bande se khud puchhe bata teri raza kya hai*

> *Raise yourself to such an eminence*
> *That before writing your Destiny*
> *The Divine is compelled to ask*
> *What is your will?*

I don't know whether these few words made an impact on the other students, but they touched the core of my soul as even then I had a strong spiritual bent of mind. I could immediately connect the profound inherent meaning to the knowledge propounded in the *Bhagavad Gita*. My mother used to read the Gita daily and would discuss what she read with my father, conversations that I must have stored and absorbed, for I am blessed with the three faculties of what philosophy calls the foundation of gaining knowledge—observation, retention and reproduction. I was fascinated by the way so much wisdom was being condensed into just two lines!

***

After I recovered, my father sent me to visit my eldest brother in his hostel at Roorkee in May 1970, more as a reward for all the efforts I had put into setting up the shop again. The trip helped to enhance my outlook, adding new experiences to my life. My brother had brought his scooter from our home and we roamed around, venturing as far as Haridwar, 30 km away. There was a strange freedom in being away from parental constraints! While staying there, I came across a book, *How to Win Friends and Influence People* by Dale Carnegie and became a big admirer of his work. The book proved to be life-changing! I had always been fond of reading and now delved deeply into this one. It gave me innumerable tips on how to win friends, a knowledge which helped tremendously in later years. It taught me the value of admiration and how to be practical and convincing. I used to make notes on it and finally my brother gifted it to me!

When I returned home, the book became my staple diet and I would sit in the courtyard in front of our house, reading it. In the house opposite ours, lived the Sharma family. Ramya was their adopted daughter and she would often look out of her window and watch me sitting and studying in the courtyard. I was at an age where awareness was just beginning to set in and those covert glances did not go unnoticed. I too began looking out for her, a thrill overtaking my budding senses, for I was spellbound by her beauty and her silent encouragement. Those were the days when possibility of a verbal interaction with the person of the opposite sex was against the norms of society, so furtive glances had to suffice! Ours was a pure romance, a fascination sprouting from our hearts, a meeting of eyes across all hurdles! Nothing more came out of the scenario as there was no chance to meet. She used to travel by car to school and later on to college as well, and got married in 1974 in our courtyard, itself. Though my attraction towards her had waned somewhat by then, I still felt like one of those forsaken suitors, whose paramour was being stolen right under his nose!

Love ignites your being, your heart, your desires, your muse and unrequited love, even more so! Just the act of being in love rouses a whole new dimension in one's life.

Those surreptitious glances with Ramya laid the foundation of my poetic creativity, for the nuances in a heart's journey are a lucrative field for a poet. The more unrequited a soul remains, the more depths it is able to fathom. I later found my sentiments echoed in the words of another well-known poet, Sumitra Nandan Pant:

> *Viyogi hoga pehla kavi*
> *Aah se upjaa hoga gaan*
> *Nikal kar aankhon se chup chaap*
> *Bahi hogi kavita anjaan*

> *The first poet must have tasted bereavement*
> *For from a sigh emerges a melancholic song*
> *Unobtrusively from the eyes*
> *Verses flow with tears sublime*

This intensity, combined with the unfortunate event in my life, paved the way for the first ever poem to emerge from the depths of my soul, presenting such a profound thought that it really amazed everyone.

> 'Who am I'
> From where have I come
> And where would I go
> I do not know
> For what have I come into the world
> What does it want from me
> I do not know

My poetic journey started with this composition, for I began to contemplate my existence and my role in this world. The excruciating circumstances I had faced due to the fire had stirred deep emotions and shaken our whole world. It was my nature to think deeply and it intensified after this event. Many philosophers and saints have asked, 'Who am I?' and have asked questions about their very existence.

Before Swami Vivekananda became an enlightened soul, he had gone to meet his Guru, Ramakrishna Paramahansa for the first time. When he knocked on the door, Paramahansa asked from within, 'Who is it?' Narendra Nath Datta, as Vivekananda was then known, replied, 'That is what I have come to find out!' an answer which really impressed Ramakrishna, for it is only such a thought that has the capacity to take one to the Divine! Then and there, he accepted Vivekananda as his disciple, the only one he ever had!

From sixteen to seventy, I feel I am still seeking the self and even named the French translation of my poetry book, *In Search of the Self!*

Chapter 6

Discovering the Poet's Voice

DIVINE BLESSINGS CONTINUED to pour on me and the next year, I was able to clear my school with a first division and join college. I took admission in Ramjas college in the B Com Hons stream without consulting my father, else he would probably have redirected me to the science stream! This was also the time when I got more deeply into reading great poets and writers like Mir, Momin, Faiz, Firaq and others, and was especially fascinated by the Urdu language, even going to the extent of buying an Urdu-Hindi dictionary to comprehend the nuances. My forays into the world of books and poems opened a whole new plethora of life-molding experiences, honing me to be ready for whatever life brought to me.

Initially, I used to commute to college by scooter, but would invariably be late every other day.

Unable to tolerate my tardiness, Dr B P Singh, my Business Management lecturer finally cornered me.

'Young man, there is a need to adhere to discipline! What is the reason that you are unable to reach on time?'

'Sir, I live in Sitaram Bazaar and it takes time to come from there.'

'That's not very far. Why does it take you time?'

'Sir, I leave fifteen minutes before the class starts!' A wave of muted laughter flowed through the room.

'As it is an effort for you to reach on time, I excuse you from my classes in the future! Hurrying up to attend my lecture is not so important!'

'Oh no, Sir, please do not deprive me of the privilege of listening to you! You speak with such elegance that it is hard to explain in words! Your diction and manner of speaking English is truly amazing.'

He was amused, and asked, 'Why do you like listening to my lecture? It is not an English class, rather a grave subject.'

'Sir, it is my favourite subject! I belong to the business community, and business management is already in my DNA! I am gaining tremendous knowledge from your lectures and am really keen to attend, but unfortunately, I get late.'

The professor large-heartedly gave me permission to attend even if I arrived late!

In the latter half of the first year, I had learnt to drive and began to commute to college by car. My father had become more indulgent towards me after he had seen the way I had held things together after the fire. Consequently, I had the prestige of commuting to college in my own car. At that time, very few students did so and I was lucky to be one of them!

The parking area used to be behind the main building of the college, but I would park my car right outside the principal's office, next to his car. The girls' common room was adjacent to this area and it used to give me a thrill that the girls noticed that I came in a car. Unfortunately for me, it didn't seem to impress the one girl I really wanted to—Rama, a very attractive girl, with looks like my favourite actress, Madhubala! Later, I realised that she was also quite like my first love, Dev's Rama, and I was amazed by this quirk of destiny! For me she was the most fascinating girl in college, who made me conscious of my own average looks and below-average height! Yet my feelings were pretty intense, at an emotional and mental level! She, too, was affected by my presence. Falling in love became a stimulus for my own growth, for when you are in love, you try to improve yourself, as you are looking for appreciation. You get onto a path of self-improvement, and want to dress and behave well. So, it was the best version of myself for Ramya at home and Rama in college, so I was constantly on my toes! Rama made my life worthwhile in college, inspiring me to emote my longings, poetically.

> *Mera sabra besabra ho gaya*
> *na mila jo saath tera mujhe*
> *mila sare sabra ka muaawazaa*
> *hai mila jo saath tera mujhe.*

> *(Impatience has become my patience*
> *as bereft of your camaraderie, I remain*
> *yet attain will I all and be recompensed*
> *By your closeness, when I gain)*

***

I was pretty active and loved to participate in events, which made me quite popular. Many were the greetings that I exchanged with other students daily, and as it was difficult to remember so many names, I got into the habit of calling everyone *Dost*! So much so, that by the final year, I began to be referred by everyone affectionately as Dost and even adopted it as a pen name for my compositions during my college days. I would be actively involved in seminars and literary circles, my creative and curious mind taking me to the forefront of things. I thus engaged in many competitions and debates, going to neighbouring colleges like SRCC, St. Stephens and Hindu to do so. My circle of friends expanded beyond my own college and thus, I developed a friendship with Arun Jaitley, SRCC Students Union President, who later went on to become DUSU president. It was then that he became actively involved in politics under Jay Prakash Narayan, moving onto the position of president of the BJP Youth Wing in 1980.

Under Modi's first tenure as Prime Minister, he held the portfolios for both Finance and Defence, a precedent not normally followed, but ill-health and his untimely demise in 2019 eclipsed his charismatic persona. He has even been referred to as an 'intellectual giant' by another renowned politician for he was extremely well-read and was an excellent orator, well-versed in both national and international affairs, right from his early days. Our friendship sustained even through all the ups and downs of life, as he was a regular visitor at both IIC and Lodhi Gardens, my favourite haunts, and we often ran into each other.

As I had become involved in the business world so early, I naturally got to know many people and soon had my own group of friends, some quite older to me! One of them was Shyam Narula, with whom I developed a deeper friendship. At that time, he got a job with Indian Airlines and marked the occasion by taking me to a well-known restaurant in Darya Ganj, Moti Mahal. It was a new experience, and I was fascinated at the spacious, ornate environment, hidden lighting enhancing the splendour of the courtyard garden. A glamorously dressed lady was intoning a ghazal accompanied by a few musicians, added a sort of excitement to the air! Shyam ordered alcohol along with a roasted chicken dish, neither of which I had partaken earlier, as it was not prevalent in our family to have them. So, for the first time, I tasted both things, non-vegetarian food and whiskey!

Another such event was when I visited my brother Devender in 1971 at Banaras, after joining college. The fire incident and the way I had handled everything had elevated me in my brothers' books, for they realised I had been instrumental in them continuing their studies. So, my brother went out of his way to indulge me to show his appreciation and took me on a trip to visit Allahabad, Lucknow and Kanpur. I enjoyed the choicest of foods everywhere and even had whiskey and non-vegetarian food once again, as my brother believed in living well!

***

Raj Kumar Kaushik was the College Students' Union president and used to appreciate me. We became quite good friends. He would occasionally discuss important issues with me, as he liked my unbiased perspective about things. He would laugh at the way girls easily became friendly with me and said they did so as I was a 'harmless creature'! My diminutive stature may have proved to be a boon in this regard, for I didn't come across as being overbearing, unlike my better endowed companions!

At about this time, I wrote my first couplet inspired by the exuberance filling my life.

> *Bura karen ya bhala karenge*
> *auron se kuchh juda karenge*
>
> *(Whether I do good or bad,*
> *I will do something different from others)*

He encouraged me to participate in elections, but I wasn't interested. I had not joined the National Congress wing meant for college students, but I liked to understand and dabble in party activities. I think it was due to what my father had inculcated in me. He would say that the task of our class, of Baniyas, was to make money and not to become kings. We were supporters of the king, but couldn't aspire to be kings, ourselves! Besides, I could see how much support and power, apart from money, was needed in fighting elections and maintaining one's position. I was not interested in recruiting an army of followers or hangers-on, as I preferred to remain a one-man army!

I came to the notice of my principal in my final year, when I happened to write a 4,000-word eco-political article, titled 'Inflation and Revolution' for the college magazine. It had been inspired by a talk on the current socio-political times given by a Communist intellectual, Mohit Sen at our college in November 1973.

Our principal, Dr Gobind Rai Chaudhary, tall and authoritative, who usually wore kurta-pajamas with a waistcoat, was impressed by my article and commented that it had uplifted the tone of the college magazine! Once he even took me to meet the vice chancellor at his residence. Since I had got into his good books, Raj Kumar Kaushik would at times send me as the bearer of messages to the principal. I had approached him one day just as he was getting into his car and requested for a few moments of talk. He had an appointment with the VC and asked me to talk in the car while he was driving there, so by default, I accompanied him to the meeting! A few gentlemen were already seated there, but the VC, Dr Sarup Singh, asked us to sit down. He had done his PhD in English from University College, London, and had taught at Hindu College before moving up the ladder. He was reminiscing about how some mischievous students once wrote some adverse comments about him belonging to the Jat community, speculating, 'How can a Jat teach us English,' on the blackboard. He said that it had him feel quite hurt.

I spontaneously said, 'Sir, please excuse me, but if some rowdy students said something untoward about you, how can a great personality like you take that to heart to such an extent?'

He looked at me carefully, 'That's a very mature observation young man, how old are you?'

'Twenty years, Sir!'

'And such profoundness!'

'All my mother's guidance, Sir! She always tells me that I should not pay attention to the thoughtless words of immature people but should just laugh them off.'

'That's very well said, indeed!'

Such was my confidence that the VC even casually told me to visit again. My principal was delighted with my forwardness and the way I had been so articulate! I did subsequently visit the VC a couple of times, even bypassing the principal to do so. On a visit once, I noticed that he was having fruit, so the next time, I took along a gift of apples, and that went down really well with him as he seemed to like my gesture! It also showed me the importance of taking gifts for the people you go to visit as it generates a lot of goodwill!

My college years culminated with the declaration of the final year results in which, as expected, I had passed in the second division, just missing the first by a few marks! I had always been an average student and here too my memory, rather than any strategy of studying, helped me to clear the exams. But I was quite happy with my performance and felt emboldened to approach Rama. 'Can we talk?'

She looked me up and down and disdainfully tossing her head, said, 'Now, there is nothing to talk!' and turning, walked away quickly, leaving me standing there, flabbergasted! Never had I felt so belittled and could not understand the reason behind her attitude. Much later, I got to know through a common friend that she too had liked me a lot and had hoped to translate the liking into a closer relationship, but I had left it too late to approach her. That is destiny at its best, tossing one around on winds of angst! The agony that dismissal generated in me led to a churning of tormented emotions which flowed out in the form of intense words that I wrote wondering at the reality of love.

Kya yahi hai ishq
Ki ek shakhs me kho jaiye
Iss tarah bezaar iss duniya se
Kyun ho jaiye

(Is this what love is
drowning entirely in another
alienating self from the world
but why should I?)

THIRD DECADE

YOUTHFUL YEARNINGS

Chapter 1

Proximity to Power

BIDDING ADIEU TO Ramjas College, I found my way into the adjacent Delhi School of Economics to pursue my Masters in Commerce. My graduation years had inculcated in me a love for the subject and I wanted to take it to the next level. This time round my father had no issue to my continuing in this stream of study and magnanimously agreed to my proposal of working during the day in our shop and going for classes in the evening. He even gave me a 40 per cent partnership in the shop, an unprecedented act for the times! I had literally earned it, the way I had rallied things after the incident of the fire! I thus had the privilege of becoming financially secure immediately on graduating, for Pitaji even gave me a salary of two hundred rupees per month! My father had always been encouraging towards us and had similarly facilitated my eldest brother to establish a chemical factory near Faridabad by giving him over one lakh rupees, after his engineering. He later made it possible for my second brother to also open his clinic once he had completed his post-graduation in medical studies.

During my admission process, I had to visit the campus a number of times. On one such visit, I happened to see our Prime Minister Indira Gandhi's younger son, Sanjay Gandhi, along with a few friends, being conducted around the campus. Such was my fascination for power that I couldn't resist its lure and soon I included myself in the entourage. Opportunity always presents itself to those who seek it and in a turn of conversation, I found mine. Standing behind him, commenting on something he said, I interpolated, 'Genuine love and genuine work never die.'

Sanjay Gandhi turned around in wonderment and looked at me piercingly, maybe evaluating me as the speaker of such a profound truth, a thought which surprised even me!

With a smiling countenance, he caught my wrist and asked, 'Are you in Congress?'

'No, Sir,' I responded.

'Why don't you join Congress, then?' was his casual invitation.

I couldn't contain my excitement at the honour being bestowed on me. 'Yes, Sir!' I replied.

That was indeed a befitting start to my journey beyond the perimeters of college life, for though it did not catapult me onto the political scenario immediately, it did put me in the proximity of power.

Soon after gaining admission in my Masters, I also got a chance to apply for MBA, so I sought my father's permission to simultaneously pursue it, to which he agreed. So I sat for the entrance exam and much to my delight, cleared it. It was a real achievement as my engineer brother had also appeared but was unable to succeed! It just goes to show that degree or age are not relevant, as one's rationality, power of reasoning and judgement is what makes a difference.

The next step was the interview, and I was pretty confident about that too, even though I had suddenly lost interest in actually gaining admission in MBA, for I realised that this couldn't be done on a part-time basis, whereas. I had a responsibility in the shop. But the desire to see if I could crack the interview made me go for it. Soon I found myself facing the panel and was at my articulate best! I launched into the story of my work and partnership and my future plans without surfacing for breath, much to their consternation! Finally, when they were able to get a word in, one of them said, 'Young man, so what are you doing here? You already seem to be well set in your life and obviously don't require this degree!'

'That's not so, sir! Definitely, business is in my very DNA but I think doing an MBA will polish and hone my skills further!'

'But from the way you are describing your work and life, I think you are just wasting our time and yours as well!'

One of them said jokingly, 'Are you here to give the interview or take ours?'

That put paid to my MBA interview and though I walked away with the satisfaction that I had somehow scored, I didn't clear it in any way!

I think the easy way I had gained recognition in my college with regard to authority, in the form of the Principal and VC, had made me over-confident. I felt I could go anywhere and do anything and get away with it! I realise that this attitude has coloured many aspects of my life throughout and has actually been my undoing, for treating others with a little dignified diplomacy is essential to create a sense of integrity.

Life fell into a pattern thereafter, with me being occupied in our shop during the day and rushing from there to attend evening classes. One evening in November, while work season was at its peak, I called out to my father while preparing to leave for my class. My father acknowledged my call and I suddenly noticed the deep weariness on his face. In that instant, it struck me that my father must miss my helping hand at this time of the evening, for customers tended to come then. I had taken charge of the shop quite extensively, directing things, handling sales, calculating long bills in the days before calculators, and my rushing away for classes every evening must be proving to be a burden for him. In that moment, I decided I didn't need an M. Com degree, definitely not at the cost of my father's health and peace of mind! The very next day, I withdrew from my studies and made my father and our shop, and growing our business, my complete focus.

Chapter 2
Joining the Youth Congress

MY LIFE FELL into a set routine, going to the shop, tending to customers, then returning home late in the evening. After dinner, my father and I would watch television and discuss the day's happenings. Our connection deepened during that time as we literally became each other's shadow!

It was a busy, lucrative life yet my heart yearned for something more. I was circumscribed into a mundane timetable which did not appeal to my aesthetic sense! I decided to plunge into reading once again, for that is the one way to keep a mind fertile and agile, so I set about refurbishing my collection of books. I added some to my poetry stock but my interests had expanded to include philosophy, and psychology, and I bought Gandhi's *Experiments with Truth*, *Kamasutra* by Vatsyayana, an ancient Indian treatise on the art of fulfilled living, for I was no different from the other boys of my age and had a healthy curiosity about what life entailed.

I also purchased my own copy of the *Bhagavad Gita* to read on how to live a life of spiritual fulfilment! Another treasure was a book on Numerology by Cheiro, for numbers fascinated me, enticing me to master them! Time took on newer hues. I got into the habit of reading late into the night and consequently had difficulty in waking up in the mornings. Pitaji obligingly allowed me to come late to the shop. I would always be around to take charge whenever he had to fulfil any social obligation, for he did not like to shut it for any reason. Consequently, I rarely attended weddings, not even those of my cousins, or other functions, for my father attended while I was at the shop.

My interest in political ongoings had also deepened. Ever since I met Sanjay Gandhi, I had begun to take more interest in what was happening in our country. There was a bit of a chaos as this was the time before Emergency was imposed in the country. Sanjay Gandhi was becoming quite visible on the national front, for Indira Gandhi was in a way grooming him for a more supportive and prominent role. Though he was an authoritarian, he had a sharply focused political mind, which allowed him to grasp any situation and handle it powerfully. His rising popularity roused a fervour within me, and I was reminded of his casual invitation to join the Congress Party, and decided to join the Youth Wing in February 1975, with a half-formed thought that whenever I encountered Sanjay, I would be able to tell him that I had followed his advice. Thus began my official political journey, just before a very dark period of our history. Soon an atmosphere of apprehension prevailed, curtailing many activities, curbing the press and media freedom, even instigating unwarranted and unjust arrests of opposition leaders on the eve of the declaration of Emergency on 25 June 1975. Business came to a complete standstill as everyone was more concerned about saving their skins and keeping out of controversial situations.

Despite my disapproval of what was happening, I felt that since I was a part of the Youth wing, I should show solidarity and started to wear white khadi kurta pajamas, which are now synonymous with my identity! It was the norm for Sanjay Gandhi's followers to do so, as it made us stand out as his Brigade and vested some sort of authority in us. And it was very comfortable too. Once I got to know that Sanjay Gandhi had secret pockets stitched in his pajamas, so I too began to do so, and very useful have they proved to be, especially while travelling!

It was only about two months later that life began to limp back to some semblance of normalcy and we once again got involved in business. Despite the sword of Damocles in the form of Emergency hanging over our heads, my father had the prudence to stock up our shop and that stood us in good stead. About that time, my grandfather passed away, and my father had to go to his ancestral home for fifteen days. The management of the shop thus came onto me and I pride myself in thinking that those fifteen days became the most profitable in the whole season of that year, for I could make an unprecedented sale of our items.

***

Faith in the Divine had always been inherent in me right from the beginning and one incident really deepened it further. I accompanied my friend Shyam Narula, his brother and sister-in-law to Vaishno Devi. I was feeling pretty excited about it, but in the last 14-km climb to the shrine, Shyam's brother developed high fever. We were in a dilemma as to what to do. But Shyam's sister-in-law decided to put her entire faith in the deity and we commenced the climb. The main shrine of Maa Vaishno Devi is approached through a narrow tunnel, through which icy waters keep percolating and falling onto people's heads. The moment the water fell on Jagdish's head, he trembled violently and suddenly was perfectly fine! The fever vanished within a moment! This apparent miracle right in front of my eyes had a profound effect on me, strengthening my belief in the Divine unequivocally.

***

My English teacher in school, Ram Nathji had inculcated in me the habit of reading in the seventh class itself, and that is one aspect of my life that has been an immense resource of knowledge! I loved to understand the views behind all news and therefore made an effort to seek more, sometimes even going to hear the opposition leader, Vajpayee's speeches, for he was an excellent orator. I was in constant quest of deeper insights to life and thus my analytical mind sharpened. I began to explore the ramifications in the imposition of Emergency and realised that there was a caucus of four dignitaries, Siddharth Shankar Ray, V C Shukla, Om Mehta, and Bansi Lal, who had supported Indira and Sanjay Gandhi in their decision to impose Emergency. A yearning arose in my mind to meet these people and obtaining their addresses, I set out to do so. Power had always attracted me and I felt that they were really powerful as they had a strong hand in pushing Indira Gandhi to declare emergency in the country!

I had already met Siddhartha Shankar Ray at a felicitation ceremony for the Indian Cricket team who, under Ajit Wadekar, had returned victorious after defeating England and West Indies in 1971. My penchant for attending ceremonies and going to the centre of things had naturally made me a part of this felicitation as well. Ray was sitting on a small couch along with the captain, while his wife Maya was sitting on another. She presented a very charming picture in a sleeveless blouse and crisp cotton saree and I was impelled to sit next to her. We naturally got into a conversation, and to my delight, a picture of us talking together was published in a sports magazine! I felt that I knew Siddhartha Shankar Ray well and could connect with him anytime, so decided to meet the others first. I went to meet V C Shukla, but unfortunately it was a Sunday, and I was unable to do so. I could not meet Bansi Lal either, for he lived in Chandigarh, as he was the CM of Haryana.

So only Om Mehta was left and I went to meet him at

his residence on Prithviraj Road. It was a pleasant meeting where I got acquainted with his son, Rajesh Mehta, who was four years younger to me, and I am still in contact with him, meeting him often at IIC. In those days, there were not as many restrictions in meeting ministers as there are now, and people would mostly go to pester them for letters of recommendation or endorsements. But I have never asked for any favours. In fact, my favourite request to them used to be and still is, 'Babuji, I need your blessings and patronage,' a request that always paved the way for cordial relations and it did so with Om Mehta as well!

Chapter 3

A High-Flying Flag Idea

OCCASIONALLY, I WOULD visit the offices of the All India Youth Congress and All India Congress Committee headquarters hoping to meet Sanjay Gandhi, who would often come there. Going there would also provide me with an opportunity to interact with eminent personalities like Hari Krishan Shastri, joint secretary AICC and Lal Bahadur Shastri's eldest son, Margaret Alva, the joint secretary and also the general secretary V B Raju and so on. One day, I learnt that Sanjay Gandhi was to pass through Sadar Bazaar the very next day and he advised me to create a welcoming atmosphere for him. I felt quite excited with the prospect and so proposed to the President of the Sadar Bazaar Trader's Federation, M L Kumar to decorate the whole market, to which he readily agreed, as he held me in high esteem. He felt that I had a spark that would take me places! We then decided to put up colourful pennants and banners along the streets and Congress party flags on the shops. It also gave me an idea! Quickly, I went to my father and told him that we needed to make flags. He became a bit hassled as to how it could be done but I insisted on summoning one of our tailors, who did the stitching of quilts for our shop, and asked him the viability of the proposal. He approved it and we immediately set about procuring material for the flags. By evening, we had about a hundred flags, eighteen by twelve inches, ready. But how to get the party emblem onto them? The tailor suggested maybe we could get a printing block from a printing shop, nearby. The idea worked and a block and ink were procured and we had a perfect flag ready to be sold! It had cost us about fifty paise. Pitaji decided to price it at sixty paise, but I insisted on selling it for one rupee, saying that I had put in a lot of effort. Those flags began to sell like hot cakes, for every shopkeeper felt it was a good way of showing their support for Sanjay Gandhi and consequently the demand began rising. I had to constantly keep getting the raw material while the tailor had to continue stitching well into the night! We sold more than five hundred flags on that occasion, the last few even going at five rupees per piece!

As the day progressed, my shrewd mind snatched the opportunity to earn even further by creating a sort of pseudo shortage of it which naturally made prices shoot up! It was a super profitable time for us. A simple idea became the basis of a whole flag industry in that section of the market, for though initially we had complete monopoly over its production, other players joined in. It was the humble flag and even humbler small cotton towel that sold at precisely twenty-five paise that laid the foundations of my later day prosperity and I have no hesitation in accepting that I began my journey by selling this inconsequential item!

Chapter 4

The Excesses of Emergency

ANOTHER INCIDENT THAT stands out clearly in my mind as a time of great terror is when my father got arrested during the Emergency. I still grow cold when I recall his arrest, for it was completely unwarranted. What I have realised is that those in power desire to keep the affluent class in subjugation, else, being secure in their life and in possession of intellectual faculties, they might pose a threat to authority! Therefore, a number of cumbersome laws and rules are created to keep them occupied. A similar rule that we had been found violating was that there should be a price tag on every item in a shop. Ours was a sort of mini departmental store for household linen where we did more of wholesale work, with some retailing. It was thus a very difficult task to mark each and every item spread over the three floors of our shop. It was neither possible, nor practical to do so. In a random raid, a few unmarked items were found and that was enough to formulate a case against us. In a packet of ten hand towels, a few had remained untagged!

Unfortunately, when the team came, I was not present in the shop, as I had gone to Gurgaon for collection of dues. When I returned that day, I was shocked to see my father being herded with four other shopkeepers towards police vans, followed by a crowd of protesting traders! It was a totally unexpected sight and I could only run after them stammering, 'Where are you taking my father?' My father was completely unperturbed as he reassured me that it was only a minor thing and would be soon resolved. I begged the team to take me instead of my father for I was a partner in the shop. However, they refused to comply, saying my father was the one present in the shop and had signed the papers. To make matters worse, it was a Friday and courts were closed for the weekend. So Pitaji had to stay in Tihar jail for two days before we could do anything to get him out. Those were the most agonizing forty-eight hours for us.

Monday morning found us in the court with our lawyer, where we somehow managed to expedite all the necessary formalities for his bail and soon had him out of jail and back home! We had expected his morale to be down after spending two days in a dreadful atmosphere, but my father was unfazed. On the contrary, he had spent two very enjoyable days being catered to and taken care of! The moment he entered the prison area, he had been hailed by a local hooligan of Sadar Bazaar who was shocked to see him there. When he got to know the circumstances, he made every effort to make my father comfortable, for he knew the respect Pitaji had back home. Consequently, not only was everything being done for him, he was also being given massages by the goons there, as that is the easiest way of showing respect! In two days, he had made a number of friends, and was fondly seen off by them when he was allowed to leave!

The whole incident was really hurtful as I felt I had been let down by the party I had joined! After all, as an active party member, one who was at an All-India level, did I not deserve some consideration?

I shared my agony with my father, but with his wisdom, he was able to alleviate my anger. I was blaming Sanjay Gandhi for the whole incident, but my father assured me that he could not be responsible for the raid, for such decisions are taken only by overzealous lower echelons, who want to get into the good books of their seniors. So, rather than being victimised by Sanjay, as I was thinking, Pitaji had become a victim of the system. Sanjay Gandhi was not even aware of it. But I did not agree with him, and still held Sanjay Gandhi morally responsible, for was he not the one to instigate the formulation of such weird policies? My helplessness was utterly overwhelming and poured itself out in another of my much-appreciated couplets:

Sabke muh me hain zabane bolta koi nahi
Aankhen sabki hain khuli per dekhta koi nahi

(Tongues loll, sans speech
Eyes gaze, noticing nothing)

The incident filled me with fear about the extent to which power could be wielded over common people. It was this fear that kept me attached to the party as I felt incapable of being able to stand up against it. Maybe I felt more secure in being a part of it. The various policies of the Five-Point Programme, formulated under Sanjay Gandhi were ideal, but they were being carelessly implemented. The one point that drew major flak was his sterilisation programme where innumerable men were forced to undergo compulsory vasectomy. Rewards were being given for the numbers achieved, leading to the most unequivocally outrageous of all Emergency excesses. It was indeed a rule of terror during those times with seemingly no checks at all!

Chapter 5

A Nation in Turmoil

MARCH 1977 BROUGHT some relief for the country with the lifting of Emergency, and finally, people could breathe easy. The imposition on the Press was lifted, all opposition leaders were set free and enterprises began to limp back to normalcy. However, the Emergency had created a lot of pressure on many facets, especially in political circles, as many faced limitations and suppressions.

The immediate effect was that one of the senior leaders, Jagjivan Ram, walked out of the Congress Party, along with five others. His dissatisfaction against Party leaders had been festering since the 1971 Indo-Pak war, when no acknowledgement had been given to him, the defence minister for the victory, and it was credited to the Prime Minister. He was totally overlooked and in his own words said, 'This—was not even facilitated with a garland of shoes!' But then this was nothing new for the ruling party, for such manipulations were common for them! When India was defeated in the Indo-China war in 1962, all blame was put on the then defence minister, V K Menon and he was forced to resign. Now when a victory had happened, credit for it naturally had to go to the top level. That is another matter that forty-one years after it won its Independence, Bangladesh posthumously honoured Jagjivan Ram as being instrumental in helping the country gain liberation from Pakistan! It must have been a balm to his soul that at least his contribution had not gone unnoticed!

But immediately after the Emergency, he resigned from his position along with Hemwati Nandan Bahuguna and a few others and together they formed a new group, Congress for Democracy, which later merged with the Janata Dal. This was the point from where the ruling Congress party began to slide towards its downfall, with the PM even declaring in the newspapers the next day that she had been stabbed in the back. In actual fact, the downward movement had begun in 1973 itself, when Indira Gandhi had appointed A N Ray as the Chief Justice of India, superseding three senior judges, J M Shelat, K S Hegde and A N Grover. It was a great blow to the judiciary, one of the most important pillars of Democracy, for by interfering in its ordained processes, she was trying to manipulate the system in her own favour, challenging the hundred-year-old Congress institution! This was naturally criticised by many senior opposition leaders who began to demand a Presidential system, instigating a state of chaos in the country. Even President V V Giri had warned her against the appointment. There are two people at the highest posts, and both must defer to each other to run the country harmoniously, and yet she chose to ignore Giri's advice, paving the way for her own eventual downfall!

The newly formed CFD party held a huge rally at the Ramlila Grounds where H N Bahuguna's opening statement drew accolades from the huge crowd—'Till now the country was being ruled by only a "one and a half" person strong government...,' referring to Indira Gandhi and her son Sanjay Gandhi, who was not regarded in good light, being of a very rash and ruthless nature. Though he chose not to hold any official position in the government, he was vested with extra constitutional powers, which he unfortunately misused. It was no wonder that both mother and son lost the ensuing elections, an unprecedented defeat for the Congress party for the first time after Independence. It is said that the devaluation of politics began with them, for their intent seemed to be only to grab power!

***

Our initiative to get party flags made was a great hit and we began receiving big orders. Prior to this, a few flags were being made by party workers themselves, with decorations being done with colourful pennants and banners, but once it was seen what gaiety they added to the atmosphere, flags suddenly became an essential accessory. As we held the monopoly for making them initially, our renown spread far and wide, heralding a lucrative period for us! Our very first order for Rs 2.5 lakh worth of flags came from the general secretary of the AICC for the upcoming general elections. It was a huge order, giving us almost 50 per cent profit! And it was just not for us alone, but a whole lot of people associated with us; those supplying raw swathes of cotton, dyers, tailors, and transporters, also got a chance to earn well. Looking back, I feel a deep sense of satisfaction that a simple flash of an idea had such brilliant consequences, becoming a source of income for many! I pride myself for having given birth to the readymade flag industry in our country, for it was seen that it was easier to order rather than to get party workers to make them.

***

It encouraged my father to get our house renovated. It had not been done ever since we had shifted there! Other than my eldest sister, none of my siblings had got married, so there had been no need to do up the house. Father took over things at the shop and for the next nine months, I was involved with bricks, mortar and carpenters as the first and second floors were renovated. Both my brothers were at home, but neither helped in any way in the construction procedure. One evening my father blasted them for their indifferent behaviour, for when he returned from the shop, both were watching television while I was rushing around madly trying to get the cement and steel unloaded from a truck and dealing with payments to the labourers!

***

There was naturally no question of raising a voice against any injustices in the country. But that did not spare us from being at the receiving end of the anomalies of the system. There was a raid by the Municipal Corporation on our shop in 1975, when they partly demolished the roof of the two rooms on the top floor, declaring them unauthorised. My father filed a case against the Municipal Corporation and DDA saying that the rooms were present when he bought the shop. He felt I should utilise my expertise in learning law in college, even though I had clarified innumerable times that what I had studied was Mercantile law and different from what was needed in such cases, but to no avail. And so, I ended up going to court and dealing with all legal matters.

On one such visit, I inadvertently witnessed a murder there, in broad daylight. That was the most appalling moment of my life as I helplessly watched a son stabbing his father multiple times, blaming him vociferously for not giving him his due share in the ancestral property. There were a number of people standing by, but no one came forward to help the poor man. An inherent apathy has set itself in the hearts of all humanity, denuding it of compassion, so that no one wants to take any initiative. That moment of acute powerlessness was so intense that it put a subconscious fear in my mind about the thought of a son, which maybe was responsible for later manifesting a distressing relationship in my own life.

Chapter 6

Trouble at the Personal Front

NARESH BHUTANI WAS one of my good friends from college, with whom I would often share my feelings. Once I told him that I was going through a lot of stress because of my innumerable responsibilities.

'You know what, I know a very good way of relieving stress. Why don't you come with me to experience something different?'

I demanded a little suspiciously, 'What is that?'

'Come on! Trust me! You will feel uplifted!' was his jolly response as he refused to divulge more.

He took me to a small house on the first floor in Sarai Rohilla, where a plump, middle-aged lady welcomed us warmly. Understanding was beginning to dawn on me, but in that moment, I could do nothing as he gaily introduced me to her. Soon she summoned her two daughters and it was obvious that Naresh was quite familiar with them. He turned to me and said, 'You can take your pick!' In a rather bemused fashion, I indicated the fairer of the two and soon found myself alone with her in the next room. I suddenly realised that the girl had already removed her lower garment and was lying down on the bed. It was as if I had gone into shock. My knowledge about mating between couples had come from the books I had read, mainly the *Kamasutra*, which even discouraged it with one's own wife in the initial few days after marriage! The emphasis was on revering the coming together of a man and a woman, of valuing each other and spiritualising their intimacy. As I stared transfixed at the sight of her bare legs, a short story *Khol Do* by well-known Urdu writer, Saadat Hasan Manto, flashed through my mind. It was about a young Hindu girl who had to face innumerable onslaughts on her body during the partition holocaust but was in the end rescued and admitted into hospital. She was lying half-conscious in a closed room when the doctor entered and immediately ordered the nurse to open the window. Even in her half-dead state, the girl had begun to open her lower garment. The helplessness and apathy inherent in that simple gesture was now apparent to me in the form of the girl in front of me. I almost shouted at her, 'What are you doing?' She stared back in astonishment, then hastily straightening her clothes, sat up, muttering under her breath that this was all everyone wanted. That one action of hers was enough to show the bestiality that she too was being forced to endure and it really broke my heart. She burst into tears and I could only talk soothingly to her and even gave her some personal money, even though I had seen my friend making a payment to the lady outside. That encounter really made me wish I could do something concrete to alleviate this social evil of society!

I came back home, not only more stressed, but more disillusioned and dejected as well!

Another instance that shook me involved my friends, who took me to a cabaret dance bar. When the female dancer approached me, feigning passion, I stammered, and asked, 'What's your good name?'
Pat came her reply, 'I only have bad names.'
I never went back to that kind of place in my life.

***

My father had been right in his observation that the renovation of the house was needed for things to get unstuck, and the new year brought a new member into our family. My other sister, Simran, married a handsome Naval Lieutenant Commander in February 1978. Pitaji held the wedding in Oberoi Intercontinental and it was a wedding filled with wonder, for many of us had never entered such a fancy place before, including myself! The icing on the cake was that my father walked in coolly just minutes before the groom had to be welcomed, as he didn't need to oversee any preparations. No one is ever happy to see anyone rising from amidst them and whispers began circulating as to how Lala Bhagat Prasad had made so much money that not only had he renovated his home but had also got his daughter married off in a five-star hotel! It was inevitable that someone would have lodged a complaint against us, for the demolition squad of the MCD landed at our house soon without notice. Panic stricken, we hastened to meet our lawyer, who advised immediate application for a stay order and another senior officer of MCD, Om Prakash Gupta, who was a distant relative as well, helped us to get the necessary papers and the demolition squad was thus sent back. The incident sent my mother into a state of depression from which she couldn't recover for the rest of her life, even needing electric shocks. The countdown for the downfall of our family started from there, proving once again that the evil eye does exist!

My trips to the court continued as I had to follow up some case or the other, but once I had finished appearing for our case, I would peep into the other courtrooms, for the varied scenarios of life that they presented were truly intriguing! That is when I happened to see Sanjay Gandhi and V C Shukla sitting in the District and Session Judge, O N Vohra's courtroom one day. I was astonished, as they were the two most elusive beings and despite all my efforts, I hadn't been able to meet them and here they were, in front of me. I was curious and made my way into the courtroom to sit next to them, choosing V C Shukla's side rather than Sanjay's.

As the proceedings went ahead, I realised that the case was connected to the recent release of the movie, *Kissa Kursi Ka*, a satire on the politics of Indira and Sanjay Gandhi. It had been banned by the Indian Government during Emergency and all prints along with the master print were confiscated from the office of the Censor Board. Later they were taken to the Maruti factory set up by Sanjay Gandhi in Gurgaon and were burnt. Once the Emergency was over, a Commission had been set up to look into the excesses committed during that time and Sanjay Gandhi, along with V C Shukla, the then Information and Broadcasting Minister, were found guilty of burning the prints. A legal case was launched against them by the director of the movie, Amrit Nahata, and that was the hearing I had walked into.

During the court proceedings, Sanjay turned towards Shukla to ask him the meaning of a law term. With all my court visits, I was well-versed with its terminology, and as I was always in that space of supreme confidence, I immediately answered Sanjay's query! They both looked at me in surprised admiration, taking in my outfit of white kurta pajama which showed that I was a party worker. Such would be my attitude that the other would automatically value me, considering me to be someone of importance! They connected to me immediately as an equal, accepting me as one of them. As I introduced myself, I told V C Shukla: 'I am a great devotee of yours, Sir, and have been wanting to meet you for so long!' That was enough to put me in his good books and I was able to strike up a closer relationship with both of them. Subsequently, I made it a point to be present in court whenever they had a hearing and would remain there the whole day, impressing them with my proactiveness. During one of the hearings, he imparted a jewel of an advice to me which has stood me in good stead my whole life.

He gently admonished me for being overly loquacious, saying that when you meet a senior personality, you have only a couple of minutes to put your concern across, so it is essential to choose words carefully! Always do a little homework beforehand, gaining knowledge about the person or the situation you have to interact with. It shows presence of mind and brings in a personal touch! Later, I realised that V C Shukla had been indirectly admonishing Sanjay Gandhi as well, for he had been clueless about the hearing, asking innumerable questions all through the day.

My relationship with V C Shukla carried on till his unexpected demise, with him even visiting my home, much to the astonishment of other people! He took an interest in me and guided me as a mentor, thus becoming my foremost political Guru! Under his guidance, I got my first visiting card made, as according to him, it was the best way of introducing oneself. The card had the Congress flag on top followed by my name with Youth Congress Activist written prominently below, and also 'Manufacturer of Election Publicity Material' and 'Supplier to AICC.' It was impressive and opened many doors for me later.

Despite the defeat of the Congress in the elections, I felt that I somehow owed allegiance to them as I had earned a lot through their offices.

Consequently, I decided to go and meet Indira Gandhi on the occasion of Diwali that year at her residence at 12, Willingdon Crescent to express my gratitude. I loved to associate with power and she was not in power then, so it was easier to meet her. When I was ushered into her presence, it struck me that she seemed to have somehow shrunk in size! The authoritative aura around her was completely missing, leaving her as a somewhat washed-out version of her earlier self. It reinforced my inference that loss of power denudes a person's personality, the same is what I had felt on Bill Clinton's visits to India while in office and after leaving it. I felt a deep emotion welling up from within me as I empathised with her condition but somewhere in the back of my mind, the thought lurked that when things go beyond limits, nature takes its own course and brings about redemption. The extreme atrocities that the mother-son duo had inflicted on the country were against the very precepts of humanity and someday things had to fall apart.

Indira Gandhi and Sanjay Gandhi, had therefore, faced a resounding defeat in the General Elections of 1977.

However, the new Janata Dal government was not stable, and a lot of infighting was already taking place within it, much to the disappointment of Jai Prakash Narayan who had pioneered the revolt against the ruling government. There were four contenders for the top position—Morarji Desai, Jagjivan Ram, Charan Singh and Chandrashekhar.

I recalled how aptly I had summed up the current political situation in the concluding remark of my popular article, 'Inflation and Revolution' published in my college magazine. I concluded the article with a remark; 'Our country is facing two main crises, first is the crisis of character and second, the crisis of leadership.' It seemed prophetic!

The Gandhis had inflicted a lot of atrocities on the country but the subsequent government were bent upon disillusioning the people completely! No one was emerging as a strong leader and the issue was finally resolved by allotting a shorter period to each so that each could be in power for some time, like we resolve fights among children!

Chapter 7

A Poetry Mentor

MY LOVE FOR *shayari* had led me to many *Kavi sammelans* and *mushairas* right from 1971 itself. The most well-known was held annually at Red Fort on Republic Day, attracting many venerable poets, some from foreign lands. This had become my favourite haunt, listening and learning from estimable poets, well versed in their art.

My sociability had taken me to the forefront and I had made my presence felt by appreciating and fraternising with as many poets as I could. Makhmoor Sayeedi was one such revered poet, a dignified personality, who I really looked up to and through whom I met my first poetry Guru. He would often anchor the programmes, coordinating the poets who were reading their compositions. One day, I spotted him standing casually outside Delite cinema house with a few friends, enjoying a *paan* at a local shop. Parking my car, I approached him enthusiastically, my attention completely focused on him.

'Sir, I really appreciate the way you compered at the Red Fort meet! If you remember, I spoke and appreciated you then, itself!'

Then suddenly, I said, 'Sir, I would like to visit you at your home.'

'Why do you want to come home?'

'Sir, I would like to become your *shagird*!'
'*Shagird*?' He seemed astonished.
'Yes, please, Sir, I need your guidance on my work.'
'You write poetry?'
'Yes, Sir, in Hindi and Urdu.',
'Really, in Urdu too? Can you write it as well?'
'Not write, Sir, just a little composing and I would like your opinion about it.'

He acquiesced and invited me to his home in Turkman Gate the very next day.

Early the next morning, I presented myself at his small house tucked away in the bylanes of Old Delhi, carrying a box of sweets and my treasured book of thoughts.

He took my diary and began going through it. 'Oh this is quite thick!' he commented.

'Yes, I have been writing for many years.'

A line suddenly caught his attention:

Kya yahi hai ishq
Ki ek shakhs me kho jaiye
Iss tarah bezaar iss duniya se
Kyun ho jaiye

(Is this love
That you get lost in one person, and forget the world?)

'What?! You have written this?'
'Yes, Sir.'
'How old are you, young man?'
'Twenty-four.'
'And when did you write this?'
'When I was in college.'
'In college you were writing such elevated thoughts?'
He shook his head and said, 'I cannot be your mentor, for your

poetry has a modern form and I don't write that. It would be better if you approach Kumar Pashi. He will be able to guide you in a better way.'

I was puzzled. 'You have not heard of him? He is indeed an excellent poet and more of your genre. He was standing with me last night. Didn't you notice the other gentleman with me?' Makhmoor added, 'I will call him and let him know about you. You set up a meeting and visit him.' I agreed and left with Kumar Pashi's contact details, unaware as to how momentous the upcoming meet was going to be, for in him I found what I had always been looking for in a mentor and our relationship lasted his whole life. I connected with him even more when I got to know that his real name was Shankar Dutt Sachdeva, as the name Shankar has always had a special place in my heart. In fact, such is my attachment to the name that Divine Providence sent another Shankar into my life, Mani Shankar Aiyar, as my political Guru much later in 1991.

The very next day, I called him up and found that he stayed quite close in the Delhi Gate area. A convenient time was decided for the subsequent evening and I presented myself at his house at the appointed hour. Simplicity seemed to be the essence of his life, evident from his casual clothes and surroundings, and I immediately launched into an introduction of myself.

'Sir, I have been writing for many years but have never been fortunate enough to get any guidance. I don't even know if my work is up to the mark or not. I depend on you for a true evaluation.'

He took the diary I offered him and began flipping through it, his attention suddenly caught by a couplet I had written during Emergency, inspired by Ghalib.

Sabke muh me hain zabane bolta koi nahi

His reaction was as full of disbelief as Makhmoor Sayeedi's, exclaiming in astonishment, 'You have composed this? But it is echoing my thoughts exactly!'
'Your thoughts, Sir? May I hear them?'

>*'Wo hukme zababandi lagane bhi na dega*
>*Per Dil ki koi baat sunane bhi na dega'*
>
>*(He won't impose though curbs on speech*
>*Yet won't allow speaking out our heart, either)*

We were both amazed at the similarity of our themes and felt immediately drawn to each other.

'Sir, will you become my mentor?'

'Absolutely! I will be happy to mentor you! But you know I don't like to make disciples or followers, so I think I will regard you as a good friend.' 'I am truly obliged and delighted, dear Sir! First teach me how to write a ghazal! I don't know how to do that.'

'But you already are writing this form; you only have to extend it a little more,' was Pashi's immediate response.

'Just continue rhyming the last words, keeping the same scheme. Like you have said *'Sabke muh me hain zabane bolta koi nahi'*, then you have said *'.... dekhta koi nahi'*, continue with *'...sochta koi nahi'*, *'.... jaanta koi nahi'*, and so on, along with a connecting thought. First write the rhyming words and then put in the relevant ideas.'

That really impressed me and so inspired was I that I sat up late into the night to complete it as my mentor had suggested. I went back the very next day. He was delighted with my enthusiasm and even more with my work. Thus began my real journey on the path of poetic literature under the mentorship of Kumar Pashi, changing my thought processes and life altogether! It was he who taught me to be a great observer of humankind and all the trials they were embroiled in and to make that the subject matter of my poems. I had been focused more on love and its ramifications, but Kumar Pashi was of the opinion that it was an outdated notion, that there were more dimensions to life than just love, which had become an overrated emotion and a topic for everyone to toss about. His perspective was so utterly relevant that I immediately adopted that thought. We had deep discussions about the variegated hues of life and how to present them in minimal words. Thus began the golden period of my profound ruminations, turning me into a prolific poet.

April 1978 dawned bringing a new thrill into my life. With Makhmoor Sayeedi's help, my first ghazal got published in the literary section of the Urdu newspaper *Milap*, along with my photograph. Within a few days, another one got printed in Pratap. I was ecstatic and framed and hung both the cuttings in our drawing room. I began to add 'Manzar' to my name, for the sobriquet of 'Dost' didn't seem to fit into the now elevated scenario. So, at my Ustaad's suggestion, I researched and came across this new name, which really appealed to me. And thus, I appeared in print for the very first time under my new pen name, Mahesh Manzar, adding immensely to my stature!

The publishing of my poems in newspapers opened many avenues for me, the first being an interview on All India Radio in a programme called *Nai Nasl, Nai Roshni* where I was asked questions by Suraiya Hashmi, a senior radio anchor, about my interest in shayari and in the Urdu language and how I had become a poet. I got a cheque of Rs 20 from All India Radio for that interview, which I treasure to this day. Soon after that, both my Gurudev and Makhmoor Sayeedi put my name down for another annual public *mushaira*, at the Ghalib Academy Auditorium on Independence Day. My compositions attracted a lot of appreciation.

The interview paved the way for many further interactions

and I got the chance to participate in a mushaira on AIR for the first time. It was a small group who were reading their poems, with only one lady, Kanta Shabnam Grover, one of the most beautiful ladies I had ever seen, the wife of a Justice of the Supreme Court, about forty years older than me.

After the programme, she approached me and said, 'Manzar sahib, you really dive into the depths of your poetry.'

'Madam, I not only dive deep into my poetry but can dive deeply into love as well!' was my instant rejoinder, making her feel charmingly flustered. Was this slip of a boy flirting with her, disregarding the immense years between them? But that was my nature, always ready to make the best of any situation. Laughing off my audaciousness, she invited me to come to tea with her and her husband. Nothing happens on its own— seeds have to be sown along the way for the fruits to be gained and here I gained a lifelong association with her whole family!

***

About this time, my brothers got married within a span of fifteen days, adding two more members to our clan. It is an accepted belief handed down from our forefathers that two weddings should not be held within a short span of time. It brings ill luck into the family and subsequent events did prove that to be true!

For the eldest brother, we went to Agra as his father-in-law was a magistrate there. It was a lavish event at a five-star hotel as my father desired. From among the guests, one very delicate looking, fair, slim girl caught my attention. Later, I got to know that she was my new sister-in-law's cousin. We stayed overnight in a haveli-like house, which we thought had been hired for the wedding guests. Imagine my surprise when in the morning, as I came out after my bath, I found the same girl waiting outside with her clothes and a towel!

I blabbered, 'Oh, what are you doing here?'

'This is our house.'
'Really? I thought it was hired!'
'No, I am Prabha Di's cousin and we live in this house.'
'And what is your name?'
'Megha.'
'That's a pretty name and so are you!'

Going pink with embarrassment, she hastily retreated into the just vacated washroom, leaving me staring at her disappearing figure.

I found myself deeply drawn towards her as a warm flame began to glow within me. Such was its strength that even after returning home, I couldn't get her out of my head. A few days after the wedding, I asked my brother to get his sister-in-law's number so that I could talk to her and see if she too was of a similar mind. Thus, I connected with her and got her acquiescence for our match. I was quite thrilled and informed my parents that I would like to marry my elder *bhabhi's* cousin. They agreed with my choice and approached her parents, who were equally delighted, for not only was ours a reputable family, but they had seen how proactively friendly I had been during the wedding. Unfortunately, my sister-in-law refused her acceptance of the match, saying that it was not a good idea to have two sisters in the same family! I felt betrayed in some way, but naturally things couldn't progress after her vehement denial!

***

Ten days later, in the first week of March, 1979, my second brother too got married to a gynaecologist, leaving the way clear for me! My father had got three of his children settled within a year, that too with beautiful alliances from reputable families. He now began to look for a bride for me, but I was more difficult to please. I felt that as I was on the slight side, my wife should be a little heavier. I refused a very good match on this ground itself! People thought us mad as the family was very well off and ready to spend a lot on the wedding. Pitaji had left it entirely to me, his only condition being that the wedding be held in a five-star hotel! Indeed, that is one of the aspects of my community that I don't like at all, making open monetary demands at the time of weddings with families even haggling and bargaining! This had even put my father and myself into a very embarrassing situation once while looking for grooms for my sister. When I refused the match, the middleman gave the excuse that the boy concerned was a little eccentric as he was a poet! He would shake his head at how we had refused an offer from a family willing to spend Rs Three lakh on the wedding just because the girl was neither fair nor plump! He got me thinking about what sort of girl did I really want! I had always been fascinated with the song, *Chand si Mehbooba ho meri tum, aisa maine socha tha...* meaning that 'My love is no less than the moon, that's how I thought of her...' The song now became the basis of my inspiration. A deep soul-searching ensued and all my aspirations poured out in the form of a much-feted *nazm*, a love ballad of fifty lines, which was even printed in one magazine! Another poet asked how a young, unmarried boy could describe his would-be bride with such clarity, for it was a precedent in itself! This composition is quite close to my heart and is the longest of all the poems that I have written to date!

The middleman put us in touch with another family whose daughter was exactly as I demanded, quite fair and a little plump, but who wouldn't be able to spend above Rs one lakh! That was perfectly acceptable to us, making him realise that we actually meant what we had said!

A meeting was set up to see the prospective bride and I was really impressed by her milk and peaches complexion, but found her to be heavier than my expectations. A confusion ensued in her mind as she mistook my brother, Dr Devender, who had accompanied me, to be the intended groom!

When she learnt about the confusion, she was not very enthusiastic, expressing her doubts about my stature to her sister-in-law, but then her brothers convinced her that she was getting a very good match in only Rs one lakh! That at least gave me the pleasure of knowing that they did realise my value though subsequent events did not support the initial reaction! I wasn't very happy either, as I felt her 55 kg weight would be too heavy for my sprightly 45 kg frame!

I had always read that the husband should be a little superior to the wife in all regards, but here I was feeling a little disadvantaged. But my sister and father convinced me to look at the match favourably. According to my father, one never got everything that one desired and so had to compromise at times while my sister was of the opinion that marrying someone slighter than myself would only bring forth a brood of even tinier children!

Not only was my family pressurising me, but even the girl's brothers would often turn up at my shop. I would be quite high-handed with them at times, impressing them with my knowledge and links. I even handed them my *nazm* to make them understand what kind of a match I was looking for. But they only began to regard me as a genius and were even more eager for the match.

Finally, the one who had suggested the connection pinned me down one day. Why was I dilly-dallying so much? 'It is not as if I had the looks of a hero or something extraordinary,' he said to me. 'Why the delay?' he questioned. I took my dilemma to my mentor, Kumar Pashi, for I regarded him next to my father. It was only when he assured me that it would be a good alliance, did I agree. Besides, who can withstand the force of Destiny? Both of us were reluctant for the match, and yet were persuaded against our better judgement to agree. I think the fate of our volatile married life was fixed then and there!

Another meeting was subsequently arranged with the family. I was again asked for my answer and being fed-up, I gave my acceptance. The relief on their faces was quite evident, and the girl even surprised me by suddenly touching my feet. I hastily pulled her up, castigating her not to do this and felt quite smitten by her dimpled smile! I asked her if she had read and understood my *nazm* and she nodded.

Later events clearly showed that she had not. But blissfully unaware of the veiled future, I accepted her answer, giving her the name of Sandhya and promised to be her support throughout life, as my heart filled with empathy for her. She had never seen her father, for he had passed away before she was born. In my mind, she had been bereft of a father's support, so she must not have been as indulged or fearless as a child is under her father's mantle. It was only later that I got to know that on the contrary, she had been a really pampered child, used to having everything done her own way, and was, therefore, quite intolerant. When I looked back at my life, I realised that I too had been no less pampered by my father thus having the qualities of intolerance and impatience in myself, too! If two people with such traits are put together, it is nothing but a recipe for disaster and that is exactly what my married life turned out to be!

Chapter 8

Distress in Person and in Politics

I GOT ENGAGED on 15 July 1979, and the turbulent essence of this significant event of my life got reflected at the national political level as well, for on the same day, Morarji Desai's government collapsed as Charan Singh and Raj Narain pulled out of the Janata Dal, forcing Desai to resign. Chaos continued to reign in the country as with the outside support of Indira's Party, Charan Singh became PM, only to resign twenty-three weeks later when the Congress Party suddenly withdrew its support, paving the way for elections.

Those were not very open times, so naturally there was not much interaction between my fiancée and myself other than an occasional call. I was wrapped up in my composing and symposiums and in our shop. After the radio presentation, I participated in a television programme with amazing success! Another poem was published in a well-known Hindi literary magazine, *Sarika*. December found me neck deep in work, for we had received a big order for the upcoming elections paraphernalia. It was a lucrative period, creating an atmosphere of auspiciousness for the family!

Elections were in January 1980, with Indira Gandhi winning with a clear majority. Euphoric, I felt like doing something exclusive and took a bouquet for Indira Gandhi to congratulate her. This gesture was the beginning of what I termed, 'Bouquet Politics,' for I would make it a point to give bouquets on special occasions to the politicians I admired. Later, I added sweet boxes for those whom I wanted to show major regard. My 'Bouquet Politics' was an inspiration of my poetry Guru who opined that relationships need investment!

I attended a national symposium in Gwalior on 14 January, encouraged by my Gurudev, Kumar Pashi who accompanied me. It was a huge platform, with a 10,000-strong audience, but by now I was a pro and read my compositions with great aplomb, nattily dressed in my father's black sherwani! I was appreciated and had my picture published in the local newspaper the next day with the title, Junior Mirza Ghalib! Never had I felt so acclaimed and the euphoria continued into the next month for my nuptials. My engagement took place the next month at the hotel Taj Mansingh, with many dignitaries not only from the world of literature, but even from the political scenario, for there too, I had been making my mark!

The wedding at Ashok Hotel was a magnificent affair. As the evening progressed, I began to feel overwhelmed and reached out to Pashi who fetched a laced drink for me. It pepped me up and before long, I had merrily joined my sisters and sisters-in-law who were dancing to the shehnai. I was dancing in the centre, surrounded by them all! Makhmoor Sayeedi, who often moderated at big poetical meets, took centrestage at my function, for not only my own composition for the new bride was being read by none other than Mujeeb Siddiqui, who was on deputation with the BBC, but Kumar Pashi, too, had composed a special sehra for the occasion. Mujtaba Hussain, a world-famous satirist, honoured me by presenting a pen sketch about my personality, designating it as my wedding gift. Quite a few eminent luminaries like the former Justice of the Supreme Court of India, A N Grover and his wife, former CM of Haryana, Banarsi Das Gupta, eldest son of Desh Bandhu Gupta, Vishwa Bandhu Gupta and his very beautiful American wife, poured their blessings on us. Many complimented us on our looks and the picture we presented together, comparing me to Rajendra Kumar and Sandhya to a popular heroine of the times, Sulakshna Pandit!

I spent the next few days at home, wrapped in the euphoria of a new relationship. The initial days after a marriage are the most crucial ones, as both partners have to build a base for their whole life. That's why couples like to go away from the family scenario so that they can have exclusive time with each other. Unfortunately, I had not planned to go on a honeymoon as I was not very clear about the concept. We had got a new room built on the roof, opposite to my brothers' rooms, and so spent most of our time there.

By March, I was back in my routine, and soon after that Sandhya realised that she had conceived, as she was beginning to remain quite unwell. She did not seem very happy, as it was too early in the marriage and one day, voiced her dissatisfaction, saying that everything had been in a hurry and that I had not even taken her on a honeymoon. I received a jolt, never having considered the matter to be of importance. But now, egged on by her insistence, I booked a trip to Goa, a destination I had wanted to visit.

However, the whole tour turned out to be a complete disaster, as I had no experience of organising an out-of-town trip, ever before. We flew down, the first time that either of us had flown. She wasn't comfortable as it made her queasy and I didn't know how to handle the situation. Our first stop was at Bombay and the hotel was not very good, spoiling our mood right at the beginning, itself. Besides the travelling had made her feel even more unwell. Goa proved to be equally uninspiring, especially as her bouts of sickness continued. We had booked a cottage near the beach, but the fishy smell proved to be intolerable for her. Thankfully, we returned in a few days, completely disillusioned with the charisma of a honeymoon!

Some days later, a few of my eldest brother's friends came to visit him. His wife was resting as she was in her last trimester and not feeling well. I requested my wife to see to the serving of refreshments to the guests. 'That's not my task! His wife is upstairs, she can come and do it,' she replied. I was shocked at her response and said, 'That's not right! We live together and everyone contributes to the work. Were my sisters-in-law not feeding me before you came?' In fact, I had a very good relationship with them.

'I will not cater to your brother's guests. You can call Bhabhi to do so.'

I was furious and scolded her severely, 'This is not done in our household. We all help out whenever needed.'

My father was sitting nearby and overheard our exchange. He added, 'We live in a joint family, my child, and there is no division that one will not cater to another's guests!'

Sandhya stood up, red-faced, and without a word, marched out of the door and down the stairs. Within minutes, she was out on the street, leaving father and son staring at each other in consternation. We caught up with her and persuaded her to return, for she even threatened suicide. We were completely taken aback at this hitherto unknown facet of hers!

Soon after, she went to stay at her close relative's house. A few days later, he invited me for dinner so that I could bring my wife back. I drove down to their place, an hour away. I was not welcomed with warmth, but invited to partake of dinner. Once that was over, he announced that Sandhya would not return that evening as it was late. I was surprised, for hadn't he himself invited me to take her?

'So what! Now I am saying that she will not go today. You can stay and take her tomorrow or come again!'

I was thrown aback by this autocratic diktat, but refused

to comply. Sandhya's mother was silent and so were her elder brother and his wife. Her brother also blamed my mother for oppressing his sister, another totally baseless accusation, as my mother had been in a state of depression for more than two years, so how could she oppress anyone? I was furious at his unjustified comments and massive disrespect on the part of the whole family that I gave an ultimatum that either the brothers could bring her back themselves, or else we could divorce. I had been insulted, and so saying, I left. The drive back home was the worst ever in my whole life. I was so agonised that I couldn't even drive properly, and was forced to stop a couple of times to calm down. My dignity had taken such a beating. How would I face my family's queries?

By now, both of us were fed up with each other, myself because of her volatile nature and she maybe because of my over-passionate one! In actual fact, my body could not match the intensity of my spirit, being on the slighter side, and the initial overindulgence after our wedding had taken its toll on it!

Moreover, her attitude seemed so unreasonable, as I was never sure when she would erupt and retaliate. One cannot live such a life; the very charm of living is lost. I poured the whole story out to my father on my return and he, too, was equally shocked by this undefinable behaviour and supported me completely.

At the time of my brothers' marriages, my father had checked out the prospective families, but had overlooked doing so at mine. He now decided to dig into their background and what we uncovered, traumatised us! Her father had not had a natural death; he had been murdered! We were unable to decide what to do and finally my father said that I would have to cope with the situation in the best way I could, accepting it as Destiny. Though I had threatened a divorce, those were not times when it was readily formalised. Marriages were regarded as long lasting!

A month later, one of her sisters-in-law, who lived in Karol Bagh, got in touch with me and persuaded me to visit. I was on good terms with her, so I consented. When I reached there, Sandhya was also present. She began to cry and ask for forgiveness, melting down all my anger and resistance. She even requested that I should take her back from there itself. However, I remained firm on my decision that her brothers would have to bring her back, especially after having faced so much ignominy. They had made it seem as if we tortured her when nothing was further from the truth.

My elder sister-in-law was a doctor and yet she did her fair share of work in the house, overburdening none. I told her once again that even if she came alone, she was welcome, for she was a part of the family and was pregnant, as well. A few days later, her third brother, along with the eldest brother's son, brought her back home. It was a real victory for me, for till now, I had been a little on the backfoot, but this incident made me gain the upper hand. I gave her the name of Chhaya, for I was mythologically connecting my life to a story of the Sun God where his wife was unable to tolerate his brilliance and so changed places with her own shadow, bringing her to the forefront. Sandhya was now just a shadow of my dreams and my hopes, and I, therefore, felt that Chhaya was a more befitting name for her as she had indeed cast a shadow on my life!

My father had always stood like a rock behind me and gave me his full support, totally unlike my brothers, who seemed to be enjoying my discomfiture.

Chapter 9

A Corrupt Congress Creeps Back

THE COUNTRY FACED another jolt with the death of Sanjay Gandhi on 23 June 1980 when he was only thirty-three. He was an avid aviator and that became the reason for his demise while on a manoeuvre over Safdarjung airport. I made haste to reach Indira Gandhi's house and was among the first few to arrive.

Sanjay's inert body lay on the patio covered with a white sheet while Mrs Gandhi stood towards his head, as if carved out of stone, her eyes hidden behind dark glasses. A grieving Maneka Gandhi was sitting in a distraught manner nearby, along with ten-year-old Rahul and eight-year-old Priyanka, surrounded by a few women. I unobtrusively went and sat with some other people on the other side.

The country had lost a dynamic leader and his going had left a void. He had been a forceful personality with a brilliant mind, but unfortunately seemed to be in a hurry to experience everything, bringing an element of rashness into his life. All his projects that included setting up the Maruti factory, regaining power for his mother in the country, imposing strange laws with good intentions, but bad planning, even down to driving rashly and his ultimate death reflected his impetuous character.

He, however, had a very strong vision for the country, wanting to bring in radical change, but perhaps, the country was not ready for it. He was indeed a true patriot very much in touch with his roots, with a healthy respect for all sections of society. At the same time, he was not blind to the anomalies happening in the system! Somehow, I was deeply impacted by his untimely demise, for he had become a sort of connect with the Party for me.

***

Chhaya expected to be taken out on Sundays, but I preferred scouting marketing opportunities and had earmarked Sunday for collection of dues. She thus had a big grudge against me as her brothers habitually took Sunday off and kept it for family outings. But it couldn't be helped; that was how businesses were run!

November saw the birth of my son on Diwali day, bringing a wave of joyousness into the family. I named him Karan, the name of the Sun God's son! However, the thought did cross my mind that he was, after all Chhaya's son and may display traits of Shani!

***

Sitaram Kesri was the treasurer for the Congress Party from 1979 and I had to approach him for my payment cheques for supplying flags and banners. We had developed a very good bonding with each other, and I would always make it a point to touch his feet whenever I met him. One day, he asked me, 'Why do you touch my feet?'

I replied, 'Babuji, you are my senior, nothing less than a Godfather to me! It's just my way of expressing gratitude!'

'But I am only giving you what is rightfully yours! You work hard and deserve it.'

I responded, 'My father says that traders gain happiness

from only three things: when they stock up their shops for trading; when they are able to sell their stuff on credit with good profit, and most of all, when they get their investment back, as they are never sure whether they will! You always make it a point to give me my money back well on time. Why should I not be happy or pay my respects to you?' He found my reasoning hilarious and commended me on my witty repartee. I was elated.

***

Politics took a downward trend once Congress came back into power. It was a surprise victory only going to show that public sentiment mattered and couldn't be taken lightly. People had voted against the party earlier but when they saw total mismanagement with Janata Dal, they decided to support Congress as there had at least been a semblance of stability in the country during their regime. But unfortunately, the unexpected victory made some of them arrogant One of my favourite senior leaders, Vasant Sathe, even commented, 'See? The people had to bring Congress back! It is just not possible for any other party to run this country!' It made them feel invincible and some began to act very highhandedly. The situation paved the way for corruption to steal in, for Congressmen became a little insecure as they realised that power was not permanent, so decided to make good as the sun shines! I was shocked when a very senior politician told me to bring some liaison cases for monetary gains. In politics, mental faculties alone were not of relevance, for wealth and women, too, played an important role! He also assured me that I too would benefit greatly from it, not only financially, but also where power was concerned. However, the inherent merchant mentality in me felt revolted at the prospect and I hastily excused myself.

The Congress coming back to power also gave rise to a situation of mobocracy, for gathering numbers became the game now, giving rise to rent-a-crowd politics. Activists were encouraged with incentives to bring in the maximum number of people they could. A mammoth rally was being organised on 16 February 1981 and people were coming from all over the country! Everything was catered for, right from transportation to supplying meals to putting them up in tents, as if they were cattle! This was the first time I had seen people being lured to attend, for till now, crowds had always been ready to support their leaders!

Indira Gandhi had become insecure after her earlier defeat, so on regaining power, she was making her position stronger by managing support for her next term! The general secretary of AICC, Vasant Dada Patil, had been appointed as the chief organiser by her and he was also in-charge of giving orders for flags and such things. I became so involved in the ongoing excitement that I would spend the entire day at the Congress offices, helping with the other Party workers. Vasant Dada needed milk every hour for his health, as he suffered from ulcers. Sometimes, his wife would come to ensure he did so and sometimes his PA. I too began to take care to remind him or serve him his milk, thus gaining his goodwill.

Simultaneously, I would be getting orders for my flags as well! From just that rally alone, I was able to earn a good amount by supplying 50,000 flags within three days!

Also, I was being appreciated for my 'three-language formula', being proficient in Hindi, Urdu and English and would offer my services to senior leaders for their writings. Poetry was embedded in my soul and I excelled in giving poetic touches to my interactions which would make me stand out from the crowd! It was such antics that made me known to all, expanding my circle immensely, for there were only a few who were as proactive as I tended to be! Mujtaba Hussain, my satirist friend said to me, 'Manzar, you are indeed remarkable! You're neither a very good poet nor a very good politician! Yet how impressively you manipulate poetry in politics and politics in poetry!'

Though Rajiv Gandhi was not active in politics, he would sometimes visit his mother and brother's offices and that is how I got acquainted with him. He was always polite and courteous and later became my inspiration in actively engaging in the party, for after Sanjay's demise, Indira involved him more seriously, nominating him to contest from Amethi.

Earlier, I was only supplying flags, but once Rajiv participated, I began to take interest and would often ask if I could help. Rajiv Gandhi would always receive me graciously, his charming smile lighting up his face! He was the most handsome and magnanimous man I had ever met! His was the first election I fervently participated in at ground level, even going to Amethi with Rajiv for campaigning.

The supply of flags was, of course, totally my prerogative, for I had a complete monopoly on that and I think I must have supplied at least 80,000 flags for just one seat! Over the years, I made crores of flags, earning handsomely from them! We were very jubilant when Rajiv won his seat. Rajiv Gandhi recognised my calibre of being able to interact with people and so included me in his offices, putting me in the team responsible for co-ordination and publicity. However, Maneka Gandhi was not very happy with the turn of events, for Amethi had been her husband's constituency and she had expected to inherit it! But things move in their own way in politics. She had a small son to take care of while Indira Gandhi had another son to cater to!

Endowed with a strong personality, Indira Gandhi was no less a 'Woman of the Millennium', a title she gained in a BBC poll in 1999! Even after being expelled from the Congress party in 1969, she formed a new faction called the 'New'

Congress and won the 1971 elections, just when I began to take an interest in politics, reading up voraciously about events and going to rallies. It was her support of the insurrection in East Pakistan that led to the victorious creation of Bangladesh, inflicting a resounding defeat on Pakistan, a feat which made other countries wary of us, till date!

The first peaceful nuclear experiment was also conducted during her regime in May 1974! It put across a strong message that India couldn't be trifled with!

Indira Gandhi also facilitated the Green Revolution, encouraging the adoption of modern methods and technology, in farming, bringing in self-sufficiency in our grain production. Earlier, shortage of food, forced us to import a red variety of coarse wheat, PL 480, to meet our requirements. But her efforts brought in a refined type that grew in abundance.

Another major achievement during her governance was the nationalisation of fourteen private sector banks, a move conducive to strengthening the 'priority sectors' of agriculture, small industries, traders and entrepreneurs. Along with that, she did away with the privy purse, a payment made to the princely states as an incentive to merge into the country after Independence. Indira Gandhi's initiative thus helped finish this extra burden on the Central Government.

Chapter 10

A Momentous Blow

DISTURBANCES WERE HAPPENING in my personal life, a continuation of the state of the country perhaps! Ours was a full house, with parents, three daughters-in-law and the next generation, not to overlook my two sisters who were often at home, so naturally things could escalate a little. Before any of our marriages, my mother had gone into depression, so had never wholly been at the helm when the daughters-in-law came into the family. All three of us were doing well, had got married and it seemed to attract people's envy, which can affect in a powerful manner.

The daughters-in-law would ask the mother-in-law what dish to make at every meal and she would invariably suggest pulses or gourd or some such vegetable, as the doctor had asked her to eat light. Even when she had been in charge of the kitchen, our meals were simple, though there were always homemade snacks like *laddoos* and *mathris* including treats from outside. The three new members would take turns in making the food but whenever Chhaya had to make the meal, though she would ask my mother what to make, she would invariably make a second dish as well, an innovation much liked by us all!

January 1982 became the stage for the next part of the drama! It started with my eldest brother protesting at the insipid meals being served daily. We were all doing well and money was not an issue. I was doing a roaring business, my eldest brother had set up a second factory, while my doctor brother was a senior consultant at RML hospital, and his wife a senior doctor at AIIMS.

That day, we had watery potatoes for lunch and gourd for dinner! 'How do you expect us to relish a full meal with such stuff?' he implored.

I added my bit, 'Yes, why can't we have some other vegetables or cheese dishes? Pitaji, how do you accept such bland food?'

Pitaji kept quiet. However, my mother did not. Her illness had made her very sensitive, and she overreacted. 'Nobody has ever complained till today! I am sure it is all this fatso's work (indicating Chhaya)! She is never satisfied with what is being served!' Chhaya had not said a word, and obviously took offense immediately and retaliated, 'Shut up, you noxious woman!'

Shock cruised through all of us and I even moved forward as if to hit her! But I checked myself, remembering an earlier incident where I had just raised my hand and she had retaliated by catching and twisting it painfully. Instead, I said, 'Pitaji, please forgive me but enough is enough! She will not live here anymore!'

My father was too stunned to respond, for never had he come across such misbehaviour! I literally pushed Chhaya out of the room, ordering her to go upstairs and not to come down at all. Thereafter, I made arrangements for a makeshift kitchen in our bedroom itself, warning her not to dare set foot in the kitchen downstairs. I too had my meals upstairs, though it was breaking my heart to do so.

Meanwhile, I hired a very good three-bedroom house in Malkaganj, a locality near our shop, for Rs 1,100 and we shifted there within five days. But before we left my parents' house, I instructed her to return the four gold bangles my mother had gifted her on our wedding day. I didn't feel that she deserved to have anything from her marital home, especially as because of her, I was being forced to leave my parents!

I think my family was very relieved with our move, and except for my father, no one came to see us off as we were leaving. I feel that I had never been popular with my brothers as they were jealous of my closeness to our father, who would often say, 'He is the youngest and yet works the hardest!' Also, Chhaya had not been able to make a loving connect with anyone in the family, so it was natural that our leaving was looked upon with relief.

Soon after, my eldest brother also moved out, and only the doctor couple remained at home, I feel for their own convenience, as both were working and they needed someone to look after the house and take care of the children that would be born, and who better than grandparents! This trend is reflected in today's society, where the relevance of grandparents is confined only to their ability of being good caretakers for the next generation!

It took time to settle into a new place as I had never lived apart from my family and was sad at leaving the family home I had renovated so lovingly! Something very precious had been torn away from my heart! My father gave his full support, always asking if I had enough money or needed anything, for while shifting, I dropped all claims to my father's house. I had a partnership in the shop and felt that was enough for me. Those were not very expensive times and life could be lived comfortably in Rs 3,000, which is what I began to take from the shop. I even managed to buy a second-hand car.

Surprisingly, Chhaya's attitude changed when we shifted. It was something she had wanted right from the start, so she was naturally very happy and it put her in a mellow mood towards me. I too began to relish the freedom of living apart from the family, and we began to go for outings and movies more often.

Soon after, a friend told me about an upcoming Group Housing Society in Rohini and asked if I wanted to become a member. I had been dabbling in the stock market since 1979, buying Reliance shares and debentures, and that stood me in good stead now.

***

My relations with Sitaram Kesri deepened over time, and I would meet him for many frank discussions about life. He proved to be an experienced guide and before long, I was sharing all the challenges that I was facing in my marital life with him. I would make myself useful by running small errands for him. Whenever anything was required in his home, even condiments, I would not hesitate to rush to Khaari Baoli, well-known as the spice market of Delhi, and everyone would laugh that Mahesh Manzar was so deeply involved with Sitaramji that he had free access to his kitchen as well!

I had seen Dhirubhai Ambani, alone and sometimes along with Mukesh and Anil at the PMs house and Sitaram Kesri's house. One day, I saw them waiting in the dining room. I was naturally excited at seeing them, as they represented success in its ultimate form to me, and rushed to Kesri's room, to tell him of their presence outside.

He was drinking tea and said indulgently in his Bihari accent, *'Oh Mahesh! Kaahe chhalak rahe ho?* (Why are you getting so agitated?) I know they are there! Go and order some tea for them from the kitchen!'

During the Congress rule, donations had become a general practice, for there were many who found this an easy way of molding things their way. Ultimately it was the common man who was the victim, as industrialists would hike up costs of goods and services whenever they gave donations to political parties, and the common man thus became an unwitting pawn in the hands of a nexus formed by politicians, industrialists and bureaucrats.

Despite being so exploited, even basic amenities are yet to be provided to a large part of the general public. It struck me that I too was receiving a part of this ill-gotten money, for the money was paid into the Party fund, and that was from where I was getting my payments. Ill-gotten money has never benefited anyone!

Life has shown me that when money comes easily, it brings anarchy as well. Though we worked hard, having a monopoly in the flag market allowed us to earn without much hassle. Taking advantage of our profits, we had renovated our house in 1977. Soon after, my mother slipped into a state of depression, which lasted till the end of her life.

It also reiterated the thought that life followed a compulsory cycle of joy and sorrow, and that it was essential to work and earn in a balanced, reasonable manner, not in fits and starts. My marriage had sent ripples of dismay through my mind and though I was rising in the outer world, my personal life was plummeting to darker depths!

My awareness of how things transpired in political circles grew as time went on, giving me deep insights into the conspiratorial machinations that went on beneath the surface.

Once, I commented to V C Shukla on the unprecedented rise of Dhirubhai Ambani and his response was an astonishing eye opener. He said: 'He is the first industrialist who has actually taken the art of obliging to an entirely different level! He not only gives tribute to the ruling party, but also to the opposition! That way, he ensures that he gets support from all factions!' This was a consideration which not everyone could think of and truly had placed the Ambanis in a league apart! I got a clearer understanding of their distinctiveness many years later when I happened to discuss our top industrialists with my political mentor, Mani Shankar Aiyar.

'These Tatas and Birlas are well-known for setting up various institutions, and making hospitals and temples. What have the Ambanis made?'

Mani Shankar Aiyar's answer was phenomenally, unforgettable. 'Ambanis make governments!' he said and the whole persona of the Ambanis got encompassed in this one, cryptic comment.

***

Pitaji visited me one morning in September, his face looking grave. We went into the drawing room where he said, 'Mahesh, come back home! Nothing feels right without you there!'

Suddenly, we both were hugging each other and crying. Though I had left eight months earlier, the feeling of being cut off from my roots had never left me and all the angst of parting from the family surfaced in that moment! Even though I met Pitaji at work daily, both of us felt a deep chasm in our life. I said to him, 'Pitaji I would love to do that but her nature is the same, and she is not going to change! How can I come back?'

'Son, the house feels so deserted. Your eldest brother has also left with his family. And the other two are busy the whole day!' Pitaji said to me.

'Pitaji, what if Chhaya again says something hurtful to you or Ammaa? You know I will have to support her because of Karan. How odd would it look if I have to leave the house again!'

'No, this time I will leave, you don't have to do so!' he said. Little did we know then how prophetic his words would become.

***

Chhaya did not show much enthusiasm about returning, but submitted to shifting back; we returned to the family house on 2 October.

Other than my father, none in the family were glad to have us back. My mother had been happy living on her own while my brother and his wife felt uncomfortable with our presence. And our whole clan was amazed at the turn of events, for it is very rare for a son to return to the fold once he has left! It made people realise how indispensable I was to my parents, especially my father, and how strong our bond was! He was indeed more of a life partner to me than my wife!

Life once again began to settle back into a routine, as I shuttled between our shop and the All India Congress Headquarters on 24, Akbar Road. I was pretty popular for I loved to mix freely with everyone. I considered 24, Akbar Road my temple since I received everything I desired and everyone appreciated my sincerity and integrity. Once an administrative officer jokingly commented: 'Why don't you insert a *danda*—a stick in your *jhanda*?' Much to everyone's merriment, I said that I was just a humble businessman, and the danda was in our esteemed PM's hands, and, therefore, how could I use it!

***

Preparations were underway for the Asian Games, and together with senior Youth Congress leader and my good friend, Lalit Maken, we approached Indira Gandhi for work. She cordially told us to go to Rajiv, as he was overseeing preparations for the Games!

When we reached 2A, Motilal Nehru Marg, Rajiv was leaving for a round of the Jawaharlal Nehru Stadium. Lalit Maken informed him that Indira Gandhi had sent us to cooperate, and he told us to follow his car as he was going there. I still wonder at the sight we must have presented in the stadium—Rajiv Gandhi being escorted by Dr Bhishma Narain Singh, followed by us and various other officials while the construction managers and workers hastened to show the sundry aspects of the project!

I became a regular visitor at Rajiv's office, interacting with high-profile people like Vincent George, his secretary, and Shree Kant Verma. I became good friends with George, who went on to become his right-hand man once he came into power.

Verma was also an old friend, whom I had met through Kumar Pashi. I was surprised to see him there. He was a renowned poet and a speech writer for the Prime Minister and was in charge of teaching the finer nuances of vernacular Hindi to Indira Gandhi and later to Rajiv.

He sometimes required stationery and would ask me to pick it up for him from Chawri Bazaar, which I would gladly do.

In December, Shree Kant Verma was appointed general secretary in charge of publicity for the Congress, and he gave me an order for flags for elections for the Metropolitan council and MCD in February 1983. I was able to bag a huge order of ten lakhs to be delivered before the end of January!

***

Although we had shifted back home in October, there was a feeling of insecurity among us all. I had told my father to give Chhaya a free hand in the kitchen as she was fond of food and was a good cook. But my mother was not very happy with the situation because her authority had been undermined. She had tamely accepted my return as Pitaji's decision, but that was all.

And so, she began cribbing, finding fault in almost

everything. Consequently, squabbles became a regular feature and sometimes, I would feel impelled to support Chhaya, especially when criticism was unwarranted. In retrospect, I feel guilty in contributing to the general turmoil in the house, but in the heat of the moment, it is difficult to check oneself! The household would alternate between resounding altercations and cold wars!

***

Pitaji felt totally helpless in the face of their continuous bickering. There was also some misunderstanding about the jewellery that had been made for eldest daughter-in-law. It was handed to the next daughter-in-law, and later to my wife, as well and so it became a bone of contention between the three of them, adding to the general dissatisfaction.

Unable to handle the situation, Pitaji retreated within himself. None of us, including his doctor son and daughter-in-law, noticed his failing health. My eldest brother was struggling with a financial crisis and even had to shut down his second factory. Suman, my doctor sister-in-law, was suspected of breast cancer and had to be admitted to AIIMS for a biopsy. Towards the end of December, I drove Pitaji to the hospital to visit her. The car stalled on the way and needed to be pushed and Pitaji got out and pushed the car, single-handedly and although he was panting and perspiring, he said he was fine and we continued towards the hospital.

The pressures of work and the stress at the home front were slowly taking a toll on Pitaji and on 4 January 1983, he suddenly collapsed. He had been working hard the whole day to fulfil the flag order and home was stressful too. We had just retired for the night when he threw up violently and went into a semi-conscious state. We called a close friend, Dr Krishan, a cardiologist, and he said that Pitaji had suffered a massive heart attack. We rushed him to AIIMS, where he was admitted directly into the ICU. The HOD wanted to know what medications my father was taking and was shocked to know that he was not taking any! He knew that my brother and his wife were doctors, so gave them a good dressing down for ignoring their own father, and for not even monitoring his blood pressure! According to the doctor, my father was a chronic heart patient, and the state of his heart showed that he had already suffered a couple of mild attacks! I was stunned to hear that, realising that maybe one had happened right in front of me when he had pushed the car, but I had not understood the gravity of the situation. Now it was too late to make amends.

Those were indeed traumatic days. On the one hand, my father's condition was really serious, while on the other, I needed to fulfil our pending order for flags. My father had always looked after the production, buying cloth, dealing with tailors, and getting everything done on time. Now suddenly, everything fell onto my shoulders. But work had to be done and that is when I began to feel that a Divine Higher Power was at hand, supporting and helping me. Somehow, I was able to organise everything, even checking a few malpractices by the team of twenty tailors.

Once I got the hang of things, I began to feel confident that I would be able to pull off the order, singlehanded. I would be in the shop the whole day, then go to the hospital to be with Pitaji, however late it was. He was too weak to be able to say anything, but his eyes would speak volumes! He was aware of our finances, for businessmen don't have much working capital in hand, and money was now needed for both hospital expenses as also for the production of flags. Despite all my assurances, I could not alleviate that stress.

***

In January, veteran Congress leader, Kamlapati Tripathi, was made acting President by Indira Gandhi. She was going through tough times: the Khalistan movement had gained strength, and the Asian Games were around the corner. There was trouble from Maneka Gandhi as well. Rajiv Gandhi was nominated as the general secretary, AICC, by her, and somehow, this made me feel empowered, as if my own position was elevated! I went over to congratulate him in his office, where he was surrounded by Party workers, and after initial greetings, I indicated to Rajiv if I could speak privately to him. The humbleness of this great man still overwhelms me, for he not only immediately stood up, but took me out onto the lawns, and to cover the difference in our heights, bowed his head to listen to my quiet appeal! I informed him about my father's serious condition and also that Shree Kantji had given a big order for flags, but unfortunately, I was facing a cash crunch. He went back inside and issued a note for an advance payment of Rs 2.5 lakh without delay! I went to Kesriji's home for he had left by then. He too issued the cheque right then, for he was well aware of my situation. Later, when I went to visit Pitaji, I took the cheque along and showed it to him, feeling truly euphoric. Pitaji was stunned and couldn't say anything, while silent tears coursed down his cheeks, the heartfelt relief very much evident in his eyes! There was an inner relaxation in him, as if a burden had been lifted from his chest. This perhaps brought about a little improvement, for he was shifted to a smaller ICU room with only two beds.

The other occupant of the room was an elderly person, who became quite friendly with my father. One day, he called me over to his side and said, 'You know your father said something quite exceptional to me today. He said that he has three sons, one a doctor, one an engineer and one who is everything to me! I deeply desired to meet such an outstanding son! Those are no mean words for a father to say about his son!'

'And he said that even if this son of mine works for only two hours a day, he still manages to achieve a lot!'

I couldn't find any words to respond. I silently touched his feet and returned to Pitaji's bedside, giving him a tight hug! I couldn't have got a bigger compliment in my whole life! My father had always been a huge support for me and even from his deathbed, he was doing so, keeping my morale strong, encouraging me, always telling me, 'Don't worry, I will be back soon!' I believe he already knew that his end was near but such was his will power that he didn't let me think along those lines at all. Later, the elderly gentleman told me that my father had tremendous strength of mind but that he would sometimes cry at the reality of the situation. Pitaji's thoughts about me turned out to be truly divinatory. Later in life, I actually would work for only two hours and yet manage to earn more than adequately.

His blessings worked miraculously, for by the due date, I was able to load the final consignment of over five lakh flags onto three trucks to be delivered to the Party offices!

***

Once I got to AIIMS, I jubilantly told him, *'Pitaji, kaam pura ho gaya!* Mission accomplished!' A look of tremendous succour spread over his face, and a tear rolled down from the corner of his eye. I had decided to devote myself completely to my father now as there was now not much work at the shop, little knowing how less time there was left. It was as if a Divine power had been holding him back, for the very next day, his condition deteriorated. He had been delighted to hear that the huge order had been fulfilled satisfactorily, but it was a sort of signal as well for him to let go. I think it was his sheer will power that had made him hang on till the order was completed, for he knew me well enough to know that if he went, I would have broken down completely, and work would have suffered. That would have caused a phenomenal loss, both on the home front as well as the shop. Even in his going he was only thinking of me and how he could support me!

Some internal bleeding started; a vein had ruptured inside and blood began to come from his nose and mouth. Doctors tried to work on him to stem the flow and bring stability in his condition. My mother, brothers and myself stayed overnight in the hospital. The next morning, the doctor asked us brothers to donate blood, as they felt our father might need a transfusion. We made our way to the laboratory, leaving Amma with him, but before we could proceed further, an acquaintance asked us to rush back.

In the little time it had taken us to go to the lab, Pitaji had moved to the next world! I felt totally disconsolate, shattered, as if robbed of the only opportunity to serve my father in his last moments! At least if he had received our blood, I would have had the satisfaction of knowing that I had done something tangible to prolong his life! Though it was 26 January, we decided to perform the cremation the same day. It was hugely agonising and once the last rites had been done, we three brothers were hugging each other and crying, that supreme moment of sorrow uniting us, as the realisation of our irreparable loss hit us. It was as if all uncertainty had dropped, leaving a space of relief in which the stress of not knowing what may happen next had vanished! The three of us were feeling that respite. Much later, I could empathise with Sonia Gandhi when she mentioned a similar alleviation after Rajiv Gandhi's death, for the tension of a threat hanging over your head is more traumatic than the actual event itself! But unfortunately, the bonding with my brothers happened only in that moment, and then was forever lost in the dark annals of our lives!

Pitaji's demise left a huge void in my life; the light had

literally gone out of my being. He had been my soulmate, my real-life partner, the only one who had actually understood me, the only one who had mattered to me or who cared for me. A part of me died that day, a part which I have not been able to revive till date, despite having had some close relationships with both men and women. The Republic Day of our country, has forever become a black day for me, coming back to haunt me every year, reviving excruciating memories. Through the years I have spent it alone, just being with the Divine, paying homage to the most valuable person in my life!

The days following Pitaji's death were traumatic. I felt morally, emotionally, spiritually, even financially shattered. Just thinking about how I would manage my life and work made me feel insecure! Home appeared desolate, the shop even more so, and the only place I found solace in was the temple! I began to go there daily, spending time in solitude. My connect to the Divine began to deepen, making me feel that this was the actual touchstone of life. Meanwhile, the rituals associated with the peaceful transition of a soul were being done at home, culminating with a *Brahm Bhoj* on the thirteenth day after Pitaji's passing.

***

Two days later, as I was relaxing after dinner in our main hall, my eldest brother approached me and demanded, 'Mahesh, show me the account ledgers tomorrow.'

I looked at him, nonplussed and asked, 'What accounts?'

'The shop's naturally!'

I could only stare open-mouthed! On paper, I was a 40 per cent partner with my father, and although my father had intended me to take it over completely after him, he had not put it down in writing. During his lifetime, he had set up both his elder sons, opening a factory and a clinic for each, respectively, without adding himself as a partner, which he easily could have done. The only one left was me and there had been a tacit understanding that the shop was to be mine. Despite that, my brother was asking to see the accounts of what was supposedly mine!

'Why should I show you my shop's accounts?' I had been working in that shop since I was sixteen. 'What your shop? Do you think you are going to become the sole inheritor of all Pitaji's assets now that he has gone?'

'What do you mean by that? You were set up in your factory by Pitaji and that is yours and so is Devender's clinic, but are they also not Pitaji's assets? Am I asking you to show me your accounts?'

'All that was his, belongs to us all,' was his retort.

'So that means the factory is also mine and so is the clinic!'

Things began to suddenly turn ugly as we raised our voices to shout at each other. The middle brother joined him against me, while the rest of the family kept quiet. The three of us were getting really worked up, hurling hurtful words at each other. This commotion made our young children restless and they began to cry. Somehow an uglier situation got diverted and we all retired to our rooms. Devender made an unexpected conciliatory gesture and gave us brothers a tranquilliser, so that at least we could have a peaceful night and deal with the situation in a better manner the next day!

That was the first time I had taken a tranquilliser and it became a precursor of many more, for that night heralded a turbulent period in my life which to date seems unending!

The following day, I continued to be defensive saying that Pitaji had always made it clear that the shop was my prerogative even if he had not penned it down anywhere, indeed an oversight on his part. I even appealed to my mother. 'Amma, Pitaji used to say that the shop was mine, isn't it so?'

Maybe my brothers had pressurised her in some manner,

but she did not support me. 'That is all very well, but then I am also there,' was her ambiguous response. Maybe, she too was feeling insecure.

As things began to escalate once more, with my brothers even threatening to lock the shop, I told my brothers to get somebody else's opinion on the whole situation. My very existence had suddenly come under a threat, making me struggle to find a way out. I consulted a couple of friends connected to law and the consensus was that I did not have a strong stand. There was no Will and he was 60 per cent owner of his shop, so it had to be divided among all us siblings. The problem was I considered it all to be mine including the goods stocked in the shop and even the bank accounts and was beginning to feel cheated!

A few days later, Chhaya requested for an extra quilt for the baby. The quilts were in a huge trunk. As I was rummaging through the trunk, I came across two bundles of notes hidden there. Pitaji must have stashed the money away. As I held the twenty thousand in my hands, a thought crept into my mind that this amount could secure me for the next few months! The dark cloud of closure was hanging over my head, and if that happened, I had no savings at all. I had opened accounts in both my wife and son's names and would deposit Rs 200 per month in each, but I didn't want to touch that. I decided to keep the money with me, even though my mother had more right to it! It left me with a feeling of guilt but my desire for security, settled it. Not a single family member supported me, leaving aside my eldest sister and her husband. Even the younger sister's husband had left the Navy to start a business venture, which was not going very well. So, she too had an iron to burn! It was only Kumar Pashi who backed me to help me uphold my claim, even pledging to rouse his community to be there for me if anyone tried to take over the shop!

Feeling totally cornered, I approached Rajiv Gandhi for a

solution, pouring the whole story into his ears. My brothers had even threatened to seize all bank accounts and I was expecting the payment of Rs 7.5 lakh for my last order to come into them. If that happened, all the money would go into their hands, money which was rightfully mine, as I was the one who had done all the hard work to earn it!

Over the years, I had slowly built up our business, and it definitely had been my efforts that had brought the shop a long way from the time when we sold 25 paise worth, napkins! Integrity matters and I had always done my work with transparency. When you are in that space of credibility, even the Divine Powers support you.

Magic now came into my life through the offices of Rajiv Gandhi! He was the general secretary of the Party and had the power to sanction things.

'My father has passed away, and I am not even sure how I will manage my business. I think I will shut it down and join you!' I told him.

Knowing that my payment was still pending and understanding the gravity of my situation, Rajiv Gandhi immediately sanctioned a check for a phenomenal Rs 4 lakh! I was filled with a sudden surge of energy, making me feel as if I could now take on the whole world!

Feeling totally buoyant, I set about investing the money in a freehold plot of 200 sq yards near Ashok Vihar. Chhaya was truly delighted that things were panning out in our favour, and she proved to be a real support to me in those days. So, quietly, with the help of friends, I took steps to secure myself, making my position stronger.

About this time, Chhaya disclosed that she was two to three months into her second pregnancy. She told me she did not want to burden me more since I was so involved with father's condition and work. Now, with my mind a little settled, I could accept the situation with more ease!

Meanwhile, the situation at home continued to deteriorate. What a paradox it was, for among my friends, I was known to be able to resolve relationships and any kind of issue, but here I couldn't handle my own! Though I was pretty sure my brothers couldn't lock the shop, they were definitely creating an uncomfortable scenario. One day, when they were in my shop generally asking detailed questions, two of Chhaya's brothers happened to pass by and saw us. Well-built, and presenting an impressive persona in white outfits, they hailed me, 'All good, Maheshji?' giving the perception that they were with me, when in actual fact they had not even tried to find out how things were going! Somehow in that instant, their presence made my brothers a little wary, making them think that I was not alone and had some backing.

My eldest sister persuaded her husband and father-in-law to step in to help resolve our issues. With their efforts, we were finally able to formalise an agreement which allowed me to keep the shop, but I had to relinquish all claims to the house. My legal advisors were of the opinion that all assets should be clubbed together and then divided, so I suggested this to Babuji, my sister's father-in-law. He, however, said that it was better not to go the legal way and do what is practical. Besides, he made me understand that I was the one who was so pressurised, while the others were not! 'I know, Mahesh that you will set yourself up in a very good way despite being put at a disadvantage! Also remember, son, that the one who accepts a little loss in the division of property is blessed with largesse from the Universe! You will definitely never be in a space of lack!' True words that have showed their veracity, time and again in my life!

Babuji and my brother-in-law however, reiterated, that I should give Pitaji's share from the shop to the family as they did have a right to it. I accepted, but insisted that sisters had equal rights, too, so it should be divided into six parts, as

Amma too had a share! Finally, some amount was disbursed among us all. I made four FDs of Rs 25,000 each for the two sisters. However, along with the money, the eldest brother also wanted shares from the bank accounts. The ownership of the house was divided between my mother and the doctor brother, with the stipulation that the mother's share would be divided between us three brothers after her death. As I was living at home, I was to give rent of Rs 1,000 to my mother, along with Rs 3,000 from the shop. Every condition was acceptable to me other than this, and I would often not be giving it regularly to her later on, for I continued to feel it was unjustified! But I wanted to keep the shop so badly that I was ready to accept even these unwarranted demands!

Babuji insisted that we should draw proper legal documents. We got our Partition Deed registered at the Registrar's office. But despite this, I was both morally and legally negating my commitment by not giving the whole of the promised amount to my mother every month!

Much later it struck me that the moment my brothers began to bother me, I forgot to grieve for my father! Every living being has an innate sense of survival and the moment it is threatened, an instinctive struggle for existence comes into action. That is what happened to me! My world had already turned upside-down with my father's departure, but my brothers' actions further upset it dramatically! Consequently, all my focus was on saving myself from drowning in a traumatic sludge of fearfulness, generated from the possibility of losing my life's work. I was so caught up in it that it took precedence even over my great loss!

FOURTH DECADE
THRIVING THIRTIES

Chapter 1

A Harmless Poet in a Political Scenario

MY YOUNGER SON, Lakhan was born in August 1983, but his birth was not marked with as much fanfare as the elder one's. My father's demise still weighed heavily on my mind. I was in charge of the shop and at home too, things were peaceful. We were on the second floor while Devender was on the first floor with my mother.

A couple of months later, I participated in a private symposium at the Rashtrapati Bhawan for President Giani Zail Singh, who was very fond of Urdu and was also a *shayar*. Many illustrious poets were invited, my poetry Guru among them. That was a God-sent opportunity for me and I cajoled Kumar Pashi, to allow me to present one of my compositions—for wasn't I connected directly to the Congress Party? I deserved a chance! Pashi included my name, thus giving me a wonderful opportunity to recite in a really elevated society. It helped deepen my links with dignitaries like Balram Jakhar, Vasanth Sathe, Khursheed Alam Khan and so on, and they were happy that one of their Party workers was so active in the literary world, too! I was happy that even senior poets were beginning to appreciate the compositions that spontaneously poured out of me!

Once, Kumar Pashi, Makhmoor Sayeedi and Ameer Qazalbash were returning home with me in my car at about

2.30 am after a wonderful evening of shayari and drinks. At the Delhi Gate crossing, Kumar Pashi encouraged me to take the wrong side to avoid a long detour.

But I refused, spontaneously declaring, 'No Kumar Saheb, *Safar Taveel hai isko na Mukhtsar karna* (The journey is long, shorten not its span)! Any vehicle can be coming from the other side.'

Makhmoor said loudly, 'Stop the car!' He got out of the car and started dancing in the middle of the road, saying, 'What a beautiful thought! What words!' Amazed, the other two joined him, much to my delight! It was a rapturous scene as all four of us danced with abandon in the wee hours of the morning at a main crossing! Makhmoor added the next line:

Jo ho sake toh mujhe aur darbadar karna
(Let me be a nomadic wanderer forever)

We all went into ecstasy at the impromptu couplet! We ourselves were surprised as to how the Universe sometimes makes one utter Divine, spontaneous thoughts!

***

In mid-April 1984, I got a call from Kesriji's office to meet him in the evening at his home. I still had to receive my pending payments from the Party, so wondered what it could be about.

'How much profit are you going to earn from the Party?'

'I didn't get you, Babuji?'

'You have already taken Rs 6.5 lakh against your order....'

'Yes, and Rs 3.5 lakh is still pending.'

'Exactly! But I am going to cut Rs 2.5 lakh from that amount. I have done a survey and the flag costs you only 60 paise, for which you're charging us Rs one.'

' Babuji! It costs me 65 paise. Then there are overheads and losses as well....'

'No, I have decided to trim your charges a little!'

'Please, Babuji, don't do this! You know I lost my father recently and since then, it has been so tough for me to handle everything by myself. Besides, I have to look after my mother every month and there have been additions in my family too.'

Unconcerned, he said, 'That's all very well, but cut I will!'

'Please Babuji, I can wait for another year, if you like.'

'Don't you trust me?'

'Absolutely, Babuji! You're no less than my father!'

'Then rest assured that if today I am cutting 2.5, I will help you earn double that amount! It is essential for me to cut your amount for there are a few others I need to deal with! If I am able to talk about your cut, my actions will carry more weight. Besides I know you can turn things in your favour and will rise despite setbacks! After all, you are a king in the flag market!'

I allowed myself to be persuaded, content in the fact that even the one lakh he was offering was pure profit for me! He immediately signed the cheque, finally wrapping up what had started in my father's time!

***

Another call a few months later, on 12 September, made me euphoric, for it came from the PM's house! I was invited for a meeting with the PM's personal secretary and confidante, R K Dhawan. With great enthusiasm, I presented myself there at the appointed hour and was asked to wait in an anteroom. Some others were waiting there too, two of them, national level poster makers, one a jeep supplier and a banner producer. Were elections being scheduled? Soon Dhawan Saheb informed us that the PM herself wanted to convey something important to us and so we entered Indira Gandhi's spacious office. This was the first time I would actually be face-to-face with the PM of our country. I would be intimidated by her, for she had a very commanding personality!

She motioned us to sit down and came straight to the point.

'We are going to hold the elections at an earlier date. You'll have to work hard and fast on a war footing! Dhawan see to all the arrangements!' That was it! She motioned towards her secretary, a signal for our dismissal as well, so we trooped out of the room. A few minutes later, R K Dhawan indicated that I should come into his office.

'You make flags, right?'

'Yes, Bhai Saheb.'

'How soon can you supply us with flags? Can you supply us with a crore of flags?'

I stared at him in astonishment at the sheer number I was being asked to prepare. Somehow, I managed to ask, 'By when?'

'In three months.'

'What? One crore in three months? That is not possible! I am sorry, but my father passed away recently and I am still trying to manage everything on my own! I can try for 50 lakh in three months, but I won't commit that too.' I was not sure if I could even actually pull that off, for till now a 10 lakh order was the maximum I had dealt with!

Then I asked Dhawan Saheb about the payments. 'How do you want to take them?' he asked.

'Against delivery, Bhai Saheb! I am not sure how many I can deliver at a time!'

'Then it would be best if you meet Shyam Kumar!'

'If you say so, Bhai Saheb! But for what purpose?'

'You go and meet him, but rest assured, your payment will be in cash.'

So, I took myself off to meet Shyam Kumar, who had an office near Pusa Road, and found that he was the sole distributor in North India for a big company. Wondering how he was connected to my supplying flags, I approached him, giving R K Dhawan's reference. He welcomed me heartily, saying that he had a deal for me. I looked at him in surprise, which slowly turned into astonishment, when he said, 'Your flag is priced at one rupee, and I will be taking 25 paise from it!'

'What? Twenty-five? But why?' I said, flabbergasted.

'Do you want your payment in cash or not?' was his calm response.

'Yes. Without cash, I won't be able to continue production.'

'And how much does your flag cost? I have already got estimates. It costs you only about 55 to 60 paise.'

I tried to tell him that competition was rising as other players had come into the field, but he was adamant.

'Twenty-five paise will be cut, besides Kesriji also gave you 75 paise, so what is your problem?' He had obviously done his homework well!

Meantime, I quickly calculated the profit I still would be making and accepted his terms, though I insisted on being paid in cash. At least I had a prestigious order in hand, directly commissioned by the High Command!

I rallied my forces for the marathon task ahead! Soon, a rumour began to do the rounds in the market that Mahesh was getting almost a lakh of flags ready every day! The truth was being exaggerated by almost 50 per cent, but it made me feel good that people thought me so capable! When I look back to those times, I really felt that some Divine force was supporting me, helping me do even the impossible tasks easily, for it was far beyond my capacity to do so!

Barely a month and a half later, however, tragedy struck, for the PM was gunned down by her own guards on 31 October 1983! To crush the Khalistan movement and to eliminate Bhindranwale, Indira Gandhi initiated Operation Blue Star. She had been forced to send the army into the Golden Temple, which is regarded as a truly hallowed shrine of the Sikhs. The Sikh community was naturally upset and stood up in arms against her. Through RAW, the offices of her Intelligence

Agency, Indira Gandhi was warned of treachery from them and told to remove the Sikhs who were her personal guards. But she refused to comply, saying that the ones who were there were like her children, as they had been with her for a long time. Unfortunately, her trust was misplaced, for her two main guards, Satwant Singh and Beant Singh, finally took her life, firing innumerable bullets into her chest and abdomen.

I learned about the shooting from Shyam and it was as if the ground had been pulled from beneath my feet! Only a few days ago, I had met her personally and the news of her unexpected demise was a huge emotional shock. Her strong personality had been a reassuring support, and now, it seemed to have collapsed.

I quickly made my way to the PM's house but her body had been taken to AIIMS by Sonia Gandhi so no one was there. The AICC office was also deserted. But Kesriji was in his office and suddenly, I was crying uncontrollably, placing my head on his knees! He too was in a state of complete shock, and incapable of soothing me. She had been one of the most gracious ladies I had ever seen, with an unforgettable, captivating smile that would light up her whole face! I even felt that perhaps I had not proved auspicious for her, as she had met her end soon afterwards. Her departure was definitely a tremendous loss, not only at the national level, but even at a personal level for everyone.

Officially, the news was not declared till late evening, for Rajiv Gandhi had to return from a tour in West Bengal. He was travelling back with Balram Jhakhar, the Speaker of the Lok Sabha, Uma Shankar Dikshit who was Rajiv's mentor, Subhash Kashyap, Secretary General of the Lok Sabha and Sheila Dikshit, Uma Shankar's daughter-in-law, all of whom later became quite well-known to me. Everyone was concerned, especially about who would fill her position. Balram Jhakhar consulted Subhash Kashyap to understand whether it could be possible to make Rajiv Gandhi take the oath straightaway, without consulting the President or other senior leaders or Congress Working Committee or even calling a Cabinet meeting. After all, it was a moment of great emergency for the whole country, and it was imperative to fill the vacant position immediately, without considering any interim option. When Balram Jhakhar suggested this to Rajiv, he was taken aback, for it would indeed be a colossal responsibility. He turned to Uma Shankar Dikshit for guidance, who also approved of the idea, only suggesting to check if there was a provision for it in the Constitution.

It is not normal to carry a copy of the Constitution everywhere one goes, but by some stroke of fate, Sheila Dikshit had her copy with her! She, thereby offered it for instant clarification and by the time the plane landed, all plans had been set for the prince's coronation! On landing, they went straight to the Rashtrapati Bhawan, and after convincing Zail Singh of the need for immediate action, administered the oath to Rajiv Gandhi that evening, itself! I got to know the inside story from all four of them on separate occasions, for I was on good terms with them all.

I had already supplied twenty lakh flags in forty-five days, in itself, a remarkable feat. Another two lakh flags were ready in my shop. An image of these flags suddenly began to flutter before my eyes, as also the picture of the hundreds of people who were being sustained by their production and who expected to be paid. A whole industry had been set up with twenty-odd contractors and over a hundred women workers from neighbouring slum clusters beneath each! A niggling worry began to bother me now. What would happen now? When I got to know that Rajiv Gandhi had been sworn in, it was as if a weight had been lifted from my mind, for I regarded him as a truly beloved leader and knew that things would pan out well.

Indira Gandhi's death was immediately followed by arson and mayhem as more than 3,000 Sikhs, were massacred in Delhi itself, while the police remained silent spectators. Only three days later, could the military bring the riots under control. Innumerable Sikhs were forced to cut their hair to save their lives. It was one of the blackest chapters of the Indian National Congress, a throwback to the communal lynching experienced during Partition. Rajiv Gandhi was in no way responsible for some overenthusiastic senior Congressmen initiating this action against the Sikhs in his name. Thankfully, it didn't reflect on his popularity for in the ensuing elections in December 1984, the Congress Party won 414 seats in the Lok Sabha, the euphoric victory completely overshadowing Indira's tragic end, showing how a consequent event, whether happy or sad, can make one forget a past event. Something similar had happened with me after my father's demise!

I have noticed that often the position you are in, gives you the strength to do justice to it. That is what I had seen in Rajiv Gandhi's case. He did not have much political inclination but the fact that he was Indira Gandhi's son placed him in that position of power. It reminded me of *Autobiography of a Yogi* where Paramhansa Yogananda found himself heading for America without much knowledge of English, yet when he was faced with an expectant congregation, he was able to do full justice to it. In my own life too, the very first time I had to face a public meeting in the Chandni Chowk area during the 1984 elections, a Divine blessing seemed to descend on me, allowing me to hold the crowd's attention for a good twenty minutes! That was the kind of divinity that I saw in Rajiv Gandhi! He had no hankering for either power or position; it was an accident of fate that bestowed these on him along with the acumen to deal with it all!

***

I had a good relationship with Chhaya's third brother, a lawyer. He would often invite me to his home on Rohtak Road. Once he invited me for dinner and I went to his place, directly from the shop. I happened to be carrying Rs 2 lakh, as I had just received a payment in cash. He told me that he had just finalised a deal for a 400-square yard plot in Pitampura and that he was short of Rs 2 lakh. 'Two lakhs are needed?'

'Yes, for the deal to be completed.'

'I have two lakhs with me right now. Should I give it to you?'

Both he and his wife stared at me in bewilderment at the unexpected solution to their dilemma. 'That would be really helpful!' was his exuberant response.

Both he and his wife had a soft spot for me and would shower a lot of respect and affection on me. Such was my trust that I didn't even take a written receipt, an oversight that proved to be rather costly, later.

***

My personal life had never been a bed of roses, for our natures were totally contrary to each other. Chhaya had always regarded me as being inadequate in all aspects, even though we had been blessed with two children. Time has made me realise how essential it is for partners to be cordial towards each other before bringing a child into the world, for if they are not, the progeny of such an alliance can only be aggressive. Both my children were conceived in an atmosphere of strife and turmoil, and showed prominent signs of it! How true was Osho when he said that the act of procreation should be approached as something sacred, for only that can lay the foundation of a healthy offspring! No wonder there is so much aggression in society now, as most relationships are dysfunctional.

***

Family apart, I did not have relationship problems with the people I met through my work. I had a very comfortable relationship with Shree Kant Verma, the general secretary of the Congress party, and once, when he learned I was getting my sons admitted to Delhi Public School with Justice Grover's help, he requested me to get his son into the school through the same reference.

I was flabbergasted. 'Bhai Saheb, I myself am obligated to Justice Grover, then how can I ask for your son as well? Besides, you hold such a powerful position, and I am sure Justice Grover would be only too happy to oblige!' I understood the reasoning behind his request. Those in high positions do not want to ask a favour from anyone, for then they are under an obligation and are compelled to reciprocate! Moreover, Justice Grover was doing me a favour, and courtesy demanded that I should not take undue advantage!

Shree Kant Verma was simple and uncomplicated and despite being a renowned poet, he was quite humble. He surprised me once by asking me to teach him to write a ghazal. 'You must be joking, Bhai Saheb!' I said, but nevertheless, recited the first line of my popular couplet and asked him to continue.

Sabke muh me hain zabane bolta koi nahi...
Sabke muh me hain zabane bolta koi nahi...
Aadmi ke mun ki gaanthen kholta koi nahi

'Oh, that is even more wonderful than mine! And you say you don't know how to write a couplet!' I said, enthusiastically.

He laughed delightedly, like a child! I have often noticed that good people have this quality of being childlike, which remains a part of their personalities, even after they attain a high position.

He had done me several good turns and I wanted to return

the compliment and got the idea of having his book on modern Hindi poetry, *Magadh* translated into Urdu. Along with being the general secretary of the Congress party, he was also a prolific writer, much appreciated by Indira and Rajiv Gandhi. He had also given the winning slogan for the party, 'Vote for the Government that works!' I approached Kumar Pashi for the translation and working together, we soon had his book printed. I still recall the look of delighted appreciation on his otherwise impassive face when I presented him the translated version of his own book!

My Guru, Kumar Pashi had once said that with all my verve and vitality, and the way I marketed myself and connected to people so easily, I deserved to be in his shoes! I was deeply moved at my mentor's appreciation of my qualities, ecstatic that he had such high regard for me. Much later, Makhmoor Sayeedi also said, 'Manzar Saheb, you will one day be among one of the decision makers of this country! You have the calibre, but it is all in the hands of Destiny!' The fact is that to be in politics, one not only needs to be brilliant and resourceful, but must also have a restrained personality, the self-effacing kind, which I could never be! Even V C Shukla had said that I needed to be less loquacious and more reticent if I wanted to move up the political ladder—a sentiment that many others voiced over the years!

Shree Kant Verma was the chairman of the media committee and soon after, I went to meet Rajiv Gandhi, telling him how I had got Shree Kant's book translated and appealed to him to release it.

'I am a technocrat, Mahesh, and a pilot to boot, far removed from books! Better if you get hold of Vasanth Sathe or Khurshed Alam Khan!'

'But, Sir, you are a man of deep insight! See how you have suggested both a Hindi and an Urdu litterateur to facilitate the release!'

He laughed and promised to send a befitting message for the occasion. I accepted his decree gracefully, captivated by his humbleness, as always. 'That's why I thank you, I love you, I admire you and I adore you!' I said.

'Oh, come along!' was his amused response.

***

With great enthusiasm, both Kumar Pashi and I set about organising a grand event, *Ek Shaam Shree Kant Verma ke Naam* at the FICCI Auditorium, inviting the cream of political society, with senior Urdu scholar Prof Gopi Chand Narang being the guest of honour. The hall was jam-packed, and dignitaries like Justice A N Grover and his wife, high-profile secretaries, ministers, and senior Hindi and Urdu poets and writers attended. Both Vasant Sathe and Khurshed Alam Khan had accepted and Justice Anand Narain Mulla, an 84-year-old senior poet, agreed to preside over the function. My mentor, Kumar Pashi asked Uma Sharma, a Padma Shri-awarded Kathak dancer and a friend of Vasant Sathe, to present a dance to the lyrics of Shree Kant's compositions sung by Jawala Prasad. She also danced to a couple of my ghazals, as well. This was a great hit, elevating the very tone of the function! The event catapulted me to greater heights, for I got the chance to share the stage with eminent politicians and scholars, making me become more prominent in both the literary and political worlds!

By the end of the evening, Shree Kant Verma was visibly moved, pouring accolades on me for giving him the most memorable evening of his life! Vasant Sathe commented, 'Mahesh, you have given Shree Kant Verma today the feeling of becoming a bridegroom all over again!' That July evening in 1985 became a landmark date in my life. Kumar Pashi and I worked together spectacularly, acting like catalysts for each other, creating miracles!

That evening sowed the seeds of my political ambitions, for I realised that I too could be a part of these circles in a more proactive manner. I was earning well and could hold my own anywhere. I had a huge circle of high-profile friends and I could converse on innumerable subjects with all kinds of personalities! To cultivate relationships, one must understand the other's acumen and relate to him or her at that level.

One of the first maxims Kumar Pashi had drilled into me was that a connection needs to be both forged and nourished, or else it would lead to nothing! I would thus make it a point to often visit people and gift them something or the other, thus making my presence felt! That is the secret of maintaining relationships and I pride myself that very rarely has any of my connections dropped from my circle of contacts. I believe that once a person comes into my life, he becomes a permanent part of it. I also believe that no one comes into your life unless they are destined to play a deeper role. Osho even reiterates that having eye contact with someone happens only if destined!

The euphoria of the colourful evening, however, was suddenly overshadowed by the tragic end of Lalit Maken and his wife Gitanjali, who were brutally murdered by Sikh militants. He had recently won from a South Delhi constituency and was leaving for Parliament when he was gunned down. I had a deep emotional connect with him and felt as if I had lost a sincere friend and well-wisher. People would often even take us to be brothers, as we somewhat resembled each other. But that is what politics is all about—unexpected events await at every turn!

***

Once I was with Justice Grover, and his family, when he commented melancholically, 'Mahesh ji, my biggest regret in life is that I could not reach the position of Chief Justice!'

'That should have been in 1973. Are you still holding that grievance in your heart after all these years?'

'If only things had been different!'

'I don't think you should agonise so much, Babuji! Had you become the CJI, your name would have been recorded in our country's records, but you would have just been another in a long line of Chief Justices!'

'What do you mean by that?'

'By resigning, you actually sacrificed your position for a cause. Even God loves sacrifices! Circumstances deprived you of your rightful position, but you had the courage to stand up to what was not correct. That puts you in a unique category in our history!'

'That's a totally different perspective, one which I have never heard before!'

'Jean Paul Sartre refused to accept the Nobel prize in 1964 on the grounds that such prizes force writers to institutionalise themselves, confining them to a mould, thereby limiting the impact of their writings. Of course, gossip has it that he was envious of his former friend, Camus, who won in 1957, and that he did not like being thought of as an afterthought! But Jean Paul Sartre went down in history for refusing this tremendous honour and is remembered even today!'

'Maheshji, you will definitely gain great stature, with your thought process!'

When I had first heard of the Sartre incident, I had opined that by refusing to accept the Nobel, he had conveyed his displeasure at being side-lined earlier and also proved that he was much above such awards. 'He made a point that he didn't need them and his greatness was definitely not dependent on them,' I had said, adding that many receive awards and are forgotten, but the one who refuses or questions such honours creates a niche for himself!

Justice Grover was reassured by my words and with moist eyes, said, 'You have lifted a decade-old weight from my mind! Injustice was done to me; in fact, Indira Gandhi was unjust to three other Justices!

'Not just with three Justices, but with the whole law system! The Supreme Court was made to adhere to her judgements, and so courts ceased to be impartial! Those who should be behind bars are roaming free!'

'Mahesh ji, you have tremendous potential, the kind that can take you places! I know so many senior IAS officers and judges; yet no one ever came up with such an interpretation!'

***

For me, politics was a social platform. I had no political ambitions and all I wanted was to be known to people and to know them, for people were my passion! I revelled in connecting with different people and being in the centre of things. I had developed links with all echelons of society—from the guards at the doors of the highest level of people to the ones at the helm of the country's affairs, managing to create an inexplicable bond with each!

I seemed to know everyone, right from the PM to the peon outside his door! Such were my interactions that I used to distribute over a hundred and fifty boxes of sweets every Diwali!

Once, I got a very valuable lesson on political interaction from Vasant Sathe who asked, 'Mahesh, do you go to the Party's regional offices? Do you know anyone over there?'

'No, I have never visited these offices.'

'Don't you have any concrete political ambitions?'

'I have, Babuji, I would like to be more involved.'

'Then go regularly to visit the regional offices. Meet the DPCC President, H K L Bhagat and other senior leaders. Attend meetings to understand how the work is done. Become more visible, for if tomorrow you manage to get a ticket for a seat, at least people will know and support you.'

'I will definitely do so, Babuji.'

'Politics operates at three levels—national, state, and local. The local level is connected to districts and blocks, from where MLAs and councillors stand for elections. You should be familiar with all aspects if you want to gain a foothold.'

Soon enough, I was a part of the regional scene, in charge of polling booths and as an agent for counting votes. I was naturally gregarious and easily created a niche for myself. H K L Bhagat made me a part of the reception or food committees of several national programmes and AICC sessions, where the PM was expected. I would manage refreshments and facilitate the seating of VIPs in the audience, as I ushered them to their seats in a dignified manner.

At one of the informal get togethers held after an event, Sajjan Kumar sarcastically commented, 'Manzar Saheb, you are neither from the bride's family nor the groom's, yet you're all over the place! Have you been appointed the Master of Ceremonies?' Bhagatji spoke up immediately in my defence: 'Let him think he is the Master of Ceremonies if it makes him feel so happy,' thereby effectively silencing dissenting voices and garnering the goodwill of many.

***

Begum Noor Bano, an extremely gracious former princess of Rampur in UP, would even take my arm to support herself! Many would accuse me of dallying with the ladies, young and old alike, but mostly people indulgently laughed at my antics, regarding me as a harmless poet who had wandered into the political scenario!

A huge meeting was organised on 2 October 1985 to commemorate Mahatma Gandhi's birth anniversary by the

Delhi Pradesh Congress. It was addressed by Rajiv Gandhi and attended by AICC members and MPs. I happened to meet a beautiful lady, a former princess of an erstwhile North Indian estate. Fascinated by her delicate looks, I conducted her to a seat in the second row, even though these were meant for senior leaders and she was not one. I could feel her eyes on me as I seated other dignitaries and when I neared her seat, she softly asked me, 'Are you an MP?'

'Hardly! I am only a PN (peon) ma'am.' Her tinkling laugh kept echoing in my ears for the rest of the evening.

'And how do I address this PN?'

'Mahesh Manzar! May I know your name?'

'Shivani Singh.'

'Great! We are both squares, numerologically speaking. M square and S square!'

At the end of the event, I ran into her yet again in the parking lot. Distinguished guests were allowed to park within the complex, but as a Party worker, I had to park outside the perimeter of the complex. Her car stopped near me as I was making my way towards my own car and she asked if I had a vehicle.

'Yes, ma'am, but it is parked at a distance.'

'Oh, okay! Can I drop you till there?'

'That is so good of you, thank you!'

She opened the back door and I slipped inside, feeling a little overwhelmed by her tantalising perfume.

'What do you do, Maheshji?'

'Ma'am, I am an election publicity coordinator with the AICC and a businessman as well.'

'You're pretty active in politics, aren't you?'

'I am an organising secretary in the Delhi Congress. Politics is my passion, but I am not a full-time politician.'

'Oh really! But I am sure there's plenty of time for you to get involved. How old are you?'

'I'm thirty-one! May I ask your age? I am a student of numerology so I love to know people's date of birth!'

She was about three years elder to me.

'Why don't you have a cup of coffee with me? I am staying at the Oberoi,' she said.

What more could I have asked for? A most gracious woman was inviting me for coffee, so how could I refuse! With a thumping heart, I accepted her offer and soon we were seated in her room, sipping our coffee. There was a sensuality in her being which was affecting me tremendously, giving me the courage to take her hand in mine and gently caress it. She seemed to like the gesture and suddenly somehow, we found ourselves kissing each other, with me showering gentle passionate kisses all over her face and neck. I have always felt that real love can only be displayed through kissing and embracing, as it shows reverence for your partner. The intimacy of the setting was so overwhelming that we could not resist the magnetism and succumbed to it. Our rendezvous however, strengthened my belief that a woman's reciprocity plays a substantial role in alluring a man, for his very vitality depends on it!

Was there a lack of love in her life as it was in mine? Maybe that innate desire for fulfilment drew us close to each other. But unfortunately, we could not meet more than once or twice a year. She even visited my home and met my family and later attended my sons' weddings.

Chapter 2

Arguments and Misunderstandings

SITARAM KESRI HAD promised to compensate for the cost–cutting he had introduced during the previous elections, and one evening, he called, asking me to meet him. I was in for a pleasant shock!

'Elections have been declared in Punjab and I want you to handle the entire flag requirement order.'

'What will it amount to? Five lakh flags?'

'Twenty-five!'

I was taken aback by the enormity of the order! Images of my previous colossal order flashed through my mind. I was confident that I would be able to cope.

But it was indeed a huge task, making me lose track of the number, sometimes. I realised that a few had gone missing, so overwhelmed was I with the order! Money literally began pouring into my coffers, something which I felt I didn't deserve. I appealed to God to restrain the flow, for anything in excess is definitely poisonous! I believed that it was actually my father's love which was being showered on me in the form of money!

It became impossible for me to handle on my own. I engaged a cousin along with a few others, but they all proved unreliable as they began lining their own nests, stealing my business from me! One good thing that happened was that I became detached from the activity of amassing wealth, and this made me more generous.

The order had to be completed within a month, and eventually, I was able to deliver only twenty lakh flags. It helped me earn enough to think of moving out of our family home in Sitaram Bazaar to Nizamuddin West in South Delhi.

To express my gratitude, I thought of gifting silver lemon sets to my mentors. Sitaram Kesri refused to accept, chastising me that I should try to bribe someone I called Babuji! Sree Kanth Verma accepted only on the intervention of his wife. I even gifted a semi-precious necklace to Vasudha Kumari, yet another former princess of an estate in Uttar Pradesh, who graciously accepted. Thus, I began my practice of gifting to strengthen my relationships. Vasudha Kumari's post of joint secretary was later taken over by P Chidambaram with whom, unfortunately, I had a disagreement. He was very meticulous and did everything with perfection. He had been especially invited by Rajiv Gandhi to join his cabinet, and, therefore, took pains to fulfil his responsibilities with great loyalty. He would meticulously check the supply of flags and rejected various lots, on grounds of colour, size, stitching and even the material.

I retaliated by saying, 'Sir, can you even purchase a cigarette for only seventy-five paise? That's what your treasurer gives me for a flag!' We got into a heated argument, with me expounding how impossible it was to make a flag in that amount.

'I will request Kesriji to enhance the price.'

'On the contrary, he has cut the price from one rupee to seventy-five paise,' was my volatile response.

He remained quite calm and humble and rounded off the argument with a promise to speak to Kesriji. A number of officers had surrounded us as I continued to rant, claiming to be senior as I had been associated with Congress since 1974, completely ignorant of his calibre.

Chidambaram had spoken in immaculate English, and I found myself responding equally fluently, confounding onlookers with this hitherto unseen side of mine. In actual fact, I was flustered by the thought of having two lakh flags rejected, especially as I had another consignment of four lakh flags ready in the shop. I had complete monopoly on flag supply, with vendors trying their best to sell their flags to me. Meeting criticism was new to me and I couldn't digest it. Moreover, I was banking on my connections with the president, treasurer and general secretary, and a joint secretary just did not match up to such a hierarchy! It was only later that the chief administrative officer, B R Dutta told me that I had been trying to outwit a renowned Harvard barrister!

Later, Kesriji said, 'Mahesh, you speak too much! Can't you hold your tongue? Do you know whom you were arguing with?'

'He's a joint secretary, isn't he?'

'He's also Rajiv's close friend, especially summoned to be a part of the Cabinet. If he complains to Rajiv about you, even I won't be able to help you!'

***

At one point, a lot of stock was disappearing from my shop and I suspected my own cousin to have a hand in it, together with a few of the employees. I knew what was going on, but decided to keep quiet for how many employees could I fire? What guarantee was there that their replacements would be better? Kumar Pashi offered a solution.

'My eldest brother has retired. If you like, he can work in your shop as a supervisor. His presence will act as a deterrent.'

I decided to pay him the maximum, more than the other employees, but unfortunately, I overlooked offering him tea and snacks in the evening, which I always ordered for myself. This was a real discourtesy on my part to an elderly person, that too my dearest mentor's brother. Once, when I was visiting Kumar Pashi, his brother's wife specifically accosted me and told me that her husband was very fond of food and would love to try the delicacies available in the market. Despite this hint, I still didn't offer refreshments to him, my logic being that I would then have to offer snacks not just to him, but to my cousin and a couple of old employees, as well.

The consequence of my oversight was that I lost a friend, for it alienated Kumar Pashi and a few months later, his brother left my employment. My own flirtatious nature was also to blame. Whenever I visited their home, I would talk freely with his nieces, who also loved to interact with me. But once inadvertently, I had recited a couplet with a double innuendo to which Kumar Pashi took immediate offence and ordered me to leave his house! I tried to apologise, but to no avail.

Kumar Pashi's backing out of my life was a big blow, for we had been together for so many years that we were like soulmates. To this day, I am embarrassed by the way I treated his brother, not taking into consideration even his advanced age.

I made an effort to reconcile with Kumar Pashi a while later, for my life felt empty without him. I went to meet him in his office without an appointment, with the excuse of getting a composition I had recently written, checked by him. It was a five-couplet-long ghazal, and Kumar Pashi seemed visibly moved by it. I had actually written it for him, appealing to him to let go of his antagonism and to accept me back in his life, for to me, he was the best person I had come across after my father.

People often say that Multanis are not very cordial, but Kumar Pashi was an exception. I find the practice of attributing particular traits onto different communities rather distasteful, for all kinds of people exist everywhere.

Kumar Pashi was a very fine personality, never ever trying to capitalise on our friendship. Though he was affected by my words, he didn't respond to them, merely saying that the composition was good and that there was nothing to correct.

A few days later, he invited me to speak a few words at his book release function. It was a great honour, as I would be speaking before many dignified personalities. I was happy because it meant that somewhere, Kumar Pashi's heart had melted towards me. I recited the same ghazal that I had composed for Kumar Pashi, dedicating it to him as my mentor.

> *Mere yaar mujh se khafaa na ho*
> *Meri zindagi se judaa na ho*
> *Tere ghum ko sah na sakunga mai*
> *Kahin tu hi mera khudaa na ho*

His wife had tears in her eyes, while the audience was deeply appreciative, drawing applause from one and all. But, though it bridged the rift between us, the earlier closeness couldn't ever be achieved.

The episode made me more aware of the need to share and I began to give more freely to others, even not having food until I had fed someone! Giving or keeping a little of our food, before eating our meal, is an old Indian custom, followed by our forefathers. I now adopted this custom vigorously. Once I happened to meet a venerable sadhu who said that by nourishing plants and feeding ants, birds and animals, daily, can avert an unnatural death. I added that to my routine, finding satisfaction in giving back to Nature in some way. Humanity lies in serving others, for the joy of giving is supreme, as is bringing a smile to someone's face even while expressing feelings through a poem!

Chapter 3

Lessons from Mr Clean

JUST AS BEAUTY gives an alluring aura to a woman, so power adds a magnetic aura to men and that fascinates me. I have always sought the company of learned and successful people and they, in turn, have left a profound impact on me. Though I was immersed in my business, I took care to nourish my mental faculties by attending innumerable literary and political discussions and seminars. I found political discussions fascinating. Once, when President Jimmy Carter visited during Morarji Desai's regime, I drove all the way from Sitaram Bazaar to Palam Airport to catch a glimpse of him!

How could I miss the opportunity of seeing these two charismatic personalities from up close? I would follow their speeches and was impressed by Morarji's lessons in humility and diplomacy and by his witty wisdom, which I found endearing. I had been greatly influenced by him ever since his visit to Delhi University in 1974 to motivate students against Indira's regime. I heard him again in 1977, after the Emergency, when he was released from prison, just before the General elections.

The 1984 elections gave the Congress a sweeping victory with 414 seats, completely decimating the BJP, the principal opposition party, which won only two seats in a House of 541.

In a democracy, the Opposition has an important role to play, but now there was no one to oppose the ruling party.

It is said that when there is no resistance from outside, strife appears from within. Rajiv Gandhi had his own crosses to bear, for this whopping majority only served to arouse jealousy and resentment in many hearts. Along with that, his reputation of being 'Mr Clean,' was a complete turnaround from the earlier government! He rejected an offer of funds from Dhirubhai Ambani himself, sending a clear message to the whole country that such tactics wouldn't be encouraged. In the presidential address at the Bombay Congress Session in 1985, he declared he would oust power brokers from the system, a jab at big industrialists who influenced financial decisions of the government.

The then Finance Minister, V P Singh, supported Rajiv Gandhi's policy, much to the dismay of several party supporters and financiers, for industry moves forward through interdependencies. V P Singh gained the epithet of 'Mr Cleaner,' for he, too, wouldn't entertain industrialists.

Dhirubhai Ambani approached the issue from an entirely different angle, telling Rajiv Gandhi that his mother had left Rs 100 crore in his custody, and that he only wanted to return it. Rajiv was aware of his mother's dealings with Ambani, but was unsure about what to do in this case. He turned to Sitaram Kesri for guidance, who told him to accept it. The Party needed funds to function, and if the PM refused all and sundry, where would the funds come from? Kesriji was a practical politician, who had risen from the grassroots and he now offered to take care of the situation. Rajiv was relieved. Kesriji also instructed Ambani to deal directly with him without bothering the PM. The whole scenario made Kesriji a very strong Congress leader, as he became an important link between the Party and Dhirubhai Ambani. Later, other prominent industrialists joined the link and Kesriji rose to prominence. In Congress circles, a rhyme related to Kesriji became very popular:

Na khata na bahi,
Jo Kesri kahe sahi!

(No writing matters
Only Kesri's words do!)

It is natural that when someone rises, there are many more willing to bring him down. Some senior leaders connived to persuade Rajiv Gandhi to clip Kesriji's wings by not re-nominating the latter to the Rajya Sabha. This proved a real jolt for Kesriji, for he did not fancy himself as just being confined to being the treasurer of the Party, with no real clout. He approached Vincent George, Rajiv's personal secretary, literally weeping before him, asking him to convince Rajiv to change his decision. 'He had served the Party his whole life, managing funds honestly and carefully,' was Vincent George's observation to me, for he knew I was close to Kesriji. Ultimately, Kesriji did get re-nominated to the Rajya Sabha, for he was an experienced lobbyist and Rajiv, a man of great compassion! Politics truly is full of entangled paradoxes!

***

A web of palace intrigue was being woven around a highly ethical politician, the meshes slowly tightening around Rajiv's oblivious persona, making him a victim of circumstances. It was as if the people held his innocence against him, considering themselves more capable, and forgetting that the masses saw the reflection of his lineage in him.

Things went further downhill for Rajiv Gandhi in 1986 with the resignation of Arif Mohammed Khan, minister of state, who was protesting against the government's stand in the Shahbano Case. The Supreme Court had passed a judgement in favour of Shahbano, an aggrieved Muslim divorcee, supporting her appeal for maintenance. Arif Mohammed Khan brilliantly defended the decision in Parliament and in the media and was commended by Rajiv Gandhi for his rhetoric. Later, giving in to the pressure of many senior cabinet ministers who regarded the judgement to be contrary to the Shariat laws, Rajiv Gandhi was compelled to enable a law in Parliament that overruled the Supreme Court judgement.

I was impressed by how Arif Mohammed Khan stuck to his stance, even at the cost of giving up his ministerial post. I went to him to express my admiration.

'Bhai Saheb, I have been your admirer since my college days when you were the President of the Aligarh Muslim University Students' Union. You, along with Harikesh Bahadur, President of the Banaras Hindu University Students' Union and Arun Jaitley, President of the Delhi University Students' Union, were my role models! I hope to be forgiven, but I would like to ask whether your resignation will be harmful for Rajiv Gandhi's image?'

Arif Mohammed Khan showed me a handwritten letter from Rajiv appreciating his defence of Shah Bano's rights and commented, 'How am I wrong in resigning? First Rajiv Gandhi praises me and then without any intimation, changes his decision! At least he could have taken me into confidence! Definitely his image has taken a beating for he has turned around his own decision, forgetting that he has the support of 414 MPs who voted him into power.'

'Isn't he a victim of his circumstances? Don't you think he's too young to hold such a responsible position? Sanjay's untimely death made him an MP at 37, while his mother's unfortunate assassination elevated him directly to the position of PM at only 40! May I ask you what would you have done in his shoes?'

Arif Mohammed Khan remained silent at my question, but from his expression it was evident that he was somewhat impressed by my reasoning and straightforward communication. I think, that was the moment when the foundation of a lifelong camaraderie between us was laid!

Harm had indeed been done. The same thought was echoed by Uma Shanker Dikshit, Rajiv's mentor, who said, 'Arif has irreparably damaged the credibility of Rajiv Gandhi!' P V Narasimha Rao tried to persuade Arif Mohammed Khan to take back his resignation. 'We are politicians, not social reformers! We have to win elections to come to power. If the Muslims themselves want to live in ditches, what can we do about it?' he told him to no avail!

I had felt let down too, for Rajiv Gandhi had vowed to bring power brokers under control during the Bombay Congress session, and here he had buckled under fundamentalist pressure! Many senior ministers were also of the opinion that the religious sentiments of the Muslim community shouldn't be touched, as it would mean that they would withdraw their support. It had become a raging discussion topic and, therefore, a strong decision was needed, to the extent of passing a law to override the Supreme Court's judgement. Rajiv did not have the experience to deal with this delicate matter and he was too young to stand up against the stalwarts of the Party, and thereby went against his own word. V C Shukla concurred with my observation: indeed, age and experience were not with Rajiv Gandhi, neither did he actually understand what politics was all about. Destiny had catapulted him into the highest position, in too short a time.

Indira Gandhi had been trying to initiate him gradually by nominating him as the general secretary of the AICC, but time was not on their side. After all, it is no mean task to handle such a huge, multicultural country!

***

In February 1986, I had booked a new house for myself in Nizamuddin West. I had been looking at areas near Sadar Bazaar, where my work was, but a good friend, Swatantra Kapoor, suggested South Delhi. The Vaishya community was concentrated in north Delhi. South Delhi sounded remote and was considered taboo in our circles, being considered too advanced.

'You have such elite connections, so why do you want to live in such congested areas? Consider Lajpat Nagar, Defence Colony or Nizamuddin.'

It made sense to me, so I did as he suggested. South Delhi had wide open roads, and was relatively free of traffic. It was enough to convince me! After an intense search of one year, I found a three-side open house, facing a park and immediately gave the token money. The house belonged to a widowed teacher, Shashi Anand, a gracious and charming lady, who had taught the Gandhi brothers in junior school. Unfortunately, it was a disputed property as she was in a tussle for the ownership with her sisters-in-law. She asked if I could help, since I was resourceful and well-connected. I soon had the case resolved to everyone's satisfaction, gaining the house and also a good friend.

The adjoining house belonged to her elder sister-in-law, Nirmal Anand, and when she saw how I had helped Shashi, she requested me to buy her house as well. I didn't have enough money, so I decided to buy it on instalments, and it made me a proud owner of 400 square yards, open on all four sides! I would pay as soon as I got my payments from the Congress office. Only once was I forced to borrow Rs one lakh from a friend to pay my instalment.

***

In October 1986, my Aggarwal community, the Vaishya Sangathan Sabha, honoured me with my very first award, usually given to people who had achieved some position or helped society. I was being recognised for my achievements, for at the age of thirty-two, I had accomplished huge tasks in my line of work. I had links with well-placed dignitaries and was prominent in the literary world as well.

On the night prior to the award function, six distinguished members of the Sabha visited my home. 'Our award function is tomorrow. We had invited the minister to preside over it and present the awards, but we have just been informed that the PM has sent him out of town for urgent work,' one of them said to me.

'That is unfortunate!' I responded sympathetically.

'You are receiving an award and that's why we decided to approach you for help. You have great contacts. Can you rope in some dignitary to grace tomorrow's event?'

I was stumped, for my own honour was now at stake, and they expected me to conjure up a minister, immediately! I thought of Sitaram Kesri, who was not only a minister but also part of the Aggarwal clan. I immediately called him up to ask if I could visit him and soon after, two car loads of us landed at his place! I explained the situation and said, 'It's not just my honour at stake, but that of the whole community; we depend on you, entirely!' Kesriji willingly agreed to preside over the function. I was the youngest in our community and in my family to receive such an award.

Chapter 4

A New Home and New Alliances

THE RUSSIAN PRESIDENT, Mikhail Gorbachev, was to visit Delhi in November 1986, and a nine-member committee was set up to give him a very warm welcome. Delhi was to be decorated with flags and banners. Sajjan Kumar, Tytler, H K L Bhagat were prominent members and, I, too was included, as I was close to the High Command and also had experience in organising and publicising. I could manage the production of flags, but I took up the production of banners, as well. Sajjan Kumar said that I was handling five lakh flags, so surely, I could manage 50,000 banners as well.

Unfortunately, I was not familiar with banner production and got them made using offset printing. It was taking time, and people began to get impatient and critical. At a meeting at Gaylords, Sajjan Kumar cornered me and tempers rose high. I said that I didn't have a factory at home. That shocked him and he threatened to throw a cup of coffee at my face! 'These Black Commandos have been given to you as a defense, and not for you to be offensive!' I said and this infuriated him. He castigated me for taking on a task I couldn't handle. I said that it was he who had forced me to agree. Others tried to placate us, but I was so incensed that I threw the cheque of Rs 2.5 lakh issued by Kesriji, on the table, refusing to proceed with the work. Bhagatji took me aside to calm me down.

Later, Sajjan Kumar was quite friendly, impressed by my confidence in taking a stand.

***

We shifted to our new house in 1987 and in hindsight, realised that it was a big mistake on my part to lock up the part of the family house which I was using. This alienated the whole family as my mother had a right to the whole house. Consequently, only my eldest brother and his wife turned up for our housewarming along with other paternal relations. My wife's family attended in full force, but I could feel their envious vibrations at my obvious elevation in life, especially as they were all still living in rented premises.

Soon after moving in, one of Chhaya's brothers got a ticket in Maneka Gandhi's newly formed minor party in the Haryana elections and he roped in Chhaya for campaigning, but she went off with the kids without informing me, just a fortnight after we had moved. When I reached home that night, I found the house dark and empty. I started calling up her relatives to locate her, and when I finally did, I ticked her off, literally ordering her to return immediately. A cousin dropped her off and I tapped her on her head, insisting that it was wrong of her to go off like this. Her cousin returned to the family with the tale that I was beating her up! Her youngest brother, who was quite hot-headed, accompanied with her elder brother's wife came later that same night, and insisted on taking her back. Fortunately, better sense prevailed and Chhaya refused to go back with them.

***

Corruption and arrogance go hand-in-hand with power and only a handful of leaders are exceptions to the norm. I know of several instances where two different letterheads are released, one to placate the supplicant that action is being taken and the other to negate it, officially. Then there is the cunning act of calling up someone ordering that the work should be done, but nothing happens at the end. Often, the ruling party becomes infected with this malady, ultimately leading to their own downfall. Workers and visitors are thus, both taken into the loop, but in reality, work is only done for those few who are of use, either socially or financially. The others are told that ninety per cent effort had been put in, while the rest was their destiny! Sometimes, just the assurance that one is being listened to is enough to placate people. Sometimes, things naturally get resolved over a period of time, giving enhancement to the politician's image!

***

Over the years, I had the opportunity to work at various levels: as a polling booth agent, a counting agent, and an office bearer at the block, district, and state committees. I campaigned, participated in rallies and demonstrations. Once, my photograph appeared on the front page of *Jan Satta* showing me standing alone in front of a water cannon. It was captioned, 'One-man army!' It was another story that my short height allowed the water to go over my head, leaving me untouched, or else it would have just swept me along! But it cannot be denied that mob mentality rouses one to frenzy and one is ready to face anything, even at personal risk!

I also made press notes for the media. Bhagatji had once remarked, 'Mahesh ji, you have a way with words, so write a press release for the DPCC meeting today. I will guide you.' And he proceeded to do so immediately, instructing me on how to talk about the agenda, describing the meeting and the attendees, and adding the names of some of the prominent dignitaries. It was the first time I drafted a report in English, a precursor to many more. These would then be translated into Hindi. I found in myself, yet another talent and gained much fame in the process!

***

Despite being given so much responsibility in multiple areas, a real, solid position of importance always eluded me. In retrospect, I think maintaining a low profile is essential, otherwise one antagonises others, especially in political circles. But my work has always spoken for me, giving me a place far above any position. My direct connections with several top leaders—from the PM to the President and governors—added to my prestige.

It also gave me a distinct advantage and I was able to foster several friendships with women politicians, attracting even the All India Mahila Congress office bearers. They would regularly interact with me, encouraging me to flirt, even designating me with the epithet of 'Great One'! I would often be invited to high tea or lunches where we would have a verbal battle of wits, with all of them ranged together against me! Though I tried to forge closer relationships with some, I was never successful and later learnt that almost all of them were connected to some senior leader or the other. It also made me realise that no woman got easily into a relationship unless there was strong chemistry involved. My liaison with them was just a light-hearted one, but the message did go into various circles that Mahesh had close connections with several senior lady leaders, some many years older than him. My ego got a big boost, but this too, proved to be my undoing, for I managed to antagonise some senior leaders who doubted my relationship with their women; these leaders made sure that I never got a position of relevance in the Party.

The following couplet aptly sums up my situation:

> *Na Khuda hi mila na wisale sanam*
> *Na idhar ke rahe na udhar ke hum*

> (I attained neither the Lord, nor a loving beau
> Deprived I remained, unfulfilled, ever and anon)

***

About this time, I came into contact with yet another of my mentors, Mani Shankar Aiyar. I had noticed him a number of times with Rajiv Gandhi, so one day, I asked Kesriji who he was.

'That's Mani Shankar Aiyar, an IFS officer, and Rajiv Gandhi's star campaigner. A very able gentleman; both are alumni of Cambridge. Now he's a capable support for the PM.'

Later, I learnt from G V G Krishnamurty that he had led a delegation in March 1985 to Washington to arbitrate on one of Rajiv Gandhi's favourite subjects, the import of dual-use high technology supercomputers, used both for peaceful purposes and in war-like conditions; such computers could predict both the weather and also launch missiles. The Americans had some reservations about sharing this technology with us, as we had close relations with the Soviet Union and were afraid we would pass it on to them. He was asked to negotiate an agreement with the Americans that would safeguard their interests and also cater to ours. Aiyar skilfully achieved his objective, with an undertaking that the technology would never be shared with either Russia or China. G V G Krishnamurty who had been part of the delegation was all praise for the way Mani Shankar Aiyar handled the situation diplomatically. It was after this that he joined the PM's office.

His persona left a deep impression on me and later after

Rajiv Gandhi's martyrdom, I once met Mani Shankar Aiyar at the gates of the Congress Headquarters.

I introduced myself and said emotionally, 'Bhai Saheb, I saw you many times in Rajivji's company and honestly see glimpses of him in you! Just meeting you has made him come alive for me. I would be honoured to receive your blessings and patronage!'

This made him equally emotional and he silently hugged me, this one action laying the foundation of a lifelong friendship. His humbleness was heart-warming and he won my heart completely. He had indeed been Rajiv Gandhi's backbone, helping to prepare the initial drafts for the innumerable speeches that the PM delivered both in and out of the country. It was a mammoth task, for after the first draft, Rajiv Gandhi would suggest relevant modifications. His famous speech on Disarmament in the UN went through seventeen major amendments and many more minor ones!

Together, they initiated many achievements during his regime, with Mani Shankar Aiyar working closely with Rajiv on his Constitutional amendments to Panchayati Raj, a strong step towards strengthening democracy in India and empowering women in rural areas. Rajiv was undoubtedly a modern visionary and it was his farsightedness that brought computers into the country, aided actively by Sam Pitroda. This was among the first major initiatives Rajiv Gandhi undertook as Prime Minister.

When the idea of digitising the country with computers was first proposed by Rajiv Gandhi, the Opposition leader, Vajpayee actually came to Parliament in a tonga to show his displeasure with the idea, and people sarcastically referred to Rajiv as 'Computer Boy'! The argument put forward was that it would cause more joblessness among the already struggling population. But Mani Shankar Aiyar had vociferously supported the PM saying that on the contrary, Indians were capable of rising above that drawback, and would turn it into a booming industry. The prophecy proved true. Soon after, Rajiv Gandhi was branded as the 'Father of Information and Telecom Revolution of India'.

Chapter 5

You Win Some, You Lose Some

A MONTH AFTER I shifted to Nizamuddin, Vijay Diwan, the friend from whom I had borrowed Rs One lakh tried to convince me to let him buy the other half of the house. I had wanted to return the money to him, but he refused to accept, saying that I should consider it as an advance for the house on his behalf. I was not interested, but he along with others continued to ask what I would do with such a big, dilapidated 400-sq yd house.

Better to rebuild half, and I could stay in their half of the house while I was doing that, they suggested. This made sense, as I had neither the money nor the muscle power to do this, and so, I reluctantly agreed to shift to their house and began to demolish my house completely. I had a *Bhoomi Pujan* before beginning the construction and invited my family for the celebration. This time, my entire family, including my mother came to shower their blessings. I was only thirty-four at this time, and I already had a VIP registration number for my car, the same as my house, D 15!

With the help of well-known architects, a very unique kind of house was made, along with a basement covering the whole plot, the first of its kind in the colony.

The new residence gave me a lot of pleasure, and it also gave a sense of unbridled freedom to my wife, who realised that there was now no family to answer to. Gradually, she became more abusive in her behaviour towards me, shocking even our neighbours, who were mostly from very elite backgrounds!

Regrettably, I too would retaliate, hurling insults back at her. Despite that, I retained my neighbours' sympathies, for they had begun to understand my conciliatory nature.

On 1 October 1988, I lost my mother. Over the years, when she had become detached from life, we brothers had got a room constructed for her in an ashram in Haridwar, where she would go to stay for a few days every other month. An aunt would sometimes go with her. On one such visit, coinciding with the full moon, she did not wake up, moving on peacefully to the other world in the early hours of the morning. Though there was grief in losing her, we marvelled at her smooth transition into the next world. It set me wondering at the nature of things. My father, who had been a better human being, had suffered at the end of his life, while my mother had gone so easily. It definitely proved that our past life karmas played a great role in our present lives!

Her last rites were performed at Haridwar itself. Both my parents were cremated on public holidays, ensuring that the family didn't need to take an off from their respective enterprises. We would often wonder at their thoughtfulness! Once we were back in Delhi, my brothers and their wives suggested that we should get our mother's jewellery evaluated before distributing it equally among ourselves. Consequently, I asked Chhaya to hand over the pieces of jewellery that my mother had given her.

A month later, when I asked my eldest brother about the jewellery, he said, 'Which jewellery?'

'The jewellery I gave you for evaluation. That jewellery!' I replied.

'You can forget about it. It was not yours!'

'What do you mean?'

'You didn't fully pay mother as per our partition deed, so you owed her.'

'But she also didn't go according to it! Neither have you completely followed it.'

I was stupefied at his reasoning, especially as my mother had not even given me a share in the ancestral home, preferring to favour her daughters, even though she was legally bound to give her share of the house to her sons. It is quite strange that a mother-in-law feels distraught if her daughter-in-law is leading a good life, forgetting that she too is someone's daughter! My mother had never appreciated all that I had done for the family. I had started working at sixteen, and had indirectly contributed to my brothers' education, and later in their marriages.

I naturally retaliated with some sharp words, and even tried to resort to legal action, my ego pushing me to demand for what was rightfully mine. How could they manipulate me so, they, who were my own blood? A senior lawyer friend, K L Hans counselled me: 'Mahesh ji, one should never carry out litigation against one's own family! It will be very difficult to prove anything. Best to forget and move on!'

Kumar Pashi, too, counselled me, 'Mahesh ji, it will be best to drop things, for you will definitely tarnish your father's name by your family squabbles!' I decided to back out, washing my hands of the whole affair. Another good friend, Shivani was also of the same opinion, 'Mahesh, you are destined to be someone great. Don't waste your precious time, energy and resources in these petty family matters. You have an image to uphold, and this is such a negligible issue!' I allowed my better sense to prevail and decided to put my trust in Divine Grace! When my eldest sister got to know the whole story, she felt really bad and came all out to support me, for she was appreciative of the role I had played in upholding familial ties. Without hesitation, she offered me a 200 gram ornament worn around the waist, a *tagri*, which had been our grandmother's and our mother had given it to her. She said that it was only right that my wife should have some jewellery of her mother-in-law.

***

On the political scenario, Rajiv Gandhi lost his position, while V P Singh's small party won the day with the help of some regional parties and the outside support of the BJP. It was a real paradox that despite having such a small party, he was able to become the PM while Rajiv Gandhi was relegated to being an opposition leader with his huge party! V P Singh had positioned himself as a strong contender for the next elections, actively working to undermine Rajiv Gandhi by uncovering scandals, including the infamous Bofors case. This happened just when the state home minister, Arun Nehru had reopened the Ayodhya temple locks following a court ruling, and Arif Mohammed Khan had resigned over the Shah Bano case. These events together pushed President Giani Zail Singh to consider dismissing Rajiv Gandhi—a dramatic turn for a leader who had enjoyed the support of 414 MPs just two years prior to these events.

However, controversies continued in the ruling Party, for there was no unity among party leaders, as each one was waiting to grab the chair for himself, especially Devi Lal and Chandrashekhar. Devi Lal was appointed Deputy PM while Chandrashekhar opted to cut away from the Party and form his own Janta Dal. In V P Singh's government, Arif Mohammed Khan was given two portfolios, that of Civil Aviation and Energy. He was a great support to the PM, often even conducting press conferences for him at his home.

V P Singh opened a Pandora's box by raising the issue of the implementation of the Mandal Commission Report, which had been suppressed by both Indira and Rajiv Gandhi. The objective of the Commission was to identify socially and educationally backward classes and create reservations for them, paving the way for caste to hold centre-stage. This led to unprecedented communal turmoil and great disharmony. There was strong resentment in the upper castes, particularly among the youth of India, as it was a sort of reverse discrimination. Taking advantage, the BJP too had entered the fray by picking up issues of religious sentiments, referred to as Kamandal to counteract V P Singh's Mandal.

Meanwhile, L K Advani undertook a 'Rath Yatra' from Somnath in Gujarat to Ayodhya in Uttar Pradesh to support the construction of a Ram Mandir at the site of the Babri Masjid, and this changed the course of India's history, for communalism is a far stronger weapon than casteism in dividing the country.

K K Tiwari, a union minister tried to hamper proceedings in Parliament to stop the dismissal by alluding that the President, himself, could be implicated for entertaining and allowing terrorists to stay in Rashtrapati Bhawan. He said to Jaipal Reddy, a vociferous critic of Rajiv Gandhi, 'Mr Jaipal Reddy, your mind is as twisted as your body,' creating a furore on the floor! K K Tiwari belonged to the 'shouting brigade' which supported Rajiv Gandhi. Elections were declared for November 1989 and I was inundated with work, with sales of almost Rs one lakh daily. Sadar Bazar was the hub for the election paraphernalia and I was the uncrowned king for the supply of flags! I would set my own prices and had an extensive clientele.

After Kumar Pashi's brother had left, I had invited my maternal uncle from his village near Palwal to help me. He was sixty and had been running the small departmental store inherited from my grandfather. He was happy to stay with us, although my wife was not very cordial to him, as she resented having to serve him meals.

Seeing my wife's often rude attitude towards me as well, my uncle commiserated with me as to how I had managed to live ten years with her.

'I am paying for my past life sins, I think! It is my karma coming back to me. Besides one has to pay for one's success. It demands sacrifice, and one can't just have everything in life!'

***

A few days before the polling date, a requirement for flags and other items came from some VIP constituencies. Vishwajit Prithvijeet Singh was put in charge of arranging them and Kesriji handed over a large amount to him for these. I was given the order for 5 lakh flags and was funded with Rs 3 lakh, with a commitment for Rs 2 lakh more. But unfortunately, that commitment was never fulfilled. Once Narasimha Rao, became president of the Congress Party, I had four meetings with him in his five-year tenure, along with the others who supplied other items for the elections. In my last meeting, I even told Narasimha Rao, 'Honorable Prime Minister, you are the Party president also, so kindly honour the liabilities of Rajiv Gandhi.' The other suppliers were shocked at my temerity, but Narasimha Rao remained his nonchalant self. He was a great listener, but where he couldn't do anything, he would adroitly start discussing Urdu poetry with me, for he himself was as adept at Urdu as with eight other languages. No solution was offered by him, though Kesriji had even accused Vishwajit of embezzling funds, of almost Rs 20 lakh.

All in all, the situation left two PMs indebted to me, for morally they become responsible for ceding any payments incurred during their tenure. It became a standing joke later. 'From one I didn't ask, as he was a good friend and the other did not give!' I would often say.

Once my house was constructed, I would invite various

VIPs, ministers and even renowned poets to come and bless my new home and my family. Chhaya was an excellent cook and would serve amazing meals to my guests, making them heartily appreciate her culinary skills.

On 25 January 1990, I invited Prof Gopichand Narang, esteemed Urdu scholar for drinks and dinner at my newly constructed house. He had headed the Urdu department in Jamia Millia University, later becoming its Vice-Chancellor, and after a decade, became the President of the Sahitya Akademi. He was accompanied by his family and the evening was very congenial. The next morning, I read in the newspaper that he had been conferred with the Padam Shri Award. Astonished, I called him immediately, 'Please accept my congratulations, Bhai Saheb, but I am a bit perplexed. We had such a good time last night, yet you did not deem it fit to share such a big honour with me?'

'Manzar Saheb, don't you know that such things cannot be taken for granted until they are officially disclosed?'

It was a lesson for me. Later, at a felicitation ceremony held by the Jamia Millia University in his honour, the Professor invited me to be one of the speakers to congratulate him. It was a great honour, for at the young age of thirty-six, I was sharing the stage with a number of illustrious names! My natural wit came to the rescue and I decided to speak what was in my heart. I had prepared a congratulatory ghazal which I recited after a short speech and it was much appreciated by everyone.

Chapter 6

A Change in Fortunes

IN APRIL 1990, my eldest sister's daughter got engaged and she said that she depended entirely on me to get all the arrangements made as her husband wouldn't be able to manage on his own. She was not only my favourite sister but had also stood by me when my brothers had not. For the next couple of weeks, I devoted myself entirely to planning and organising the whole event, staying at my sister's house.

A few days after the wedding, a fire broke out in the area behind my shop in Sadar Bazaar, bringing back haunting memories of a similar night back in 1969. I had recently started a new business, processing of grey rexine linings in partnership with a friend, Bhushan Kumar, and a lot of material was stored on the upper floors of the shop. However, the fire was brought under control just as it reached the back part of my building.

However, a bank, a few shops away from my shop, was not so lucky when yet another fire broke out in the area, a few weeks later. Almost all the ledgers got burnt, destroying the records of thousands of clients, all in an era before computers. But by tallying all records with their system resources, they were ready to cater to their clients within a couple of months. The manager requested that the Federation of Sadar Bazaar Traders Association felicitate their zonal manager for the extraordinary work done by their branch. His zonal manager, also got directly in touch with me.

He said, 'It would be good for the morale of the bank employees. Clients too would feel valued.'

'If your chairman, Mr Mistri will also come, I will try to help,' I said.

The chairman was quite happy with such a function but wanted me to invite the finance minister, for he knew I had strong links in the government. Though the Union Cabinet Minister for Finance didn't agree, he deputed the Union State Minister for Finance in his stead, which was an equally great honour!

Thus, a huge event was organised on the main road of Sadar Bazaar, with the tent extending from Bara Tooti to Qutub Road. The chairman of the federation, one of the largest in Asia, was Manoharlal Kumar, a prominent builder, known for his aggressiveness. He requested me to compère and manage the show, even making the thanksgiving speech. Consequently, I was the MC, anchoring the event and interacting with the dignitaries.

***

Around that time, Ashok Kamal, a partner in a reputed finance company, MGF, and who lived in New Friends Colony, turned up at my house with a few prominent residents of the area.

'Maheshji, we have a club adjoining the colony, and the management committee has decided to make you one of its founding members.' Not being acquainted with club culture, I was wary of the proposal and tried to wriggle out of it by saying that I was too busy with Party work. My friend continued, 'We want to nominate a few people who have achieved some social status and will enhance the value of the club. I can sponsor you,' he said. Feeling pleased that I was being considered, I immediately made out a cheque for Rs 10,000 for a life membership.

Thus, I got introduced to club culture and soon got acquainted with its numerous benefits—huge bar, big halls, restaurants, courts for tennis and badminton and a swimming pool, all of which proved to be a big boon for my family. It also widened my circle of friends as I got to know many more people, and came in handy for what I called, 'my dinner diplomacy'.

***

A fresh wave of delight was brought into my life by Ayesha, a very well-educated Muslim lady and a senior Government official. I admired her greatly, and soon, she began to reciprocate, leading to some wonderful evenings together. Later, she would visit my home, almost as a family member and became Chhaya's best friend. It was very strange that Chhaya could not make friends on her own, but usually became really close to my lady friends. Kumar Pashi would often encourage me to make friends with both men and women, as he himself was a great worshipper of women. He was tall, dark, with a deep sonorous voice, and was quite a popular, modern Urdu poet. He held an important position in Irwin Hospital, and women always found him attractive. He would advise me, 'Don't get disheartened that your married life is not a bed of roses; it happens with the best of us! If it was so, you wouldn't have achieved the heights of expression that you display in your poetry, for only an injured soul can speak thus. The conflicts at home have helped you channelise your passion into other aspects of your life. You thrive through your words, your politics and your friends!'

Socrates' thoughts on this are equally relevant when he said, 'By all means, marry. If you get a good wife, you'll become happy; if you get a bad one, you'll become a philosopher.' I am a true representation of his quote, for indeed, only the unhappily married men touch heights in the fields of poetry and politics!

***

Once, Justice Grover expressed dissatisfaction that I had not progressed in life. He had foretold that I would rise to great heights, but here I was, still making a living out of a mundane, mercantile existence! It's true that I was more interested in making money than in taking on a leadership role. My main focus in forming friendships in political circles was aimed at getting orders to improve my business, rather than being actively engaged in politics. Justice Grover's wife insisted I consult their very good astrologer friend, J C Mendiratta, a former Chief Commissioner of Income Tax, to understand what the blockages in my life were. Glancing at my horoscope, he said, 'Maheshji, you will become a leader of a very high order! But…after initial failures.' He added: 'Maheshji, you will never experience the solace of one woman's constant companionship, either at home or outside.' This second statement was a bit of a mystery, because at that time, I was getting the best of both the worlds, for Chhaya was a bit compliant at home and I had forged great friendships with both Shivani and Ayesha and with a few more women. He continued, 'There will be plenty of lady friends, but none will be a real companion. Also, your children will not be a source of comfort for you.' He stated that I would get fame in the fields of poetry and politics, grow socially and economically, and have good health as well, so what else does one need?

Bemused, I asked him, 'Will I become an MP, as that is the extent of my ambition?' He laughed and said, 'Not just an MP; you might even become the PM!'

This, I found difficult to digest, but he explained, 'After all a PM emerges from an MP, and there's only a very slight difference between the two. Every MP is entitled to become a PM, who is like a monitor in a class.' I shared this with others, even creating a kitchen cabinet and nominating my family and friends to various posts, much to everyone's amusement!

J C Mendiratta's analysis changed my concepts about life and deepened my belief in astrology and Destiny. He said I had a better bonding with my father than with my mother. He advised me to accept the inevitable and that allowed me to have a sense of detachment towards my own family. He had warned me of future betrayal from them all, and added that it would be better to prepare myself for it. He became a close family friend, even attending all our family events later. He had lost his wife early and once I said to him, 'Yes, good wives move on quickly while the bad ones stick around for a long time!' He found my observations quite amusing.

***

V P Singh's government was soon on shaky ground, and this encouraged Rajiv Gandhi to initiate a change of power.

On 2 October 1990, a massive rally was taken out to gain support for the Congress Party. The rally took ten hours to cover the 5-km distance from Rajghat to Fatehpuri, for not only were all Party workers present, but the public too had turned out in unprecedented numbers. At almost every step, Rajiv's cavalcade would be stopped and he would be presented with flowers or garlands, sweets and shawls. I was in an open jeep right behind him. Every little while, he would toss the flowers or sweets that he was receiving, back into the crowd and a few times, into our jeep as well, even as we shouted slogans like 'Rajiv Gandhi *sangarsh karo, hum tumhare saath hain, Congress Party zindabad*' and so on! It was an exhausting day and we were all jubilant at the public showing their allegiance to the Congress leader.

On Diwali, I went to wish Rajiv Gandhi, taking along with me a box of his favourite *pista barfi*. He was in the lawns of 10 Janpath, along with Ghulam Nabi Azaad, Ahmad Patel, R K Dhawan, Buta Singh, Jagannath Pahadia and his wife, Shanti Pahadia. Rajiv Gandhi gave me a charming smile, rousing an overwhelming love in me. I opened my box of sweets, demanding that he should open his mouth. Everyone was surprised at my temerity to demand this of an exalted dignity! It goes to his credit that without taking offence, he obliged, allowing me a deep satisfaction, but those standing around did not like my behaviour. I chose to ignore them and commented 'Bhai Sahab, you are not carrying a pen in your kurta pocket. In poetry circles, this is equal to being bare and barren!' And taking an ordinary pen from my own pocket, I placed it in his. Rajiv Gandhi simply laughed at my antics while the gathering marvelled at my boldness and laughed half-heartedly along with him! Nonetheless, I was forgiven and regarded as a mad but lovable poet!

***

To meet the expenses for constructing my house, I had to sell the plot I had bought earlier. The last election had helped me make money, but a house needs constant funds for construction. My work was suffering and my uncle had gone back to his village, fed up with my wife's attitude.

I took the momentous decision of changing my fifty-year-old, cloth merchandising business to that of home appliances, for there, at least, everything could be counted. Thus, on 16 January 1991, the day the Persian Gulf war started, I took on a dealership of Racold and reset my whole shop.

Chapter 7

A Poetic Tribute to Rajiv Gandhi

21 MAY 1991 proved to be one of the most disastrous days of my life, for our beloved Rajiv Gandhi was assassinated on a visit to Sriperumbudur. It was about 9.30 am when I got the news. I switched on the television to crosscheck and then barged out of the house shouting loudly that they have now killed Rajiv Gandhi also. At the back of my mind, I felt the Sikhs were once more responsible and a Sikh lived right opposite my house! My grief was intense, but no one reacted to my volatile display of grief and I went back inside. Just then, Shahid Siddiqui, a prominent Urdu newspaper editor and a senior Congress leader, and also a good friend of Rajiv Gandhi, called me. Rajiv Gandhi had visited his home, which was on the opposite corner to mine, a couple of months earlier. He had also invited me. Once we had had dinner, I asked Rajiv ji to visit my home too as I was practically next door. Rajiv almost agreed, but his security stepped in, saying a prior recce was essential to ensure his safety. Rajiv assured me that he would visit my home some other time. This thought flashed through my subconscious mind!

He asked me if I had heard the news, then asked if I had a driver available.

'I drive myself, Siddiqui Sahab. Please come here and we will go together.'

When he came, we both broke down, hugging each other desperately, unable to contain our despair! We wanted to meet Sonia Gandhi and the children for even though she was not very amicable towards people, we didn't know what else to do to mitigate our grief. While, on our way, another senior leader, Prof Saifuddin Soz, called Siddiqui and asked us to pick him up as well. We were overwhelmed by the tragedy and could only wonder at Rajiv's going away at forty-seven. He could have easily won another term as PM but now nothing was possible.

I turned to Siddiqui and said, 'You know how I am feeling? It is like:

> *Apne hone ka bhi ahsaas nahi hota hai,*
> *tu na ho pass toh kuchh pass nahi hota hai.*

From the back seat, Prof Soz said, 'Manzar Sahab! Stop the car!' Perplexed, I did so.

Prof Soz exclaimed, 'That's an amazing couplet! Quite akin to what Momin once composed and was appreciated by Ghalib himself. You must write it down immediately.'

> *Tum mere pass hote ho goya*
> *Jub koi doosara nahi hota*

Encouraged by both, I did so by, borrowing paper from the Professor. We continued to 10, Janpath but found that all the gates had been closed as the family had been put under high security. Many other senior leaders were also present at the gates, but none were being allowed entry, and so we had to return home without meeting them. The next day, at an emergency meeting of the CWC, Sonia Gandhi was unanimously nominated the president of the Congress party, but she declined.

After being brought back from Sriperumbudur, Rajiv

Gandhi's body was kept in state at Teen Murti house. Within hours, I was there along with my wife, Siddiqui and his wife. Sonia Gandhi was sitting on one side with her children and a few family members, and to my utter amazement, when I bowed my head, nineteen-year-old Priyanka actually stood up to acknowledge me. It was a really emotional moment for me, for I was not expecting any recognition at all.

I spent the next three days there before the cremation took place in the afternoon of the third day. The procession started on its final journey with many VIP cars following, while thousands lined the sides of the road. I followed in my car but when we reached the India Gate roundabout, policemen were stopping the cars. When the car immediately in front was stopped, a gentleman got out and started scolding the policemen saying that they were stopping the future PM's car. I was curious to see who this was, and immediately got out of my car to check.

N D Tiwari was in the car and to press my advantage, I greeted him with great gusto and he responded with equal fervour and demanded to know how I was there.

'I am your born follower, Babuji, so I am right behind you.' I definitely did not want to lose ground in case he did become the PM though it is another story that he didn't even become an MP.

We finally reached the cremation grounds and despite tight security, I managed to reach right next to the platform on which the funeral pyre was. Only very important dignitaries were standing there and yet no one stopped me, even though I had no right to be there. The final logs were being put on the body, first by Sonia Gandhi, then by Rahul and Priyanka and finally by Amitabh Bachchan, who was almost like a brother to Rajiv. As Amitabh descended after putting the log, like lightning, I slipped up the few stairs to place the final log. No one stopped me as I paid my final respects to my beloved leader and before anyone could even become aware of me, I was off the platform, with a deep sense of spiritual gratification for having performed that final rite. In that moment, I recalled a sarcastic comment once made by H K L Bhagat, when I had taken an unwarranted liberty with the PM: 'Do you have any past life relation with Rajiv Gandhi?' I really felt it to be true, else how could I have been the one to place the final log for his last journey? I forever treasured my final moment with him! *Alvida Rajiv!*

***

A couple of days later, H K L Bhagat asked me to compose a ghazal on Rajiv Gandhi which he would have me read at the *Sarvdaliy Shok Sabha* (All Party Condolence meet) at the Ramlila Grounds. I expressed my reservations but he encouraged me to try, as I had been close to Rajiv and knew him well. I mulled the topic over and recalled the *sehra* written for my wedding day by Kumar Pashi where he had used our names as an alliteration. I now used Rajiv's name in the same alliterative manner and took my composition to Kumar Pashi for approval. He wholeheartedly ratified my eulogy, tweaking a word here or there. The final presentation was so mesmerising that it was read at innumerable events all over the country, with requests to translate it as many couldn't understand some of the Urdu words. On the day of the condolence meeting, I felt overwhelmed, for that was the same platform from where Vajpayee had paid his heartwarming homage to Lal Bahadur Shastri, years ago! Besides, it was the first time I was being given a chance to do something on a personal level as a poet. But although I was present on stage, I couldn't read my ghazal due to crowd sentiments and some political machinations.

***

One morning, as I was hanging my towel in the balcony of my house, I noticed Prof Gopichand Narang walking down the road accompanied by a well-known Pakistani poet, Qateel Shifai. In my usual exuberant way, I hailed them loudly, oblivious of my semi-clad state. They stopped outside, while I quickly pulled on my clothes and joined them. Narang introduced me as a poet who recites Urdu couplets in Hindi. They accepted my hospitality and came in to have a cold drink.

Qateel Shifai said, appreciatively, 'Manzar Sahab, *isse kehte hai daane daane per likha hai khane wale ka naam.*'

I exclaimed, 'But Huzoor, you haven't tasted a morsel yet. So can we say, "*Qatre Qatre per likha hai peene wale ka naam?*"' *(That every droplet has a name on it?)*

He stood up and hugged me! 'Never have I heard such instant creativity! In my whole life, I have not used the words that you're using nor ever heard them being used.'

His enthusiasm was infectious. 'Bhai Sahab, you must have heard that too—'*Zarre zarre per likha hai rehne wale ka naam*, you had to come and grace my humble abode today. It was not me who invited you here; it was the very slivers of my house that did so.' He was again amazed at my ingenuity, 'I never realised that even zarre can call out to one!'

We spent a congenial hour together and then they continued on to their original destination, to the house of a neighbouring poet, Mumtaz Mirza.

***

On P V Narasimha Rao's initiative, a Kavi Sammelan and Mushaira was planned on Rajiv Gandhi's birth anniversary on 20 August 1991. Ghulam Nabi Azad was in-charge of the event. The cream of the literary world was invited, besides senior leaders and I realised that my name was not in the list. I approached Ghulam Nabi Azad, but he expressed his inability to do so, saying that the list of Hindi Urdu poets had already been submitted.

I then approached Vincent George and requested a meeting with Sonia Gandhi. When I told him the reason, he said, 'I will see to it that your name is included. You deserve to be a part of the event.' And thus, on the day of the Symposium, I, too was sitting on the stage with many great names. The organisers had put my name down as the last speaker, not realising that this honour was usually for some senior poet! I read the ghazal I had written extolling Rajiv Gandhi, but with such intensity of emotion that the whole hall resounded with euphoric applause, with poets and politicians alike showing unbridled appreciation, making me repeat each couplet twice or thrice. When the PM arrived to attend the event, Ghulam Nabi Azaad presented a silver shield to him. After I finished my recitation, Narasimha Rao summoned me and presented the shield to me, as he was delighted by my composition. That one event elevated me in the eyes of many, as I got love and approbation from the higher echelons of governance.

Chapter 8

Unseen Battles, Unspoken Wounds

MY SHOP WASN'T doing well as the stuff I was selling on retail was also being sold at wholesale rates in the same market. Since I had changed my line of merchandise, my reserves were depleting. I had invested in the construction of my house, and had even sold my plot, which I had bought in 1983 as a kind of reserve against future calamities. Moreover, our community has a fetish for saving for the future! The newly constructed house was like a huge ship, demanding maintenance on an equally grand footing.

With Rajiv Gandhi's demise, I felt as if my support system had collapsed, just like I had felt at my father's death. Even the Rs 2 lakh due to me after the 1989 election campaign had been denied to me. With the change of government, I didn't have any hope of reclaiming it, either. Eventually, Congress came back into power in June 1991 under P V Narasimha Rao.

I also got caught in a serious family crisis, as my wife Chhaya and my younger son fell ill after dinner in Bengali Market. Leaving my elder child with a neighbour, I rushed them to the Holy Family hospital where they were diagnosed with cholera. I shifted them to the R P hospital for Communicable Diseases in Kingsway Camp, dealing with this single-handedly, as in the stress of the moment, I didn't think of informing the family until the next morning when Chhaya needed glucose intravenously for forty-eight hours, as she was serious. My son was better the next day, but it took three days for Chhaya to recover.

***

My dwindling resources were putting me into a state of panic. I approached V C Shukla, who was now a cabinet minister, and shared my concerns with him. He directed me to meet the textile minister who helped me to get the franchise of Gurjari, the Gujarat state emporia. They were opening outlets in residential areas and my residence basement was perfect. All the infrastructure, staff and the merchandise was their responsibility. It was a lucrative deal, for I was to get a daily rent of Rs 2,000 and a 10 per cent commission on sales. The opening was done with a lot of fanfare, with the event being promoted in prominent dailies, attracting the jealous attention of some of my neighbours. Film actress Vyjanthimala and Rajesh Khanna visited the newly opened emporia, besides elegant ladies from the neighbourhood and from nearby posh areas. A group of residents, however, visited me, raising objections to commercial activity in a residential area. I tried to reason with them saying that I needed the earnings for my family's upkeep, as my shop was not doing well. But they were adamant and wanted me to close down. I refused, recommending them to go and complain wherever they wanted. I couldn't have foreseen the conspiracy they would weave.

A few evenings later, a young girl of the locality, whom I knew came to look around with a friend. The girl asked me what could I give her for free, so I told her that only I was available for free and she could take me! They laughed and left, but in a while, some youths entered accusing me of sexually harassing the girl. They threatened me with dire consequences if I didn't shut down the emporia. After they left, I called up the SHO, a friend, and narrated the whole incident to him. He took a serious view of the matter, saying that they could easily trap me, for weightage would be given to the girl's accusations, even if inaccurate. The incident made me realise that there was more politics happening in society than in political circles, for people have lower value systems! After that, I began to phase out the emporia, reducing the rent as sales were coming down. Soon, I had to bid goodbye to it totally, bringing myself back to square one!

Throughout my life, I've dabbled in about sixteen ventures, including the share market and property, mostly ending in losses. Only the last two were more sustainable, as running a shop alone proved impossible. However, by 1993, investing in properties paid off, and I owned a plot and a couple of flats.

Meanwhile, my electrical goods shop, too was on the verge of a shutdown. I now really needed to get my act together. How times had changed! The very shop from where I had sometimes earned a profit of up to Rs 50,000 a day was not even giving me Rs 50 now! It just went to show that time and Destiny were more powerful than either space or individuals.

I was at my wit's end, and recalled a chance meeting with the Medical Superintendent of Irwin hospital, Dr M K Trivedi. A hospital needed so many things, could I not supply something or the other? With this in mind, I asked Dr Trivedi if I could supply any of the hospital's requirements. Thus, I began to supply small cleaning items and glasses to the hospital. Once I invited the chief store officer for dinner who asked me pointedly why I was only supplying such inconsequential items. He explained that it was acceptable practice to dole out at least 20 per cent to the person who was responsible for placing the orders. I told him that margins were low in the items I was supplying. He responded that I could supply only

50 per cent of the requirement but charge for the whole! This came as a real shock and I realised the extent of corruption, that too in a government-run hospital!

I categorically declined as I had never used any such underhand tactics ever in my dealings with the Congress party, and certainly wouldn't do them where a hospital was concerned! That line of work too didn't last long and I backed out of it a year or so later.

However, here I met Dr Ragini and we became good friends as she loved Urdu poetry. Beauty always attracts me and she was also quite attractive. She had divorced her husband as he had a habit of belching! I told her that she was a double MD doctor, and could have found ways of treating him rather than divorcing him!

***

In 1992, I got a chance to play a significant role in the Congress session in Tirupati. I was included in a newly formed 'special invitee category'. Narasimha Rao had established a new rule under which twenty new members were to be added, ten nominated by him and ten elected. Kesriji asked me to lobby for his candidate Tariq Anwar, and I readily agreed, for he was also a good friend and neighbour. I stood at the entrance of the area where voting was happening, requesting each voter, all AICC members, to support and vote for Tariq Anwar on Kesriji's behalf. Film actor-turned-politician, Sunil Dutt, was quite amused by my tactics, and highlighted them later by saying that this is how campaigning should be done! Meanwhile, R K Dhawan approached me with the same request, 'I too am standing for the election. Please campaign for me as well!' I was delighted to do so and added his name to my appeals! This brought me to everyone's notice and my picture standing there along with Arjun Singh even made it to an article about the session in *India Today* with the caption, 'One step below the peak'. Arjun Singh was a likely candidate for the PM's post. The Congress session proved to be a great event in my life as it catapulted me into the limelight strongly, especially as R K Dhawan won!

A while later, by-elections for a seat in New Delhi were announced. Rajesh Khanna was a contender, and R K Dhawan proposed my name for the campaign committee. Thus, I remained in very close contact with the actor, becoming almost inseparable till the election results were declared. Rajesh Khanna kept me constantly by his side, even when his wife and daughters came for campaigning. He appreciated how I was canvassing in his favour, calling out to people to come and vote for him, and categorising him as the first and last superstar of the film industry! Rajesh Khanna would laugh at my exaggerations, and I would tell him that the world of politics was even more artificial than the one he came from! He gave me the name of Toofan at the way I energetically managed everything! Our efforts paid off and he won the election, defeating Shatrughan Sinha by a big margin.

***

After Rajiv Gandhi's demise, I got another shock in mid-July when my best friend and poetry Guru, Kumar Pashi passed away due to brain haemorrhage. It caused me a lot of grief, especially when I learnt that after taking ill, he had to walk to Irwin hospital from his house in Delhi Gate. I felt really sad that I had not been able to support him in his last moments. He had been the humblest person in my circle of friends. He had received international accolades, but would constantly worry about the future of his five daughters and had become addicted to smoking and drinking leading to his early demise.

All the pillars of my life had died early, my father when

he was just fifty-nine, Rajiv Gandhi at barely forty-seven and now Kumar Pashi at fifty-seven. I felt as if my life had lost its sheen for a huge vacuum was created by Kumar Pashi's departure, one that no one has been able to fill till date.

Chapter 9

Scams, Corruption, and Some Priceless Moments

1992 WAS ALSO the year when a major scam came to light. Harshad Mehta, a well-known share broker, had been caught in a security scam and alleged that he had delivered two suitcases of Rs 10 million to the PM's house, to gain his goodwill. There were twenty-seven CBI cases against him and he had expected Narasimha Rao to bail him out. However, nothing could be proved, since, naturally nothing was on record. The PM remained his impassive self, completely unrepentant, with no signs of resigning. It was pretty shocking, disclosing the inherent corruption of politicians, for no Party is free of it. Vajpayee used to vouch for the integrity of the Bhartiya Janta Party, claiming that BJP's *'chaal, chehra, charitra'* were completely different from the Congress party, yet it too had many similar facets, for in another incident, the national President of the BJP, Bangaru Laxman, was the victim of a sting operation by a private television channel, Tehelka, which exposed him accepting a bribe of Rs 2 lakh in a defence deal. Though no action could be taken against Narasimha Rao, Bangaru Laxman was forced to resign. Indira Gandhi once said 'Corruption is a global phenomenon', justifying its existence, for it is an inherent aspect of political life, proving that 'Power corrupts and absolute power corrupts absolutely'.

On Rajiv Gandhi's first death anniversary on 21 May, a huge event was organised at the Indira Gandhi stadium where almost 30,000 people had gathered. The PM was delayed and the crowd was getting restive, many moving to leave. Sajjan Kumar, the organiser, suggested to Bhagatji, that Mahesh Manzar read his ghazal till the PM comes. Bhagatji immediately invited me onto the stage. This was the first time I faced such a huge gathering, that too a non-poetical one! I began to recite the ghazal with a little trepidation, but the response was phenomenal! Everyone was euphoric, appreciating every couplet, even making me repeat it a number of times. With this unmitigated adulation, my whole being was totally involved in that rapturous moment! The stadium resounded to deafening applause, as laurels were loaded onto me along with innumerable garlands from senior leaders of the Congress party!

***

When Shankar Dayal Sharma was declared the President, I went over to congratulate him, and found many others also present at the gate. When our names were sent in, much to my delight, only I was allowed to enter, with the others being asked to come the next day. Inside, a small function was in progress, where Shankar Dayal Sharma was being formally presented the decree of Presidentship. Only the newly elected President, his wife, Arjun Singh, T N Seshan and myself were present. There was extensive media coverage for the event was being telecast live on television. It was a very remarkable memory for me as I too became a part of one of the country's historic moments!

A meeting was organised at the AICC Headquarters on Rajiv Gandhi's birth anniversary, where Narasimha Rao had to pay his tributes to the departed leader. However, he spoke for only two minutes on Rajiv Gandhi, but spoke at length on Mani Shankar Aiyar, praising him profusely! I, was standing in the VIP enclosure and remarked to Bhagatji, 'Babuji, Mani Shankar Aiyar is definitely going to gain a ministry soon!'

In a dismal tone, he responded, 'You either get a ministry or accolades in the Congress party!' His observation was accurate, for that was all the acknowledgement Mani Aiyar got. But I became more enamoured by Maniji's persona, making efforts to get closer to him, subsequently even inviting him for dinner to my house the next year. I already had the privilege of hosting many senior Congress leaders like V C Shukla, Bhishma Narain Singh and Vasant Sathe. Maniji was also an MP, but he still maintained a humble lifestyle, even driving himself in a small Maruti car! Along with him I had also invited Tariq Anwar and his wife, Yasmin, and this turned out to be a pleasant surprise for Maniji. Yasmin was a very good friend of Chhaya's and came over quite often. Chhaya has always been an excellent hostess and has always dealt very warmly with my friends.

Maniji and his wife Suneet were quite happy to visit my home and meet my family. His tuning with his wife is amazing, especially as his marriage was an intercaste one, she being a very gracious Sikh lady and he a Tamil Brahmin. It is indeed a truth of life that a wife's beauty adds to a man's prestige while a man's success is like a jewel in a woman's life. They form a perfect foil for each other, and stand out in society!

Politics has a trend of superseding merit over seniority and this is what had happened with Mani Shankar Aiyar as well. P V Narasimha Rao wanted to appoint him as a cabinet minister, but some senior leaders from Tamil Nadu restrained the move, saying he was only a first-term MP, and many were way ahead of him! His qualities were totally overlooked, as normally happens in games of power.

***

23 November 1992 was another important date in my life, for I was conferred with the C L Nepali award for National Integration by the Union Cabinet Minister H R Bhardwaj. It was a public recognition of the work I was doing without any position or returns. Towards the end of the function, I was requested to recite my already famous ghazal on Rajivji, and received unmitigated appreciation and love from the jam-packed audience, comprising many political and social dignitaries, my friends and family members.

Soon after the Babri Masjid demolition on 6 December, Tariq Anwar came over, sounding very worried about the turn of events. I proposed meeting Kesriji and he agreed. Once there, I asked Kesriji, 'Babuji, there were thousands of people at the site, mostly supporters and workers of BJP and its allied groups. If the police had opened fire, how many people would have got butchered?'

I was amazed by his crisp response, 'Only about four or five!'

'How can you say so?'

'Well, they were firing to protect the centuries' old structure, and not to butcher. Besides, when one person gets shot down, a thousand immediately run away! Only a few actually reach a fatal end.'

I spontaneously said, 'That means our Central Government is responsible to some extent for the demolition!'

While I had the dealership of Racold, I was on very good terms with the managing director and in 1993, he included me in the group going to Kathmandu, Nepal, even though I was not doing much business. This was the first time that I went abroad. There were about thirty of us and we stayed in a five-star hotel. As was my nature, I had soon made myself the life and soul of the party, cracking jokes and generally entertaining everyone. Here, too, a few were interested in meeting some local women, but I chose to stay in the hotel with our organiser. It was not in my nature to trifle with a woman, since I preferred deep, meaningful interactions with them. I also had my first experience of a casino and gambling, besides visiting the famous Pashupatinath Shiv temple. It was a memorable trip for me!

***

My business at the shop was not going well, so I turned my attention to the share market and also into property dealings. I would subscribe to lots of magazines on the share market and would go through them thoroughly. I even hired a full-time employee to work for me and was able to get some very lucrative returns. I owned shares of more than two hundred companies, but I couldn't fully take advantage due to some later events.

Meantime, Tariq Anwar was nominated by the Congress President, Mr P V N Rao, as the chairman of the Minority Cell in AICC on Kesriji's recommendation in 1993. About ten months after the Babri Masjid demolition, he was asked by the PM to organise a conference of the Muslim faction at the Talkatora stadium. He knew that the Muslims were very angry with the incident, so he consulted me.

'I am sure you can gather 10,000 Muslims from all over India! Why don't you call out at least two hundred party workers from each state? If you get even half your number, you can add people from other frontal organisations, who would get to know.'

Tariq asked me to start the conference with my ghazal on Rajiv Gandhi, but I refused saying that it would show the PM in a bad light. I suggested he invite another senior poet, Gulzar Dehalavi, who was also a loquacious orator. How one presents things makes a big difference, just as Narasimha Rao had done earlier in his speech about the demolition, *'Neeyat galat nahi thi hamari, niti galat ho gayi'*. (There was nothing wrong in our intention, but our policy somehow misfired.)

Gulzar based his rhetoric on similar lines, as both did not wish to offend the Muslims, and at the same time, had to defend the Congress. He continued speaking for almost twenty minutes, far beyond his designated time, drawing great applause from the audience! Tariq tried to stop him, but was restrained by the PM, himself. Kesriji and the other leaders were all praise for me for arranging Gulzar's talk.

Around this time, I was asked to edit the Hindi section of *Tasveer-e-watan*, a fortnightly Urdu newspaper, run by a friend. I was now designated as an editor as well.

Arjun Singh, the then Minister of Human Resource Development in Narasimha Rao's government, resigned in 1994 and joined N D Tiwari, forming Congress Tiwari, with the tacit support of Sonia Gandhi. Their aim was to topple the Narasimha Rao government, but he was able to counteract their intentions by buying off some MPs. The Congress Plenary session was held in Suraj Kund, but dissidents like Sheila Dikshit, Natwar Singh, and M L Fotedar were not invited. They, therefore, rallied together and sat on *dharna* outside the venue. I was there, this time as editor of a newspaper.

At that time, Bhajan Lal was the chief minister of Haryana, and a few days later, a big car came to a stop in front of my house and some officers of the Haryana state government came in with gifts and sweets for me. It was customary to oblige journalists in this way back then. I was quite surprised that even a humble writer like myself was being feted in this manner!

Soon after, Arjun Singh's personal secretary invited me to tea at the leader's house. Arjun Singh said to me:

'I thought you were only a poet activist, but you have turned out to be an editor as well!'

'That's just something I do part-time.'

'Why don't you join our Party then?'

'I need to consult with my political gurus, Kesriji and

Shuklaji, so can I please respond later?' I asked.

I was in no position to join politics, full time, for my financial condition was not stable. Besides, my priority was my business not politics, even though I had a passion for it. My mentors also felt it was not the right time, so I backed out gracefully.

A multi-party meeting was held at the Mavalankar Auditorium, following the Babri Masjid incident. Many senior leaders were present, the Congress outnumbering the other factions. During the question-answer session, I posed a few very pointed questions to L K Advani, demanding validation for the demolition. He was unable to give precise, clear answers, and there was much hooting in the hall, to such an extent, that he had to leave the stage. People appreciated the way I pinned him down, and this added to my stature!

The Delhi Assembly elections were held in late 1993, and persuaded by friends and mentors, I applied from the Nizamuddin constituency for a ticket, but did not get it. Bhagatji asked me to support a Kashmiri lady who had been a sitting MLA from Minto Road and an associate of Indira Gandhi. So, I hosted a dinner for all the prominent people of my society to introduce her to them. I would accompany her for campaigning and some people would mistake me for the candidate. My speeches were impressive, and people would garland me, much to her discomfort. She gained a majority, but when a victory march was taken out, I was completely overlooked, which made me upset. I complained to Bhagatji and he placated me saying that the credit goes to you too, for your candidate was one of the fourteen who won among seventy Congress candidates. 'It will help to lay the foundation of any future position you might undertake.' My respect for Bhagatji deepened for I realised that indirectly he had helped me.

FIFTH DECADE
EXUBERANT EVOLUTION

Chapter 1

A Time of Liberalisation

NARASIMHA RAO WAS well-versed in Urdu *shayari* and encouraged *mushairas* as these were regarded as innocuous ways of beguiling people. The Union State Home Minister, Sayed Sibtey Razi, would be in charge, with the Delhi Police organising it. He was a good friend, so I would invariably be invited to such gatherings, as he liked my Urdu poetry. Two consecutive events were held in January 1993 and 1994, at the historic Ghanta Ghar in Chandni Chowk, with the PM and his Cabinet as chief guests. At the January 1993 event, I read my poems along with many well-known poets like Javed Akhtar, Shahryar and so on. I sat next to Javed Akhtar, for I felt a close affinity to him, as in my youth, my recitations had once been appreciated by his father-in-law, Kaifi Azmi.

I had a deep connection with Mujtaba Hussain, an internationally acclaimed satirist, who composed my pen sketch read out during my marriage. He once brought Shaharyar, composer of the *Umrao Jaan* film ghazals to stay overnight at my home, as he couldn't accommodate him at his own house. Shaharyar was a recipient of the prestigious Jnanpith award and I could only wonder at my luck at hosting such eminence! For a long time, we drank and talked, but then after my customary limit of two pegs of 30 ml each, I dropped off to sleep about 2 am. When I woke at 5 am, both he and Mujtaba Hussain were still talking and drinking!

Shankar Shad Mushaira was another symposium organised regularly by Kamna Prasad. Poets from Pakistan and Europe also participated. I wanted to be a part of it as a favourite Pakistani modern Urdu poet, Ahmed Faraz, was participating. Kamna Prasad readily agreed to my request and also roped me in to pick up and drop off Ahmed Faraz from IIC, where he was staying. This gave me an opportunity to interact with him personally.

On another occasion, I was requested to host Ali Sardar Jafri, a celebrated progressive poet, and I felt truly honoured to do so! He was also a Jnanpith awardee, and he took a deep interest in my compositions. We had an enjoyable evening together, with both of us becoming a bit tipsy by the end of it. In the morning, Ali Sardar Jafri had a bit of a hangover, so I served him an apple, telling him that my father regarded it as an excellent antidote, even though he himself never touched liquor! Jafri Sahab happily told me that this sort of practice is also prevalent in Russia!

My interactions with these well-known personalities added a lot to my confidence. I would appear charismatic to many, especially to the ladies. And quite a number of younger divas too have shown their fascination for me, with some of them even encouraging me to steal kisses from them whenever I got an opportunity, while my male friends would just roll their eyes at my imprudence when I recounted my encounters to them!

When Bhagatji lost the elections, he had also been the President of the Delhi Congress Committee. Sajjan Kumar, who had won the 1991 elections, now demanded that he be made President in place of Bhagatji. However, politics is never straight, and Deepchand Bandhu, a low-profile Jat MLA, was given the presidency in 1994. Sajjan was an overly dynamic personality, sometimes given to aggression. I, too, have faced similar discrimination, for I had often been told that I was too overpowering for the position I wanted!

Under Deepchand Bandhu, for the first time, I got a specially created official post in the Delhi Congress Committee of Organising Secretary. I was so happy at the appointment by Bandhu that I got innumerable posters printed and pasted all over the city.

Deepchand Bandhu was part of the so-called premier league and, therefore, was willing to give a chance to politicians who had not won any elections so far, like myself, a Vaishya, or Hazarilal Chohan, an aristocratic scheduled caste, whom he appointed as General Secretary DPCC, and Prem Sarwariya, a Brahmin, whom he nominated as treasurer, DPCC, to support him. He would feel comfortable with us, his B-team, with people appreciating the fact that he had roped in efficient leaders, even if they were not high-profile ones. Every evening, dressed in crisp whites, we would congregate at the United Coffee House and hold deep discussions about the political temper of the times. I would often accompany Deepchand Bandhu on his tours, for I proved useful in helping him in his interactions and speeches. I was also very actively participating in demonstrations against the Delhi BJP CM Madanlal Khurana's policies.

Both Mani Shankar Aiyar and Bandhu thus played a major role in my growth at the national and regional levels. But despite the support I got from so many senior leaders, I remained a junior leader, never actually fighting an election.

Manmohan Singh, an eminent economist, had recently become the Finance Minister and the economy was on the path of recovery. Liberalisation was thus being ushered into the country under the dual leadership of P V Narasimha Rao and Manmohan Singh. The foundation that had been laid by Rajiv Gandhi was now being carried forward by them. The country was, however, witnessing riots in the post-Babri

Masjid demolition phase, and Muslims were feeling very insecure, leading to many incidents of violence and serial bomb blasts.

***

Meanwhile, my relations with Mani Shankar Aiyar were deepening, and I had even started work on the translations of his political works from English to Hindi-Urdu. He was very appreciative of my work and promoted me further!

One such event was a small symposium organised at the AICC office by Mani Shankar Aiyar on 21 May 1995, on Rajiv Gandhi's death anniversary. A few well-known poets presented their compositions before Narasimha Rao and other senior leaders. Rao asked Mani Shankar Aiyar to bring the poets for tea at the PM's house the next evening. Meanwhile, Mani Shankar Aiyar had got an appointment for 5 pm with Sonia Gandhi as well, to meet the poets, as she could not attend the function. Mani Shankar Aiyar mentioned to Sonia Gandhi that I had composed a ghazal in honour of Rajiv Gandhi. Naturally, she asked me to recite it and picked on a couple of the Urdu words, articulating them very well in her Italian accent and asked me their meaning.

Nafasat Rajiv Gandhi Latafat Rajiv Gandhi
Nazar aate thhe kitne khoobsoorat Rajiv Gandhi

It confused me and made me nervous, but Mani Shankar Aiyar cordially stepped in to translate my ghazal for their benefit. Priyanka and Sonia both appreciated my recitation. After the meeting with Sonia Gandhi, we went on to the PM's house, where we were welcomed warmly with snacks before an early dinner.

***

Every summer, I would take my family for a long holiday to the hills. We would drive down in our own car with a driver. Once, while manoeuvring those hair-pin bends, I decided that one must write a will. What if we plunged over some cliff? There was my three-storey house in Nizamuddin, my shop, a couple of plots, jewellery, FDs and more. I wrote it down immediately in my diary, ear-marking almost 50 per cent for donation. At least 10 per cent would go to the Congress party, and the rest for orphanages, old age homes and for the physically challenged. One per cent I designated for a close lady friend. The other half was to be distributed among mine and Chhaya's relatives. This draft was amended every year, according to the current status of my relationship with the concerned relative and accordingly, the percentage would either go up or down! It proved to be a good way of assuaging my feelings of revenge.

***

I was very fond of and still am, of getting myself graded! I once asked my elder son, 'How many stars will you give me?' And he replied, 'Papa, you are my perfect father. I will give you five stars!' The younger, however, gave me four stars. The same question elicited three stars from my wife, which was most unexpected. I was surprised that she was willing to give me as many as three! I countered, 'Chhaya, I am sorry, but you're not a good wife to me! However, you are a very good housewife!'

We shared a love-hate relationship, which has only intensified over the years. Despite being at constant loggerheads with each other, we would go for morning walks together to Lodhi Garden after dropping the children at school. Sometimes, we would go swimming at the club. I have even taken her to a disco in the early years of our marriage. We would go regularly for dinner to the club and also to popular restaurants. On every special occasion, I would gift some precious ornaments to her, adding to her collection for almost two decades. She had a habit of fighting with me, then getting angry and refusing to have her food, occasionally even going on a hunger strike. That would bother me, for I believed that the lady of the house who cooks the food shouldn't ever go hungry. I used to try my best to reconcile, even bowing my head at her feet. Sometimes, I think I spoilt her and that made her even more aggressive towards me. We would curse each other and squabble, yet there's a deep concern for each other, which still surfaces whenever the other is in trouble.

***

Once, when my elder boy was sixteen, we attended a function in Chhaya's family. Liquor was being served and I encouraged my elder son to taste it. Everyone later criticised my action to Chhaya. I socialised with many political and aristocratic families and had seen sons and grandsons of a few families drinking with their elders. But I overlooked the fact that we were not of the same backgrounds, and later, with my unthinking encouragement, my sons became inclined towards drinking early, drawing disapproval in our family circles.

I often listened to Osho's discourses; he would say that when we prevent a person from doing something, they feel all the more inclined to do exactly that. But this made my wife even more critical of me, blaming me for our sons' waywardness. She would say that I tended to copy others' negative aspects, never their positive ones. Perhaps my lifestyle of entertaining and allowing liquor in the house had led to the discord prevalent at home.

Chapter 2

Politics and Family Matters

EARLIER, THERE WAS a trend of holding large press conferences where correspondents from national and international media were invited. A foreign journalist once asked Narasimha Rao why he was not taking a decision on the Babri Masjid issue. Pat gave his spontaneous response, 'Not to take a decision is also a decision!' This witty one-liner showcased his acumen for instant rejoinders! But by now, he was embroiled in a number of shady conspiracies, which were throwing a shadow on his persona.

***

Whenever Bandhu accompanied the PM, even if it was to go to the AICC, he would take us along with him. Narasimha Rao favoured him and made him a member of the CWC, a coveted position that was denied even to Bhagatji, who was more senior. It showed clearly that loyalty matters more than talent in politics.

Once I presented Bandhu with an invitation card for my nephew's wedding. He examined the card, then asked, 'Where are the accompanying sweets?' Flustered, I responded, 'Oh, but we are not distributing sweets,' as it isn't our custom to do so. 'Bhai Saheb, please accept Rs 500 to compensate for the deficit.' Casually, he took the money and said, 'This is good! Now we can buy sweets of our choice!' The corporation leader, Ram Babu Sharma, who was Bandhu's rival, happened to be present and had heard this exchange. Later, he maligned him for being small-minded. Such power games are always being played in politics!

***

Nachiketa Kapoor was a prominent youth leader, and together with him, I was invited to attend a small diplomatic get-together organised by Jennifer Tytler, as he had spoken about my poetic talents to her. She was a gorgeous lady with a magnetic personality and we hit it off instantly. There I happened to meet the Italian ambassador and became quite friendly with him. During our conversation, he encouraged me to stand for the MP seat from the Chandni Chowk area, as I belonged to the business fraternity. I was quite surprised at his grasp of local matters and his deep knowledge about our political system.

***

On Narasimha Rao's birthday on 28 June 1995, I felicitated the PM at his home and hung around with the Delhi Congress President, Bandhu. This was my way of making my presence felt. I happened to meet a former minister, who had also come to wish the PM well along with his daughter. My eyes were immediately drawn to hers, as I was always on the lookout for a beautiful face. She had a solemn look and as a gracious smile crossed her face, I was instantly smitten! The minister regarded me with affection and introduced his daughter, Hema, a lecturer, to me, adding that she had been the wife of a senior IAS officer, but was unfortunately widowed a year ago.

That shocked me intensely, for she was not only youthful, but good-looking too and perhaps just a few years older than me. When I called her a couple of days later, she burst into tears on the phone while talking about her late husband to me. I was overwhelmed at her loss and it was as if she was reaching out to me for comfort. I managed to calm her down, assuring her that I would always be there for her. Soon, we became very good friends, and over the years, she proved to be not only an emotional support but also my spiritual guide. At get-togethers, she would warn me to keep my distance from women and not get carried away! A man must have humility, dignity and vanity to maintain a respectable image in society and her constant prodding would help me adhere to it. She had a way of calming me down, adroitly countering any romantic overtures on my part. She would say, 'Mahesh ji, you believe in Destiny, then why don't you leave our friendship to God and Destiny?'

***

The very next month, Delhi was witness to a ghastly incident that made headlines. Sushil Sharma, the Delhi Youth Congress President, suspecting his wife, Naina, of infidelity, shot her dead in the heat of the moment. To cover up his crime, he tried to burn Naina's body in the tandoor of his restaurant's kitchen, with the help of the manager. As fate would have it, some people got suspicious and called the police. I knew Sushil Sharma well and this incident shocked me deeply. Power can be truly corrupting, making one feel that one has a license to behave any which way. Rajesh Khanna said to me, sadly, 'Mahesh Bhai, wearing a white kurta in public is making one feel insecure now!' Sushil Sharma's act had ruined a hundred-year-old Party's reputation. 'This stain will definitely not get wiped out easily,' I said to him. Indeed, the Party didn't fare well in the ensuing elections.

***

Around Diwali that year, for the first time, I rented out my shop. It went against my conscience, but I couldn't help it. I was running into losses, and not earning anything from the shop. Moreover, I was eating into my capital, which was making me feel insecure. So, when a firecracker dealer in the market approached me for renting my shop for just ten days at Rs 10,000 daily, I went ahead, thinking it was a very lucrative offer; for the first time, I realised how valuable my shop was! Subsequently, I began renting it out on festive occasions like Rakhi, Christmas, New Year and Holi, thus ensuring that money would flow in.

***

The next year was a landmark in my elder son Karan's life, as he topped the Class 10 Board exams in DPS. The school authorities even published his photograph in an advertisement in *Hindustan Times*. Nothing like this had ever happened in our family before, so naturally we were ecstatic and I presented a new, AC Maruti car to him. Thus, at sixteen, without a licence, he started commuting to school in the car along with his brother. I had always considered myself to be above the law, sure of my political connections, and this attitude had percolated down to my son. So fearlessly he would drive around in his car. He had been made head boy in his school for topping the exams and was also the captain of the football team, and this added to his cockiness. My friend, Makhmoor Sayeedi, once confronted me about my foolhardiness in allowing him so much freedom, letting him drink and encouraging him to drive without a licence. But I was taking pride in his proactiveness, and his driving had taken the pressure off myself and Chhaya, as it was otherwise our duty to drop and pick up the boys from school. I was quite interactive in the school, and the principal requested me to become a part of the parent-teacher executive committee. Despite his support, some others saw me as a typical politician and consequently, I lost the elections. But the next year, the principal nominated me as a member of the committee, by using his special discretionary powers.

***

1996 was also the year of the general elections, and for the first time, Congress outsourced all the election paraphernalia. Kesriji was aware of the money owed to all of us suppliers, so he wasn't sure if we would cooperate. He played it safe, hiring Graphisads, to supply the materials needed. When I approached Kesriji, he directed me to meet the MD to see if I could supply one of the items. The payment was against delivery. It worked out well and I earned handsomely by supplying a large quantity of flags.

Chapter 3

The Dark Side of Politics

THE PRIME MINISTER has immense powers vested in him. The problem arises when he utilises them to further his own ends. The temptations are irresistible and the strongest of characters can get swayed. Allegiances then don't matter at all. It was the Congress Party that nurtured Narasimha Rao, helping him rise to great heights, yet his actions later were traitorous, sowing the seeds of downfall. The Babri Masjid demolition clearly showed that someone powerful was facilitating it, and this fact really damaged the secular image of our Party. Mani Shankar Aiyar said to me that this PVN Rao government seems to be the first BJP govt. Bribes were now openly being accepted from the top downwards. The Jain Diary Hawala case was opened by the PM, implicating many of his own senior leaders, including V C Shukla, N D Tiwari, Balram Jhakhar, and Madhav Rao Scindia from his own party and L K Advani, Devi Lal, and M L Khurana from the opposition.

V C Shukla said to me, 'This is beyond comprehension! I supported and even saved his government from falling, and this is how I am repaid!'

It was as if Narasimha Rao wanted to remove all competition, not realising that it would eventually reflect back on him as well, for politics is a dirty game, where no one can remain unscathed. Treason and betrayal are a part of a politician's DNA, weakening their position.

That's the primary reason why we were overpowered by invaders and ruled by outsiders for more than a thousand years, as there was no fidelity among us.

While discussing it with Jennifer later, I said to her, 'Jenny, don't you think politicians can literally kill their conscience to retain power?'

'Mahesh, I regard them as insensitive people; you have defined them exactly! Insensitive is a very lukewarm word for them!' We shared a good comradeship, talking daily every evening. Once she said to me, 'Manzar, while talking to you, I keep a diary handy. Sometimes you say such unique things that I feel I need to note them down immediately, as I forget quickly!'

It made me euphoric that she appreciated me so much! Her support elevated me immensely, especially when I asked her to rate my personality, she put it at hundred, much to my delight! Her reply is still etched on my heart, to this day. She disregarded my concerns for my diminutive height, for she said, 'Mahesh, I don't even notice that! To women, emotional, intellectual and spiritual heights matter more than physical height. And in that regard, your height is tremendous, camouflaging any shortcomings easily!'

***

My morning walks in Lodhi Gardens proved beneficial, for I would meet well-known personalities and form friendly liaisons with them. It was here that I got to know top editors such as Khushwant Singh, B G Verghese, Hiranmay Karlekar and H K Dua, and got deep insights about the political situation in India. Khushwant Singh shared an incident about Pandit Jawaharlal Nehru. In 1957, the first ambassador car made in the country was priced at Rs 14,000, and it was presented to the PM by Birla. Dr Rajendra Prasad, the President objected, saying that he was setting a wrong precedent.

In discussions with other editors, more intriguing facts came to light, highlighting the dark underbelly of the political world. They thought Indira Gandhi was responsible for promoting unethical practices. In a case of fraud, the cashier of State Bank, Mr Malhotra, was asked to release Rs 60 lakh to Nagarwala, purportedly by the PM's office in 1971. He did so, but when he went to confirm the receipt of the money from the PM's office, they denied all knowledge about it. When allegations began to be thrown around, someone commented in the PM's defence that surely the money wasn't to be used for her household expenses! Some speculated that it may have been needed for the innumerable Bangladeshi refugees who had barged into the country in the 1970s. It was a puzzle back then, although later, the amount was recovered.

It was said then that the PM has to spend sometimes for the welfare of the country, and this cannot be reflected in the exchequer. Indira Gandhi was a very shrewd politician and had to often juggle things to manage the country. The unacceptable trend that had started in thousands had moved into lakhs in the 1970s, then ran into crores during Rajiv Gandhi's time and had multiplied into billions by the time Narasimha Rao was PM! Lal Bahadur Shastri is the one PM that stands out like a shining star, for he had a very honest reputation in complete contrast to the PMs before and after him.

In retrospect, Nehru was cautious, but his daughter, Indira Gandhi, was not so. Rajiv Gandhi, however, got entangled in the mesh and Narasimha Rao made it seem as if all was acceptable. The devaluation of the rupee over the years was directly proportional to the devaluation in political values of our political leaders. It was as if the very destiny of the country was clouded over, for none of the leaders who could have steered her to greater heights were given a chance to do so.

Circumstances soon forced Narasimha Rao to resign as the President of the Congress Party. Bandhu, along with his executive committee members, including myself, visited Narasimha Rao to assure him of our allegiance, but his reply was remarkably woeful. 'Do you want to see a Congress President being arrested? If I resign, at least the Party won't have to face the ignominy of having its leader arrested!' he had said.

Narasimha Rao, though, along with Manmohan Singh, greatly contributed to stabilising the country's economy that had been ravaged by the preceding PMs, Chandrashekhar and V P Singh, although they had held office for only six and twelve months, respectively. Many agreed that Narasimha Rao had been a good PM, but unfortunately, he proved to be detrimental as the Congress President. Subsequently, even his own working committee members had voted against him.

Before relinquishing his post, Narasimha Rao promoted Sitaram Kesri as the next President, thus ensuring that he would continue to be involved in power, but things often don't work the way one may want.

I was truly happy to see Sitaram Kesri become President of the Indian National Congress in September 1996. Kesri ji soon appointed Tariq Anwar, my good friend and neighbour, as his political secretary.

***

On my son's sixteenth birthday in November, I threw a party in my basement and invited many senior leaders of AICC and Delhi Congress, including my good friends Mani Shankar Aiyar, Devanand Mishra and Bandhu, besides Jennifer Tytler, Uma Sharma, and Hema Chaudhary, to congratulate the newly appointed political secretary. My guests, including my family, were astounded at the VIPs and luminaries present at my party that night!

Chapter 4

The Decline of the Congress Party

IN 1990, I met Dev Anand Mishra, son of former CJI Ranganath Mishra, at Rajiv Gandhi's residence. In 1995, he was appointed as the secretary of the AICC, by Narasimha Rao. Though he was not a Congress party activist, he was well qualified, an IAS officer, an English professor and also a lawyer. Sometimes, such qualified people get appointed to political posts on their own merit. I went to congratulate him and we clicked there and then, especially when he learnt that I was a poet! We would meet sometimes and have long conversations till late into the night. Once, I invited him and his family for dinner. His wife turned to me and said in a very melodious voice, 'Maheshji, you play the role of the 'other woman' in my life!'

I was astonished. 'How so?' I asked.

'He is always talking to you, especially during the time he should be spending with me! So, are you not my *soutan*?' That drew laughter from all of us. But it was true that we loved to discuss every topic under the sun and would often lose track of time.

Once even Mani Shankar Aiyar had commented, 'Mahesh, you are like my wife—you interrupt me often.'

By the start of 1997, my fortunes improved somewhat when my shop was rented out, assuring me a regular monthly income of Rs 50,000. With the shop thus sorted, the pressure of looking around for a regular source of income was taken care of, leaving me with more time to pursue my literary and political interests. Every evening, I used to be invited to a symposium or a political meet. I was, therefore, able to make a name for myself, for I would participate enthusiastically in both, adding value to the event. I could now count innumerable dignitaries, including some very gracious ladies, as my close friends, which boosted my confidence.

My younger son, too, was in his early teens by now and would often get into trouble and be quite a handful. Once, he was sulking after receiving a scolding, so I took him shopping. Even the shopkeeper noticed my son's recalcitrant expression. When I told him that indeed he was quite a handful, he suggested that I should get him blessed by a very enlightened Swamiji in Barsana, Radha's birthplace, near Vrindavan. I took down all the details from him and drove down the very next day, as a special *bhandara* was to be organised there.

When we entered the ashram, one of the devotees took us to the Swami and introduced us. The moment he heard my name, Mahesh, he spontaneously exclaimed, 'Kailash himself seems to have graced our abode!'

I said, 'Swami ji, I had an intuition that you will accept and appreciate me as your devotee.'

He wanted me to explain what 'intuition' meant, so I shared my favourite quote with him—'In prayers we talk to God; through intuition, God talks to us,' which really impressed him.

He asked the reason for our visit. 'Destiny must have brought us,' I said, but he replied, smilingly, 'Not your Destiny, but the Divine Grace of Radha. Vrindavan is Radha's drawing room. Anyone can visit, but very few people are able to come to Barsana. This is regarded as her boudoir; that's why it's not easily accessible, except to those who have her Grace.

so know yourself to be truly blessed' This thought filled me with bliss and I asked, 'Swamiji, are Destiny and Grace two entirely different concepts?'

'Grace is miraculous and much more powerful than Destiny! Destiny is connected to your Karmas, but Grace is not. It can be unexpected and infinitely Divine,' he explained.

Ever since, I have been using this term, 'Divine Grace of God'. That was also the moment my first prayer took shape in my mind. 'Dear God, I am under Your Divine Grace and not under my Karmic law as I have full faith and total trust in You!'

Swamiji was usually taciturn, so it was quite amazing to the other devotees that he was interacting freely and warmly with me on our first visit to the ashram! My ability to influence people had again come into play, forging a lifelong bond with Swamiji. The visit to Barsana proved to be a turning point in my life!

***

Kesriji had been very appreciative of Narasimha Rao initially, but eventually, he took a stand and set a time limit for him to step down from his position as CPP leader. Much later, I asked Kesriji: 'Babuji…how could you deal so harshly with him?'

'I prostrated before knowledge, earlier! But when I felt a deficit of integrity, it was time to back out!' he replied.

In 1996, when the Congress party under Narasimha Rao couldn't get a majority in the elections, they decided to support Deve Gowda's very small party, making him the PM. Such an appointment is normally done after a process of elimination that brings forth a nonentity, reducing the possibility of ego clashes, and also paving the way for future abrogation, similar to how Indira Gandhi had made Charan Singh, PM in 1980 and then withdrawn support after six months. Rajiv Gandhi had supported Chandrashekhar to become the PM after V P

Singh, but later the Party had pulled back.

Once Deve Gowda was nominated to office, elections for the Party presidentship were to be undertaken. Sitaram Kesri had become bolder and more ambitious, wanting to be an elected President of Congress and, therefore, initiated talks for inner party democracy, proposing elections, to which most of the senior Congress leaders had agreed. Sitaram Kesri, Sharad Pawar and Rajesh Pilot were in the fray, having an electorate of about eight thousand among the Pradesh and All India delegates. Kesriji had changed almost all state Presidents and appointed his loyalists in top positions. Deep Chand Bandhu had also been replaced by Chaudhary Prem Singh as Delhi Congress President. Sitaram Kesri was thus able to manipulate the voters in such a manner that he got almost 97 per cent of the votes! Sitaram Kesri was the first to be nominated and then elected as President in the Party's 111-year-old history.

Subsequently, Kesri thought that he could even be a candidate for the position of the PM. Addressing Delhi Congress workers at the AICC Headquarters, Kesriji was very discourteous towards the PM, shocking everyone. He had become overambitious. There was also a suspicious case where a man's arm was found in a drain connected to his house. It was eventually identified as being that of Dr Surender Singh Tanwar, who would visit regularly to check Kesriji's BP.

Although nothing could be connected to Sitaram Kesri, Deve Gowda had somehow managed to get wind of it, thus posing a threat to Kesri, who promptly summoned Pranab Mukherjee to draft a letter to send to the President of India, withdrawing the Party's support. This was akin to self-sabotage and his popularity instantly plummeted.

A new PM was needed as Deve Gowda did not have enough supporters, but senior leaders were reluctant to name Sitaram Kesri because of his high-handed and cunning behaviour. However, he was a wily politician and was able to win the confidence of not only the CPI(M) doyen, Comrade Harkishan Singh Surjeet, but almost all other regional party heads like Laloo Prasad Yadav, Mulayam Singh Yadav, and Kanshi Ram among others. I remember, once, Laloo Prasad Yadav touching Kesriji's feet, thanking him for advising him in appointing his wife, Rabri Devi, as the CM of Bihar when he was in prison.

Yet, there were several lobbies within the Party and stalwarts like Sharad Pawar, N D Tiwari, Arjun Singh, P V Narasimha Rao, and Sonia Gandhi were not willing to back him, as he had become known as a leader favouring the Muslims, scheduled castes and backward classes mainly. A senior leader had said, 'Kesri equals three Muslims plus one Meera,' referring to his closeness to Tariq Anwar, Ahmed Patel, Ghulam Nabi Azaad and Jagjivan Ram's daughter, Meera Kumar. Moreover, he was very vocal against Sonia Gandhi and her followers. Kesriji thus lost the confidence of the strong ruling castes, the Brahmins and the Kshatriyas.

Sitaram Kesri once sent some confidential papers through me to Communist leader Comrade Harkishan Singh Surjeet, his friend, philosopher and guide, seeking his help to resolve the deadlock. The PM's post was empty, and he wasn't being nominated for it. He was apprehensive that Deve Gowda would become PM again and appealed to Harkishan Singh Surjeet to prevent that from happening.

Harkishan Singh Surjeet confided in me: 'I tried to stop him from withdrawing support, and had even told him he would lose everything and end up empty-handed! He could have handled it more diplomatically.' 'Babuji, that is what we call Destiny!' was my response.

As a result, I K Gujral, who had retired from active politics, was named the next PM. Political machinations don't remain hidden and neither were Sitaram Kesri's intentions. In his farewell address in Parliament, Deve Gowda highlighted this by coining the phrase, 'an old man in a hurry' clearly alluding to Kesriji!

Then again, at the Congress Plenary Session in Calcutta, Kesri committed another blunder. He declared that if Sonia Gandhi wanted to become the Congress President, he would step down. Ultimately, Kesriji proved too cunning for his own good and ended up devaluing the august office of Congress President.

I had always been loyal to him, yet he took me for a ride as well. He once told me that he was thinking of appointing me as a secretary in the Party, but nothing ever came of it. Another time, just before the Delhi Municipal elections, he told me to start preparing for the Corporation elections. He claimed that it could open my way to get a ticket for the MP elections, which were not far away. But Tariq Anwar deprived me of the opportunity. He said that Nizamuddin, from where I could have stood, was a hardcore Muslim seat.

I, however, continued visiting and meeting him. 'Who have you come to meet, the Congress President or Sitaram Kesri?' he asked me once.

'I have come to meet my Babuji! This is his residence; I could have gone to his office if I had wanted to meet the President!' He was delighted with my reply and lovingly patted my back.

He would interact with people from all over the country daily for an hour at his residence, to know everything at the grassroots level. He would then go to the AICC office to meet MPs and senior leaders. His office doors were usually open, signalling that all could approach him. Once he saw me crossing his open door and called out, 'Mahesh, why are you roaming around in such a frustrated manner?' How could I tell him that his own actions were what was bothering me? He was wise enough to conclude that himself. Neither did he ever give me any appropriate post, nor did my destiny in doing business with the Party allow it!

He was trying to calm me down by indirectly conveying that Destiny matters most, even more than merit or loyalty and so should be accepted gracefully.

Kesri ji sometimes took me along to visit Baba Nagpal at the Chhatarpur Katyayani Devi temple. He told me that the Baba had special powers. Once, when he was not being renominated to the Rajya Sabha, he was planning to resign from his post as treasurer, AICC. The Baba advised against it. He said that it was that position which would take him to the highest post and it happened so. Once, he was invited by the Law Faculty of Delhi University and on the way, he commented to Tariq Anwar and myself: 'Just look at how time deals with one! I have never been to college, not even to a proper school, and here I am going to address University students!'

'Babuji, Kabir never saw the face of any school or madrasa, and yet he has become immortal!' He once said:

Tum kahte ho kagaz lekhi,
mai kahta hun aankhan dekhi!

(You say what is written on paper,
I say what my eyes observe.)

Neither of the two reacted to my comment, but when Kesriji started his address, he used my words to draw applause from the audience. He was not only blessed with practical wisdom, but was shrewd, too. I was also reminded of Aristotle's quote: 'Wisdom comes from observation, retention and reproduction.'

Bandhu, aware of my frustration at being unable to secure a position of note, consoled me, 'Mahesh, there are about twenty secretaries in AICC, about a hundred and forty MPs, two hundred and seventy-two municipal corporators, yet do any of them receive the importance that you do?' It was indeed a valid point, convincing me to make peace with my Destiny! What did it matter if I hadn't gotten a deserved post, because being recognised for my capabilities was also a source of satisfaction? Gaining a post or power was not exactly my cup of tea, either, for I didn't have the temperament to fight elections, which entailed going door to door, and begging for votes! One needed money and muscle power to campaign, a manipulative mind and also, team spirit. Perhaps I was lacking in all of them.

I had to be honest with myself. Wasn't I using the Party as a platform to acquire knowledge by meeting accomplished dignitaries? I was more interested in fraternising with them and, in the process, upgrading myself.

***

In 1997, I began attending monthly symposiums organised by well-known writer Ajeet Cour at her Academy of Fine Arts and Literature in the Siri Fort area. I had met her by chance at a literary gathering and she had invited me to her home, where I also met her daughter, Arpana Cour. They roped me in to participate in their monthly recitation events, which were attended by several dignitaries, including former PM V P Singh who was fond of poetry. I, however, regarded him as a traitor who had not been true to Rajiv Gandhi even though the latter had given him so much importance, even appointing him Finance Minister in his Cabinet.

On one such poetical evening, I found him distracted, so addressing him as Singh Sahab, I asked him to listen to what I was reading. He was visibly displeased, but didn't say anything. I presented a *sher* of my *ghazal*.

Mere zakhmo ko seene jo Massiha ban ke aaya hai,
Mujhe dar hai wo mauka paa ke mujhko qatl ker dega

*(The Messiah who has come to heal the lacerations of my heart,
I fear that seizing the opportunity, he may stab me)*

It became clear to everyone that I was alluding to V P Singh. The mother and daughter had a soft spot for V P Singh and didn't appreciate my innuendoes, but they kept quiet.

***

I was pretty popular among the morning walkers in Lodhi Gardens, as I was very enthusiastic. We often held contributory parties in the Garden. I used to be the life and soul of these parties, for it was easy for me to bond with others. Some would even joke that if Mahesh stands for elections here, he would win hands down! On one of our walks in Lodhi Garden, the President of the Walkers Club, O P Malhotra, approached me and Chhaya to accompany a group of twenty-five of the morning walkers on a visit to Shirdi as a guest. That was the first time I got to know about the significance of Shirdi and Sai Baba. I turned to Chhaya and asked casually, 'Should I go?' To my surprise, she gave an immediate assent, when normally her first reaction is to deny. I laughingly turned to Malhotraji and said, 'Baba definitely wants me to come! This is the first time my wife has given her acceptance so promptly!'

It was a very memorable trip, opening up a new chapter in my life. The immense peace that I felt was amazing, filling me with total bliss. Sitting in front of Sai Baba's statue, I went into deep, mesmerising meditation. It was as if Baba was smilingly welcoming me for finally coming to his Samadhi. That's when I got connected to Sai Baba and my bond has only deepened over the years. Besides the company was so very wonderful and I, as usual, threw my heart and soul into spreading joy all around. I recall those four days as a whirl of laughter and good food, so much so that when we got off the train back home, one Mrs Khanna, actually had tears in her eyes, as she said to me, 'I will miss your company.' Everyone could relate to her, for all of us were forlorn that our trip was over.

My newfound love for Sai Baba got a further impetus when O P Malhotra held a lavish *Bhajan Sandhya* at his Golf Links house a couple of months after our return. I was so mesmerised by one of the bhajans, that I, along with the host danced uninhibitedly to it. The wordings, *Sai tera naam Bhola hi Bhola*, another name for Lord Shiva, reminded me of my father for he would say that I was a part of Shiva, and that my birth had brought blessings into our family. The evening paved the way for a deeper connection with Sai Baba and I began visiting the temple on Lodhi Road regularly.

My devotion to Sai brought many miracles into my life. The very first was Chief Justice, Supreme Court, Ranganath Mishra with his son Dev Anand Mishra, my very good friend, visiting my house for lunch. Justice Mishra was the chairman of the National Human Rights Commission and lived near India Gate. He was very reserved, but we shared a good bond. Dev Anand would often lovingly invite me for evening tea and crisp *moong dal pakodi* at their place, saying, 'Pitaji loves your company.' I would never go empty-handed, as that was one of the first lessons I had learnt in life.

Justice Mishra was the second Chief Justice of India to have visited me at home. He was also the one who gave me the formula for judging people by giving them points out of a hundred, 'Ten points for *vesh*, twenty for *vani*, thirty for *vichaar*, and forty for *vyawahar*' (appearance, speech, thoughts and behaviour). He complimented me, saying that I was good in all four! But unfortunately, his magnanimity proved to be another nail in my floundering household; my family couldn't cope with my high-level connections, as it gave them a complex, making them feel inadequate in socialising with them.

V C Shukla had said that in politics, one should be aware

of the direction in which the water is flowing to know about upcoming future changes. I had integrated this maxim into my life, and that was the reason I had begun meeting Rajiv Gandhi much before he came into power. That was also the reason I had cultivated a friendship with Vincent George, even going to wish him a happy birthday in November when few had done so. After I had gifted a pen to Rajiv Gandhi, I made it a habit of gifting similar pens on special occasions to VIPs, friends and close relatives. Once when I presented yet another pen to Vincent George, he said much to everyone's amusement, 'I already have four of these! How many are you going to give me? At least, change the design of the pen!' My frequent visits proved fruitful for he was always benevolent. Hiranmay Karlekar, who has been editor of *Hindustan Times* once commented that the Congress was responsible for its own downfall with their unethical policies, which were in existence right from the time of Indira Gandhi. Even before Indira declared Emergency, the Congress party was broken into two factions and Indira Gandhi had set up V V Giri against the official Presidential candidate, Sanjiva Reddy. V V Giri, was thus able to defeat Sanjiva Reddy on a very tricky appeal by Indira Gandhi, who solicited the people to vote by listening to their inner voice. The victory brought Indira back into the harness, vesting her with unbridled power. Such practices were responsible for the way I K Gujral was removed from office, with the allegation that he was not cooperating in the Jain Commission enquiry into Rajiv's murder. It became the reason for the party to withdraw support.

***

General elections were announced for February 1998. Vijay Bhaskar Reddy, the ex-CM of Andhra Pradesh, was sent to talk to Jayalalitha, the AIDMK chief as Congress was seeking her support in Tamil Nādu. She made it clear that her first choice was the Congress party because of its secular character. She was also being courted by Vajpayee. She wanted Kesriji to come the very next day as the other party was demanding a quick alliance. Mani Shankar Aiyar hastened to meet Kesriji with her proposal, but Sitaram Kesri refused to travel to the south before tying up matters in the north. Mani Shankar Aiyar, disillusioned by his repudiation, resigned from the Party.

Lamho ne khataa ki thi
Sadiyon ne saza payii

(Moments fell into blunders
Making eons face a retribution)

It was indeed a momentary lapse on the part of Sitaram Kesri to refuse the proposal from Jayalalitha. Her support was needed to win the election. A senior Congress leader, Thanga Balu also told me that it was one of the lapses that cost us dearly for a long time as Congress couldn't come back into power until 2004.

R K Dhawan, Indira Gandhi's close associate, approached me much to my surprise, as he had never given me any consideration earlier. He wanted me to campaign for him in the coming elections.

'I was really impressed by the way you campaigned for Rajesh Khanna in 1992 for the New Delhi constituency.'

'Thank you, Bhai Sahab,' I responded, adding, 'I did the same for Tajdar Babar for her Nizamuddin Assembly Constituency in 1993!'

'And both won despite being tough contests! Now I want you to recreate that victory for me.'

I readily agreed but he tried to make me distance myself from Mani Shankar Aiyar and work entirely with him. I adroitly turned the situation around by saying that my association with MSA was more literary and emotional than political, as I occasionally translated his English works to Hindustani and working for R K Dhawan was a political assignment. 'I am a soldier of the Congress party and can definitely campaign for you!' I told him.

Subsequently, I organised a very good meeting in my basement, inviting the cream of New Delhi voters. I had an extensive circle, both in the Nizamuddin area and beyond it, and innumerable were the bouquets R K Dhawan received that evening. In my opening speech, I said, 'This gathering here today of the creamy layer of your New Delhi constituency is not only that of your voters but also your supporters,' drawing applause from the audience. R K Dhawan acknowledged it as the best meeting of his entire campaign, praising me for organising it. It was his last public meet before voting day, two days later.

R K Dhawan kept me with his close team to organise polling booths and appoint counting agents. I was the Nizamuddin booth incharge since I was familiar with the area. On the results day, I met our opponent, Jagmohan, and reminded him of an earlier meeting in 1977 as part of Sanjay Gandhi's small delegation of Delhi Youth Congress, when he was the Lieutenant Governor of Delhi. His family had accompanied him and we became quite friendly, making people comment on my familiarity with the opponent. I said that our ideologies may be different, but we were not enemies. Doesn't Hinduism teach us the philosophy of *Vasudhaiva Kutumbakam* meaning the entire world is one family?

Despite our best efforts, R K Dhawan lost, mainly because the Congress party's graph was down, due to the lapses and ego clashes of senior leaders, who were more obsessed with themselves and less for the Party or the country.

In these elections, Congress got 141 seats with 9 crore fifty-one lakh votes, while BJP gained 182 seats with 9 crore forty-two lakh votes. Vajpayee thus came into power with the Congress being relegated to the position of opposition. The paradox of democracy is that despite getting fewer votes, the BJP became the larger party. The country's secular vote bank got split between the regional and Congress parties, while the Hindu vote remained consolidated with the BJP.

Soon afterwards, Sitaram Kesri was removed in a rather immoral manner, literally being thrown out of office. At a public rally at Ramlila Grounds before the elections, Sonia Gandhi made Kesriji wait for an hour, showing him in an inconsequential light. Keeping the President of a national party waiting is equivalent to making a laughing stock of the Party. It made him lose credibility in the public eye. That's when Sitaram Kesri realised that things might slip out of his hands completely. Once the elections were over, almost all the CWC members, barring Tariq Anwar, voted against him, passing a no-confidence motion. Kesriji shared with me later that he had been elected by some eight thousand delegates, so how could just about twenty members vote him out of office? An AICC session should have been summoned if any such step had to be taken, but it was not done.

Earlier at the Congress Plenary session in Calcutta, Kesriji himself had said he would step down if Sonia Gandhi wanted to become the President, but when senior leaders reminded him of his words, he backed out. Even Comrade Harkishan Singh Surjeet advised him not to go back on his word. He didn't accept his advice and subsequently had to face a lot of ignominy. I continued to remain close to Kesriji in later years, and had thus gotten to know how things had been panning out. I would visit him even when no one else was ready to talk to him after his downfall.

A few senior leaders asked me why I was still meeting him and I had replied that he had always given me time, even when he was Congress President.

'Is there anything more valuable than time? How can I forget all that now?' At one time, during the Indira-Rajiv era, he was regarded as being next to the Congress President and could even keep the Ambanis waiting, a fact that I had witnessed for myself. Besides, he deserved appreciation, for he had literally risen from the grassroots to the highest position of a party President with his own efforts. The person mattered more to me than his position.

***

On 14 March 1998, Sonia Gandhi became the President of the Congress Party with George as her close associate. Vincent George had already hinted at this possibility when I had met him for Christmas about three months earlier. The newly elected President is usually felicitated by Party members and I requested time from Vijayan Pillai, additional private secretary to congratulate Sonia Gandhi. He and P P Madhavan, officer on special duty, were next to Vincent George in the President's staff and were regarded as Sonia's 'eyes and ears.' I was on good terms with them. Both had come home for dinner, though separately, more than once. They were usually at loggerheads, and I would try to resolve their issues.

I was given time for the very next day and reaching well before time, I found some senior leaders already there, waiting to congratulate Sonia Gandhi. She was not yet in office, so we had to wait, not in the waiting room attached to Vincent George's office, but on the grounds. Meanwhile, more people were joining the queue. A while later, I noticed Madhav Rao Scindia in the line a few places behind me. I said immediately, 'Bhai Sahab, I am truly embarrassed that you're standing behind me, a humble party worker, while you are such a senior leader! Please come forward and change places with me.' But he smilingly refused, 'It's perfectly all right! Please don't give it any consideration.'

I could only retreat, marvelling at the newly elected President's hauteur in keeping such a senior leader waiting in line! A while later, this feeling got even more intensified when I realised that Sharad Pawar had also joined the line! He was in an even higher position having almost become the PM in place of Narasimha Rao, and yet he, too, was in the queue! I couldn't stop myself from exchanging my place in the queue with him, but, he too gracefully refused the offer. This was making me feel agitated. Was no consideration being given to seniority? Where would things lead to from here?

Finally, we began to be allowed in, some fifteen minutes after the designated time. I was feeling self-conscious and somewhat nervous as I entered the office to greet her. Sonia Gandhi was standing at the other end of the room and no chair seemed to be available. My mind registered this fact, making me wonder if she would make the senior leaders follow the same pattern. This indigestible thought filled me with a strange kind of fear. I approached her diffidently and proffering the single flower that I had brought, said, 'Madam, may you succeed in your mission.' She acknowledged me rather condescendingly, waving me on. I realised I was expected to exit from a door at the side, and I did so with trepidation in my heart. Never had I seen such superciliousness even on my visits to the PMs in their office!

***

Two years later, when Mani Shankar Aiyar was appointed as the chairman of the Political Training Department, AICC, he put in a recommendation for me to Sonia Gandhi for the post of national coordinator. For the first time, I was given a post with his help, a post that brought me onto a national platform and gave me a chance to work in close proximity with Mani Shankar Aiyar. Once, I asked him, 'Bhai Sahab, may I ask why you were the first to revolt against Sitaram Kesri?' His resignation was the first pebble that started the avalanche of Sitaram Kesri's complete downfall.

MSA explained his position, 'I was really disappointed with his lack of national allegiance. Ultimately, it was this very attitude that helped the formation of the Vajpayee government, which lasted for thirteen months, after crippling the Congress party! If we had made that pact with Jayalalitha, things might have been a lot different.'

He had earlier shared that when he would write speeches for Rajiv Gandhi, he had experienced Sitaram Kesri's immature behaviour. He had been pushing Rajiv Gandhi to contribute some talking points for his speeches, crediting his vast experience in the political arena. Rajiv Gandhi had asked Mani Shankar Aiyar for inputs from Kesriji, and reluctantly, MSA had done so.

Kesri had asked MSA to note down the points, the first being to add, 'I am Indira Gandhi's son.' Mani Shankar Aiyar had been perplexed when Sitaram Kesri reiterated the sentence, telling him to put it down, so rather reluctantly he did and waited for the next input. But the third sentence had made him lose his patience. 'Indira Gandhi loved the poor and that's why I, too, love the poor!' At this point, MSA snapped his diary shut and stood up, saying, 'Alright, I understand you wish to present their love for the poor, so I will do it in my own way.'

'Yes, you can bring this point in very well that Rajiv Gandhi follows what his mother was in favour of.'

When Mani Shankar Aiyar reported to Rajiv Gandhi, he laughed a lot.

'That's exactly why I sent you to him! I didn't want to waste time on his frivolous talks!' said Rajiv.

Chapter 5

Upwardly Mobile on the Personal Front

ON MY BIRTHDAY in 1998, one of my close relatives informed me that he had saved a huge amount of money, much beyond my imagination. He had politics in his blood.. I told him that I would try something big for him and immediately called Sitaram Kesri, requesting a meeting with him. He called me the same evening at 9 pm. I put forth his case in front of him just like a lawyer, and succeeded in convincing him that he could add value to the Party.

I added that since he was ready to contribute substantial money to the party fund, he deserved a Rajya Sabha ticket!

'Babuji you have unsuccessfully been trying to teach me patience, tolerance and reticence for years! All these qualities are already present in him.'

Kesriji assured me that he would seriously consider my proposal.

On our way back home, he was highly delighted at the way things had shaped up. 'I could never have thought of such a post even in my dreams!' he said to me.

But unfortunately things didn't take off, as Sitaram Kesri himself got displaced within a month.

***

One more incident that stands out in my memory is when by Divine Grace, I was guided to a tiny temple in the bylanes behind Ram Manohar Lohia hospital. It had only a Shivling and a statue of Nandi and I offered my prayers there. Something in my bearing inspired the priest to approach me and request for adding *murtis* of Shiva's family, Parvati, Ganesha and Kartikay to the existing Shivling. I felt blessed that I had been chosen to bring that temple to life and within a few days, I went back with my family, and got the murtis consecrated there, with a small *bhandara*. It proved to be a real blessing, for since that day in February, I have experienced much all-round growth.

***

My elder son Karan had appeared for his Board exams in 1998, but he did not score as well as in his Class 10 Boards two years earlier. He was involved in other activities, and put studies on the backseat. Admissions in good DU colleges are based on high percentages and he did not make it to the required cut-off. When he realised the seriousness of his situation, he was quite agitated and fought with both Chhaya and me.

One night, just before dinner, he walked out of the house in anger. It reminded me of the time when Chhaya too had staged a walkout years before, and also a few months after our marriage. At that time, my father and I had been able to bring her back immediately. We were worried for his well-being. My main prayer that night was to Sai Baba, entreating him to keep Karan safe from any mishap. Both of us awaited the morning with apprehension. I had decided to wait till the next evening before going to the police, but halfway through the evening, he returned. I reasoned with him about the futility of arguing with us and running away and assured him that he would get admission somewhere through my connections.

Karan had wanted to study in the north campus and with his marks, this was not possible.

He wanted me to try in Ramjas College as I had studied there and still had links with the faculty, but we had to face disappointment. When we were returning from there, something pulled me towards Hindu College. Karan asked me why I was even thinking of going there, since admission there was not possible at all, but I insisted on checking it out.

I sent my visiting card to the Principal, for I always present my case to the seniormost person. Almost immediately, we were ushered into her room and I was pleasantly surprised to see Dr Kavita Sharma in the principal's chair. I had met her a couple of years earlier at an event at Red Fort. She was compering eloquently in Hindi and then translating it into English for Kathak dancer, Uma Sharma, who was a dear friend. At the end of the Red Fort event, I had complimented her, asking Uma Sharma where she had found such a gem. At that time, Kavita Sharma had been an English lecturer at Hindu College and now she was the Principal! The head of the Hindi department, Professor Harish Naval was also present and he was quite familiar with my work. When he understood the purpose of my visit, Professor Harish gave a suggestion. Karan's marks did not meet the cut off levels of the college and his performance on the sports field as the captain of his school football team was also not enough to get him admission, as only national or state level players were considered. The professor, therefore, proposed that they consider him in the extracurricular activity category if he could learn one of my ghazals and present it in front of a five-member committee. He would then gain the extra 5 per cent needed to get admission in the special quota.

Professor Harish was the chairman of the Cultural Committee and could project him as an upcoming poet. Kavita Sharma readily agreed to the proposal. The plan worked beautifully and Karan was soon in the prestigious Hindu College. I was so grateful to Professor Harish that I went to thank him with sweets, fruits and flowers, offering him a substantial amount of cash in an envelope as a special present. But he flatly refused to accept this, saying he had done it out of his love and respect for me. Values were strong then!

A difficult task was thus accomplished with the goodwill that I had earned over the years. My friendship with Dr Kavita Sharma deepened over the next few months and I even went to wish her on her birthday later, taking along sweets and flowers. Her husband, Jagdish C Sharma, was a senior IFS officer posted in USA, and was given the post of secretary of the NRI section a few years later. I met him when he returned from the States and we really hit it off.

Chapter 6

Kingmaker and Right Hand of Sheila Dikshit

JAGDISH AND JENNIFER Tytler's daughter, Radhika, got married on 7th June 1998 at a magnificent function at the Hyatt Regency. My family and myself had always shared a special bond with Jennifer, so I was thrilled to be invited. At the venue, we found Jennifer Tytler dressed in a beautiful gown, and she and Jagdish stood on either side of the newlyweds on the stage and guests proceeding in a line to wish them. When I reached to congratulate and bless the couple, I couldn't resist complimenting Jennifer, 'Madam, you are looking even more gracious than Jacqueline Kennedy!' Jagdish Tytler turned aside to hide his involuntary smile at my flagrant magnification while Jennifer bashfully retorted, 'Oh, come on, Manzar!'

I discovered that the groom was from my community, and a distant relation. It made me feel even more connected to the Tytlers! I was impressed by the elegant sobriety of the event, rousing a desire in my mind to conduct my children's wedding similarly.

Sitaram Kesri also attended the wedding and was seated alone at a corner table. It is a shortcoming of our society that when someone loses power, he is immediately ignored. I made it a point to go and sit with him, for I considered him to be my mentor. I procured snacks for him and escorted him to his car when he left. This attitude of being indifferent to those ousted from power is equivalent to thrusting your parents out of the house once they are old!

Shiela Dikshit was also a guest at the wedding. I had met her a decade ago when she was a minister in Rajiv Gandhi's government and we had clicked well together. My reputation as a reliable Congress activist had risen after my campaigning for Rajesh Khanna and I was regarded as an asset by senior leaders. As she got off the dais, she noticed me and immediately took my hand to step down.

'I have something very important to share with you,' she said.

'Today, I have been appointed as the Delhi Congress President.'

I immediately congratulated her. Still holding my hand, she continued, 'Maheshji, I need you to be with me. Promise that you will not betray me.' Her behaviour manifested anxiety and insecurity, for she had been losing elections since her only political victory in 1984, when she had become MP from Kannauj in UP. After her husband's demise two years later, things had not gone well with her. It was only after Rajiv Gandhi's death that she became close to Sonia, who brought her from Uttar Pradesh to Delhi. She, however, lost from East Delhi in February 1998 in the General Elections as she was an outsider. 'I have always had deep admiration for you from the day you came to Nizamuddin in 1991 and told me you had shifted into my neighbourhood. I am always there to support you and am sure that you will uplift Delhi Congress, bringing all the leaders together,' I said reassuringly.

'In that, too, I will need your help, because you are the only one I know who has a good relationship with every faction of the Delhi Congress,' she said.

'That is the reason why I have never been given any senior position in the Delhi Congress, for each considers me to be the other's supporter! They don't realise that I am a Congress person and, therefore, compelled to cooperate with everyone,' I replied.

'I want you to come daily to the Congress office.'

The evening laid the foundation of a beautiful relationship with Sheila Dikshit that lasted till her last breath.

***

I began to go to the Congress office daily, but I would do so only when Sheila Dikshit was there, usually in the second half. I would call her secretary or he would inform me when she was in office. Once she didn't come to the office for three days and when I met her, she petulantly informed me that she had been hospitalised with gastroenteritis and I hadn't even kept in touch! Sheila Dikshit then shared with me her personal mobile number. She was very action-oriented, not believing in wasting time in words and managed everything efficiently and practically. Almost daily, there were tasks of drafting, translation, writing, and responding to letters—all activities that kept me busy.

Once I had just got back from the Congress office and was settling down to a late lunch, when she called, requesting me to return to the office for some urgent drafting work for the press release of a resolution to be submitted by 6 pm the same evening. She said that she would order a meal for me. Prof Purshottam Goyal, former chairman of the Metropolitan Council, had already prepared the initial draft of the resolution, yet she trusted only me to frame the matter in the right way.

I hastened to the Congress office, where a number of leaders were present and quickly drafted the release to her satisfaction. But she completely forgot her promise, as no meal was arranged for me! I finally went back home to a really delayed lunch!

Shiela Dikshit knew how to get work done very diplomatically. No wonder that she could pull a hat trick in remaining the chief minister of Delhi for three terms! Despite that, she was not without her insecurities. Elections were declared and I decided to take a chance as V C Shukla had once advised that even if one didn't win, it was essential to be in the race as it kept one at the forefront of things. Sheila Dikshit, however, said that she needed me to be with her and help her with her campaigning. I accepted and during those days, we were constantly together from morning to late evening. At the outset, she had handed Rs 5,000 to me, saying that she didn't carry a purse, and that she would take whatever she needed from me. I refused to take the money, gently admonishing her that I could afford to sustain petty expenses. 'Besides, I am not your paid worker, with whom you have to maintain accounts. If you need to spend a larger amount, you can always give it to me later. You don't have to give me anything in advance!'

'Maheshji, you are truly one of a kind!'

'Madam, it is because of us few that the country is surviving! Such people are a rare breed, but they do exist!'

A couple of days into the campaign, Sonia Gandhi wanted to include Nafisa Ali, a former Miss India and a film actress in the campaigning. She thus became a part of our team and would sit in the back of the car with me, while Sheila Dikshit sat in the front, as she was not too happy with this. We would sometimes stop for refreshments and once Nafisa Ali requested me for something non-vegetarian. I told her that Sheila Dikshit was a Brahmin, so might object to that. But when I returned with three or four different kinds of snacks, it was Sheila Dikshit who commented, 'Only vegetarian snacks, Maheshji?' making Nafisa glare at me. I had not known Sheila Dikshit's predilection for nonvegetarian foods. A few days later, however, Sheila Dikshit arranged for Nafisa Ali to travel in another car, saying she couldn't take confidential calls in her presence, as she was a recent addition to the Party. Nafisa Ali was upset and did not come after that.

***

Once, at a campaign meeting, when Sheila Dikshit handed the mike to me, people began asking me to recite a few lines, as by then, I was an established poet. But instead of reciting one of my own *shers*, I recited someone else's, giving it a twist to match the times, drawing appreciation from the crowd.

BJP me sakdon tan makar aal
Akl ka kharcha toh ek do ounce hai
Inki jamhoori siyasat ka mizaj
Dheenga mushti dhandhali aur dhouns hai

(Cunningness pervades the BJP
And combined with a bit of brains,
They make a show of democratic politics
But what you get is nothing less than a circus of corrupt capers)

More was demanded, so I carried on, reciting a sher which categorised everyone as a beggar, for aren't we all always desirous of something or the other?

Ab bheekh mangne ke tarike badal gaye
Lazim nahi hai haath me kasa dikhayii de

(The process of begging has changed
A begging bowl is not necessary)

I felt that I, too, was always seeking to fulfil my desires. The audience enjoyed my satirical musings, but some leaders looked askance at my boldness. However, Sheila Dikshit didn't say anything, and I carried on, unchecked. But later when we were in the car, Sheila Dikshit castigated me gently, shaking her head in despair. 'Maheshji! How you do go on and on! You should know when to stop and not just float away in a deluge of words! People might even think that you are speaking on my behalf.'

Once D C Bandhu had given me the mike, and he too, regretted it. That's when I had quoted a sher on corruption.

> *Na jane kaise achanak ameer ban baithe*
> *Ye sub the bheekh mere saath mangne wale*

> (Amazing, how suddenly affluent they have all become,
> Those who once begged with me)

That was my take on my contemporaries, for they had been at my level but after winning elections, had become endowed with power and wealth. D C Bandhu was uncomfortable with my outspokenness and from that point onwards, avoided handing me the mike! My blunt nature has come in the way of my political growth over the years! But I was happy that I had got a chance to present my ghazal on Rajiv Gandhi at a commemorative event on 21 May 1998, his death anniversary, which Sonia also attended. People were familiar with the ghazal, and I was once encouraged to recite it at a function at the AICC grounds.

> *Nafasat Rajiv Gandhi latafat Rajiv Gandhi*
> *Nazar aate the kitne khubsoorat Rajiv Gandhi*

***

Sheila Dikshit wanted her biodata updated and requested me to draft it. 'You write such ornamental English, so you have to write my biodata,' she said. Two days later, Pawan Khera was at my doorstep to collect the biodata, but as I had constantly been on the road with Sheila Dikshit, I had to ask for more time to complete it. She was pleased with the result.

Some such task was always being given to me as I had a good grasp of both politics and literature. Before elections had been declared, Mani Shankar Aiyar had asked me to formulate a chargesheet, tabulating points against BJP's misrule. This was a mammoth task, but he encouraged me to take it on, saying he would help. I came up with forty-six points that highlighted rising prices, mismanagement of water and electricity supply and other such civic issues that impacted the common man. After Mani Shankar Aiyar's excellent editing, the final version of my chargesheet became popular among the Delhi Congress leaders, with Sheila Dikshit carrying it around for reference. The favourable response it got brought it to the attention of the general secretary, AICC, Oscar Fernandes, who then thought of presenting it to the manifesto committee. I felt it was a great honour to have my points become the basis of a policy document.

Campaigning threw us constantly into each other's company and I got a lot of time to converse with Sheila Dikshit. Her past experiences had left her feeling pretty insecure and when such thoughts overwhelmed her, she would hold my hand, rousing envy in many hearts. It added to my stature —that I was a man of substance, and not to be taken lightly. At a meeting, Sheila Dikshit paid me the biggest compliment saying, 'All know Mahesh Manzar, and what can I say about him? He is truly an angel! No one has supported me as he has. If I win and become the Chief Minister, I promise to make him a chairman of some Board or Corporation, equal to a ministerial rank!' I was overwhelmed; later, I thanked her profusely for this most beautiful gift of acknowledging me!

An acquaintance, Kirti Azad, a BJP candidate, and Sheila's opponent, whom I had met during the campaign, had warned me that she won't give me any credit for my loyalty, I had told him that I wasn't looking for any. She was already giving me unprecedented affection and respect, and that was a reward in itself. Sheila Dikshit had noticed my interaction with Azad and had wanted to know what we had been talking about.

When I told her that he was warning me, she laughed merrily. She asked me to tell her what people were saying about her, but I refused saying it went against my principles.

Towards the end of the campaign, she said, a trifle amused, 'Maheshji, you not only talk too much but also force others to do so! I don't think I had ever talked as much to even my husband as I have to you!'

'You honour me, Madam! But I would like to ask, how did you get so close to Soniaji?'

'After Rajiv's demise, I would called her often and visited her every week.'

'You must have talked a lot then to each other.'

'That's the surprising thing! We didn't talk much as neither of us are talkative; we would go into deep silence sitting together. Sometimes, just your presence matters a lot, since it gives strength to the other.'

On voting day, Sheila Dikshit looked nervous. We visited every polling booth in her New Delhi Gol Market Constituency. In the evening, after voting, refreshments had been arranged and when I asked her if she would like to have something, she refused. She hadn't eaten the whole day, so I fetched a few *puris* and insisted that she eat. I stood outside her car window, handing her one *puri* with *subzi* and like a child, she submitted to my entreaties. I cajoled her to have another, then another… till she had eaten all the six *puris* I had got! It was indeed a dramatic scene witnessed by booth workers and media, with a reporter even clicking a picture! When she had finished, her eyes were moist. 'Maheshji, you are truly like an angel! You're feeding me as if you were my mother.'

Spontaneously, I said, 'But my wife considers me crazy!'

'And yet you take her name half a dozen times, daily,' was her instant rejoinder. Indeed, this was true. 'Well, she does serve me my meals every day,' I acknowledged.

On the eve of counting, her youngest sister, Rama

Dhawan, her election-in-charge, was allotting tasks to all family members. Sheila Dikshit was tense, even though chances of her victory were high. When Rama was deciding a task for me, she intervened and catching hold of my hand, insisted that I would be with her in her room till the results were declared. Her attachment was a bit obvious, drawing censorious glances. During the fifteen days of campaigning, a mutual affection had arisen and I had never received the respectful regard which she accorded me! The next morning, I reached early to find that she was still in her room. Rama and Tripathi, her personal secretary were on the computer in a small lobby adjoining it.

Even in the turmoil of elections, each member was busy with his or her allotted task. I found her lying down, exhausted and anxious on her bed. I presented her with a bouquet of roses, saying, 'Madam, in anticipation of your grand victory!' Her eyes welled up with tears.

Counting had begun, and as time progressed, it became evident that she was winning. Suddenly, she became energised. Within no time, she was out of bed and quickly dressing, bounced out of her room calling enthusiastically, 'Come on Maheshji!'

Her victory made the Party euphoric, for it was a Congress win after many years. The *Times of India* carried a picture of a victorious Sheila Dikshit on the front page, with myself beside her. I delightedly pointed it out to her, telling her that she was looking like a 'smiling doll,' much to her amusement. Rama and Latika, her daughter, looked at me askance! For the next three days, revellers kept turning up at her house, dancing to drumbeats. There was an air of intense celebration as people from all walks of life poured in to congratulate her, including family, close friends and senior Congress leaders.

Sheila Dikshit was never in the best of health, and even back then, had problems in going down the steps. I insisted that she should look to her health first, since she was diabetic. 'Maheshji, this day has come after fourteen years!' she said to me. For her oath ceremony, many senior Congress activists wanted passes, which were being distributed by Rama Dhawan and Latika Imran. She told me to bring my wife, but I told her that I had received only one pass. She promised to rectify that.

It was obvious that some of her family didn't quite like me. Was it because I seemed to be more focused on Sheila Dikshit than they? She was aware of this and grateful for my contribution to her success. Many of her family were also appreciative, considering my presence to be like a lucky charm for her.

She assumed office and from the first day, a whirl of activities began. First, there was a meeting at her home with senior Congress leaders. I was expecting her to give me some position, but nothing materialised, and sometime later, it was alleged that the chairmanship of Delhi Tourism Development Corporation had been conferred with some consideration involved. I didn't say anything about her promise and instead planned to honour her with a felicitation gathering on my birthday in February at my house. She attended with her entire family and interacted cordially with my family. Other senior leaders, including Mani Shankar Aiyar were also there. Towards the end, former Chief Justice of India, Ranganath Mishra walked in with his family, causing a stir. Even Sheila Dikshit seemed awed at his presence and moved forward to greet him. The evening in my jam-packed basement was a super success!

***

Govind Kapoor, a friend, introduced me to the concept of *chaliya*, a practice of visiting the temple daily for forty days to deepen one's connect with the Divine. He came from Mayur Vihar daily for this. I found it very intriguing and decided to start on it after my return from Shirdi, a trip that had been already planned. I brought back *Tulsi malas* and Sai rings as gifts and even gave them to Sheila Dikshit, who graciously accepted them, touching them to her forehead. She placed them on a small altar in her bedroom, which had a small statue of Ganesha and a picture of her husband. This profoundly moved me.

I initiated my forty-day '*chaliya*,' by visiting Sai temple on Lodhi Road, daily. On 25 February 1999, I saw a very delicately-featured lady in a cotton saree outside the temple, exuding a divine charisma that instantly attracted me. I approached her with the age-old line, 'Have we not met before?' She refuted it with a gentle smile. I pressed my advantage and quickly introduced myself, handing her my visiting card. She took it hesitantly and moved away. More than three weeks later, she sent a message, reminding me of our meeting at the temple and apologising for the delay in contacting me. Her name was Dr Mahi Malhotra and I regarded her getting in touch with me as a Divine blessing, for I had just returned from a visit to Barsana.

***

For Sheila Dikshit's birthday, I decided to present a saree to her at her home. She was with her sister, Rama Dhawan and daughter, Latika Imran when I gifted it to her.

'Madam, I have bought a saree for you from your favourite Cottage Industries Emporium. Please wear it for your birthday, your first as a CM!'

She reciprocated politely, but then, I said something really inappropriate. Her sister and daughter were present there as well. I said something unintentionally which turned into a faux pas. I beat a hasty retreat. I am sure that later the others must have convinced her that she would only be asking for trouble if the CM keeps a person like me with her.

Chapter 7

My Growing Spiritual Leanings

MEANWHILE, I BEGAN frequently chatting with Dr Mahi Malhotra on the phone. She was a history professor in Daulat Ram College, very cultured and soft-spoken. Her voice was fascinating, as it was so child-like, a total contrast to her sophisticated appearance. I would share well-known quotations with her and then discuss them, delighting in her knowledgeable responses in her well-articulated English. Within a short time, I felt that she completely fulfilled my four criteria on *vesh, vani, vichar* and *vyahvar*.

A few days later, to my great pleasure, she invited me to her home in Green Park for her husband's birthday. I, thus, got to meet her family and found them very cordial and supportive. What gave me even more happiness was that Mahi served the snacks I had taken for the family, showing her appreciation for my choice. I really liked that, for it displayed a complete lack of ego. When I was leaving, Mahi presented me with Paramhansa Yogananda's *Autobiography of a Yogi*, a book that later wrought tremendous change in my thought processes. It not only introduced me to meditation and pranayama, but also helped me proceed in my spiritual journey. I came to regard this book as being next to Holy books like *Bhagavad Gita* and *Sai Satcharitra* (Sai's bio).

My spiritual journey continued with regular trips to

Barsana for I had many well-connected friends who went there from time to time and would take me with them. Even the Swamiji there was very affectionate towards me and would encourage my friends to bring 'Kailash,' as he called me, with them whenever they came. Once, when a few months had passed without a visit from me, he wrote a postcard to invite me there! I still treasure that letter! It was Swamiji who guided me to continue offering water to the Sun God, the actual source of all life. I have been doing this for years!

Chapter 8

Radharani's Blessings for Me

IT WAS ON one such visit that I received a call from Mani Shankar Aiyar making me feel that Radharani's blessings were being showered on me!

'Where are you, Mahesh bhai?'

'On my way back from Barsana.'

'Have you decided to become a sage at your age?'

I hastily denied this and asked him how he had thought of me.

'Well, your services are needed here. I want you to translate the speeches I write for Sonia Gandhi into Hindustani.'

I was overwhelmed at this great honour literally falling into my lap, for just being associated with 10 Janpath was beyond my expectations. General elections had been declared in the last week of September for the Vajpayee government had collapsed after only thirteen months. Sonia Gandhi was now campaigning and needed speeches to be written for her. So, MSA had been appointed along with Prof Janardan Dwivedi for this task. But Mani Shankar Aiyar had also been given the post of secretary, so he had his hands full. He was well-acquainted with my proficiency in translation in Hindi-Urdu, and hence decided to involve me. He wrote in English, but Sonia Gandhi had to deliver her speeches in Hindustani. She liked the Urdu touches that I added and would articulate the words authentically. I was truly impressed by her, especially when one day, I saw her delving into various books and magazines and making notes. She kept herself updated and was obviously not dependent only on her team for knowledge.

***

It was my good fortune, more the blessings of Shree Radhe and Sai Baba, that I found myself endowed with the label of 'King maker!' Earlier I had been associated with Rajesh Khanna, who won over Shatrughan Sinha and now Sheila Dikshit, who had been categorised as a non-winner, had also won! My desire for a chairmanship for a Delhi Board or corporation was truly trivial in the face of the acclaim I was now receiving.

Kesriji was the first to congratulate me on my accomplishment, followed by V C Shukla. So far, I was regarded as a poet, but after Sheila Dikshit's victory, my stature had grown in the eyes of veterans like Vasant Sathe, Ram Niwas Mirdha and Balram Jakhar, who now began to involve me in their political programmes, further enhancing my political image and making my face known beyond Delhi. Sajjan Kumar paid me a huge compliment, 'Manzar Sahab, if you were willing to support me, I wouldn't hesitate to cover the distance between our houses by prostrating all the way!' Very diplomatically, I refused, saying that our temperaments didn't match!

I now got busy with my work with Mani Shankar Aiyar, who had a room in 10 Janpath and he magnanimously shared the space with me. Formulating those speeches was hard work and meant long working hours. Many points from various states had to be integrated according to the venue of the speech. Although tea and biscuits were served from time to time, they were inadequate, so I began bringing packed lunch. Vincent

George noticed this and within a couple of days, a complete meal began to be ordered for me, mostly South Indian food.

Prof Janardan Dwivedi had a room adjacent to Mani Shankar Aiyar and also wrote Sonia Gandhi's speeches in Hindi; he had a doctorate in the language. Initially, he didn't seem very happy with my presence, so one day, I explained that I was there on Maniji's invitation and had no intention of creating any hurdles. I wanted to pay back to the Party that had given me so much! Convinced with my appeal, the Professor mellowed and understood the viability of working in a cordial atmosphere. We were both working on the same project, but were submitting our work separately for Sonia Gandhi to study and amalgamate. My initiative cleared the air between us, leading to a close friendship later.

Kesriji had appointed Ahmed Patel to the post of Treasurer and Sonia Gandhi retained him. When he came to meet her at 10 Janpath, he would often peep into Mani Shankar Aiyar's room and if I happened to be there, he would come in to chat, acknowledging and admiring my selfless service to the Congress party.

***

Meanwhile, my bond with Kesriji had deepened. One evening, I visited him casually and we had a wonderful time together, discussing many topics. At the end of the evening, Kesriji requested me to visit him often as he felt lonely and our time together uplifted his spirits. I began visiting him almost daily. If, by chance, I couldn't go, he would call me! We became quite intimate, talking about innumerable subjects ranging from politics to amorous stories to life advice! He would sometimes send me boxes of alphonso mangoes or pistachio *barfi* from Mumbai, both regarded as quite lavish foods! He once even invited me for lunch. There were at least fourteen different kinds of dishes!

I invited him home, and it was a real honour for me that he accepted. I had invited him many times before as well, but he had always refused, citing limitations of protocol. But now he was not in office, and it was easier for him to visit my home. I asked him his preferences in food, including the sugar, salt and spices quotient. He was delighted at this gesture. I made it a habit henceforth, asking my senior guests their preferences, drawing admiration from them. Kesriji, however, did instruct me not to invite anyone else so only my family was present. We welcomed him with a shawl and a bouquet.

A few evenings later, while we were deep in our discussions, he stood up and folding his hands, begged my forgiveness, very emotionally. I was shocked and hastily denied the need for him to make an apology. But he continued, saying, 'In all these years that you have been with me, I couldn't realise your worth!'

'How can you say that, Babuji! You have always stood by me and uplifted me.'

'But I didn't recognise your true value! What immense depth you have, in all aspects, political, social, literary, emotional, and spiritual. You're blessed with both intelligence and compassion and yet I couldn't help you to evolve as you were meant to. You have very positive vibes, and that makes you really charismatic!'

I reassured him, 'Babuji, no one can give anything to anyone, unless God so desires! Only He has the power to do so, and not even parents can give anything to their children. If they don't have comforts of life, how can they give them to their child? But if it is in the child's Destiny, no one can stop him from gaining them! Please don't feel regretful; it was not in my Destiny to achieve any position. You once wanted to make me a secretary, but it didn't transpire. Now even when Sheila Dikshit promised to give me a position, nothing is happening! Your recognition is of great value and that is enough for me! The love and affection that you are giving so abundantly is all that I want!'

Kesriji became really emotional and marvelled at my wisdom, as I continued, 'What have you been able to give to your own son, Amar Nath! But to me, you have truly given a lot. When I started, I used to be a humble businessman, and see the heights you have helped me reach!'

***

In May 1999, Sharad Pawar raised the question of the credibility of a foreigner being the National Congress President. Sonia Gandhi's highhanded ways were making her unpopular with some of the senior leaders. Tariq Anwar and P A Sangma supported Sharad Pawar and the whole plan of bringing up her antecedents was discussed at Kesriji's residence, who too was irked by her behaviour and, therefore, encouraged them to revolt. It was decided to bring up the issue at a meeting of the Congress Working Committee.

Kesriji also had to attend that meeting, being an ex-Congress President. As he was getting ready to go, I happened to visit him. He asked me to accompany him, maybe because of a premonition. I was in the back seat with Kesriji, while his personal assistant, Mohan, was in the front. As soon as our car entered the AICC driveway, some Youth Congress and Sewa Dal members approached the car from either side. The moment Kesriji stepped out, they grabbed him roughly. Shocked, both Mohan and I rushed to protect him, throwing our arms around him from either side. However, somebody still swiped his cap off his head, while another tugged at his dhoti. I shouted at them to leave him alone. He was not only our past party President, but also an octogenarian. Only a few months earlier, when he was in office, people were touching his feet and now they were roughing him up! Somehow, we propelled him into the building and helped him straighten his clothes, feeling completely unnerved. Kesriji attended the meeting, while I waited outside. As a result of the challenge to her right to be the leader, Sonia Gandhi offered to resign, but her supporters refused to accept that and subsequently the three who had protested were expelled from the Party, paving the way for the formation of a new party, the Nationalist Congress Party.

I accompanied Kesriji back home, and once back, he broke down and cried like a child, still overwrought by the ugly incident. I consoled him, but it had left me also completely shattered. I had come face to face with the dirty side of politics, which showed no consideration for either loyalty or age. No explanation seemed evident so we could only dismiss them as overenthusiastic activists!

'God has blessed you with great heights; regard this too as an act of God and accept it,' I said, trying to calm him down.

'No one can be so unruly without some encouragement! Who would dare to accost an ex-Party President in such a manner?' Kesriji retaliated with deep anguish, silencing me effectively.

Surprisingly, within half an hour, Sonia Gandhi visited him to apologise for the untoward event. Later, he shared with me that he had told her that being much senior to her, he had experienced all kinds of conspiracies, so was well aware of what went on in political circles.

***

I got so involved in my work that it left me with no time to visit the DPCC office or even Sheila Dikshit. When I met her a few weeks later, she greeted me warmly and invited me to her newly allotted house on Mathura Road. That was the only time that I reminded her of her promise to make me a chairman, to which her response was, 'Mahesh ji, hopefully next week!' For the next three months, this phrase became her catchline whenever we met. A few leaders had even begun to taunt me, saying 'Oh, here comes our CM's chairman!' Over time, I began to get a sense of the helplessness behind her evasive attitude, for sometimes matters are not in our hands, so I declared her free of the promise she had made to me, much to her relief!

***

Another one of my close mentors, V C Shukla had been very affectionate towards me and after my role in Sheila Dikshit's victory, his affection became even more apparent. He promised to give me a wonderful gift, and a while later, he did so helping me forge a close bond of friendship with an ex-princess, Shefali Singh! She was interested in entering politics, and V C Shukla asked me to guide her.

Sonia Gandhi lost the elections, getting only 114 MPs, much to Kesriji's delight. He gloated that he had gained more than her, so how could she be more powerful? Her white skin was praised, but that had not helped her pull in more MPs, and it was his tanned skin that had proved more resilient. 'I am neither photogenic nor telegenic, while your new President is both, yet where has she reached?' he said.

Once Kesriji had been removed from office, I had begun to visit Narasimha Rao, as I liked to be in the centre of activities. I told him about the attack on Kesriji at the AICC office, but he was not very sympathetic.

'One doubtlessly reaps what one sows! Definitely Karma has a prominent role to play in everyone's life.' I agreed with him, for I was aware of the blunders Sitaram Kesri had made.

Mani Shankar Aiyar had lost the 1996 and the 1998 elections, so as the 1999 elections approached, I was quite concerned. I prayed for his victory at the Sai Temple and brought back prasad for him. Both he and his wife were surprised that someone had gone to such trouble for his victory and deeply appreciated the gesture.

'Though I don't have much belief in God, I respect your faith in Him and praise your efforts in thinking so much for me. But I would like you to respect my non-belief in God, too!' he had responded.

'Why not? Everyone has the right to have their own opinion and you have a unique thought process of 'Work is Worship' which I heartily applaud.' He was always deeply immersed in work and totally distanced from the world around him, almost like being in a meditative state. He would himself say that 'Others like to go to temples, but I prefer going deep into my work.' I agreed, adding that Mahatma Buddha also endorsed this thought that even if you did menial tasks with dedication, it was equivalent to going into a spiritual state.

By Divine Grace, he won the elections and both Venkat, his PA, and I went to receive him at the airport with garlands. His wife suggested that he should go directly to the Ganesh Temple in Connaught Place, before doing anything else. Years earlier, the temple had been established by his father, a prominent chartered accountant.

Mani Shankar Aiyar was given room six at the AICC Headquarters since the time he had been appointed as the secretary in 1998, and now, after becoming an MP, he was allotted a house in Tilak Lane. As he used the main office set up in his residence, I would be in his AICC office, along with another secretary of the AICC, Mukul Wasnik. The adjoining room was used by Jairam Ramesh, secretary of the Economic department, whose chairman was Dr Manmohan Singh. Jairam Ramesh was impressed by my dedication and commitment, and one day suggested that I should join him in his department. I felt very good and happily accepted, 'I would love to! Besides, it will give me a chance to interact more frequently with Dr Manmohan Singh, for once my poetry was appreciated by him!'

'But you will have to leave Mani Shankar Aiyar!'

I was astonished at this. 'That I cannot even think of doing! I will be happy to work with you in any way, for I am a Congress worker and can work for anyone.'

Jairam Ramesh was not very happy with my reply and somewhere it reflects even today in his attitude towards me! It disturbed me as to why anyone would want me to break away from Maniji, for earlier, too, R K Dhawan had attempted to make me do the same thing.

After Sheila Dikshit, Subhash Chopra had become the DPCC President and he, too, was interested that I should work with him. Everyone was aware of how I had supported Sheila Dikshit. I politely informed him that I wouldn't be able to do justice to the role since I was already involved with MSA's (Mani Shankar Aiyar's) office at AICC.

Once Sajjan tauntingly commented that I seemed to flatter almost everyone, like a sycophant. I retorted that I considered myself to be a merchant of love and had only love to trade in my shop; there was no space for hatred. It drew a few chuckles from those who heard our exchange. Another time he aimed a barb at me, 'Manzar Sahab, the kind of press releases that you write, I can get done from any journalist for Rs 500.'

'That's very good to know! But then you cater to the trend of paid mobocracy, and that's your style of politics. I deal in the politics of mind and heart, and that's my style. I seek the blessings of Devi Saraswati while you invoke Devi Laxmi!'

I continued, 'Bhagatji once commented that Manzar handles his political connections very diplomatically. He spends about two hours every morning, calling up his contacts, setting up meetings, getting titbits of information and sharing them around, generally chatting comfortably and making them all happy! That sums up my political style, devoid of any money or muscle, only focused on mind power!'

That effectively silenced any further attempts to belittle

me and subsequently, Sajjan became a good friend.

***

The year 2000, brought another wonderful opportunity into my life. One evening as I was going to Sadar Bazaar to collect my money, I received a call from Anil Shastri, Lal Bahadur Shastri's second son and a good friend. He asked me to meet him at the AICC offices. Once there, Anil Shastri took me to meet Ghulam Nabi Azad, the general secretary of the Party, who came to the point directly. 'Manzar Saheb, will you be able to go to Orissa? We would like to give you the responsibility of an observer for the election campaign.' I was astounded at the honour being given and accepted eagerly. This was the first time I had been asked to do something of importance outside Delhi and felt God was compensating me for not giving me a position in the Delhi government. My association with Sheila Dikshit and the way she had reposed faith in me so entirely had helped to prove my mettle and now I was being regarded as a competent party activist. I had reservations of going to a completely new place, but Anil Shastri assured me that both he and Ghulam Nabi Azad would be around.

Besides, I was already acquainted with the preceding chief minister of Orissa, Giridhar Gamang and his son, who had recently been replaced by a tribal leader, Hemanand Biswal. Two MPs had been chosen from Delhi to go as observers to Orissa, Jai Prakash Aggarwal and Jagdish Tytler. But unfortunately, Tytler was unable to go and the task had fallen to my lot.

Before going to Orissa, I went to seek the blessings of PVN Rao who advised me to keep my distance from money and women as prospective candidates may try to lure me. He warned me that there will be a lot of people watching me from AICC and OPCC. He gave a special packet of sweets for J B Patnaik, OPCC President. On my return, J B Patnaik reciprocated the gesture by giving Orissa's Jaggannath Puri temple's holy prasad.

There were twenty-four observers from different states and each had been given a district to oversee. I was in charge of two remote districts, Koraput and Malakangiri, and for the next twelve days, I shuttled between Bhubaneswar and these districts. Giridhar Gamang was from Koraput and everything was catered for very efficiently, from arrangements in state guest houses to a chauffeur-driven car! An Orissa state Congress leader accompanied and introduced me around. It is the task of an observer to choose the most suitable MLA to contest and I had to recommend seven for the tickets, after interviewing and selecting the best candidates. Later, I would have to justify my choices before the State Election Committee in the presence of the AICC general secretary and secretary.

My Orissa visit was pleasant and left no scope for feeling homesick. I was given much love, respect and importance. I was often invited by the chief minister or the State Congress President and other senior leaders to their homes for dinner. I became quite popular in Orissa!

***

I submitted my list of seven potential candidates for the ticket once back in Delhi and four among them were approved; two of them, won later. A few days after returning from Orissa, Ghulam Nabi Azad told me that I should go back again as everyone was appreciating my work and wanted me to be a part of the campaigning for the selected candidates. This time, Ghulam Nabi Azad was given a helicopter to visit the different districts and I would accompany him with either a State leader or Anil Shastri. It was a thrilling experience! The chopper rides were noisy and once when I was trying to convey something to Ghulam Nabi Azad, he said, 'Manzar Sahab, if you spoke just 50 per cent of what you currently do, you would have been more successful! You talk too much!'

Anil Shastri intervened, '50 per cent? It should be more like 25 per cent!'

'Actually, I just can't control my exuberance when I am happy!' I replied, a trifle abashed.

'But you have to take into account your circumstances. The chopper is making so much noise above my head and you are constantly speaking into my ear! Who should I listen to?'

We were staying in the same hotel in connecting rooms and would often work late as candidates would drop in to collect funds for their campaigns. Once I had suggested that we should leave it for the morning. He refused, saying that it would prove to be a hindrance to their schedule. Our task was to facilitate their work and not look to our own comfort. It showed his dedication to his work, inspiring us all. Being close to Ghulam Nabi Azad meant that we would also be sharing our meals together, sometimes even eating from the same plate!

One day, we had to tour remote and sparsely populated villages. He asked me to visit them beforehand to meet the block Congress Presidents and gram panchayat heads and motivate them to mobilise the crowd to be present at the designated time. This was not part of our regular programme and Ghulam Nabi Azad handed me Rs 5,000 for expenses. I took it reluctantly, but had no occasion to spend it, as everything was catered for, so when I tried to return the amount to Ghulam Nabi Azad, he refused to accept it. Ultimately, I purchased ten sarees from local weavers, as gifts for the family and for two of my best lady friends back home.

In a public speech during the campaigning in the presence of Ghulam Nabi Azad, I happened to say, 'We accept that we have failed to provide schools, dispensaries and toilets to all villages in Orissa, but if you vote us back into power, we will definitely take care of making *Vidaylay, Aushdhalaya*, and *Shauchalaya* in all the villages of Orissa.'

Later, Ghulam Nabi Azad reprimanded me for being so truthful! 'Keep your honesty for your poetical and literary activities; such transparency is not good for electoral politics!' he told me. It showed that even after a quarter century of political association, I had yet to manifest political common sense.

It was my luck that thanks to the campaigning, I was able to visit Jagannath Puri, one of the four main pilgrimage Dhams of the Hindus, thrice in the same month. I also visited Cuttack, the hometown of former CJI Ranganath Mishra, and when he got to know of my visit, he invited me home for dinner and even arranged a trip to a popular Devi temple in the city.

I also met Sheila Dikshit in Bhubaneswar as she too had come for campaigning, for two days. She was staying in another hotel and invited me for dinner. We had a heart-to-heart talk especially about her inability to fulfil her promise to me. Subsequently, when we returned to Delhi, she issued a letter of appointment designating me as the chairman of the Delhi State Industrial Development Corporation. The MD of the Corporation, Atul Sharma called me to congratulate me on being appointed chairman. I was very surprised for I had not received any intimation about this. Just before this call, a Mr Kanaujia had called to tell me that he had been given the chairmanship of the Society for Prevention of Cruelty against Animals. He somehow managed to make me speak against Sheila Dikshit, for I did feel a momentary surge of anger at again being overlooked and not being given a post. Unfortunately, this was a conspiracy, for Kanaujia had recorded our conversation and replayed it for Sheila Dikshit, making her antagonistic towards me.

So when I received the MD's call but no follow up, I

realised the game that had been planned against me. I was sure that those around her who didn't want me to come into any position of authority, were responsible for this conspiracy and ousted me yet again. I suppose it was the Destiny I had been born with! But somehow, I was also thankful, for being made a chairman or secretary would have limited me. I was happiest as an all-rounder and receiving unprecedented laurels.

Still, there was a part of my heart which was a bit melancholic, for the situation reminded me of my friend Balraj Komal's famous poem *Circus ka Ghoda* in which after exhibiting his enticing acrobatics, the circus horse would return to his stall and cry, for his own brethren couldn't see him!

Chapter 9

Trouble on Several Fronts

I WAS SO involved in events in Orissa that Chhaya had to enlist the help of her elder sister to send a message to me to return home, with the excuse that the children were missing me! But I think it was Chhaya who was missing me! She had begun to feel ignored, for I had got so set in my life that I didn't need her. I had a good circle of friends and spent most of my time away from the house, for whenever I was at home, we were always getting into some argument or the other.

Since I was getting a steady rental income from my shop, I didn't need to do much work and remained absorbed in political activities. Chhaya would routinely taunt me for being a useless layabout. It would fire me up, for I was actually doing a lot of work in political circles, which the world was praising so much, but at home she never lost any chance to insult me!

My relations with one of Chhaya's close relative were not good, and to win me over, he had assured me that he had guided Chhaya to handle me tactfully. He had encouraged me to let him know if she behaved otherwise. But when I complained to him after returning from Orissa, Chhaya had somehow convinced him that it was she who was being victimised. And now, he, too, had turned against me. He told me that it would be better if he took Chhaya away, to which I agreed readily. She demanded that both sons should accompany her, but they refused and she had to leave the house without them. Once she had reached there, they must have realised that the three of us had ganged up and she was all alone. He began calling me on her behalf telling me that Chhaya was feeling very sad and that I should come and take her back home. I resisted, saying that this time, she had gone too far and it would be better if we separated. This was not acceptable either to her family or to my sons, for they were still quite young, the elder being nineteen, and the younger, sixteen. They now began to egg me on to bring her back and finally I submitted, making her promise to behave well.

***

On my return from Orissa, former CJI Ranganath Mishra called me early one morning; he wanted to know when he could visit me. I felt so emotionally overwhelmed, that I immediately responded, 'Babuji, you are most welcome any time. In fact, let me know and I will come to visit you!'

'No, no, we will come to meet you.'

'I will be truly honoured! Please let me know when would you like to come—for lunch or dinner?'

'Only for coffee.' Time was set for the same day about 11 am, and both father and son came home. Ranganath Mishra came straight to the point, 'Mahesh ji, you know that my son Dev Anand has not been gainfully employed for the past three years. It is unfortunate that no office has been detailed for him by the Party. Kesriji didn't give him any post and now even Sonia Gandhi is not doing so. If he could be made secretary in AICC or given the chairmanship of some Corporation, it would occupy him. You are close to both Sonia Gandhi and Sheila Dikshit; if you could put in a positive word for him?'

I responded, 'Babuji, both these posts were promised to me as well, but to date, nothing has materialised. But I will do my best to push them for Dev ji. He is much more qualified than me and I am sure something will work out for him.'

***

With my gregarious and audacious nature, I counted a number of the finest ladies as my friends. Associating with them made me feel gratified intellectually, emotionally and spiritually. Talking with Mahi invigorated me and I once said to her, 'You are a blessing of my Gurus to me!'

'Maheshji, that's a really big thing to say! I don't think I deserve that!' she replied.

***

On my birthday, in February 2000, , I had bought a Ford Ikon, as both my sons were driving now. We went to the Hanuman temple and after dropping my family home, I drove to Kesriji's house for blessings. He demanded a ride in it. It was a real touching gesture and his way of showing his affection for me! We took a short round from his residence on Purana Qila Road to the India Gate circle, my pride knowing no bounds!

Seeing my driving, he commented, 'You will soon reduce this Rs 6 lakh car to a Rs 6,000 one!'

'Is that a blessing or a prediction, Babuji?'

'The way you're driving, it has to be a prediction!'

'Oh Babuji! The car is new and I am excited about driving you!' I said.

'I think you'll benefit by taking some driving lessons.'

***

Ram Niwas Mirdha, one of my revered mentors, was appointed chairman of the Congress Election Authority, a body which regulated elections within the Party. A few days later, a dispute arose in Rajasthan between chief minister Ashok Gehlot and the President of the State Provincial Congress Committee, Dr Girija Vyas, whom I knew well as she too was a poet. Mirdha detailed me to accompany a high-powered committee as a coordinator. I asked Kesriji about the reason for such a dispute, especially as the Party had just come into power again after a long hiatus, and he gave me insights into this. 'It's a manoeuvre by the High Command to appoint leaders from different factions to key positions, satisfying everyone. In that way, those leaders are more interested in checking the other rather than ganging up together. It's a divide-and-rule tactic, to check and balance power.' Later, I got to know that it was Indira Gandhi who had initiated this system. It had been perfected by other followers.

We were going as Party representatives to resolve internal issues by meeting the leaders concerned. We were treated royally and even visited Chaukidhani. At one meeting with the leaders of both camps, arguments took place and I began to feel very uncomfortable and short of breath. I went back to our hotel to rest, and later decided to go to my sister's house in Ajmer to rest and recoup. I decided to get a thorough check up on returning to Delhi, but before I could do so, another incident really shook me up. One night, my sons fought fiercely as both had very strong egos. Both Chhaya and I tried to intervene, but they continued beating eachother. I was deeply affected and realised that the strife between Chhaya and myself was getting reflected in them, pushing them to become even more aggressive. The same feeling that I had experienced in Jaipur engulfed me and I had to sit down, drawing the attention of my wife and elder son, who backed out of the fight. They realised something was seriously wrong and took me to Moolchand hospital. The doctor found I had a heart problem and said that I needed a stent.

The next day, a friend, Mahender Aggarwal took me to a senior doctor in Escorts who voiced the same diagnosis. Eventually, I contacted another friend at MS Ram Manohar Lohia hospital, Dr C P Singh where the chief cardiologist found that the condition could be managed with a tablet. A tremendous feeling of thankfulness welled up within me and I was immediately reminded of the temple behind the hospital, where I had helped to establish the Shiv Pariwar *murtis* a couple of years ago. I was convinced that the Lord's blessings had guided me back to the hospital for the correct diagnosis to be made!

***

I was good friends with one of the general secretaries, AICC. Once when I was visiting him at home, he jokingly asked, 'Maheshji, when are you inviting us to your house?' I did so at once and soon, he and his family came over to my house for dinner. A few weeks later, they took me for dinner to Lodhi hotel and later, I invited them to my favourite Pandara Road restaurant for non-vegetarian dishes. Some days later, I received a call from his wife, asking me to get her those tasty non-vegetarian dishes from Pandara Road. She also invited me to have lunch with her at home. I took my children along when I went to drop the food off at their place. A few days after that, the general secretary called to thank me for taking care of his wife during his absence. I suddenly realised that I could be getting into deep waters. On another occasion, she asked whether I could drop her off at her office as their driver wasn't there. I promptly conveyed her request to her husband and he affably responded, 'Brother, you are not supposed to be at her beck and call!' Somehow this episode showed me in poor light, and his attitude was as if I had initiated this closeness with his wife. Later, I heard that he did hold a grudge against me, and had vetoed the idea of giving me the position of secretary, AICC.

Many a times, there had been a lot of unnecessary smoke without fire where my reputation was concerned. I was naturally gregarious and my camaraderie was often misconstrued. Once, Mahi described me as being an 'ocean of compassion and passion' when I shared some of my social adventures with her. I told her that she had been sent specially to brighten my life, a compliment she denied hastily! Nevertheless, I gained a reputation for being an epicurean and also for being very well off, while on both counts, I was facing a reality of deficiency. Besides, I was wary of lending money, for my father had never been in favour of either lending or borrowing.

Once a staff member in Sonia Gandhi's office asked me to lend him a few thousand, which I was not carrying and couldn't spare either. Mindful of my father's words, I told him that I didn't have cash but could write a cheque. He immediately backed out, for a cheque can be compromising.

Chapter 10

Shayar-e-Azeem

IN DECEMBER 1995, I was invited by Usha and Krishna Kumar, a Union Minister in the then Narasimha Rao government, to attend their daughter's wedding reception. I happened to meet his niece, Subha Rajan, an elegant lady. I gave her my visiting card with my favourite line, 'You're looking truly gracious in this pink saree!' Out of the blue, she called me in November 1997 to invite me for a conference. I learned then that she was a Director at the CII. The conference was at Hotel Taj Mansingh, to felicitate the President of South Africa, Nelson Mandela. Next year, a conference was held to welcome the Palestine President, Yasser Arafat and I was invited to that as well. She introduced me to him as a popular Indian poet and politician! Subha would often invite me to several high-profile conferences over the next twenty years, giving me the chance to interact with many foreign dignitaries.

At one of these conferences in 2003, I got to meet Benazir Bhutto and presented her with my Urdu poetry book. The next day, she requested Subha to invite me for a poetry session over coffee, as she had read a few of my poems and wanted to meet me personally! It was one of my most memorable meetings for I was greatly impressed by her simplicity in both her attire and mannerisms, totally in contrast to her position. She was tall, well-proportioned, and with a charismatic authority. She enjoyed my compositions, reading them aloud, much to my elation. I told her that I had been fascinated by her from way back in 1972, when she had come to the Shimla Conference along with her father, the then President of Pakistan, Zulfikar Ali Bhutto, to sign the Shimla Agreement with Indira Gandhi, after the Indo-Pak war.

She marvelled at how Destiny had made our paths cross! Later, the three of us casually walked around in the corridors of the Maurya Sheraton, Benazir sure of being incognito in her ordinary outfit. The next day too, I was invited back to entertain her, with Subha remarking that Benazir was CII's guest, while I was Benazir's! Subha was delighted at how I had won her esteemed guest's heart. We often began to meet for coffee and I became good friends with her husband, Rajan as well.

Attending Subha's conferences gave me the opportunity of meeting several dignitaries, including the President of Afghanistan, Hamid Karzai and Shashi Tharoor, who was the under-secretary general for the UN back then. I was mesmerised by about an hour-long speech of Shashi Tharoor.

***

In June, senior politician, Rajesh Pilot passed away in a fatal road accident. In some circles, there was speculation that he might have been the victim of a conspiracy. I was with Kesriji when a reporter asked him for his opinion, and he said, 'I feel there is some foul play involved in this accident.' Later, I said to him, 'Babuji, the Home Minister, Advaniji was saying investigations were yet to be done. So, wasn't your statement, rather strong?'

I was really aggrieved by the loss of Rajesh Pilot for he was a very dynamic and popular leader. I was on good terms with practically all senior leaders, for they understood that I was not power hungry and as a result, there was no competition for them. They, therefore, interacted freely with me, involving me in many political or social events. Once Rajesh Pilot had organised a rally for the Gurjar community and asked me for 5,000 flags costing Rs 25,000. But it so happened that he did not give the payment even when I asked him directly. A few days later, I reminded him, saying, 'You have always regarded me like your younger brother. How can you withhold your own younger brother's money? My livelihood depends on it.' He finally paid, albeit in instalments! I invariably managed to retrieve my dues in some way or the other, with the exception of H K L Bhagat; Whenever, I meet his son, Deepak, I put in an appeal for the Rs 15,000 he owed me! He laughs it off, saying returns are timebound, and even the law writes them off eventually as irretrievable after three years.

Another time, Jai Prakash Aggarwal invited me for his son's wedding at the Mavalankar Hall grounds and deputed me to take care of his VIP guests. It gave me a chance to interact closely with them. I catered to Rajesh Pilot and Ahmad Patel, personally. As they were leaving, I complimented Ahmad Patel, '*Aap iss libas me bahut haseen dikh rahe hain*! (You are looking very good in this outfit.)'

Rajesh Pilot responded, '*Yeh be-libas aur bhi zyada khoobsoorat dikhte hai!* (He looks even better without his outfit).'

'You might have, but I have not seen him so, therefore, I cannot comment,' I said, drawing laughter from Ahmad Patel, who said, 'You can't win over Manzar Saab! He has the gift of repartee! *Yeh toh Shayar-e-Azeem hain*!' To show my appreciation, I pecked his cheek, a gesture which made Rajesh Pilot exclaim sarcastically, 'Dear Lord! Please protect the Congress ladies!' again causing merriment amongst us. I said, 'I worship Devi Saraswati while you revere Devi Durga. A sadhu advised me to recite her chants daily as I was connected to the literary world. It's her blessings that have given me the gift of repartee.' Rajesh Pilot wanted to know the mantra, instantly, so I gave it to him, written behind my visiting card.

Aim Namo Bhagwati Vad Vagdevi Swaha

***

Once, I told Kesriji, that if people were going to get positions by spending money, there was definitely no scope for the likes of me! Kesriji commented, 'Once Dhyan Chand was the hockey icon, and now it's the time of Dhanraj Pillai! So, set aside the sobriety of *dhyan* (meditation) and focus on *dhan* (wealth)! Politics requires money!' Another time, we were talking about gratitude. He responded, 'There's a lot of gratitude in you, which is a very good quality, but unfortunately, it is not valued in politics. You're still catering to the old President and it may cause hurdles for you. You have to remember that when a house is being constructed, wooden posts support the roof. But once the beams are in place, the posts have to be removed.'

'But my poetry Guru would say that ungrateful people are worse than murderers! Thankless people assassinate humanity and then selfishness will become the rule of the day!'

Kesriji reiterated, saying 'Sheila Dikshit rightly called you an 'angel!' You're blessed with the qualities of a saint!' I felt quite euphoric at his words! 'I sometimes thank God for not having given me any position for that would have forced me to compromise with my values. It would have killed my soul! Compared to the accolades I am presently getting, they are much more precious than any office,' I told him.

Besides, no one can stop you from getting what you deserve and if God wants to give you something, no power on earth can come in the way. Being garrulous and interactive were the two characteristics that won me friends and also often went against me! Kesriji and Ahmad Patel had once pointed out to me that I couldn't be trusted. Even Narasimha Rao had said that I was prone to too much hobnobbing!

Ahmad Patel looked upon Kesriji as his mentor and would often visit him like I did. Sometimes, Kesriji would politely ask me to leave since they had a lot to discuss. It was Kesri who convinced Ahmad Patel to resign, when the situation was too volatile for him. His wisdom and knowledge were indeed incredible, and he never gave up learning till his last breath. He would involve me in his plans, alluring me with the thought of a secure income for the rest of my life, but he never actually got around to translating it into action, though he could have done so with just a phone call to the Ambanis.

Jitendra Prasada had been the political secretary to both Rajiv Gandhi and Narasimha Rao and was the Congress vice President, under Kesriji. One day he asked me to deliver some papers to Jitendra Prasada at his home. He wasn't there and his wife Kanta Prasada, said that I could give the papers to her. When I refused, she said, 'But I am his wife! Don't you trust me?'

I spontaneously retorted, 'Madam, I don't trust even my own wife!'

She looked at me in astonishment and then burst into laughter, inviting me in for tea. Just then, Jitendra Prasada arrived and when his wife told him about my distrust, he smilingly approved. 'He is absolutely right in not trusting anyone. After all it's a matter of commitment, which is quite lacking in the Party as it is.' She invited me to visit again when I was in the Lutyens zone and I did do so, more than once. Jitendra Prasada remained quite affectionate till his last days.

Chapter 11

Of Politicians, Brokers and *Kalals*

ONCE KESRI JI was ruminating about who could be made to stand against Sonia Gandhi and asked for my opinion. I suggested Rama Pilot.

'Why do you recommend her?' he asked.

'Babuji, our country is prone to being sentimental. Even governments have been overthrown on emotional sentiment. Currently, she will gain a lot of sympathy from the Congress delegates due to her recent loss!'

Kesriji was all admiration for my insight and told me to go and ask her if she would stand for office. But she diplomatically refused, with folded hands. But Kesriji had already asked Jitendra Prasada to stand for the election. 'Won't it be only a symbolic fight, for after all Sonia Gandhi is the wife of our most beloved leader who has obliged thousands of Congressmen including myself?' I questioned.

'Both Sharad Pawar and Rajesh Pilot had stood against me. It's all part of the process!' the wily politician replied.

Once he had elucidated about the people who could gain success easily in politics: brokers, courtesans and *kalals*, explaining the last as a person who used wine, wealth and women to push himself upwards. I said he didn't belong to any of these categories.

'No, Mahesh, I can be called a broker! I too used to take

money from one source and give it to another, as the Treasurer.' He also told me that I was not cut out for the political world as I couldn't be a party to such dealings! Once he wanted me to set up a meeting with four people with whom he wasn't on good terms, but I was. The four were Prof KK Tiwari, Dr Bhishma Narain Singh, Dev Anand Mishra and Mani Shankar Aiyar. I called the first on the list only to get an instant refusal, 'Mahesh ji, I cannot overlook the fact that he has a tendency to abuse pundits, for he has done so in my presence. He never called me when he was in power, and now he's doing so? I refuse to comply,' he said.

Next, I contacted Dr Bhishma Narain Singh and got almost the same response. He cited betrayal as the reason, saying he had always favoured him but had got no support from him. Dr Singh said that I have come to your house many times and I would come again if you invite me. Dev Anand Mishra, however, agreed to visit him readily. I was so discouraged by the refusal of the first two, that I didn't even get in touch with Mani Shankar Aiyar, for I knew he was even more vehemently against Kesriji's ideology and modus operandi than the others. Much later, when I shared this with Mani Shankar Aiyar, he regarded it as a missed opportunity to clarify things with Kesriji!

***

On 24 October, 2000 Kesriji passed away after being on the ventilator at AIIMS for a few days. I had visited him in the ICU and was agonised to find him totally alone there. After his death, I felt quite bereft, similar to the times when I had lost my father and later, Rajiv Gandhi and Kumar Pashi. His body was kept at the Congress office, but I saw only the staff preparing the body for its last journey. It hurt me deeply and I rushed forward to take over the preparations. Ahmad

Patel also joined me. Later, a senior leader from Himachal Pradesh, Vidya Stokes hugged me to show her appreciation for taking the initiative to show reverence for Kesriji. He was to be cremated at his home town of Danapur, near Patna, so arrangements had been made to fly him there. I accompanied his PA, Veer Singh on the big vehicle that was transporting him to the airport, sitting on top of it. I noticed Sonia Gandhi gesticulating, indicating towards the roof. I turned to see that as the vehicle was moving out of the office area, I could have hit my head on a low protruding rafter. Sonia's gesture, was truly endearing in that moment.

When we reached the aircraft, I helped to transfer the body on board. Akhilesh Das, who was also quite close to Kesriji, had also reached. He couldn't control himself and bursting into loud tears, turned to hug me. I too became deeply emotional, for till now, I hadn't been able to give vent to my feelings, having been so busy with the preparations. We bid a tearful farewell to a beloved leader, forlorn that an era had ended with his demise.

Chapter 12
Keeping the Faith

I WAS USUALLY in an excitable state most of the time, so Mahi suggested that I participate in a Sri Sri Ravi Shankar five-day Art of Living course. That was the first time that I got introduced to the practical aspects of *pranayama* and its calming effects. I enjoyed it so much that I decided to make it a part of my life. Their philosophy of smile, service and surrender inspired me to formulate my own prayers, somewhat echoing the Sikh philosophy of *simran* (chanting the Divine name), *sewa* (serving) and *vand chakho* (sharing food), that former Union Minister Buta Singh had once explained to me on a visit to the Bangla Sahib Gurdwara, making me feel more closely connected with the teachings. With the help of the scriptures of different religions, I was able to give my prayers a shape and subsequently got them printed and distributed to my friends and acquaintances. Mahi suggested the addition of the power of acceptance. 'Rise and shine,' was her motivational prod, egging me on to attain greater heights! I was also inspired by Osho's thought that love gives birth to prayers and she would often tell me that I had an ocean of love within me that was seeking an outlet in some form or the other!

Later, Padma Shri Hindi poet, Prof Ashok Chakradhar helped translate my prayers into Hindi.

***

The new year found me working with Mani Shankar Aiyar translating papers on Panchayati Raj. The work was exhaustive and often took us long hours. That day, we worked late into the evening at his home in Sainik Farms, so he invited me to stay for dinner and it was almost midnight by the time I left. The night was shrouded in a swirling fog and I got lost in the confusing bylanes. Perforce, I had to call up Maniji for directions. He then very patiently guided me for twenty minutes out of the labyrinthine lanes till I reached the more familiar main road! It made me marvel at his acumen and deepened my regard for him.

A few days later, I came across an article in the Speaking Tree column of the *Times of India*, by an American scientist, proving the sanctity of the Kumbh mela, held every twelve years, at each of the four riverside pilgrimage places, in turn, according to astrological combinations. The author stated that when millions of devotees bathed together with faith and reverence, they had the power to change the vibrations of the water and it was thus auspicious to have a dip at that time.

Eager to experience it for myself, I decided to visit Allahabad that year in January 2001. C K Jaffer Sharief, the Union Railway Minister in the Narasimha Rao government in 1993, had nominated me as a member of the Zonal Railway Users' Consultative committee, North Zone. So, I called Vijay Sahni, joint secretary, Ministry of Railways, for two tickets for myself and my elder son. Lakhs of devotees were heading there, yet he managed to procure tickets for that very night through a special quota. We were told that finding a place to stay in Allahabad would be tough as everything was booked. Unexpectedly, I got a call from Brigadier Mishra, Kesriji's friend, who told me that we could be guests of his daughter's in-laws who lived there. Delighted at this easy solution, I thanked him profusely, and buying some sweets and fruits for our host's family, reached Allahabad the next morning.

They received us warmly and guided us about the best routes and places to bathe. We were amazed at the sheer number of devotees from all walks of life, foreigners and Naga Sadhus included! We managed to reach the ghat and were guided to take a boat to the confluence of the three rivers for the best bathing experience. Once we were back on the boat and dressed up, I slipped into the river and had to be fished out! On that chilly February morning, I was scared that I would catch a cold, but the boatman assured me that I must have needed double blessings and that's why I ended up in the river, once again! According to him, there would be no repercussions and it proved true! Despite roaming the rest of the day, I was fine! Such were the blessings I received that I have been able to go to every Kumbh mela since.

***

After our trip to Shirdi, Mr Malhotra of the Lodhi Garden's Walkers Club had organised another visit to Vaishno Devi. I was reluctant to go there as I had experienced a disturbing incident which had haunted me for years. In 1992, my family had visited the shrine with a friend's family. It so happened that Chhaya and my friend's wife had begun to climb up quickly while we two friends lagged behind with our children. When we reached the top, much to my shock, I couldn't find Chhaya anywhere. The friend's wife, too, was unable to throw any light on what had happened to Chhaya. I searched the shrine, then took a pony down the fourteen kilometres hill track and back up again, still unable to locate her. I was constantly praying to Baba and Maa, appealing to them not to let anything untoward happen. Night was coming on fast, adding to our tension. I once again decided to go down the slope and leaving the boys in my friend's care, I began to descend, when to my utter relief, I suddenly saw her slowly ascending the hill in front of me! She responded casually that as she had felt tired while climbing, and had stopped at Ardhkuwari, half way up the slope and had fallen asleep in a corner, the reason why I had missed seeing her when I had checked earlier. The other lady had been walking very fast and had left my wife behind and so had no idea that she had stopped on the way. I was really upset at the turn of events and even more angry with the other lady and subsequently broke off relations with my friend and his family. I shared this with Mr Malhotra, but he persuaded me not to let that one incident colour the present. "It's best to remember good things and release the disturbing ones. This will be a good opportunity to create better memories." I was glad that he had persuaded me, for it became another memorable trip.

***

After Kesriji's death, I became quite lonely and missed our evenings together. We had shared a very close comradeship, the age difference of more than forty years having no relevance at all. At home, my wife would taunt me for not doing anything constructive and my sons began to think similarly. This would force me to remain away for long periods and gave me the chance to get more involved in religious activities. Oscar Fernandes and his wife, Blossom would invite me to go to church with them on Sundays while I accompanied Buta Singh to the Gurdwara sometimes. Makhmoor Sayeedi encouraged me to occasionally visit Nizamuddin Aulia's tomb, saying that I lived so close and should visit it. I began to realise that every religious place was endowed with powerful vibrations. I would also be part of the procession carrying Sai Baba's *palki* and would find tears flowing freely whenever I got a chance to shoulder it. Noticing my emotional connect, one of the senior devotees suggested that I should serve Baba by offering a dress for his statue before the *aarti* and contribute towards community meals.

***

Boredom was, however, settling into my life as there was not much activity, either social or commercial. It, therefore, seemed just the right time to invest and sell property, which I began doing with the help of a friend, Rajesh Mehta, who was in the property line in Gurgaon. I bought my first plot of sixty square yards for Rs 5 lakh, selling it for Rs 6 lakh within two months. I had FDs of Rs 30 lakh which I now gradually invested in this business, moving from sixty to 150 sq yd plots. I also got into the construction line. I had gained possession of my town house property and was getting regular rent, along with the rent from the shop, so I was financially secure. I had another property in Rohini, so that made me the owner of three residences.

About this time, I seemed to be getting distanced from the political scenario. I mentioned this to a friend, who suggested that I visit the Khatu Shyam temple in Rajasthan to remove all blockages from my life's path. He narrated the story behind the temple, telling me that it had been built to revere Barbarik, son of Ghatotkacha and grandson of the Pandava, Bhima. Barbarik had been invited by the Kauravas to join them, but Krishna didn't want him to do so. He intercepted Barbarik and challenged him to pierce all the leaves of every tree on earth with a single arrow. Krishna hid one leaf under his foot but Barbarik's arrow discovered that and pierced it as well. Krishna appreciated his divine powers in achieving the impossible. Barbarik had said humbly, 'All this is due to your Divine Grace!' Krishna asked for his head in return for blessing him with such powers. Barbarik instantly complied and it is this shorn head that was placed by Krishna himself on the hill at Khatu, for Barbarik had asked to be able to watch the war happening. Krishna declared that Barbarik would now be known as Shyam Baba, and blessed the place, which later became known as the Khatu Shyam Baba temple. It is said that the wishes of devotees who visit this temple get fulfilled. The story fascinated me and I willingly went with my friends to visit the shrine.

Chapter 13

The Politics of Relationships

IN AUGUST 2000, Sonia Gandhi was blessed with a grandchild and all the senior leaders went to wish her. Armed with flowers and a well-thought out one liner, I also joined the queue of well-wishers. When it was my turn, I smilingly presented my bouquet. 'My heartiest congratulations, Madam! You have become the most gracious grandmother on this Planet Earth for us!' Despite her self-control, an expression of amusement crossed her face at my flowery compliment, and she inclined her head to acknowledge its uniqueness.

Earlier in the year, objections had been raised by the opposition that Sonia Gandhi had become an MP from Rai Bareli, while holding an office of profit, and hence this was not legally acceptable. Before taking on the office of an MP, candidates must resign from any such profitable position and as Sonia Gandhi had not done so, her election was nullified and she resigned from her post as MP. All leaders once again congratulated her on this sacrificial step, and I did, too. There, too, I had gained her attention by my lively remark: 'Madam, till now you were Indira Gandhi's daughter-in-law, now you have become the daughter of Mahatma Gandhi!'

***

A couple of days after my return from the Khatu Shyam temple, I got the delightful news that Mani Shankar Aiyar had been appointed chairman of the Political Training Department by Sonia Gandhi. I was happy that I would now get more chances of working with him as I enjoyed doing that, even more than with Sheila Dikshit, for with him, I got to learn much more. He was my political Guru, as he was not only very knowledgeable but also an intellectual with immense charisma. He was three years senior to Rajiv Gandhi at Cambridge University and that's how they had met again after their years together at Doon School. Mani Shankar Aiyar was an erudite scholar and won many debates in the university. Once Rajiv Gandhi had even campaigned for him, when he was running for a Presidential contest at Cambridge University. It was a play of Destiny that several decades later, Mani Shankar Aiyar was the one campaigning for Rajivji! After Rajiv's demise, Mani Shankar Aiyar had compiled his thoughts about him in a book, *Remembering Rajiv*, a deeply emotional eulogy which brought tears to my eyes as I read it. I happened to discuss it with George one day, praising the strong portrayal of Rajiv Gandhi's life and work. George must have mentioned this to Sonia Gandhi, for the next day, he called to ask if I could obtain a copy for her as she had misplaced her own. I promptly handed him my copy to be given to Sonia Gandhi.

Mani Shankar Aiyar nominated me as a national coordinator along with Dev Anand Balodhi, who also did translation work for Maniji occasionally. Maniji held his first political training camp in Patiala under the aegis of the Punjab Pradesh Congress Committee. The elegant MP Preneet Kaur, wife of Capt Amarinder Singh, and ex-MP, Sant Ram Singla were deputed by Punjab Congress to be in charge of the Camp. Senior Congress leaders and former Union Cabinet ministers addressed delegates from all over India.

It was Maniji's magnanimity that he let me share the stage and even asked me to speak. The Camp was a great success. I happened to meet a very beautiful and young delegate from Chandigarh and got very friendly with her, much to Maniji's amusement who humorously accused me of grabbing the best for myself! The next training camp on Industries and Labour was at Raipur after about two months. In both camps, we had the best of living and eating arrangements. Buta Singh was also a part of the delegation and in Raipur, took me to visit a well-known Gurdwara. The Chief Minister, Ajit Jogi, whom I knew well, invited Maniji's core group to his house for dinner. I remarked that there were only three relevant posts in the country: 'DM, in charge of Districts, CM of state and PM of the whole country. You were the DM earlier and now are the CM. Who knows, next you might be in line for the PM!' Everyone burst into laughter, with Jogi saying he was happy to be CM.

V C Shukla who lived in Raipur also invited me for lunch to his farmhouse, a beautiful heritage home. He also drove me around his farm in a jeep.

The memorable meeting gave me a chance to thank him for having introduced me to Shefali Singh.

***

The love and importance that I was receiving from Maniji was really amazing, making me feel heartfelt gratitude to the Divine for answering my prayers of being suitably occupied. I decided to express my love and gratitude by organising a felicitation for him. I called V C Shukla and asked him if he would grace the occasion and bless Maniji. To my great joy, he readily accepted and I began to prepare for the occasion on 12 September 2001. I also invited Bhishma Narain Singh, and other senior leaders, besides IAS, IPS, and IFS officers,

Justice A N Grover, Chief Commissioner of Income Tax, J C Mendiratta, former Chief Minister of Haryana, B D Gupta, and some Hindi-Urdu-English nationally known poets and scholars, including stalwarts like Dr Namvar Singh and Kamleshwar, along with some of my gorgeous lady friends and dignified neighbours. Mani Shankar Aiyar was accompanied by his wife, Suneet Aiyar, looking dignified in a beautiful saree. He was presented with innumerable bouquets and wishes and the evening took on a more rapturous note when I recited my popular, congratulatory ghazal.

> *Aaj ka din ye aaj ki shaam tumhare naam*
> *Pyar mohabbat ka paigham tumhare naam*

I requested V C Shukla to drape a shawl to felicitate Maniji along with Bhishma Narain Singh, handing either ends of the shawl to both. Cheers went up as both together honoured Maniji, who was so overwhelmed that he bent down to touch the feet of the two senior leaders. A moment later, the cameraman who was clicking pictures, informed me that due to a technical lapse, he had missed the momentous scene.

Maniji obligingly bent down once again to allow the picture to be clicked, an unexpected and endearing move on his part! The evening was an unprecedented success and when everyone had left, V C Shukla praised me in front of my family, much to their discomfiture.

'I am surprised that you have not achieved a higher stature! You surely deserve it,' were his very encouraging words to me.

'Babuji, your saying this is a tremendous honour! Is that less than any high post? There can be no greater commendation for me!'

The next morning, V C Shukla called me again, 'Maheshji, you're undeniably a magician!' Bhishma Narain Singh also called to say, 'I am absolutely sure that never must have Maniji ever touched anyone's feet in this manner, that too twice! And yet some people call him arrogant!'

I responded, 'He's absolutely not arrogant. People don't know the exact connotation of the word.'

***

My friendship with Shefali Singh, a former Princess of a *riyasat* in Rajasthan, had become quite strong. She was a Rajput, well-built and quite sensual, and we would have truly mutually fulfilling love sessions. She used to call me Shiv Ardhnarishwar as I was contrary to her figure. Maybe it was my built, but I have always had a special liking for tall women. One senior Congress leader, was 5' 10', yet she liked me despite the difference in our heights. Shefali too found me attractive and once told me, 'If you had been single, I would have stayed with you on an Osho model!' We didn't ever have even a minor argument and she never threw tantrums. She would reciprocate my mild gestures and also my elevated thoughts, words and deeds. She scored high in all my four criteria of *vesh, vani, vichar* and *vyawahar*. She had visited my home a couple of times and was well-acquainted with my family. Once she invited all of us for dinner at her place in Jor Bagh. My sister and her daughters were visiting me, so I asked Shefali if we could bring them along. All of us had a great time, as she was a very gracious host and even gave us thoughtful and relevant gifts when we left, including to my sister and her daughters.

On our way back home, my sister commented, 'Kaku, I never knew there were such cultured ladies in your Congress party!' I responded a little proudly, 'But of course! Congress is still the oldest and best party in our country.' Even Chhaya was overwhelmed to receive a precious wristwatch and a royal bedcover, which she treasures to this day.

When I look back, I find the fact quite disturbing that I never gifted anything of value to any of my intimate lady friends while they were truly magnanimous. I felt what mattered most was to care and share each other's happiness and sadness and to stand with each other in times of need.

Earlier, women were more altruistic and less demanding in monetary terms, feeling fulfilled by the love, respect and importance being given to them. I could very comfortably discuss my life with them and they, too, would do the same. I would often play the victim card to garner a more sympathetic and loving reaction from them. Whenever I looked at the way my life was going, I would recall Kumar Pashi's words 'Maheshji, if a man or a woman is able to find a truly loving partner, Heaven could be made on earth itself!' I loved to share this thought with my lady friends. One thing that stands out in my relationships with all my intimate lady friends is that none of them were liars, greedy, selfish, cunning, or arrogant—qualities that, I believe, developed in women after the advent of smartphones and social media. My friends were transparent and loyal.

It was only in 2005 that one of them pointed out to me that she had noticed that I was totally bereft of any gifting etiquette.

Chapter 14

Merchant of Love

WHEN I BOUGHT my plot in DLF, I noticed that a Sai temple was being built opposite it. I gave a contribution of Rs 5,000 for an idol and subsequently, it was completed into a beautiful temple. I had invested about Rs 25 lakh in my real estate business and gained a profit of Rs 5 lakh in a year. I was sure that it was with Divine blessings that my Rs 5,000 converted to Rs 5 lakh. When I visited the newly constructed temple, I prayed, 'Baba, you promised to match ten steps to my one but you have actually matched hundred! I bow in gratitude for your blessings.'

At about this time, on my friend's advice, I sold my town house, making a good profit on the deal. The property market was booming at that time. I met an architect who proposed that selling after constructing would be even more profitable and so, I ventured into the construction field. However, within a year, I realised the architect had ganged up with my friend and were profiteering at my expense! I withdrew from the construction venture, immediately. My family were upset because I would call dealers and clients at home for sale or purchase deals. I found it more convenient that they come home to receive or hand over cash. Besides, I had set up a picture gallery in my home with pictures of myself with many dignitaries including PMs and Presidents of India! Visitors would be intimidated at my connections and it gave me confidence that they wouldn't do any double dealings with me. But the dealers were a rough and tough lot, and I had to cater to them by serving drinks and non-vegetarian snacks. Moreover, Chhaya was allergic to smoke. At times, she would be irritated with my constant presence at home with my business associates. She would then say, 'Stop meandering around me like Rahu-Ketu!'

Matters came to such a head that to keep the peace at home, I was forced to rent a one-room set in the government flats on Lodhi Road to use as an office. I invited Mahi to come and inaugurate the place as my office, which she did on 16 August 2001. This was the first time we had been alone together and though I wanted to be intimate, I somehow felt intimidated by her magnetic persona. I was in awe of her intellectual aura and wisdom ever since I had met her at Sai temple and felt good about my association with her as we could converse about many topics, including literature. She was proving to be a very good friend, philosopher and guide in all spheres of my life and I didn't want to annoy her. A while later, as I went downstairs to see her off, she seemed amused at my nervous dilemma making me feel a trifle embarrassed!

A few days later, I realised the office wasn't viable and gave it up within three months.

***

I bonded well with Bhishma Narain Singh, former Union minister and governor who was connected to a number of cultural societies of different countries in some capacity or the other. He would often take me to various cultural shows at embassies. Once we visited the French Embassy on French National Day, where the ambassador and his wife were welcoming the guests. While greeting us, the ambassador's wife touched her cheek to mine and it electrified me, for I had never experienced such a feeling before! A memory suddenly surfaced as I recalled Nehru writing in his autobiography, 'In jail everything was available except the soft touch of a woman!' The thought came to me that he must have talked about such a contact, for it was even more intense than a kiss! It was at that same get together that I met Nirupama Kaur, an aristocratic poet and English writer, and we instantly clicked with each other.

***

Subconsciously, I was always on the lookout for a good companion, for though my links with some of my lady friends were pretty convivial, I yearned for regular companionship. She invited me to her mother's place in Defence Colony for lunch a few days later. I was astonished to find that her mother was Prabhjot Kaur, a senior Punjabi writer. We had met earlier at a literary event and after recognising me, welcomed me warmly. I also met her sister, Anupama and her husband, Lt Gen J J Singh, over a very delightful lunch. I addressed him as General, much to his amusement! It was a diplomatic ploy of mine, for I often used to address those in the Services with a rank higher than what they were. He did get his promotion a few years later and became the Chief of Army Staff.

***

People were curious to know about my sources of income, for I was always seen socialising without doing any tangible work. I had a reputation of being bold and daring, ready to participate in all activities. An aunt had even expressed suspicion that I must be involved in some nefarious activity. Once I was visiting Hema and her father, when her daughter asked me, 'Uncle, what do you do?'

With a serious look, I answered, '*Mohabbat* (love)!' much to everyone's amusement.

'And other than that?' Hema's father questioned.
'*Ibaadat* (worship)!'
'That's very good, but what else?'
'*Siyaasat* (politics)'

It only drew loud exclamations of mirth and he again demanded to know how I earned my livelihood. So, I said, '*Tijarat* (business)' explaining that I had rental income and traded in real estate.

***

One day, rather unexpectedly, a highly agitated Prof Ujjwala Sharma, daughter of Dr Sher Singh, a former Union Minister, called me. She had married N D Tiwari, who had served as CM of UP, thrice. Her mistake was that she had left her husband and moved in with N D Tiwari, without adhering to any societal or legal norms. She was so in love with him that she wanted to bear his child and let the world know of their relationship. Her husband and son had compromised with the situation earlier, as they too benefitted from the liaison, but when things became blatant, they felt impelled to take a stand. It led to some serious repercussions for N D Tiwari, as he had to step back from the chief minister's post.

Ujjwala Sharma was known to me and my family and even had my wife's sympathy in her current situation. When she called me, I felt a rage rising within me and I immediately drove off to confront N D Tiwari at his home in Tilak Lane, next to Maniji's house. I demanded belligerently, 'Babuji, why are you invoking the curse of a Devi?'

Calmly, he responded, '*Kavi Mahodaya*, which Devi?'

'Prof Ujjwala Sharma. She has been crying so desperately while talking to me. Please forgive me, but I felt compelled to accost you.'

'Oh, let it be! Along with curses from one Devi, I am

receiving the blessings of a hundred more! Calm down and have some refreshments,' he said, calmly to me.

His attitude doused my anger instantly, and I apologised for my audacity. His words clicked in my subconscious mind as I connected them to my own life where I was receiving the curses of the woman of my house, yet gaining blessings from ten other wonderful women! That encounter also showed N D Tiwari's calming thoughts in the face of my impudence, giving credence to Osho's thought that humanity was higher than morality. Later, the matter was taken to court, where a DNA test proved his parentage and he subsequently accepted mother and child into his life some fourteen years later. However, when things are forced, they rarely have a happy ending. The son suffered the most, going into depression and later meeting a tragic end.

The affair had been going on since the times of Indira Gandhi and Ujjwala had appealed to several senior leaders, but none had wanted to get entangled in the mess.

Later, she expressed her gratitude to me for standing up for her when no one else had done!

I narrated the incident to Balram Jakhar and Kesriji. Both looked at me in wonderment, with Balram Jakhar going to the extent of saying that had you done something like this with me, the Lord only knows what would have happened! He added, 'Mahesh, you advice Kesriji so often, yet you don't follow your own advice!' Kesriji also censured me, 'I would definitely have banned your entry into my house if you had done something like this to me!'

I was trying to justify their outburst and remembered my father's words that one should think deeply before speaking, twice before putting anything into writing and three times before taking any action.

'Yes, and four times before getting any work done,' Kesriji had once added jocularly.

'And five times before getting anyone murdered !' was my spontaneous response!

Naseeb Pathan and Akhilesh Das Gupta, two senior politicians from UP were present at that time and found our exchange hilarious, later telling others that such was the closeness between Kesriji and the poet that the latter would boldly disregard their age difference of more than forty years to justify his views! It became quite a standing joke in the party, making Vasant Sathe, once interrupt my effort to prove something by insisting that he was not Kesri!

Chapter 15

Admissions Saga

AS MY ELDER son had so easily got admission in Hindu College, thanks to the kind offices of the Principal, Dr Kavita Sharma, he didn't value his luck and eventually became careless with his studies, so naturally, he didn't score well. Kavita Sharma once asked me about his absence in college, thus making me aware of the situation. When I confronted him, he said that commuting 18 km to attend some boring classes didn't make sense! Chhaya supported his stance, saying that he was studying at home. Since the time she had left home after my Orissa trip, and then returned, she had been manipulating the boys so that they would take her side. I was shocked by my son's indifferent attitude, realising belatedly that things shouldn't be made easy for children too early. When he had topped in the tenth standard, I had allowed him to drive and had even got him his own car. The lack of routine at home, where I was not working in a regular job, impacts children and must have contributed towards his lackadaisical mindset.

About this time, Chhaya's brother was elected the President of the All-India Institute of Chartered Accountants. I had some thought of encouraging my elder son to become a CA and expected my brother-in-law to help. He was to hold a party at Taj Man Singh after taking the oath and wanted to invite senior leaders and so, I took him to Mani Shankar

Aiyar, CM Sheila Dikshit, and even to George's office. All congratulated him, assuring him of their presence, but other than Bhishma Narain Singh, none of them turned up. During the evening, I spotted Ghulam Nabi Azad dining in the hotel's restaurant along with his wife and friends. I requested him to grace my brother-in-law's celebratory party for a few minutes, apologising for intruding into his family dinner. He affably accepted and accompanied me to my brother-in-law's event where his sudden appearance created an instant furore.

But despite such favours, my brother-in-law didn't think of lending a supporting hand to my son. I approached another senior CA friend of mine, Manchanda, who lived in East Nizamuddin, and asked him to allow my son to do an articleship under him. That's another story that my son didn't do much justice to the opportunity, attending office, only erratically. I then requested Mansoor Elahi, another CA to take my son on. He, too, agreed, but unfortunately, my son was not very dedicated towards his work, making Mansoor Elahi say that his heart was not in his work and he should not be forced to follow this career.

I now persuaded my son to take the CAT exam, but his scores were also not up to the mark. I, therefore, requested Kesriji first and then Maniji to intervene on my behalf with Kamal Nath, who owned the prestigious Institute of Management and Technology, Ghaziabad. I knew Kamal Nath, too, but due to some misunderstanding between his PA and me, he had stopped being friendly. But now, I needed admission for my son.

My habit of instantly retaliating had already cost me quite a few good friends. Kamal Nath belonged to an upcoming generation of politicians, and I preferred to associate with the senior leaders. That's why I had to appeal to Kesriji to intervene. However, he wasn't very enthusiastic about it, and so I appealed to Maniji, but he, too, was reluctant.

I decided to meet Kamal Nath directly, and said to him, 'Bhaisaheb, I haven't had a chance to serve you in any way so I am in no position to be asking you a favour. But I need your magnanimity now!' He didn't deny my request outright, but didn't accept, either. I then requested V George, but he had also sent in a request for Prof K K Tiwari's son along with mine. Prof Tiwari's son was given admission easily, while my son's admission was kept on hold. Karan was asked to give an admission test at the Institute. After a lot of delay and drama, I was finally told that admission was not possible. Meanwhile, I had been in touch with Anil Shastri, the chairman of the Lal Bahadur Shastri Institute of Management in Delhi. But there too matters couldn't come to any conclusion. Eventually, I appealed to Bhishma Narain Singh for help and he was able to get Karan admission in the Fore School of Management, Delhi, as the Director there was his friend.

My younger son also cleared his twelfth that year and he didn't score well, either. I happened to mention my dilemma to a close friend, Shagufta, and she immediately offered a solution. 'Manzar Saab, do not worry. I know the principal of Bhagat Singh College well, Prof Siddiqui. I am sure he will be able to help you.' Such was her affection for me and my family that she called up the principal and took us to meet him at his residence in Nizamuddin East. Thus, the tension of his further studies was sorted easily and he began his graduate studies in the evening college.

The next year, I happened to meet the principal of the morning college, Dr J Kaur, and invited her for my book launch. She was impressed by the grandness of it and I was able to persuade her to allow Lakhan to shift to morning college.

Lakhan was, however, two steps ahead of his brother in wanting to impress his friends and so wanted to drive my Ford Ikon. He was only eighteen years at that time! Karan had already taken over the Maruti car and only the old Fiat was left for me, that too without an AC. We would often have arguments about this with my elder son, Karan, supporting me that I should have the Ford Ikon. And so, one day, my younger son left the house and did not return for almost twenty days! This time, I remained calm and detached, sure that once he experienced the hardships of life, he would return. Chhaya too, was equally detached and didn't push me to look for him. Later, I learned that he was staying in Gurgaon with a group of boys, including some Afghanis. We didn't have any contact with him, but one day got to know that he had tried to sell imported books to his aunt. There was a trend then of going door-to-door to sell expensive books for a commission. Almost twenty days later, I got a phone call from him and an apology, 'Papa, I am sorry.'

He asked hesitantly, 'Can I come back home?'

'Okay, but you have to behave yourself. If you don't want to listen to us, continue to stay where you are.' I was strict and a rather crestfallen Lakhan returned home. One of the first things he did after returning, was to get his head shaved, much to our amusement. We could only guess that it was his way of showing repentance!

It was a real anomaly in my life that even as my prestige was rising in the world outside, the situation at home was deteriorating. I felt I was getting no support or respect at home despite all the efforts I put in for my family.

Chapter 16

Manzar Dar Manzar Takes Shape

MAKHMOOR SAYEEDI HAD become the secretary of the Urdu Academy and as he was very fond of my poems, he wanted me to submit them for an award. An independent committee selected the best Contemporary Modern Urdu Poetry and to my great joy, my work was approved and I got an award of Rs 7,500 for their publication. Some whispered that it was due to the fact that Sheila Dikshit was in power and must have endorsed my work, but I hadn't even told her about it. The recognition really boosted my confidence, more so when Hindi poets such as Ramesh Gaur and Ramavtar Tyagi encouraged me to submit to the Hindi Academy as well, as I was, first and foremost, a Hindi poet. I did so and miraculously, I won an award from the Hindi Academy, too, receiving another similar amount! My mentors told me that it has happened for the first time in Delhi. They were delighted and pushed me to get a collection of my work published, especially as the awards I had won were enough to cover the cost of publication. The double honour had heightened my stature, for no one had been awarded simultaneously by both Academies.

Professor Gopi Chand Narang, President of the Sahitya Akademi, directed me to Amar Nath Verma, chairman of Star Publications, and with his reference, he was very happy to publish my book in both Urdu and Hindi. He suggested that since I was very particular, I should freeze on the cover with their designer, Imroz. I had heard about him, and about his association with Amrita Pritam, an internationally renowned poet and acclaimed writer. Their love for each other was phenomenal and they had been living together for the past fifty years, after she separated from her husband. She was a good thirty-four years older than me and was not in good health, but Imroz was taking wonderful care of her. My book gave me an opportunity to connect with them. Imroz wanted to go through the book before suggesting what should go on the cover and both he and Amrita Pritam were quite appreciative of my poems, and a close bond formed between the three of us. During one of my visits, I asked her why she had not dropped the 'Pritam' as it was her first husband's name. Theirs had been a loveless marriage. She responded that it had got set as her pen name; besides, Imroz was not the possessive kind. She even described the love she had felt for Sahir Ludhianvi as 'an illusion,' compared to the love she felt for Imroz, which was 'divine,' for it was spiritual. It made her feel fulfilled, bringing stability into her life.

'When Imroz came into my life, it was as if my agonised search for myself and for the Divine came to an end.' I suddenly realised that this was the actual definition of love for it represented the *Sat, Chit,* and *Anand* aspect of the Divine and when this is experienced in an earthly union, it brings bliss into life. Sat represents the eternal truth; chit is our consciousness, while anand translates into bliss. Amrita Pritam was delighted with my interpretation, agreeing that it was indeed the essence of life.

The next part of the publication process was deciding on the title of the book and I told Amar Nath Verma that I wanted to name the book I published, *Manzarnama*. For years, I had been wanting to bring out a book of my ghazals and had even requested Rajiv Gandhi to release it way back in January 1991. I had said to him, 'As not much protocol is needed now, I would humbly request you to release my book once it is published.' It was a thoughtless thing to say as it pinpointed his not being in power any more, but he smiled as usual at my impudence. But his unfortunate martyrdom had pushed all thoughts of a book out of my mind and only around 2000, Prof Gopi Chand Narang and Geeta Chandran put the thought of publishing a book back into my mind.

It had so happened that some time after Rajiv Gandhi's demise, another poet, Amir Qazalbash, who knew of my desire to use Manzarnama, said to me, 'If you're not bringing out your book, I will use this title'. And he went ahead, much to my shock. I castigated him for this unscrupulous act. Besides, he once plagiarised a line of my sher. He had asked me to 'gift' my line to him, as it fascinated him so much:

> *Woh mere rubaru hoker na kuchh meri khabar dega*
> *Mujhe pahchanane se aaina inqar ker dega*

I refused and others too berated him for trying to take someone's thoughts in this way. He himself was a renowned poet, having even given the lyrics in a few Raj Kapoor films. Later, he rewrote the thought in his own words, an acceptable practice. After all, no one can claim monopoly on thoughts!

> *Tere chehre pe kisi aur ki soorat hogi*
> *Aaina dekhne wale tujhe hairat hogi*

After a few days, at one of our regular literary meetings, Makhmoor Sayeedi informed me that even Shaharyar had written a similar idea!

> *Kya koi nayi baat nazar aati hai mujhme*
> *Aainaa mujhe dekh ke hairaan sa kyun hai*

So now, I was at a loss and asked for a couple of days to think about the title. During the night, an inspiring title flashed through my mind, *Manzar Dar Manzar* which seemed appropriate. In the morning, Prof Narang readily endorsed it, saying that it was even better than the original. The award comfortably covered the cost and Amar Nath Verma gave me the option of either taking copies of the book or royalty. I chose to take 750 copies of the book, instead, some in Hindi, and others in Urdu.

In 1982, Kumar Pashi had introduced me to a senior journalist of *Navbharat Times*, Ramesh Gaur, and over the years, we had become good friends. I would often even present Ramesh with a bottle of liquor as he was in the habit of drinking and once had even sold his blood to buy it! When my father passed away in 1983, he had even put the news of my loss on Page 3 of the *Navbharat Times!*

Uma Sharma had once danced on my ghazals in 1985, and now Geetanjali Lal, a kathak professor at the Kathak Kendra at Mandi House, had expressed her desire to dance on my shers. I also happened to meet Geeta Chandran just when my book had gone for print. She had always encouraged me to get my poetry published. She immediately offered to dance to my ghazals. I was delighted that Geeta would perform Bharatnatyam. I asked her if she could be part of a fusion performance as Kathak was performed in royal durbars, while Bharatnatyam was danced in temples. There was an allurement in the former, but a spiritual reverence in the latter, and Geeta, surprised that I was aware of this fusion form, enthusiastically agreed.

I invited Geeta home along with her husband, Rajan Chandran, a senior officer with the UNO. Shyam Banerjee came along, too. He was ready to compose the music for the ghazals. His younger brother, Sudip Banerjee, a renowned ghazal singer and a disciple of the late Jagjit Singh, would also join in from Mumbai to sing them. I asked for their charges, but Rajan smilingly said that their names on the invitation card would suffice! We decided on the venue—Stein Auditorium at the India Habitat Centre and fixed the date, 20 January 2002, a Sunday. I like to numerologically and astrologically align important events in my life, and the date was perfect. Rajan designed a beautiful invitation card and I felt blessed at the way everything was falling smoothly into place.

The next fifty-five days passed in a whirl. Veer Singh, Kesriji's personal assistant, proved to be a real support. After Kesriji's demise, he would often visit me, for we had known each other for more than twenty years. He was working for Parliament, earning an average salary, and I had asked him to work for me. He took over the task of payment of utility bills and generally putting things in order and maintaining my files, as I was always lagging behind on such tasks. I didn't have any staff and neither did my family support me in any way. He would come regularly every Sunday and had helped me organise Mani Shankar Aiyar's felicitation as well.

Another friend, Pradeep Sethi, who worked in Post and Telegraphs and was associated with O P Malhotra, also wanted to help as he enjoyed my company. I thus acquired two very good associates, easing my life a lot.

Once, in a passionate mood, I asked Mahi, 'Do you acknowledge my feelings for you?' Much to my pleasure, she replied in the affirmative.

'Do you accept my feelings?'

'Yes.'

'Do you appreciate them?'

'Yes.'

'Then will you reciprocate them as well?' was my next million-dollar question.

'Thirty per cent.'

I felt a bit abashed, but she laughingly refused to go beyond that. I shared her rating with a few friends! One even said 'You are only 30 per cent and she has very correctly analysed you! After all, you are all words and no action.' Another said, 'Only thirty out of hundred? You have failed!' It became the butt of many jokes, but I was happy that, at least, she was ready to reciprocate even that much, for she was really gracious. It was only much later that a retired senior IAS officer, Vasudha Kumar commented, 'She could easily have denied your other criteria, but she is ready to acknowledge, accept and even appreciate you! What else do you want?' Another friend, Sharmila said, 'No one can reciprocate your kind of passion, Mahesh ji; her thirty per cent is a bonus for you!' Besides, I believed in Osho's thought that there's always a 'yay' hidden in a woman's 'nay', and that made me always hopeful.

***

A positive development in my life around this time was that Divya, my elder sister Simran's daughter, who lived in Ajmer, came to stay with us. Divya had just completed her MBA and my sister sought my help in helping her settle in Delhi. She brought fresh energy into our house, neutralising the volatile atmosphere that prevailed there. She would ask after me, offer to fetch things, generally making me feel wanted, unlike the others in the house. Within a year though, a Professor living near my brother's house in the Civil Lines area, thought she was perfect for marriage to his son in the US, as she was both very pretty and capable.

Chapter 17

Politics Without Patriotism

AFTER KESRIJI'S DEMISE, I began visiting Narasimha Rao. I loved to interact with octogenarians, for they are mines of knowledge and wisdom and Narasimha Rao was an intellectual. Some say that he was the most learned PM India had ever had, besides Jawaharlal Nehru. He was, however, a man of few words and mostly I would be doing the talking. He would enjoy my whimsical observations, but rarely added to them.

Once I remarked, 'Babuji, this Sonia Gandhi is running the Party as if she was Akbar the Great!' He laughed at this comparison, and asked 'How?'

'Akbar had nine *Navratnas* in his court and she too has nine gems around her. Please check me if I am wrong. The first three are Vincent George, Ahmed Patel and Oscar Fernandes.'

He nodded his assent.

'The next three are Arjun Singh, Dr Manmohan Singh and Natwar Singh.'

'Then there is Sheila Dikshit, Digvijay Singh and Ashok Gehlot!'

He chuckled at my list in agreement with my definition of the nine gems! 'Babuji, I know all the nine gems, and they too are well-acquainted with me. Why is it that I am still unable to gain a foothold in the Party?'

'You must know that Sonia Gandhi is very reserved and dislikes garrulous people. It often comes across as if you are challenging the other's authority with your enthusiastic comments,' he replied.

I had expressed something similar to Balram Jakhar, the former Lok Sabha Speaker.

Ai shama tujh pe bhari hai ye raat jis tarah
Maine tamam umra guzari hai iss tarah

(As the night overwhelms you, o tiny flame
I too passed my entire life, similarly engulfed)

Another time, at Vasant Sathe's residence, when someone commented that we should put in more effort for the Party, I couldn't stop myself from remarking why we must do so, when there was not much motivation to do anything. The state of the Party was nothing like the pre-Partition times when it was formulated. At that time, people had joined with a zeal to serve the country, but now they were doing so only to gain power. Politics had been reduced to a profession and an industry, devoid of commitment and patriotism.

Maybe Mahatma Gandhi had a premonition of what Congress could be reduced to. That's why he had suggested dissolving it after Independence! Those of the old school who were willing to work, such as myself, were not valued anymore; middlemen, and wheelers-dealers seemed to have taken over. I expressed my angst through a well-known couplet.

Parwana hun shamma toh ho raat toh ho
Marne ke liye taiyar hun koi baat toh ho

(Ardent moth that I am, where's the flame, where's the night?
Enthusiastic am I to die, but where's the cause?)

A few years later, I shared the nine-gems conversation with Mani Shankar Aiyar, who found the comparison, amusingly appropriate. Mani Shankar Aiyar was quite the opposite of Narasimha Rao. After he was appointed chairman of the Political Training Department of the AICC, he was interviewed by a *TOI* journalist, who described him as a diplomat, and 'sometimes a little ebullient.'

'Yes, I love the sound of my own voice!' Mani had replied, a response that amused and impressed her so much that it was used as the title of the article the next day!

I was in the room during this interview and his comment aptly described me as well. I, too, was in love with my own voice! Once I had attended Bapu Asaram's congregation at Jawaharlal Nehru stadium, with a one lakh-plus audience. He was a popular spiritual leader with discourses on television, and attracted top leaders. Chhaya and I pushed through all barriers and reached the dais where Bapu Asaram was seated. I greeted him enthusiastically, adding in a rush, 'I am a devotee of yours, Bapu. You have revolutionised the spreading of Dharma by using media.' He listened to me in astonishment and then beckoning me close, said, 'Do you know you are draining yourself unnecessarily?' I was a bit fazed, but soon recovered, for my yen of being close to power had been fulfilled in my interaction with him! I am so fascinated by authority that I want to get close to anyone who represents it. That's why I always push myself to the forefront to be in their vicinity, making my presence felt.

My over-enthusiasm sometimes becomes an obstacle in my life for it's not always right to push oneself forward. It's essential for a person to have patience and tolerance and I have failed on both counts. One even needs to have control in front of the family, never going overboard to justify oneself. Bapu Asaram's words left a deep imprint on my mind and I tried thereafter to curb my exuberance.

On New Year, my neighbour Arvind Sharma invited me for dinner to meet his cousin, Deepti Naval, the actress, and her husband Vinod Pandit, as she was passionate about poetry. Dressing nattily, I took along a New Year diary and pen as a gift for her, which I presented to her with a flourish, 'Deeptiji, a humble gift from a humble poet to a popular poet-actress of India!' She laughed and said, 'Manzar Saab, you seem to be a *peshewar aashiq* (professional wooer)!' Everyone burst out laughing.

***

The addition of a Labrador pup, Cheekoo, to our household brought liveliness into our lives. He was a very frisky pup, energetically scampering around, and neighbours observed that he possessed my effervescent genes, especially as he was more friendly with women! His antics would bring us together and he brought love into our lives, even though we couldn't connect with one another, otherwise. Chhaya would feed him with her own hands or he wouldn't eat. He would recognise the sound of our cars and would tumble out of the house to demand a ride, which we had to fulfil. For eight years, he filled our hearts with a lot of love, then left us heartbroken, after a sudden illness. We buried him in a nearby ground and the sorrow was so deep that we didn't feel like keeping another pet after him.

***

During the Vajpayee government, the Ketan Parekh stock scam came to the forefront, in which his adopted daughter's husband, Ranjan Bhattacharya was allegedly involved. The Opposition demanded an enquiry and a Joint Parliamentary Committee, comprising of a number of senior leaders from all

Parties, including Mani Shankar Aiyar and Kapil Sibal, was set up. Maniji took a deep interest in the proceedings and wrote a number of powerful articles that I translated. It was a challenging task requiring many discussions. If I happened to suggest a word that he found appropriate, he would appreciate it wholeheartedly.

Once he sent me with an article I had translated to Mrinal Pandey, the editor of the Hindi edition of *Hindustan Times*, whom I hadn't had a chance to meet before. When I reached her office, she not only invited me into her office directly but also approved my article without any changes!

While conversing with George, I mentioned that people unnecessarily categorised MSA as being arrogant when he wasn't like that at all. George recalled that Rajiv Gandhi would call him up to ask how much minimum time he would take to reach him and then would jovially ask him if he could come ten minutes earlier! On the contrary, MSA used to ask me to take my time.

I shared this anecdote with MSA, appreciating his benign nature. I was lucky that both my mentors, Sheila Dikshit and now Mani Shankar Aiyar, were loving taskmasters, inspiring and motivating me to give my best!

Chapter 18

Ek Shaam Mahesh Manzar Ke Naam

2002 DAWNED, BRINGING with it, the rewards of all the good deeds that I had ever done, in the form of wholehearted support for my cherished project, my poetry book! Imroz presented me with a beautiful painting to start off the year. I asked Prof Gopi Chand Narang, President of the Sahitya Akademi to write a foreword for the book. Makhmoor Sayeedi wrote an emotional article on my persona and my poetry. Mujtaba Hussain updated the profile he had earlier created for me. Talib Rampuri, an Urdu poet-writer of repute, and editor of a couple of Hindi-Urdu magazines, helped me tremendously. I requested Kamleshwar, former director general of Doordarshan, considered the prime minister of the Hindi language, to write an endorsement for the book and also Dr Namvar Singh, professor emeritus in JNU, regarded as the President of the Hindi language! It felt as if Divine blessings were being showered on me! These blessings helped me find a forgotten write up by my poet Guru, Kumar Pashi from among my papers, in time to be added in the book! Kumar Pashi had written an article on my poetry in the Urdu literary magazine Sutoor, which he edited in 1980. He had rewritten it in Devanagari script for me and I found that now. Once I had finished my preface, talking about my poetical journey of thirty-two years, I got it approved by Prof Narang.

He gave me pertinent insights: that as in the case of poetry, not a single superfluous word should be used in prose either. He appreciated my thought that a Higher Power works, guides and writes for us in a spontaneously Divine manner, categorising me not only as a poet, but also a saint! I titled my preface, *Manzarnama*, thus satisfying my desire for the name!

Those twenty days in the New Year were hectic, for a lot of work needed to be done to make the event memorable. It was a mammoth task, more than a wedding!

I approached Dr Manmohan Singh, a little hesitantly, for being the chief guest and, he agreed. He was a connoisseur of Urdu poetry, and had appreciated my poems in the past. I succeeded in persuading Mani Shankar Aiyar to preside.

I next approached CM Sheila Dikshit. 'Madam, I have always regarded you as an esteemed mentor and would like to put your name on the invitation to receive your blessings.'

She agreed to be there to bless me.

I submitted my first invitation card at Sai Baba's feet at the Lodhi Road temple. It was his Grace that was making everything possible.

A couple of days before the event, I took Chhaya along to formally invite Dr Manmohan Singh, with a box of sweets. But there I received a jolt, for he informed me that he wouldn't be able to fulfil his commitment as he had to urgently visit Assam on Sonia Gandhi's behalf over the weekend. He gave me a signed message for the success of the evening.

Arshiya Sethi, the creative head at IHC, helped me in setting up the stage. A brass statue of Goddess Saraswati was at the front of the dais to invoke Divine Grace. I had dedicated my book to the three most important men in my life, my beloved father, my beloved poetry Guru and my beloved leader, Rajiv Gandhi and I placed framed and garlanded pictures of all three on one side of the stage. Geeta Chandran had practised enthusiastically for her performance and two days before the event, Sudip Banerjee flew down from Bombay. My only expense had been in booking the hall for Rs 5,000.

The only ones who didn't seem very happy with all the extraordinary excitement were my immediate family. Even Balram Jakhar, who was not in town, made it a point to reach back on time to attend and was among the earliest guests to arrive. I wore a black sherwani and had black suits tailored for my sons and a black silk saree for Chhaya, the colour being our dress code. Both sons and my nieces presented bouquets to the guests.

Mani Shankar Aiyar and his dignified wife, Suneet, arrived well on time. Indeed, by 6 pm, the hall was almost full, with even Nafisa Ali managing to find a seat only in the last row. Later arrivals had to be sent upstairs to the balcony, including a senior leader, Harikesh Bahadur. I was in a trance. Ten chairs had been placed on the stage for my very distinguished guests but four more had to be added. Despite that, a few VIPs had to sit among the audience, as the stage was full. Arshiya shared later that never before had she arranged for such a long table for the VIPs on the stage! The evening begun with the first flame of the eight-pronged ceremonial lamp being lit by Maniji followed by Sheila Dikshit, Balram Jakhar, Vasant Sathe, Bhishma Narain Singh and others. Makhmoor Sayeedi opened the literary half of the evening with a grand gesture, 'This evening is totally Mahesh Manzar's, who needs no introduction. Bringing out a book is like becoming a bridegroom and who is better suited to welcome the groom than his better half? I, therefore, request Madam Chhaya Bhabhi to come on the stage and present flowers to our beloved poet!' Thus, Chhaya came on stage to felicitate me and then in that moment, an instant inspiration came to my mind and taking the mike, I announced, 'I believe in reciprocating and as Makhmoor Sahab is no less than a mentor for me, I would like him also to be felicitated by his gracious wife!' And so, his wife too was invited onto the stage to present him flowers, making them both feel much feted.

Once both ladies had returned to their seats, I addressed the audience, 'I would like to draw your attention to these three pictures I have put up here on stage, for their absence from my life is like a void. It is their blessings that has brought me so far in life and I am pretty sure their souls are also present here today! First, is my revered father, an ideal and complete man. I haven't come across another like him in my whole life! Second, is my Guru, Shankar Dutt Kumar Pashi, and suffice it to say that if he hadn't come into my life, this evening wouldn't have been possible! I truly believe that he is my soul mate, the only person who actually understood me after my father! And the third we all know very well, our beloved Rajiv Gandhi, the only leader I know who was a unique blend of divinity and magnanimity. Indeed, it was his lovable personality that inspired me to enter active politics in 1981, after I worked with him in his first election campaign.'

Everyone was fascinated by my eulogy. I continued, 'And had it not been for my connection with Rajiv Gandhi, I wouldn't have gained Mani Shankar Aiyar as my political Guru!' This drew instant applause from all present.

I continued to introduce Makhmoor Sayeedi with a few words, but such was my enthusiasm that my thoughts flowed non-stop, and the audience could only marvel at my flawless rhetoric! I continued to talk about Mani Shankar Aiyar, Balram Jakhar, Vasant Sathe, Bhishma Narain Singh, Sheila Dikshit and so on, introducing them with interesting observations about themselves! To describe Prof Narang, I used the phrases *zabaan ke jadugar aur alfaaz ke badshah* (his oratory was magical and his words, mesmerising). He told me later that though he had visited some seventy countries in his seventy years, he had never been praised like this. In that moment, I myself didn't know from where all these words were flowing.

It was as if some Divine power was articulating through me! I spoke about Kamleshwar, sharing that the Nightingale of India, Lata Mangeshkar once said that she was so fascinated by him that she made sure that none of her recordings were fixed between 8 to 8.30 pm since she watched Kamleshwar's TV programme at that time! Ashok Kumar had once said 'Kamleshwarji, the world admires us, but we revere you!'

I introduced Bhishma Narain Singh as being very close to Indira Gandhi, and her trusted advisor. A while later, Bhishma Narain Singh wanted to leave early. But I jumped off the stage with electrifying speed to persuade him to return. Sheila Dikshit said from the stage, 'Maheshji! So excited?' Vasant Sathe added, 'Let him be Mahesh, he said he would return!' I was so excited that I wasn't aware of what I was doing!

Since I was refusing to stop, Mani Shankar Aiyar sent a slip asking me to cut my talk short. I commented, 'But Bhaisahab, I can't afford to be any shorter!' I continued recounting the helicopter conversation with Ghulam Nabi Azad, and how he had remarked that if only I spoke 50 per cent of what I usually did, I would have been much more successful! And Anil Shastri had halved even that figure! The hall resounded with mirth as I finally returned the mike to Makhmoor Sayeedi! My extempore elocution had brought in an atmosphere of informality and warmth.

Prof Narang released the Urdu edition of my book while Kamleshwar released the Hindi edition of *Manzar Dar Manzar*. Prof Narang now spoke, saying that there is no one like Manzar Sahab, who is totally unique!

'He himself is saying that he has been told to speak less and understands it as his shortcoming, yet he seems to be compelled to speak! I would request him to bring his volubility down to 10 per cent!' There were bursts of laughter all over. 'He says he has been a businessman, a cloth merchant. But I have known him for more than twenty years and I think his real business is that of being a merchant of love!' Prof Narang emphasised that my poetry was a prime example of modern poetry with a deep, philosophical tone. 'He is a complete poet, having experimented with all varieties of poetical forms, from *ghazal* to *nazm*, from *sher* to *doha!*' he interpreted some of my *shers,* giving them an entirely new dimension. He concluded his speech by saying, 'Manzar Sahab is such a brilliant star that his one call has gathered a galaxy of stars over here today! But it's the tragedy of life that where once literature was considered the touchstone of life, with the rulers seeking guidance from sages and philosophers, now we litterateurs are dependent on the rulers for validation. Even Manzar Sahab needs the support of politicians to add prestige to his event!'

Kamleshwar now spoke and gave me my biggest compliment, comparing me to Mahatma Buddha, saying I was filled with a compassion equal to him! He categorised my poetry as spiritual, pure and pious—as the river Ganges! 'His poems display not only compassion, but are filled with immense passion. Every word is soaked with a depth of unfathomable love.'

He shared how once in Indore he felt his speech had become a little extended and he had apologised to the audience. One of them stood up and said, 'You're our guest and we are here to listen to you so that's not a problem. But later we will definitely have something to say to the organiser who invited you!' The audience found this hilarious, especially when Kamleshwar added, 'But here the host himself is...(the organiser).'

Sheila Dikshit spoke next. She congratulated me and confessed that she had not read my poetry. 'But I am sure that his poetry must have the same mystical touch with which he lives his life! Prof Narang has said it has a philosophical element while Kamleshwarji has given it a spiritual angle, but those had to be there, for he embodies these aspects. He has worked closely with me and I am aware of his nature.'

When Balram Jakhar took the mike, he reiterated, 'There is no doubt that Mahesh is one of a kind! What else can you expect when at eighteen itself he was writing such phenomenal lines like.'

> *Bura karen ya bhala karenge*
> *Auron se kuchh juda karenge*
> *Haan ye zamane se juda hai*
> *Lekin hume faqr hai humse juda hai*
>
> *(Yes, he is different from others,*
> *but we are proud he is connected to us)*

Indeed, Congress is fortunate to have such a person associated with it. Those who are trying to curb his voice, how can they? He is like a river in full spate and it would be an injustice to stop its flow. He reminds me of a couplet:

> *Hum hain fiday e Lucknow aur hum pe fida hai Lucknow*
> *Kiski majaal hai jo humse chhudaye Lucknow*
>
> *(We are devoted to Lucknow, and Lucknow is devoted to us.*
> *Who has the audacity to take Lucknow away from us?)*

'He is an ocean of elevated thoughts and words and blessed with the power of vibrant expression, so how can you restrain his flow? Why should we restrict him? He spreads positivity with his words; it is his hallmark. If he is stopped, he will lose his identity.' His words touched the very core of my being, bringing tears to my eyes!

Vasant Sathe said that although unable to read Urdu, he loved the language, 'And when I received Mahesh's book, I got completely lost in it, reading every word carefully late into the night! I have become so enamoured with the ghazals that

I have to read out a few that I loved right now.' To my great delight, he read three of them, emphasising their beauty!

The next speaker was Sibtey Razi and he started off by saying, 'Manzar Sahab writes excellent ghazals but he is no less than a ghazal himself! You have a glimpse of his aesthetic nature in all his traits, whether sitting, walking, speaking, thinking…in every aspect. He says he doesn't know Urdu, but, he is completely steeped in the language, living and breathing it! It's literally pouring out of him. Hindi and Urdu are sisters and Manzar Sahab personifies their amalgamation. I pray to God that not only this, but every evening, every morning gets dedicated to him, so talented is he! May he forever rise and shine!'

Prof K K Tiwari was next, 'In my sixty-four years, I have not come across anyone like Maheshji! I consider him to be more than a younger brother and am really happy with all the appreciation being bestowed on him and his book. A poet is not born easily, it's only when a soul gets injured that poetry flows. A classical great English poet commented that poetry is like 'a fever of the bones.' You see a cheerful person here, but no one has seen the thorns he must have sustained to reach this point. I request Mani Shankar Aiyarji to appeal to Sonia Gandhi to give him a more prominent place in the Party, befitting his calibre. Literary people should be allowed to be a part of the political system since it enhances the level of politics which has unfortunately come down considerably!'

Sajjan Kumar had come a bit late, after Bhishma Narain Singh had left, so I invited him to come on the stage. Although many senior Congress leaders of Delhi were present that evening, only Sheila Dikshit could be invited to speak.

Finally, Mani Shankar Aiyar took the mike and said, 'What a beautifully momentous evening this is! *Oopar stage per Congress ka Adhiveshan ho raha hai, neeche Adeebon ki mahfil saji huyi hai* (A Congress Plenary session is in progress on the stage and a meeting of literary stars is happening below it!)

My heartiest wishes are with Mahesh Bhai! A lot of deserved praises have been bestowed on him and his poetry today, so nothing much is left. Instead, I would like to share the words of a friend, a Pakistani poet, Rais Amrohvi. I was the Consul General in Pakistan, and once when I was coming to India, he presented a beautiful *nazm* to me, *O Hind jaane wale, mera payaam le jaa* which I would like to read now.' It was a very touching poem, with the message of the angst of parting from family and friends, and reflected the agony the Partition must have caused on both sides of the border, mesmerising the audience that evening.

Later, Prof Narang, Kamleshwar and even Vasant Sathe heartily approved my choice of Mani Shankar Aiyar presiding over the function!

Rais Mirza took over the compering of the cultural part of the evening, creating an artistic ambience. He read a few *sher* and then lauded Sudip Banerjee for his rhythmic and rhapsodic renditions, composed by Shyam Banerjee. His soulful singing of my three ghazals captivated the audience completely, interspersed with Rais Mirza's ardent comments. Geeta Chandran danced to another two ghazals and a *nazm* also sung by Sudip, presenting an even more enthralling performance. The audience was in a state of hypnosis as all eyes were glued on Geeta's amazing fusion of Bharatnatyam and Kathak. Towards the end of her dance presentation, she suddenly stumbled. I involuntarily jumped onto the stage to lend her support and escorted her towards the wings. She was a little breathless and still excited with the enthusiasm of the performance and I gave her a quick hug of appreciation. It was a spur-of-the-moment reaction, unfortunately, Rajan who happened to come just then, had a look of disapproval on his face. I excused myself and went back to my seat.

Finally, Sudip Banerjee concluded: 'I have truly never attended such a scintillating evening! It positively belonged to Manzar Sahab. His one phone call saw me hastening from Mumbai to be a part of it!' From below the stage, I replied, 'Sudip Banerjee, this evening is no longer mine, I dedicate it to you and Geeta now!'

Later, both agreed that perhaps that evening had seen their best performance.

Rais Mirza now invited me onto the stage to say a few concluding words. I said I had been trying to bring out this book since 1991, when Rajiv Gandhi had almost agreed to release it, but for the tragic turn of events in which he lost his life. I thanked everyone and poured out my heartfelt gratitude to them all. 'I feel as if I have now fulfilled the purpose of my life and have no wish to live any further! I am entirely at the Divine's service whether He desires to take me away or wants me to use the power of my pen to make a difference in the political world. I would love to live the rest of my life serving the people for I have received immeasurable love from my friends, literary scholars and senior politicians. I have occasionally been given the honour of being an observer and have been sent to different states on these and other assignments. But my political Guru, Mani Shankar Aiyar, is the first who has given me an official position as a National Coordinator in his very important Political Training Department, and who gave me the opportunity to accompany him to different states as part of the training camps. I feel I have been divinely blessed!'

I have been a devotee of Suryadev for the past twenty years, offering water to the Sun every morning for the life-giving energy Suryadev bestows on us. I pray to the Sun God to give me fiery energy to serve like Him, for I have settled my family, published my book and now wish to be of service to humanity. I recommend you all to follow this one daily ritual of offering water to the Sun God, for we are surviving because of the Sun's divine energy!

My father taught me another very important lesson—that

we should show reverence to the five elements. Later, this was endorsed by a sadhu I met!

I then invited Mani Shankar Aiyar to present bouquets to them all.

I expressed my deepest gratitude to all who blessed me that evening, including the publishers who helped me make this *Ek Sham Mahesh Manzar ke Naam* a memorable event.

'This evening can't be complete without my fervent acknowledgement of my mentor's immense contribution in my life and in making this evening perfect! I would like to now invite my political Guru's dignified wife, Suneet Aiyar on to the stage to present a bouquet to her husband, Mani Shankar Aiyar.'

I expressed my heartfelt thanks to the audience for making the evening truly successful, finally inviting them to dinner at the nearby India International Centre. Almost all the guests came, but I realised that Chhaya's brother and his family gave dinner a miss, which upset me a little, for at my last such event in 1985, he was the one to complain about the lack of refreshments! Congratulations and felicitations poured in as we all gathered for the feast. I gifted almost 150 signed copies of my books that evening to my well-wishers. The evening had been enchanting and euphoric and I could see the same satisfaction reflected on the faces of close friends especially Mani Shankar Aiyar and Mahi Malhotra! Their demeanour conveyed it all! I believe that in my seventy years of life, it was undoubtedly the best evening of my life!

That one event made people aware of my depth! Many had doubted till then whether I was a real poet or even if I had any political connections. My family too had never dreamt that I had such an elevated persona! An uncle commented that he had been totally mesmerised by the whole evening for never had there been such a personality as mine in their clan till now! Neena, my cousin, hugged me emotionally, saying that she had never dreamt that her younger brother would bring such laurels to the family. Even my usually reticent eldest brother spontaneously praised me, 'Kaku, your exuberance kept everyone spellbound! And the way you opened your heart compelled all the other speakers to do the same, bringing in a wonderfully passionate atmosphere!' Chhaya's third brother, whom I met a few days later, said begrudgingly, 'What stamina you have, speaking non-stop!'

'All His Divine Grace! I myself don't know where the words come from!'

'No wonder you are regarded as being unique in our entire family,' he said. It made me feel good.

None in my extended family had ever heard any of my poems or speeches and were unacquainted with this aspect of my life. Very few of my family members and friends even knew that I had had the privilege of reciting at the prestigious *mushaira* held annually at Red Fort in 1999. My journey had started in 1978 when I first recited on the radio and appeared on television in 1979.

Chapter 19

Outcast at Home, but Popular Outside

AFTER THE PHENOMENAL success of my book launch, Mahi warned me to avoid attracting the evil eye, as naturally everyone is not always happy at another's rise. I laughed it off, not giving the thought much credence, but a few days later, I was forced to acknowledge it. I developed a skin irritation and no medication was giving relief. Even my wife began to treat me as an outcast, fearing it to be contagious and consequently I began sleeping in the drawing room. I finally met an old Vaid, who concluded that as I had consumed fish daily for almost fifteen days before my book launch, it had caused an allergic reaction. He gave me herbal medicines and recommended curd and buttermilk to bring down the itching. Though I recovered soon, the situation caused a lifelong chasm between my wife and myself. As it was, my family had been somewhat alienated after the function, as they had not expected it to be on such a grand scale. I didn't have much value in their eyes and it was difficult for them to digest all the accolades poured on me! None of them referred to the event in any way. Instead, they began criticising me at every opportunity, condemning or pulling me down in every manner.

I did understand why they didn't value me. I had rented out my Sadar Bazaar shop in February 1997 to two vendors for seasonal work, and had an assured annual income of Rs 6 lakh and consequently felt there was no need for me to work. I augmented my income further with occasional property deals and the share market and these, I managed mostly on the phone. I was, thus, free to devote my entire time to politics, literary meets, and socialising, activities that were considered futile in my family's eyes.

Many evenings, I would spend either with friends or with Kesriji or attend some symposium or other cultural event since I would get invited to many, almost daily. The adulation that I received outside the house compensated for the way I was treated within it! However, I was losing my family's respect gradually, for to most, only a disciplined life enhances a man's dignity.

After the function, I presented my book to the senior leaders whom I was close to, the first copy to Narasimha Rao, who was really appreciative. A book strengthens one's credentials and enhances one's accomplishments. It became a standing joke among my friends that everywhere, there was only *Manzar Dar Manzar,* for the book could be seen in everyone's house! Due to it, my status increased at Lodhi Garden and I began to count many well-known dignitaries including former PM, V P Singh, former CBI director, Sardar Joginder Singh, former Karnataka chief minister, R K Hegde, MP Bhupinder Singh Hooda, senior editors Khushwant Singh and H K Dua as my close acquaintances. Another throwback of the function was that I became more popular, especially with several prominent ladies of all ages from different professions. A senior lady from a Northeastern state had visited Sonia Gandhi along with her mother and I happened to meet them in George's office. She became so fascinated by me that she insisted on visiting me at my home to present an identical shawl she had presented to Sonia Gandhi!

The event even brought a third princess, Sulakshna Singh into my life, whom I had first met at Ahmed Patel's house.

She was from Madhya Pradesh, and whenever she visited the Capital, she would stay either at the State Bhawan or at India International Centre, making it easier for us to meet in privacy.

***

A Congress meeting on 30 September, 2001 was to bring Madhav Rao Scindia, Sheila Dikshit and Mani Shankar Aiyar to Kanpur to address it. On the same day, Mani Shankar Aiyar's daughter, Yamini, was to leave for London for further studies, so he opted out. Sheila Dikshit had some urgent official work and also had to back out. Consequently, Madhav Rao Scindia boarded the plane with a few other junior politicians. The plane crashed before reaching Kanpur and all those on board perished, raising a doubt of a conspiracy in some quarters.

For the first time, Mani Shankar Aiyar, a complete disbeliever, acknowledged the strong hand of Destiny, marvelling at both his and Sheila Dikshit's providential escape! He was convinced that he was to do some more important tasks and that's why he had been saved. Sheila Dikshit too had witnessed a propitious escape. 'I had to become the chief minister three times in a row, Mahesh ji! That was definitely not my time to go.'

In June 2002, a national conference on secularism hosted by the State CM, Digvijay Singh was organised by Mani Shankar Aiyar at Bhopal. Fourteen intellectuals from different parties were invited as panelists from all over the country. Mani Shankar Aiyar chaired it very efficiently and everyone was fascinated at the way he instantly translated from Hindi to English and from English to Hindi for the speakers, in spite of being a Tamilian.

Mani Shankar Aiyar, however, went down with fever on the very first evening and wasn't able to prepare the introductory papers for the next day. These had to be prepared in both

Hindi and English. The other coordinator, Devanand Balodi also fell ill, and I had to work right through the night, finishing only at 6 am till these introductory papers were ready! When a person is faced with a big challenge, they say that he is given Divine capability to fulfil it! Science says that such stimulating situations make the body secrete adrenaline giving one the necessary high needed to finish a demanding task!

The next day during lunch, Mani Shankar Aiyar approached me and cautioned me to eat less. 'Eat half of your normal diet!' he cautioned.

I was mystified and wanted to know the reason. 'If you eat too much, you will feel sleepy, especially as you were up the whole night and I want you to remain active during the upcoming session!' I was astonished at his concern and at the same time, felt a jubilation at being valued so. The conference was a big success, attracting coverage from both print and electronic media. I happened to have my own moment of fame when once MSA happened to hand over the mike to me encouraging me to contribute. I started off with, '*Deviyon evam Sajjano...*,' making Sunil Dutt, who was present, jocularly comment, 'Manzar Sahab likes to keep all his options open!' drawing laughter from everyone. On the concluding day, the CM had got a cultural programme organised, and during it, some of the delegates called out to me to recite my ghazal on Rajiv Gandhi. Surinder Singh Thakur, a Rajya Sabha MP, and the co-ordinator for the Conference, soon invited me onto the stage. I had barely recited three of the eight-sher ghazal when he asked me to stop, saying that the artists were waiting to present their dance. I was astonished; it was a flagrant disrespect to our departed leader! Angrily, I said, 'I am accountable to only two people, my chairman, Mani Shankar Aiyar and your CM, Digvijay Singh. If either of them asks me to step down, I will readily do so. Even the delegates present here are more interested in listening about our great leader because of whom we are all standing here in power today rather than watching some juveniles dance.'

The audience's full support was with me and they began to shout slogans in my favour, interspersed with 'Long live Rajiv Gandhi'. Immediately, Mani Shankar Aiyar was on the stage, defusing the situation diplomatically. He encouraged me to continue reading, but now a new demand rose from the non-Hindi speakers, who asked for an English translation! And so, Mani Shankar Aiyar accommodatingly translated my ghazal, *sher* by *sher,* as I recited it on stage, all over again! It was a historic moment for me!

Later that evening, Surinder Singh Thakur visited us at our hotel and apologised profusely to Mani Shankar Aiyar, conveying his deep regret for the incident. Mani Shankar Aiyar consoled Surinder Singh, telling him to forget about it.

***

A *mauni* baba from Rudraprayag would visit Delhi and used to stay at Mahi's principal's house at Kirti Nagar. Mahi suggested that since I was always ready to interact with enlightened souls, I should meet him. He had been in silence for about twenty-five years. I agreed happily, wondering how anyone could keep silent for so many years when I couldn't do so for even a few hours! Besides, I thought it would be a good chance to meet the principal, since I was always keen to connect with high-profile women.

When we visited him, I presented a shawl to him. Hearing my name, he said that he was a devotee of Shiva, Surya and Shakti, creating an instant affinity between us. I invited him to my house and to everyone's surprise, he accepted and did so a few times over the next five years, which was indeed a privilege. As it was, he hardly ate anything, surviving only on fruits, soaked dry fruits, vegetables, milk and curd. He embodied Osho's teachings, the first being to eat less: 'The lesser the load, the better the health.' Second was to enhance our energy by conserving our senses. So along with not speaking at all, the baba would blindfold himself occasionally and stuff cotton into his ears, then meditate with deep breaths and long exhales.

Another time when he came to the principal's house on Maha Shivratri, he asked her to invite me for a ritual to be performed all night. I felt very honoured and humbly requested that Mahi should also be invited, as she was the one who had connected us. It so happened that I mentioned the event to Dev Anand, who also insisted on coming along with his father, Ranganath Mishra. Subsequently, we all attended the night-long *Rudraabhishek* ceremony. It was a deeply spiritual experience, with chants reverberating throughout the night. The Baba himself said that it had indeed been a truly divine time, as all present had been fully involved! It was a matter of great joy for me at how I could form an instant and deep connect with such holy man. Our association continued for a few years but then, he stopped coming to Delhi. He was around ninety years old by then, although he looked only about sixty!

***

An astrological conference was held at Ghaziabad, organised by an NGO run by a retired army officer, Colonel Tyagi. They had invited former Union minister, Prof K K Tiwari as the chief guest through Virender Trivedi, a secretary in AICC and a relative of the colonel. But at the last moment, Prof K K Tiwari couldn't make it, leaving the organisers in the lurch, as no other prominent dignitary could be invited at the last moment. Virender Trivedi had been impressed by my book release function and he requested me to accompany him to Ghaziabad to inaugurate the event. 'But you too can do it,' I said.

'Everyone knows I am closely related to Colonel Tyagi and my presence will not create an impact. But you have a politician's crisp personality and your presence will be more appreciated! We will introduce you as a popular poet and politician and the rest you handle.' And so, the next day, I accompanied Virender Trivedi to light the inaugural lamp at the conference. Addressing the jampacked gathering, I praised the Colonel's initiative in organising the conference, saying, 'The Colonel has been given a Vir Chakra but I think he deserves a Param Vir Chakra!' This seemed to tickle a beautiful, graceful lady in the front row, so I addressed her directly, asking her whether she agreed. My attempt to start a conversation with the pretty lady brought immediate laughter from a few of those present. Later, I learnt that she was the Colonel's neighbour! On Astrology, I said, 'I revere this subject and appreciate its depth. What I have understood from various sources is that other than the relation of the movement of the planets, the universe too comprises of the five elements that make up our body. That's why we say *Aham Brahmasmi*! Besides, we are not bodies, we are souls, and are a part of the Divine! We are directly connected to heavenly bodies like the sun and the moon and are influenced by them. The full moon affects the oceans, and it also affects our body, for the percentage of salt and water present in both is the same. Many people's minds are deeply affected by the full moon and the two words, lunar and lunatic definitely seem to be interconnected. Humans and nature are integrated and greatly influence each other, so it is natural for the stars and planets to play an important role in our lives. Astrologers have a very relevant task in interpreting those roles for us, making us aware about the experiences and circumstances in our lives!'

My speech went down well with the audience as well as with the astrologers on the dais, who appreciated my knowledge of this occult science. I had been interested in the subject since my teenage years, when I had purchased books on astrology and numerology and had been applying their principles in my interactions with people over the years. I was seated next to a famous television astrologer, Pt Ajay Bhambi and he was quite inspired and ended up becoming a lifelong friend.

Virender later said that I was a talented person. 'How come you have not attained the heights you deserve?' he asked. 'All a matter of Destiny! But then a lot is happening in my life which is giving me so much value, and I am grateful for that. How much more can I demand from Him!' I replied.

During lunch, while the three of us were at a small VIP table, I saw the lady from the audience and invited her to join us. She smilingly complied, introducing herself as Minakshi Sharma. Thus was laid the foundation of yet another strong friendship, much to the amusement of the other two.

She later invited me to her home in Ghaziabad and when I went to meet her, I took along a basket of apples. 'These apples are so beautiful! Just like yourself!' she said to me.

'No dear, how can you compare them to me! They are as smooth and rosy as your cheeks!'

With a tinkling laugh, she responded, 'From your speech, I gathered that you could understand the Colonel's character, immediately. It helped me to understand you at once! 'And how's that?' I asked.

'Well you stopped your speech right in the middle and forgetting the conference, and without bothering about the audience, you began to talk to me, randomly! You know what was my first thought? If you were giving a Param Vir Chakra to the Colonel, you should be given the Bharat Ratna award!' We spent the next six hours chatting about everything under the sun!

I found her to be very principled, for though she was divorced, she refused to live with her parents, saying that if a woman could take the bold step of separation, she should be capable enough to live independently.

Chapter 20

More Trouble at Home and Outside

ONCE IT SO happened that I and my dealer had to go to Gurgaon for a registry, and realised that both the Ford Ikon and the Maruti had been taken by my sons, leaving only the old, dilapidated Fiat for me. I couldn't possibly go to Gurgaon in an old car without an AC. I called up the younger one who didn't respond, so rang the elder one and ticked him off. He told me to come and change cars with him, as his college was enroute to Gurgaon.

When I reached him, I admonished him in front of his friends, which naturally made him uncomfortable. In an undertone, he said, 'Just you come home now, I will see you!' It was a blatant threat, and even the dealer was shocked. When I got back home, my niece Divya, who was living with us, had returned from work, so my son restrained himself from creating a scene. Later, the younger one kept talking nonsense—'What will you do with all the money! You say you are earning for us! You claim that you spend very little on yourself. But you are not giving us comfort today. Who has seen tomorrow? Why should we drive an old car? And you are earning because of our Destiny! All this is due to our Destiny? We deserve it all!' The mother made no move to stop this tirade, thus giving her silent assent to this chain of thought.

I purchased a fourth car, another Ford Ikon, within a few

days. After visiting the temple, I drove to Narasimha Rao, seeking his blessings. I complimented him on his foresight in bringing in liberalisation and globalisation during his tenure, for that had enabled a simple party worker like myself to buy imported cars.

***

Around the time of the car incident, my sister had come to meet Divya along with her younger daughter, and was naturally staying with us. She witnessed an ugly scene at home in which both Chhaya and I had a horrible fight over a seemingly trivial issue over me giving some choice sweetmeats to the servant. Chhaya had objected and the boys, as usual, had sided with their mother.

Later, when I was chatting with my sister and her daughters, my sister scolded me for being responsible for the way I was being treated in the house. 'It's essential for the man of the house to go out for some time at least. He shouldn't be at home the whole day; his value goes down.'

She continued, 'Besides you were the one who used to really pamper Chhaya earlier, tolerating all her tantrums. You should have taken a stand right from the beginning.'

'I felt that was best at that time! Peace had to be kept at home! The children were very young and I couldn't let her remain hungry,' I replied.

'You should make it a point of getting out of the house for a few hours. Go anywhere, to the temple or to AICC offices, but don't remain at home,' my sister said to me.

Later, in the evening, I decided to go and meet Narasimha Rao, for I used to feel rejuvenated after meeting people like him. I was still feeling a bit disturbed and it must have been evident on my face, for he asked, 'All well?' I shared the situation at home with him, and he consoled me by saying, 'Who can win against one's wife or children?' A while later, he added, 'Even Ghanshyam Das Birla faced such domestic issues when once he gave a *mewa laddoo* to their servant. But he effectively silenced his wife saying that it was this servant who would rush them to hospital in any emergency, for all their sons were living far away from them.' It was a habit of Babuji that he would slip into a state of silence of up to ten minutes while sitting with me, sometimes snoozing, too. It reminded me of the Chinese leader, Mao Tse Tung, who too would slip into a somnambulant state during the day, even during meetings.

At times, after one of his short snoozes, Babuji would indicate with a nod that I could leave and sometimes he would break his silence and comment on the topic we had been discussing or he would ask me to recite a couplet. Sometimes, he would call his helper to serve some drinks or tea with crisp *samosas*. I noticed that he could tolerate my company for only about thirty minutes maximum, while Kesriji could have me sitting for even four hours at a stretch!

Encouraged by my sister's support, I again took office space on rent in Jangpura where I could spend a couple of hours. I think that kept me sane, or else the circumstances at home would have pushed me into a state of anxiety. Around this time, I began visiting the Yogoda Ashram on Mahi's suggestion. That too helped to keep me rational and grounded.

Minakshi once visited me at my Jangpura office and we spent a few very pleasant hours together, leaving us mutually content. As she was leaving, I presented her with some eatables from a well-known sweet shop. It was Minakshi who made me aware of the importance of gifting substantially, especially to my beloved women friends. She had once commented acerbically, 'It is so surprising that a man gives everything to his wife even if she's not giving him any comfort or respect, yet to the one who is giving him immense joy, he thinks apples and oranges are all she needs!' I was pretty taken aback, never having considered giving anything valuable and realised that it was expected. But then a thought struck me. 'You may be right, but was it only you who surrendered? Did I, too, not surrender myself? Did I not give pleasure as well?' She had no answer to my comments.

'And you are right, a man gives everything to his wife, but then she has not one, but three licenses to receive it all—a legal license, a religious and a social one. Besides, she is the mother of his children too. She takes care of his house and his social obligations. She is there when he needs care. And a man gains from her Destiny, too, or so it is said in our scriptures. In short, she enhances his life!'

Minakshi again had no words to counter my thesis. However, I continued, 'To some extent you are right though. In one of Saadat Hasan Manto's stories, one man asked the other whether he had been to a prostitute in a rather derogatory manner. The other demanded to know why it was wrong. According to him, a wife was worse than a prostitute for even after taking everything, she refused to give love or respect to her husband. 'Was that not duplicity of the highest order?' he asked.

Saadat Hasan Manto was a well-known Pakistani writer born in Ludhiana. Though he is considered to be one of the finest twentieth century writers, he was tried for writing provocative stories six times, thrice before Independence, and thrice later in Pakistan. However, he won all his cases as the judgement was given in his favour since many literary celebrities testified to support him. He had declared in court: 'I present the naked truth; I don't dress it up'. The real purpose of literature is to portray reality as it is. Like many evolved souls, Manto too faced an early demise, being only forty-three when he passed away.

I had been inspired by the stories of Munshi Prem Chand in school and by the works of Manto in my college days. Later,

Mahatma Gandhi's *The Story of My Experiments with Truth* was another influencing factor. My poetry Guru also advised me to read three popular women writers, Quratulain Haider, Ismat Chugtai and Kamala Das, to understand the dynamics of man-woman relationships.

Kamala Das's forte lay in delineating the complexities of a woman's mind besides her frank confessions, and later she became the first Indian woman litterateur to be nominated for the Nobel Prize in 1984. It is a fact that when literature speaks truth unabashedly, it becomes immortal. But to write the truth, the writer needs courage, confidence and the conviction to do so, qualities which even literary giants lack.

***

On Bhishma Narain Singh's recommendation, the general secretary AICC, sent me to resolve issues in the Palamu district Congress Committee office in Jharkhand. I first went as a state guest to Ranchi, then the next day, Bhishma Narain Singh's son, Prem, drove me to Daltonganj. During my stay, an elderly businessman approached me with the complaint that the district President was appointing him as a mere secretary when, according to age and experience, he should be either a Vice-President or the general secretary. I promised to look into the matter. Later, at a meeting with the officials to resolve issues, I was also able to put the businessman's concern forward and get an approval for his request.

To my great surprise, the next day, he quietly handed Rs 25,000 and though I refused to accept, he was very insistent. Though I had taken the money, I wasn't comfortable about it, and when I returned home, it struck me that I could present the amount to Minakshi, for she had indeed taught me an important aspect of life. When I did so, she protested that she had not meant me to do something like that. She felt it more as an affront and I had great difficulty in making her accept it. I learnt my lesson of being more open-hearted and generous with my lady friends, thereafter.

***

In 2002, Hema's grandson was born and at a small ceremony, I happened to be with her father and her niece, Sanya, who was also a lecturer and had been widowed a couple of years earlier, at thirty. I had met her a year before, for Hema had requested me to find a match for her, as she was quite young and beautiful. I knew a young Brahmin who had lost his wife but when I approached him with the proposal, he declined, as she belonged to the Jaat community.

Hema's father encouraged Sanya to exchange numbers with me, telling her that as I was very gregarious, I could prove helpful. I called her a couple of days later and during the conversation, she asked where we should meet. Subconsciously, I was hesitant in pursuing Sanya, as I had a great bond with Hema, her aunt. Later, Sanya invited me to visit her at her parent's home, saying that they wanted to meet me. I accepted the invite, taking fruits and sweets with me and spent an enjoyable evening with her family. Sanya's father mentioned my visit to Hema, and as I had expected, she was quite upset. She called to find out my reason for pursuing her niece. I tried to pacify her saying that her parents wanted to meet me. 'Besides, she's a helpless widow!' At that, Hema retorted, 'Maheshji, *aap aisa karo, ek sindoor ki dibiya jeb mei rakha karo aur jab kissi vidhwa se mila karo, toh usski maang mei ek chutki sindoor bhar diya karo!* (Keep a box of vermilion in your pocket and apply to every widow's forehead you meet!)' I apologised at once. Feeling truly contrite, I tried to placate her and after her initial burst, she said quietly, 'It doesn't add to your dignity, Maheshji! Are you the type who just goes around hunting for women?' She finally did forgive me and having learnt my lesson, I backed away from her niece.

***

My wife once had an argument with my elder son, when he suddenly moved towards her aggressively and threatened her with dire consequences. Shocked, I immediately intervened. He was a well-built young man and at that point, was full of boiling anger. My wife seemed truly apprehensive of him, a feeling she had never experienced where I was concerned. In our relationship, she would take an aggressive stand. But that one incident with Karan terrified her so much that she never ever tried to intervene with him in any way.

It's a fact that a man should not only be taller than his wife and have a better physique, but should also be more educated and earning well to wield authority. Only then is a woman able to show him real respect. It reminded me of a time when some poets, all of them, women, had been having good-hearted fun at my diminutive height, saying it made me look cute and harmless. One of them had even said that precious things came in small packets. Enjoying the ribbing, I had asked that if a man who weighed only 45 kg had married a 55 kg woman, then how could the marriage be successful? A tall, well-built senior poet had exclaimed, 'Maheshji, how can a 45 kg person be called a man!' Another woman defended me saying that 45 kg was even a category in wrestling! The fact of the matter is that I had looked like a callow youth next to my wife when I had got married.

***

At that time, the India Islamic Cultural Centre was being set up next to the Chinmaya Mission on Lodhi Road. Suhail

Khan, a senior advocate of the Supreme Court, and one of the board members and also my neighbour, had wanted to nominate me to their Centre, asking for a donation amount of Rs 10,000 from me.

'But I am sure you must be taking only Muslim members,' I said.

'No, the board wants to include a few renowned Hindu secular members as well, to give it a composite nature.'

I agreed, 'Yes, true culture should be composite. It cannot be of one colour!'

It was indeed an honour, for many prominent Muslims were wanting to be a part of it and here I was being given the opportunity. My years of political and literary interaction had helped me create a respectable niche for myself in society. The then chief minister of Orissa, Hemanand Biswal, had lovingly hosted drinks and dinner only for me from among all the observers who had visited Orissa. Later, we would occasionally meet at Orissa Bhawan, and at one such meeting, he asked when I was inviting him to my house. So, I invited him for dinner the very next day.

One day, my elder son, Karan, asked me for a few shares as he needed them as part of his MBA studies. I had shares of over two hundred companies but wasn't actively trading in them. I played safe and had invested in a variety of enterprises, which included real estate, FDRs, shares and gold. I transferred a few into my son's name and he began experimenting with them. He made a profit and that made him want to dabble with more shares. I would ask him regularly for an update, but he wouldn't divulge anything, and instead say that while I had just bought and dumped the shares, he was now finally making them profitable. He would taunt me and say that I didn't understand how to gain from trading.

I mentioned that if he was making a profit, I too was entitled to my share, as the main investment was mine. He refused point-blank, saying that he would return the principal amount later! However, over the course of a year, he reduced my shares to almost zilch, as he began speculating recklessly. One night he said to me, 'Papa, get me arrested!' It was then that he told me about losing almost all the shares that I had been nurturing since 1979 and which were valued in lakhs at that time.

'You are worthless, swindling me out of my money, not even giving any interest on it! I asked you so many times about what you were doing and you never told me anything.' There was nothing I could do and rather dejectedly, I told him to go to sleep.

I then vented out on my wife, 'What sort of children have you borne? They are scoundrels, robbing me! Are you sure they are really my children?'

***

I would give a monthly allowance of Rs 1,000 to my sons for personal expenses, plus expenses for petrol and mobiles. On their birthdays, I usually gave them Rs 5,000 to celebrate. It was my younger son's nineteenth birthday in August and he exceeded that amount while partying with his friends and demanded an additional Rs 8,000. I was already quite worked up due to my elder son's shares fiasco and refused to give him the money. 'You have bullied me into buying such an expensive car; I am not a royal treasury. I started earning at sixteen, leaving my studies also to do so, and used to earn for my father rather than asking for pocket money. You both are demanding money all the time.'

'From 1981 to 1996, I had been celebrating your birthdays lavishly, sometimes inviting fifty of your friends along with about a hundred other guests almost every year, including relatives and neighbours. And yet you have no gratitude. I stepped into the family business, even abandoning my studies to help my father as he had faced heavy losses because of a fire.

At one time, I was earning only Rs 5,000 per month from the shop, and yet I didn't let you people feel any lack of money. And look at your fanciful lifestyles!'

My taunts hurt, and within a few days, my younger son secured a night job in a telecommunication multinational firm for Rs 5,000. He attended college during the day and worked as well. It became a life changing event for him. It made him understand the importance of hard work, helped him gain confidence, and he polished his skills in the English language. He was intelligent and diligent as well, and within a short time, began earning Rs 10,000 per month. He is now earning in millions through his own hard work and acknowledges my contribution in making him so successful! By the time he was thirty-four, he was driving a Rs 55 lakh BMW! Within the next four years, he had gifted a Rs 60 lakh Audi to his wife!

Chapter 21
Making Modi Retreat

VINCENT GEORGE HAD accepted a hefty cheque from Abhishek Verma, the son of one of my mentors, poet-politician Shrikant Verma, as pin money. A cheque can be incriminating and soon he came under the CBI radar. He was Sonia Gandhi's right-hand at that time, but as soon as scandal touched his name, she moved him to the outer office. He was very hurt and refused to attend office. Senior Congress leaders finally managed to persuade him to return, impressing upon him that no one is indispensable and his actions would be detrimental to his own future. Along with some of his staunch supporters, I too frequently visited him to assure him of my support. Eventually, Sonia Gandhi reportedly spoke to Atal Bihari Vajpayee and prevented his arrest. After all, he had served her loyally, often standing like a rock beside her, even declining Narasimha Rao's offer of the post of a cabinet minister, remaining loyal to her.

***

Former CM of Haryana, Bhajan Lal would hold regular gatherings at his Golf Links house, where he would invite senior Haryana leaders. One of them introduced me to him and subsequently Bhajan Lal began to invite me, considering me to be good company. He was not interested in poetry but admired my political wisdom. I sometimes took my younger son along. He would serve tea and snacks during the meeting and one day, with his prior permission, I brought some snacks. He showed his appreciation, telling everyone, 'My youngest friend is the first to think of reciprocation!'

At about this time, I asked the CBI Director, Joginder Singh, about Kesriji's case from him but he gently told me not to open that chapter in any way.

***

Despite being neither an MP nor an MLA, Narendra Modi was directly nominated as the Chief Minister of Gujarat by Atal Bihari Vajpayee in 2001. He had been a dynamic RSS *Pracharak* and at the time of his nomination, he was the national general secretary of the BJP. Consequently, in December 2002, Narendra Modi was to stand for Assembly elections for the very first time. Ahmed Patel asked if I could go to Ahmedabad for campaigning against Narendra Modi for about fifteen days. At the Congress office in Ahmedabad, Ahmed Patel asked me to address a meeting. 'No senior leader is able to go, so you will have to go and address it.'

'Our candidate against Narendra Modi, Yatin Ojha is an SC advocate; he is going with you and both of you can manage things,' he added. Thus I got the opportunity to address a campaign meeting individually as the chief speaker. My words invariably have a poetic touch. I noticed that the audience comprised people from different religions, and so I added a spiritual aspect. I spoke of Congress as a secular party and even the Constitution displayed the word prominently. But I added that we are a secular nation, and not indifferent towards other religions. We have a uniform outlook and equal respect for all. Our ideology is *Sarv Dharam Sambhav*. We regard all as being equal, for all religions convey righteousness. My words impressed everyone, including Yatin Ojhaa, drawing repeated applause from the audience. Yatin Ojhaa henceforth took me everywhere in his personal jeep, along with his wife, to all meetings till the end of the campaign.

Subhash Chopra, Delhi Congress President was also in Ahmedabad with his team and he met me the next day. I was upset with him for when he became the Delhi Congress President the previous year, he had manipulated to make me only an executive committee member despite my name being put forward by V George for general secretary, DPCC. The post gives a dignity and a few perks like a room with a name plate, which I have sorely missed all my life. Thereafter, I had avoided him, not even going to the DPCC. Now too, he had not included me in his team and I owed my presence in Ahmedabad to Ahmed Patel! Neither did I attend any of the lunches organised by him for the Congress activists at Ahmedabad. I was fortunate as I was being well taken care of by Yatin Ojha, who would even carry me off for meals with his family.

At another meeting, Lalu Prasad Yadav was to be the chief speaker but his helicopter was delayed, and I was requested to take the mike. I spoke about Congress Party's pre- and post-Independence achievements and held fort till Lalu Prasad Yadav finally arrived. It was my longest political speech ever—of fifty-five minutes.

On polling day, Ahmed Patel assigned me to tour polling booths in the Maninagar constituency of Narendra Modi. At one of them, Narendra Modi had brought his motorcade of seven cars right up to the booth, which was against the rules of the Election Commission. It was his first election, and he was probably not aware of this rule. Each voter, VIPs included, are to walk the last hundred meters to the polling station. I approached him and said, 'Honourable Chief Minister, I have been appointed as the Observer of your Constituency by the Honourable Congress President, Soniaji, so it's my duty to point out that bringing your cavalcade so close to the polling station is against the regulations of the Election Commission.'

Narendra Modi at once indicated that the cars be moved back beyond the restricted area. He had a reputation of being a stern leader, especially after the Godhra incident, creating awe not only in the minds of Muslims but even Hindus, and yet without any hesitation, he had immediately retreated at my request. The other party workers marvelled at my courage in confronting the CM! This won me many accolades from my Party, with Ahmed Patel, Ambika Soni, and even Kamal Nath awestruck at my daringness. Ahmed Patel commented that I had done absolute justice to my presence here! A secretary of the Gujarat Pradesh Congress Committee, Parikh had been deputed by Ahmed Patel to accompany me everywhere, showing me the sights and managing my time efficiently. In one incident, a GPCC secretary asked if she could visit me in my hotel in the evening, but I gently denied her permission, saying we would meet at the Pradesh office. At the back of my mind was P V Narasimha Rao's advice that one should always be very careful of how one behaved with regards to money and women, especially while on an assignment by the High Command. All lapses were at once reported to them and it proved to be an effective way of keeping everyone under control. I think even my accepting the money in Jharkhand had been reported, for a roundabout comment once dropped by the general Secretary, Harikesh Bahadur indicated that he knew about the incident.

After the elections, I visited Dwarkadeesh temple in Dwarka, courtesy Ahmed Patel, besides Porbandar to see the house where Gandhiji was born and lived in during his initial years. It was a big, dilapidated double-storey haveli, though under the care of the ASI. I also got a chance to see the mansion given to Sudama by Krishna, and named Susheela Bhawan, after Sudama's devoted wife. A beautiful temple has been made within its precincts.

After I went to Rukmini's palace, I used the ferry to visit Bhent Dwarka, in the middle of the ocean. Krishna reportedly lived there after coming from Mathura. Next, I visited Rukmini temple, where Krishna's wife, Rukmini had lived for some time, after she left Bhent Dwarka, angry at Krishna for still being lost in Radha's love.

I was fortunate to visit the holy Shiv Jyotirling, Nageshwar on the way. In Gandhinagar, I saw the beautiful Swami Narayan Akshardham temple. In 2000, I had got the chance to visit another Dhaam, the Jagannath Puri temple in Orissa, thus completing two of our four major pilgrimage places.

At Ahmedabad, I met the tall, handsome Kuldeep K Kohli, a Vice-President of a corporate firm in Delhi. He was accompanying a senior AICC leader. Once back in Delhi, he introduced me to Colonel Anil Sachdeva, the chief security officer at Reliance, and his elder brother, Colonel Rajendra Sachdeva who lived in Defence Colony.

Colonel Anil Sachdeva had won a Gallantry Award and was one of the officers in Rajiv Gandhi's Special Protection Group. The brothers invited me to a party on New Year's Eve where snacks and drinks were flowing freely to the sound of loud music. It was my first experience of an uninhibited party, and I felt distinctly uncomfortable. Everyone was inebriated and dancing crazily. A tall, charming, voluptuous Sikh woman pulled me onto the dance floor, but I couldn't as I was feeling too conscious of her sensuality and the disparity in our builds. I was also feeling inhibited by her husband's presence, who was also on the floor, dancing with someone else. Me with my poetic-political background and my typical outfit felt out of place!

***

Though my circle of good friends had expanded after my book launch, I confided in Makhmoor Sayeedi that despite intimate friendships with a few, including three princesses, none of my connections were fulfilling, since I was dependent on their whims. He remarked philosophically that no one ever gets everything they desire! 'What Kumar Pashi once said about you has come true, hasn't it? That one day you will become the male version of Draupadi, for at least five women would come into your life and love you truly!' He added thoughtfully, 'Whatever anyone is giving you, be thankful for it and move on. Don't demand more!'

I might have lacked love, but my poetry was however going strong. Around that time, I participated in a mushaira at Sai International Auditorium to which V P Singh had been invited. A day before, I had requested P V N Rao to 'come to listen and bless me' and I was pleasantly surprised when half an hour into the evening, P V Narasimha Rao casually walked into the hall, creating an instant furore. I jumped off the stage to welcome him while everyone spontaneously came to their feet at his unexpected appearance. He refused to come onto the stage to be felicitated, saying that he had just come to listen and the event should continue. I thanked him profusely for coming and pouring eulogies onto him, I recited some couplets, dedicating them to him.

That day, I realised that he regarded me with affection despite his reserved nature! The evening was phenomenally unique for there were two former PMs in the auditorium, one as a poet and the other as a listener, but unfortunately the Press was not present, so it didn't get recorded!

***

My friend, Minakshi from Ghaziabad had once expressed a wish to be part of the All India Mahila Congress in any capacity and requested an introduction. The President of the Mahila Congress was a good friend and I invited her for breakfast to my home to put forward a recommendation for

Minakshi. During the ensuing conversation, she shared how once a senior colleague was arguing with Indira Gandhi, and had unthinkingly said, 'Madam, if you had not been Jawaharlal Nehru's daughter, you would have been working in a menial job right now!' It is a fact that inheritance does endow an unwarranted dignity.

***

Dr Hari Kishen Kaul, the chief librarian at IIC, had also attended my book release and had taken permission from the IIC President to allow me to become a member. He was the President of the 'Poetic Society of India' and liked to promote poets. He approached me through Prof Narang, who was already a member, with the offer of nomination to their exclusive centre. Prof Narang said that I should be honoured that they were inviting me to join them. 'Bhaisaheb, I am already a member of the New Friends Club, and am now too busy to visit it. Recently, I have been nominated to the India Islamic Cultural Centre as well! Please convey my gratitude and regrets!'

At one of the CII Conferences, to which Director Subah Rajan would often invite me, I met Seema Aggarwal, a tall beautiful lady. I observed her serving snacks to an older lady, and commented, 'Madam, I love your gesture of catering to your mother as she must have done when you were a child!' Both simpered at my dalliance, with Seema retorting, 'Well, since you are a poet, you naturally bring in poetry everywhere!'

I was pretty astonished, 'Oh you know me! But I don't know you.'

'Like you, I too am frequently present at Subha's events and your outfit always makes you stand out in any gathering.'

She introduced herself as a senior advocate of the Supreme Court of India, laying the foundation of another very genuine friendship.

Chapter 22

A Dinner Party

POLITICS HAS ITS own power plays and there was an ongoing tussle between V George and Ahmed Patel. The cheque incident in 2001 had tarnished George's image and Sonia Gandhi had chosen Ahmed Patel as her political secretary. I wished to felicitate him at dinner at home. He wanted it to be a small, exclusive gathering, and I made a huge mistake by impulsively asking if I could invite V George. At the back of my mind was the thought that if they worked together, it would be beneficial for the Congress President. I thought I could patch up things between these two power blocks!

Ahmed Patel had responded, 'You're the host, so you can invite anyone you like!'

Along with V George, I invited Dr Bhishma Narain Singh, Prof K K Tiwari and Nafisa Ali. V George was the first to arrive. I had told Ahmed Patel that I would send my elder son to bring him home. Nafisa Ali had also requested to be picked up as well, so I dispatched my younger son to bring her. I had arranged two huge garlands to welcome both V George and Ahmed Patel and I goofed up again, for I first garlanded V George and then Ahmed Patel, completely overthrowing protocol!

Dr Bhishma Narain Singh later asked me why I done this after being associated with politics most of my life. K K Tiwari also made a derisive comment: 'Maheshji, such unlimited loyalty!' Discordant undercurrents, therefore, prevailed throughout that evening for Ahmed Patel chose to ignore George completely, talking exclusively to me while the others remained silent, with only Nafisa putting in a comment now and then. Had I, maybe, bitten off more than I could chew?

I had also caustically chided Nafisa Ali for demanding to be chauffeured especially when she had come on her own once earlier, a totally unwarranted and undignified comment. Another faux pas I committed a little later was when Ahmed Patel asked me to support Tajdar Babar, from my constituency and I recounted how I had supported her in 1993 at Bhagatji's request and how she had completely ignored me after her victory.

Criticising the Party candidate in front of senior leaders was absolutely wrong, especially when he was asking me to support her!

Nevertheless, Ahmed Patel stayed for almost three hours, and Bhishma Narain Singh commented, 'Maheshji, I feel that he was waiting for George to take the initiative to break the ice between them. What do you think?'

In retrospect, I also felt that V George might have been interested in patching up, but his ego wasn't allowing him to take the first step. He must have felt that his willingness to be present at the dinner was enough. Ahmed Patel, on his part, was giving George ample time to approach him, but things rarely go as planned!

***

On the eve of Independence Day, Prof Harish Naval of Hindu College informed me of my selection for a Rotary Club award. This group comprised of intellectuals, mostly professors of Delhi University. That year, they had decided to honour two people, one who had made concrete contributions towards uplifting society before Partition and the other who had done so after Partition. On Dr Kavita Sharma and Prof Harish Naval's recommendations, I was approved for the second option. A citation was read out about my work and contribution. The other awardee was a veteran Congress leader, Lala Shivchand Gupta. I addressed a jam-packed auditorium and it was as if Goddess Saraswati herself had descended onto me, for I gave a speech that drew much applause from the audience.

***

Dev Anand Mishra would call me sometimes, saying, 'Mahesh, my father is remembering you, so come over for tea!' On one such occasion, Justice Mishra wanted to know what I did for a living. Everyone was curious, for my somewhat flamboyant lifestyle would puzzle them! Mani Shankar Aiyar's wife, Suneet, too had shown a similar curiosity. I told him about my real estate investments and my shop. When Justice Mishra heard that I had rented out my shop since almost seven years, he advised me to sell it off. His genuine concern was that if something happened to me, the tenants would take over the shop, without compensating my family. He warned, 'Maheshji, in our country, it's possible to manipulate things, police, judiciary included! Everything has a price! Where will your children go for justice then?' This advice coming straight from a retired Chief Justice of India immediately prompted me to sell the shop.

Another important event in 2003 was the declaration of the Assembly elections in Delhi. It had been five years since Sheila Dikshit had been elected and soon enough, I got a call from her sister that the CM was 'remembering me'. I sounded acerbic when I said that Madam was quite experienced now and surely didn't need my support. She had a team of IAS officers at her service and she was sure to be elected again as she had done a lot of work. I also informed her that this time I wanted to contest myself, and would come to seek her blessings!

I, then approached Mani Shankar Aiyar for blessings in getting a ticket in the coming elections. He enthusiastically supported me. I mentioned that Tajdar Babar was the sitting MLA from my constituency, and she would possibly be renominated. I told him that an Aggarwal had stood from the neighbouring constituency of Kasturba Nagar, but had been defeated by a small margin. I had many acquaintances among the Aggarwal and Gujjar clans in that area, and also from the Punjabi community, so suggested that I stood a chance there. Mani Shankar Aiyar wrote a remarkable letter in my support to the chairman of the Screening Committee, writing 'Mahesh Manzar has been contributing to the Political Training Department of the All India Congress Committee, the best of his remarkable bilingual talent, which makes him equally fluent in English as in Hindi, not to mention Urdu. He's such a dynamic Congress activist and deserves to be given a ticket from the neighbouring constituency of Kasturba Nagar... request you to consider him for the same.'

Next, I visited Ahmed Patel, who was equally delighted about my decision, making me feel that maybe I could gain a political opportunity with all my mentors' blessings. However, a consent was needed from R K Dhawan, seniormost leader of the Parliamentary Constituency, New Delhi, and an associate of Indira Gandhi. He wanted to oblige his good friend, Ashok Chopra, who was also backed by the President of the Delhi Congress Committee, Subhash Chopra. Ahmed Patel tried his best to promote me, and even had me walk into a meeting he was having with R K Dhawan so that I could remind him of the many meetings I had organised for him in both 1998 and 1999 elections. I had even served as his polling and counting agent. R K Dhawan acknowledged my contributions, but said to Ahmed Patel, 'I totally agree to his worthiness, but Mahesh Manzar is only my friend while Ashok Chopra is like my brother!' And that was the end of the matter! Eventually, Ashok Chopra was not able to muster the relevant number of votes and Congress lost that seat by a big margin.

Perhaps it was a blessing in disguise, for I couldn't even count on my immediate family for their wholehearted support! Neither did I have the monetary resources needed to fight an assembly election.

***

It is my experience that when the members of a family are struggling to make ends meet, they remain united, but once they become financially secure, differences begin to set in. Such was the case with Chhaya's five brothers. After their father was murdered in 1957, they had remained a close-knit family till 1996, when each had become financially strong. Today's strife among couples can also be attributed to the same reason. Women who are financially independent have started asserting themselves, in contrast to the society of a few decades ago. The situation has made them both over-confident and at times, avaricious. I remember the case of a high-profile lady who had lent money on interest, and was now seeking my help to get her money back. She had even lent money to Dev Anand Mishra. I called him telling him that as her husband was a well-placed IAS officer and a former Union minister, things could get tough if he got involved. That did the trick and she got her money back.

Too much money can be a curse for it can bring sickness or dispute in its wake. One should have only as much as brings comfort and not luxury. There is a lot of inequality in the distribution of wealth in the country and if we amass it, somewhere we are stopping its flow and contributing to that inequality, depriving the lowest layer of society.

***

2003 also marked a very interesting event for I got interviewed by the AIR FM channel. It raised me to the heights of a celebrity. Both me and Chhaya were interviewed together on our views on philosophy of life and songs of our choice were aired in-between the questions. Chhaya handled it confidently and both of us answered truthfully. The interview was quite a hit and was even re-broadcast after a few months. It expanded my reach even more and brought many more people closer to me.

***

Once I happened to meet a truly graceful Sikh woman at a traffic signal near Sarvodya Enclave, when her car stopped next to mine. As our eyes met, I smiled at her. To my delight, she reciprocated! That was enough encouragement for me to introduce myself as a poet, informing her of my recently released book.
'Can I present my book to you?' I asked.
'That would be great!'
I did so, along with my visiting card, asking her to get in touch if she felt comfortable. I found out that her name was Ruby Singh and that casual encounter was the basis of a good friendship allowing me to later invite her to the New Friends Club. It was only when we saw each other for the first time that we realised the difference in our heights. We had only seen each other seated in our cars once before. She laughed the situation off, saying that it did not matter, because after all, we were not contemplating marriage! She was an NRI from Canada who was in Delhi to take care of her sick father and was single. A few days later, she reciprocated my gesture and invited me to her home in Sarvodaya Enclave for lunch. When I reached there, she told me that her father had to unexpectedly leave for Amritsar. Circumstances were conducive, but inhibitions couldn't be surmounted as I was engulfed in desire and fear, both!

Presenting my book to a lady at a traffic signal had happened once before. My car had stopped next to Begum Noor Bano's, a beautiful royal MP, and remembering that she had not come to my book release, I had immediately offered to give my book to her, apologising at the unconventional manner of presenting it. She graciously accepted and I promised to visit her at our mutual convenience.

Later, while I was walking in Lodhi Gardens, I bumped into Jai Prakash Aggarwal, a Lok Sabha MP for around twenty years who would occasionally ask me to draft some important official letters in English. He requested me to help him regain a foothold in politics, as he had been out of the scene for five years.

'You are regarded with favour by the High Command, so please put in a word to Ahmed Patel or V George to help me get some diplomatic post or the other,' he said to me.

I told him that I would try my best, then added, 'What about people like me who have never ever been elected a municipal councillor, despite being active for almost three decades?'

'You already have an established identity of a poet. You don't need politics to prop you up any further!' he replied.

'And tell me, do you invite only ministers and governors to your home? Don't I deserve to be invited?' he continued.

I immediately did so, feeling humbled that people showered so much love and affection onto me, and thanked the Divine for His Grace.

That same year, Ahmed Patel gave me an invitation to Sonia Gandhi's iftar party, always an event in which many top dignitaries are hosted, but very few Hindus are invited. I was with some prominent leaders like Dr Girija Vyas, Rita Bahuguna Joshi, and Renuka Chaudhary along with the NSUI President, Nadeem Javed. Renuka Chaudhary asked what I was doing these days, and before I could reply, Nadeem Javed interposed, 'Oh Manzar Sahab is an accomplished poet and his book has been released recently.' I said impulsively, 'Before a *shayer*, I am an *aashiq*!' eliciting a hearty laugh from all.

On Diwali, I took my son along to wish Ahmed Patel at home. He was surrounded by a number of leaders including Shailja, a senior Haryana Congress leader, with whom I was not friendly. Ahmed Patel was seated casually, his one ankle placed on the other knee. I too sat down in the same style, for I was used to interacting informally with him. Rather acerbically, she said, 'Manzar Sahab, put your foot down!' It was an embarrassing moment for both me and my son, especially as Ahmed Patel also did not say anything. Was I being ticked off because I had never given her adequate importance? Moreover, I was close to Bhupinder Singh Hooda and they belonged to different camps. The incident made me realise that I needed to be more mindful of my etiquette while interacting with high profile people, especially in public.

***

Later, that year, I was invited for the book release function of a friend. He introduced me to an elegant professor of psychology, Radhika, and with folded hands, she bowed deeply in greeting. I became the unofficial host of the party, keeping them all in splits. One thing I understood during the evening was that the Professor was not happily married. A few days later, she called to say that she was in the area and would like to meet me, so I invited her home. We spent a wonderful afternoon together, finding a lot of things in common. When I presented my book to her, she was impressed by both my personality and poetry.

After only three short meetings, she proclaimed, 'Maheshji, you're unique! God must have broken the mould after creating you!' I was amazed at her words, for they reminded me of one of Chhaya's brothers who had also remarked that their family considered me to be unique. But he had acknowledged it after twenty-three years of our marriage, and here she was saying that after only three meetings. Pleased, I asked her to give me points on the basis of Justice Mishra's four 'V' formula and was really happy when she gave me 80 per cent! If a woman wants to be admired, men too like to gain approval!

I countered, 'You are being generous with your numbers! I know my worth for my very good friend, Mahi Malhotra valued me at 70 per cent, though I found that too to be on the higher side.'

She continued, 'May I tell you one thing more, Mahesh ji, I feel you need at least five women in your life to make it blissful.'

I laughed and replied, 'But that's what my Guru used to say! Do you also consider me to be the male version of Draupadi?'

'Of course you are! How rightly he described you! You cannot be satisfied with only one, you need a poet, a professor, a politician, an artist and also someone spiritual—all hues of life!'

'Radhika, you're no less unique! No one has analysed me as well as you have, and that too after only a short span of time! I find you to be so contradictory and complex and so complicated to understand!'

I continued: 'After my book release two years ago, at least two dozen women have come into my life, 90 per cent of whom were fake! Earlier they were humble, truthful and generous, and not at all demanding. There was a synchronisation in their thoughts, words and deeds. But now they want one to cater to them in all respects, totally unlike before! Even you have shown such traits!'

'Don't you know, Maheshji, that loyalty and gratitude are missing from the very DNA of a woman? She herself doesn't know when her mood changes and she moves on!'

I was astonished, for it was the very first time that someone had confessed the fickleness of a woman's mind. None from among the hundreds of women I had known had ever accepted this fallibility and I told her that I saluted her for saying so! There is a well-known couplet of Raja Bharthari:

> *Triya Charitram*
> *Purushsya bhagyam*
> *Devon na janati*
> *Kuto manushya*

> *A woman's character*
> *And man's Destiny*
> *Gods can decipher not*
> *What to expect from men*

Raja Bharthari was a great king of Ujjain and during his reign, India was regarded as the land of gold. The king was besotted with his third wife, Pingala. Once Guru Gorakhnath visited his court and was warmly received by the king. Happy with his devotion, Guru Gorakhnath presented him with an apple, saying that if the king ate it, he would always remain young and vigorous and so be able to serve the kingdom well. However, the king decided to present the fruit to his favourite wife, with the thought that she would always remain young and beautiful. It so happened that the queen was enamoured with the chief security officer and wanting him to be dynamic, passed the apple onto him. Now the courtesan was this officer's sweetheart, and so he presented the fruit to her. When she received it and understood its significance, she felt that it was only the king who deserved such a blessing and, therefore, presented the apple back to the king, much to his shock.

The whole story was, thus unravelled, exposing his queen's disloyalty, making Raja Bharthari completely lose faith in life itself. Subsequently, he abdicated the throne in favour of his younger brother, Vikramaditya and became a disciple of Guru Gorakhnath. He spent years meditating in the caves near Ujjain, detaching from worldly affairs. I find those caves fascinating and always visit them whenever I go to the Mahakaal Jyotirlinga temple in Ujjain.

***

Once, while we were working together, Mani Shankar Aiyar asked me that if mythologically, Chhaya was the second wife of Mahesh, who was the first?

I replied, 'Sandhya.'

'So, as you identify yourself with the mythological Mahesh, who is your Sandhya?'

'No one as such, since I have got married only once,' I clarified. 'But I would love to give that name to my dear friend Mahi, who till date is the best lady to come into my life!'

Curiously he asked, 'And why does Mahi deserve to be your Sandhya?'

'Bhai Sahab, we have never been physically close, but I feel that she's undoubtedly my soulmate. Since we met in 1999, she has become a great moral support, and indeed is my dearest friend, philosopher, guide and reformer as well!'

'I am glad that you have such a close friendship in your life!'

Mani Shankar Aiyar was an observer for the Northeast States and when an internal strife rose in Manipur, Sonia Gandhi formulated a high powered committee in late 2003, appointing him along with Dr Manmohan Singh and Pranab Mukherjee, to resolve it. The three were to have their first meeting at Pranab Mukherjee's house at 5.30 pm one day. Before the meeting, Mani Shankar Aiyar called to ask where I was. I was nearby at the DPCC offices at 2 Talkatora Road, and he told me to come to Pranab Mukherjee's house, just opposite to the DPCC office. The plan was that once the meeting was over, we could go together to his office in Tilak Lane to complete work pertaining to the Political Training Department. I was quite friendly with Pranab Mukherjee's PA Ranbir Singh, and at 5.30 pm, Dr Manmohan Singh entered 5 Talkatora Road, rousing a wonder in my heart that such a high-profile dignitary could be so conscientious about punctuality. Both the PA and myself rushed forward to welcome him, he with folded hands, while I touched his feet. However, Mani Shankar Aiyar came almost 25 minutes late as he had been caught up in some urgent family matter. Such was Mani Shankar Aiyar's elevation at that time that he could make them wait, for he was a sort of troubleshooter for the Party since Rajiv Gandhi's times and was often included in high-powered committees for resolving challenging situations. But it was also a quirk of Destiny that the two who waited for Mani Shankar Aiyar rose to the highest positions in the country, one as PM, and the other as President.

***

The year ended on an auspicious note for I visited Shirdi along with my younger son, Lakhan. I wanted to go to Tryambakeshwar Shiva Jyotirlinga temple near Nashik, as an astrological combination for *Kaal sarp yog* was in his birth chart and it could be remedied by a puja done there. He had an aggressive nature which was causing considerable strife at home. I had taken him for a pilgrimage six years earlier, but to no avail, for he often got into trouble, both at home and at school. When he was barely thirteen, his teacher had summoned me to demand what was being taught to the child. I was surprised at her question. She said that Lakhan had recited the following sentence in class: 'A woman is the supreme gift of God given to man in compensation for the loss of Heaven!' She added that she knew that I was a poet, 'But he's just a child and this is what he has quoted in class!' she said. It made me feel quite embarrassed, realising that he must have overheard me speaking the lines to a friend. It was one of my favourite couplets composed by a well-known Hindi poet, which I had translated into English and had recited it innumerable times to beguile my lady friends!

However, the head pujari in Nasik told me that the ritual had to be performed either by me, my wife or son. He suggested that I should make my son chant *Aum Namah Shivay*. One of the shlokas in the Rigveda states that God is beyond places, rituals and even prayers, and listens to the voice of the heart. The pujari's advice reminded me of one of Osho's aphorisms that people had become so lazy that they had begun to outsource even the rituals which they should be performing themselves! The visit was so blissful that I prayed to Baba to allow me to visit at least once a year, for I had missed a couple of years in between. His Grace is so benevolent that my frequency of annual visits has been increasing, year by year! Since then, I think I must have visited Shirdi at least fifty times.

SIXTH DECADE
WINS & WOES

Chapter 1

So Near and Yet So Far

THE NEW YEAR started on a spiritual note. Hema was connected to the Brahmakumaris and asked me if I would like to make a donation for their upcoming International Brahmakumaris Conference at the Jawaharlal Nehru stadium. The President was the chief guest. After the event, Hema took me on to the stage to meet three venerable ladies, respectfully being addressed as 'Dadi'. When Hema introduced me, Dadi Janki smiled and said, 'But he should be called Krishna!' In a loving gesture, she presented me with a beautiful idol of Krishna.

***

The CJI, Ranganath Mishra, had advised me to sell my commercial building in Sadar Bazar. Just as he had predicted, I found selling it difficult with tenants who had been there for seven years! My elders had always said that it was not good to live on either rental or interest income, as it turned a person into a lethargic profligate. In my family's eyes, I was unemployed, since I didn't do anything concrete. But this income had helped me grow in the literary, political and social scenarios. The income was taking care of my household expenses and my sons' education, comfortably.

The sale of the building was becoming bothersome, so I consulted my astrologer friend, Pt L R Mishra, purohit of Dr Karan Singh, who advised a Rudrabhishek with milk on a Monday and to feed green, leafy vegetables to cows every Wednesday. I enjoyed that and began feeding them almost daily. I believe it was Divine Grace that made me meet Haji Meharban, a Congress friend, within a month near Paharganj, while feeding cows. He was a builder and with his help, I was able to finally sell it, though at a reduced price, suffering a loss of more than Rs 10 lakh. The blessings I received from the rituals were plentiful and I have continued with them to this day. However, I was uncomfortable in pouring the milk on the Shivling, so I spoke to the panditji and suggested that we collect the milk in a bowl and make tea to be distributed to the poor. He appreciated my thoughts and said, 'Why just distribute it? We can have it like *prasadam*.'

'Panditji, I have been visiting Shirdi for seven years, and the *pujaris* there even collect the water used for bathing the Sai idol and distribute it as holy water. There is a long queue for it, every morning!'

***

Meanwhile, my younger son wanted to do his MBA from IMI. He had appeared for the CAT exams, but his scores were low, and he wasn't in the first list. Disappointed, I approached V George and begged him for the admission through the director general of IMI. Nitish Sen Gupta, who had been a Lok Sabha member and former revenue secretary in the Finance Ministry. I broke down and said, 'Bhaisahab, I have always given my best for the Party. Earlier, you had promised to help with my elder son's admission. I request you to help now. At that time, Kamal Nath was involved but now the DG may be more approachable.'

'Even if I have to go personally to the Institute, I will do that!' he said, pacifying me. My mind went back to the time I had garlanded him before Ahmed Patel at the dinner at my home in 2003. I hoped that loyalty and gratitude would now pay off!

Unfortunately, my son's name wasn't in the second list either. V George called Nitish Sen Gupta and told him that I would be coming to meet him for my son's admission. I introduced myself as a poet and presented my book to him. He reiterated his stand, saying that he could admit my son right then or we could wait as a third list was expected. To my great joy, my son's name was in the final list and he thus gained admission on his own merit.

A few days later, I was with V George, who was busy as the names for the general elections were to be finalised and people were coming for submissions to 10, Janpath. He was called to meet Sonia Gandhi and turning to me, he said, 'Maheshji, please go outside and accept the submissions, as these cannot be delayed.' He introduced me to the candidates as an AICC coordinator, who would collect their applications. It was indeed a prestigious moment as these submissions were accepted only by Sonia Gandhi, V George or Ahmed Patel, personally. Feeling the sanctity of the task, I tried to project myself as Rajiv Gandhi would have done, give the best in that moment. V George returned perhaps thirty minutes later and was surprised to see that all the aspirants had been dealt with!

Once V George asked me to suggest names of ten probable candidates for New Delhi, as I was familiar with the leaders there. After giving it much thought, I drew up a list with Dev Anand Mishra, Ajay Maken and Nafisa Ali, besides seven others. V George was surprised with my selection, saying the first three were already being considered and commended my political acumen! From among all the candidates, Ajay Maken got the ticket. During the campaign, his wife and mother came to my home to ask for blessings. I assured them of my support, saying I had been good friends with his uncle, Lalit Maken. But despite my requesting the two to ask him to call me, he never did and, therefore, I didn't attend his meetings.

After the selection for New Delhi, V George discussed candidates for Chandni Chowk constituency with me.

'We are confused about the Chandni Chowk Parliamentary seat; the sitting candidate, Jai Prakash Aggarwal has lost twice. He cannot be considered for a third time according to policy.'

'Yes, even R K Dhawan has not been given a chance due to that reason.'

'We can't find a suitable Vaishya candidate who will be able to win.'

I lightheartedly said, 'Don't you know there's an Aggarwal right here in front of you!'

V George was excited. 'Are you an Aggarwal? Then who better than you?'

'Don't raise my hopes! Kesriji had promised me a ticket for the Corporation, but when Tariq Anwar pointed out that it was a Muslim stronghold, my name was not considered. Even Sheila Dikshit and Ahmed Patel were proposing me as an MLA candidate from Kasturba Nagar, but R K Dhawan insisted on a Punjabi, so both times, I lost my chance!'

Pat came his reply, 'But this time we need a Vaishya, and you are one!'

'Please don't make me a laughing stock by considering me for Lok Sabha!'

Emphatically, he asserted, 'You can be the perfect candidate. You know the area well as you were born there and are well known too!'

Feeling a little hopeful, I added, 'I have an old commercial building there, almost eight decades old. I have lived in the constituency for thirty-three years.'

'There can't be a better candidate than you! Why don't you

use Aggarwal in your name then?' he asked, puzzled.

'Why should I use it? I consider myself to be a universal person, beyond all caste, creed, class and religion. Once I began to write poetry, I took on a pen name and have used only that ever since, although officially my name is still Mahesh Aggarwal. I am a universal blood donor too, as I am O positive! And a donor of love to all and sundry!'

A laugh escaped him as he commented, 'I thought maybe either your mother or your father was a Muslim!'

'You're not alone in thinking that. But that doesn't bother me.'

'Then I suggest you use your full name, Mahesh Manzar Aggarwal, or else people may get confused about your real caste. Sometimes that can create problems, especially during ethnic clashes.'

'I will do as you suggest and use my full name, henceforth!'

'This is perfect! We will use both your names. That will help to capture both the Muslim and Vaishya votes, as they form the majority of the demography there. We don't have time, so submit your biodata today, itself.'

Though I was convinced by V George's suggestion to use my full name, I however, consulted Sheila Dikshit and Ahmed Patel. It was only when both approved of my name as Mahesh Manzar Aggarwal that I went ahead and got new cards made.

The next afternoon, I got a call from Shivraj Patil's office. I had been invited for tea by the chairman of the screening committee. I presented myself at his home with sweets and my book. He was pretty impressed and as he flipped the pages, I told him about the release function with stalwarts like Sheila Dikshit, Balrama Jhakhar, Vasant Sathe, and Bhishma Narain Singh, and with Mani Shankar Aiyar presiding over it. He was astonished and asked for how long I had been associated with Congress. He was surprised to know that I had been connected since 1974. He expressed shock at how I had been deprived of a ticket for so many years!

'Babuji, there is a wonderful quote on Destiny, 'When the first layer of earth was laid, the Destiny of the last person to live on it, was written'. Destiny matters!' I informed him.

As I was leaving, he commented, 'Maheshji, I approve of your credentials and am recommending your name to Sonia Gandhi.'

'I refer to her as CP,' I interpolated.

'That's a unique way of referring to her,' he said delightedly. 'But I want you to please remember that this is the Congress party! What if you're not selected, ultimately?'

It was a subtle warning to not let my hopes soar! 'Babuji, I will then give credence to Harivansh Rai Bachchan's philosophy in his autobiography, *'Basere se door!'*

'What is that?'

'What he feels is the essence of life:

Mun ka ho toh achhchha,
Mun ka na ho toh aur bhi achhchha.

If something which you desire happens, that's good, but if it is not what you desire, then it's even better!'

'What does that mean?'

'Babuji, you are 'Shiv Raj'. I am sure you will be able to understand its meaning.'

'No, please clarify.'

'What we desire can give short-term gratification, satisfying us in the moment. But God knows our long-term future, and tries to gratify us accordingly.'

'That's a really deep thought! Excellently said!'

'So, if the ticket doesn't materialise, I will accept that there's a Divine design at work! God knows what is best for me and everything is a blessing in disguise!'

As the news got out that my ticket was almost finalised, Sajjan Kumar called to wish me, saying, 'I told you, you deserve to be only in Parliament!'

'Oh yes, I remember! But I have not reached there yet! *Dilli abhi door hai!*'

His wishes jolted me out of my dream state, making me realise the reality of the situation! A fear began to gnaw at my subconscious: if I got a ticket straightaway for Parliament, how would I manage? I wasn't even sure people at ground level would support me. Deep inside I hoped that something would happen to make them withdraw my name on their own!

I had gone to seek Sheila Dikshit's blessings. 'Maheshji, look I immediately approved your name!' she said, happily.

'Thank you for your blessings!' Even though Sheila Dikshit hadn't been able to give me the chairmanship she had promised, she had always supported me, attending all my personal functions.

I visited Ahmed Patel, who also told me that he had immediately approved of my selection. But as they say, there is always a slip between the cup and the lip, and soon, the opportunity slipped away from my hands! Jai Prakash Aggarwal called me and remarked, 'Mahesh Bhai, you too are doing this to me?'

'No, no, I am not doing anything against you! V George has proposed my name,' I replied.

I learnt later from Ahmed Patel that Jai Prakash Aggarwal had met Sonia Gandhi with the request that his ticket not be given to Mahesh Manzar as he was junior to him. He outlined how he and workers at the grassroots would have difficulty in relating to a flag merchant, even though he accepted that I was competent and cordial. Instead, he named Kapil Sibal as the ideal candidate and expressed his willingness to support him. Kapil Sibal was already a Rajya Sabha member.

A few MLAs from the Chandni Chowk constituency were not happy with my selection either, and, therefore, a delegation went to Sonia Gandhi—Haroon Yusuf, a three-time MLA and a minister in Sheila Dikshit's cabinet and Anjali

Rai, Ajay Maken's aunt, also a senior MLA. The grounds for their objection were that I had been the party's flag supplier till a few years ago and had never stood for any election. They agreed that Kapil Sibal would be the better choice!

I met Kapil Sibal, but he denied it all, outright, saying that since he was already a Rajya Sabha member, he could not contest for the Lok Sabha! I, however, assured him that I would wholeheartedly support him if he was given the chance! Shivraj Patil also called saying that my selection had generated a controversy and that the CP had sought advice from M L Fotedar, who had been a political advisor to Indira Gandhi. I immediately went to seek his blessings, and heard him talking on the phone, saying, 'But everyone identifies Mahesh Manzar as a flag merchant!' I realised that my business was hindering my growth on the political scenario. My hopes were dashed, but, nevertheless, I approached M L Fotedar and touching his feet, smilingly informed him that I was the flag merchant he had been mentioning on the phone!

He laughed aloud at the synchronicity, for we had never met before. I presented my book to him and told him that I would be perfectly happy with whatever he decided, peppering my conversation with a few of my favourite destiny quotes.

'I have tremendous faith in God and surrender myself to His will! He takes His decisions through messengers like you. Bertrand Russell has said, 'Cooperate with the inevitable,' and I have made an amendment to that.'

'What is that?' he asked curiously.

'To cooperate with the inevitable, gracefully.'

The situation was so volatile that ultimately Kapil Sibal was made to resign from Rajya Sabha and then stood for elections from the Chandni Chowk constituency. I was actually flooded with relief for it would have been a huge task for me, one that seemed almost impossible to accomplish! Ahmed Patel tried to cover up, saying that Sonia Gandhi had not selected my name as she felt I was a Muslim and she wanted a Vaishya for the seat. Rarely in the history of the Congress has the Chandni Chowk constituency been deprived of a Vaishya candidate!

Later, I felt that this turn of events had been a blessing in disguise. Fighting a Parliamentary election is a very expensive affair! A friend had done this before and lost in the assembly elections. He had had a nervous breakdown and ultimately, it led to his demise.

As it is, my family was so critical and non-supportive; and a defeat in the elections would have added fuel to fire! Besides, there wasn't a single trustworthy relative on whom I could depend on. Even after my book release, other than my eldest sister, no one was happy with the recognition I was receiving. Moreover, I didn't have either adequate money, muscle or mental power to deal with tough situations that can arise in elections.

In May, in a fortunate turn of events, Congress returned to power with a coalition and Dr Manmohan Singh became the Prime Minister. The Party wanted Sonia Gandhi, but circumstances made her relinquish it voluntarily in favour of Dr Manmohan Singh, a phenomenal economist recognised as the one person who had been an instrument of change for the nation. He had brought in globalisation and liberalisation during 1991-95, under PM Narasimha Rao.

Rahul Gandhi had won his Lok Sabha seat from Amethi, so I set off to congratulate him. I approached my friend, Kishori Lal Sharma, his PA, for an appointment, and armed with my poetry book and flowers, I presented myself at the appointed hour. After conventional greetings, I launched into a monologue, informing him I had been fortunate enough to have gained opportunities to work for his grandmother, his father and even his mother. I told him that I was a poet and had launched my book at an event blessed by senior Congress leaders.

Garrulousness has always been the bane of my life and in this instance too, my unchecked speech proved to be my undoing. It was obvious that Rahul Gandhi was not paying attention! He was not even glancing at me! In an acerbic tone, I said, 'Rahulji, I had come to congratulate you and present you my book in which there is a poem I wrote in my beloved leader, Rajivji's memory. If you say so, I can leave the book, or else…' I was going to say '…or else I will take it back.' Kishori Lal hastily took the book from my hands and thanking me for my efforts, herded me away from Rahul. I was really offended by his indifferent attitude and ever since, have never tried to visit him.

About that time, real estate prices skyrocketed, encouraging me to invest almost the entire money from the sale of my shop in investments in Gurgaon. My dealer friends, Rajesh Mehta and Vinod Rajpal guided me to invest Rs 20 lakh in a plot in Sun City in Gurgaon, facing the Golf Course. They proved to be absolutely right, for indeed, its value increased to crores in about twenty years. I decided to register the plot jointly with my elder son out of love and affection for him, but when I asked him to accompany me to sign the pre-registry documents, he refused, upset that I had woken him up from his afternoon siesta. He also belligerently told me to remove his name from the documents. I was so infuriated that I deleted his name and registered the plot in my name alone. This was a very prosperous time for me. I would purchase property and sell it soon at a profit, even before it was registered.

Once I came across a newspaper ad for the sale of a 300-square yard plot in R D City, opposite Sun City, at just Rs 36 lakh. I purchased that instantly, another investment that fetched me huge profits, later.

I drove almost daily to Gurgaon as that was the hub of the property market. One morning, I asked Chhaya for some *bhindi subzi* that she had cooked for lunch along with a *paratha* for breakfast. She refused, saying she had prepared the vegetable for lunch. I retorted angrily telling her that I wouldn't be home for lunch! That angered her and she flung the *paratha* onto the floor. Two dealers in my drawing room witnessed the ugly scene. I had always conducted all transactions at home, as I didn't feel safe conducting them outside. That day, I left without having breakfast, and later in the day, Rajesh Mehta asked his wife to send a packed tiffin for me.

Chapter 2

Man ka ho ya na ho, sab achhchha

AS MANI SHANKAR Aiyar had been close to Rajiv Gandhi, Sonia Gandhi held him in high regard for his competence and loyalty. He had been given charge of two prominent ministries in the new government, Petroleum and Natural Gas and Panchayati Raj. I went to congratulate him at his Petroleum Ministry office. He received me happily and asked if I wanted a petrol pump! I humbly refused which made him appreciate me, since many were badgering him for one!

'Even if you had asked for it, Mahesh Bhai, I couldn't have given it, as a recent Supreme Court judgement has revoked a minister's discretionary powers to allocate petrol pumps to anyone!'

As we chatted, I noticed a couple of small briefcases in one corner and enquired what these were.

'I have been given charge of this Ministry for a few years only. Any day I may be asked to leave; I would then just need to pick them up and walk out!'

I was astonished at his pragmatism! The *Bhagavad Gita* propounds the same philosophy—that one should not be too attached to power or anything else, for everything can be lost without intimation at a moment's notice. Attachment is good, but it should always be tempered with a sense of detachment and one should learn to accept things happening in the present.

'Mahesh Bhai, all such things are pretty temporary. Anytime, they can be taken back from us!'

'That's a very philosophical view of life! This is what I want to inculcate into my life and am inching forward towards it,' I replied.

***

Once I met the younger brother of my first love, Neera, at a government office, after a gap of forty years. He was at a high post and helped to get my work sorted. I enquired about Neera and he told me that she was happily settled, sharing her number when I asked for it. When I called her, she was as ecstatic to hear from me as I was to connect with her. She told me that her husband, a professor, would love to talk to me. She assured me that he was very open-minded and later in the evening, Harinder called me himself. After only a few exchanges, we felt a kindred energy, and he invited me to accompany him to Haridwar, as he was going there with a couple of his colleagues. I agreed and we entrained two days later. I had an east-facing room at the hotel and early the next morning, I was mesmerised by the sheer beauty of the rising sun, emerging from behind a distant hill and spreading its brilliance on the flowing waters of the Ganges. I had never seen such a charismatic, divine scene in my life, not even in Kashmir, a state renowned for its scenic wonders! To this day, that scene is integrated into my soul.

I had been a Sun worshipper for twenty years and many times, I have felt a close, personal bond with the Sun God. Innumerable times, when the sun is not visible when I go to offer water, I pray in my heart that it shows a glimpse of its Divine presence and invariably it does, tearing apart dense clouds to do so, before vanishing immediately afterwards!

Harinder was visiting Haridwar for a *pind-daan* ceremony

for the salvation of his parents' souls. The ceremony was performed at Har-ki-Pauri by a pandit and it encouraged me to get it done for my parents too. It gave me a deep sense of satisfaction and I thanked Harinder profusely for showing me this path! All in all, it was a memorable trip, setting the base for many more future interactions. Thereafter, Haridwar became another favourite pilgrimage place for me to visit regularly. I added Rishikesh to my list as well.

***

Sahib Singh Verma, a senior politician and earlier, Delhi's chief minister and a Union Labour Minister later in the Vajpayee government, was a good friend. I had first met him in mid 1984 at a get-together organised by one of Chhaya's relatives, who was a councillor. Sahib Singh Verma was a very imposing personality, and would invariably be clad in a half-sleeve kurta. I commented, 'Sahib Singhji, you have a distinctive spark in you! Even your birth and Destiny numbers say you have a bright future.'

'You must offer water to the Sun God every morning, for it is because of him that we are surviving. The Sun is our scientific God. Please try to feed birds and put out something sweet for ants too, daily. Keep water for birds in the balcony and make it a point to nourish a few plants every day. We keep taking from Nature and this is a good way of showing our gratitude to the Universe!'

He enthusiastically agreed to act on my suggestions and appreciated my simple thought process.

'They may help in enhancing your Destiny! I have been performing them for quite some time and feel as if I am blessed with Divine Grace.'

Within a year, Sahib Singh Verma was appointed MCD chairman. He called to inform me of his appointment and subsequently would always acknowledge my bit in enhancing his Destiny! When he became the Delhi chief minister in 1996, I called to congratulate him and he invited me and my wife over for lunch, saying that he was holding a small get together, the following Sunday. Chhaya was unwell, so I took my younger son along. It was a quirk of fate though that, due to an incongruous policy, he had to step down from his position just a couple of months before his tenure was over, in favour of Sushma Swaraj. In a span of five years, three chief ministers were appointed by the BJP! However, Sahib Singh Verma won the Lok Sabha General elections in May 1999, and when the Vajpayee government came back into power, he was appointed the Labour Minister.

I once requested him to inaugurate a friend, Mahendra Aggarwal's steel factory in Ghaziabad. He told me that he was traveling out of town. I asked if Madam was accompanying him.

After a moment, he smiled and replied, 'That's a question which shouldn't be asked! But since you're asking, let me share an entertaining story which I read in a magazine.' Once the British PM, George Llyod was going to attend a peace conference that ended the first World War. He was asked a similar question—whether Mrs George was accompanying him. The PM smoothly replied, 'When you are invited to a meal, do you carry your own sandwiches?'

I admired his wit and apologised for my faux pas. He continued, 'But I am a pure Indian, totally steeped in our culture. I am devoted to my wife and like to take her along with me!'

The UPA coalition government won the 2004 general elections and Sahib Singh Verma again lost his position. Around Diwali, I went to meet him as I always used to make it a point to visit friends even if they were not in power. To me, my relationships mattered more than positions did. As I was leaving, I said, 'Bhaisahab, I have visited your home many times; won't you come to my house, too?'

It was as if he was waiting for the invitation. He asked immediately, 'When should I come?'

Delighted, I responded, 'You may come any day, Bhaisahab! It's your house, and you're welcome anytime, even tomorrow.'

Unfortunately, even though I was enthusiastic about inviting him home, our interaction slipped my mind completely. The next morning at about 8.30 am, his car stopped at my gate much to my confusion. I had just woken up and was still groggy with sleep. He took in my appearance and lightly said, 'Still sleeping, Manzar Sahab! *Waah!* No wonder, Congress doesn't give you a post of importance! You did invite me, right?'

I apologised hastily and taking him inside, detailed my family to take care of him while I made myself presentable. He had brought a 2 kg box of cashew sweets, a gesture which was truly endearing, for rarely had any VIP who had visited me earlier, ever brought anything. I quickly ordered refreshments, while Chhaya mustered whatever she could. Once the repast was over, Sahib Singh Verma said, 'I have a proposition for you.'

'What's that, Bhaisahab?' I asked, a bit surprised.

'You have been working with Congress for the past thirty years and now, too, they have been in power at the State level for many years and at the Centre for about half a year, yet they have not shown any regard for your loyalty and commitment. Nor has Sheila Dikshit rewarded your untiring devotion in six years! It seems they are not going to give you anything, so it would be better that you join the BJP! I will arrange a direct meeting with Vajpayeeji.' Amazed at the outright proposal, I replied. 'Bhaisahab, I am overwhelmed by your proposal. But forgive me—even if Congress doesn't give me any tangible post, I will never leave it. Congress has been like a mother to me! I have received a lot from the Party, and it has given me recognition in almost the entire country. A post is not everything!'

'That's a very good thing to say!' he replied.

'It's not everyone's Destiny to even be a councillor, leave alone, a higher position.'

'Yes, Destiny has a strong role to play.'

'Also, Bhaisahab, in 1975, Sanjay Gandhi had made me coordinator of the publicity department of the All India Congress Committee. Along with that, he gave me opportunities to supply several necessary materials, since I was with the cloth industry. My family have been die-hard Congress activists. The Party is in our blood and my grandfather, Lala Shyamlal, was a freedom fighter.'

'Oh great! That goes a long way back, indeed.'

'Another more important factor, Bhaisahab, is that I don't agree with the ideology of the BJP. I cannot connect to an organisation which differentiates between people, segregating them on the basis of religion. God created only man and woman, and everything else, has been created by us humans! All are made up of the same mud and blood, so what does it matter how one worships or conducts oneself! I have tremendous faith in Sanatana Dharma and belief in *Vasudhaiva kutumbakam*—the entire world is one family.

Sarv jan hitay,
Sarv jan Sukhay
In the interest of all, for the happiness of all,
as also Sarve bhavanti sukhinah
Sarve santu Niramah
May all attain peace; may all remain healthy.

If your faith doesn't convey the message of love and humanity, it cannot be conducive. The principle of 'righteousness' applies to everyone with passion and compassion, and I don't think BJP adheres to this philosophy. They are killing the real spirit of Sanatana Dharma.'

Sahib Singh Verma shook his head in a perplexed fashion at my vehemence. 'And Bhaisahab, look at your own situation! You yourself once told me that though Vajpayee gives you recognition, Advani doesn't, and that he was responsible for your abrupt removal from the chief minister's office. So, there are multiple factions in your party too, as there are in ours. Human nature is the same the world over, so what's the point of joining your party? If Advani cannot be cordial towards such a dynamic leader like you, where do I stand?'

'You have a point there!'

'Bhaisahab, if you uproot a tree which has been standing in one place for thirty years and transplant it, how do you expect it to survive?'

Highly amused, Sahib Singh Verma commented, 'Right you are, Maheshji! I take my proposition back! I agree with every word you have said, so let things be as they are!'

'I am obliged,' I mirthfully concluded. Then I added, 'Have you come across Mani Shankar Aiyar's book, *Knickerwallahs, Silly-Billies and Other Curious Creatures?*'

'No, I have not.'

'It is an enlightening account about the actual purpose behind the creation of the RSS and Savarkar's ideology. Even Narasimha Rao is fond of this book! I got so interested in the subject that I began to do my own research and found an article by Hedgewar which showed that the RSS was inspired by an Italian Fascist force to safeguard the interests of the Hindus, their culture and national unity, without any political innuendoes. Many of the current political-social organisations are like the Jan Sangh, which is now the BJP, Bajrang Dal, Vishwa Hindu Parishad and such others that have emerged from it.'

'Is that really so?'

'Hedgewar and Golwalkar had said that the RSS would never enter any kind of power politics and see what is happening now? Gandhi had suggested the dissolution of the Congress party after Independence, but its leaders ignored it.'

'Maheshji, please donate some knowledge to me as well!'

'You are so wise yourself! How can I do that?'

'At least, give me Maniji's book.'

'That I can do, but as it is out of print, I would be obliged if you return it after reading.'

'Also, you are a poet-writer of some renown, and you must be having many books. I have set up a big library in Jaipur, so whatever books you can spare will be kept in it,' he said.

'Oh, that's a great initiative. Your party goes in for building temples and you are thinking of a library!'

'Maheshji, I was a librarian in a college before joining full-time politics!' he said, humbly.

I had a huge collection of books since other poets and writers kept gifting me their books. Much to his joy, I was able to give more than three hundred books, making him say that it was the largest number anyone had ever given him!

***

One morning, when I was asleep after having returned from a function, the previous night, our helper, Ramu, woke me up with the words, 'Sai Baba has come!' He said that a sadhu was at the gate who looked like Sai Baba. I told him to invite the ascetic into the house and I offered him some refreshments. He was traveling to Haridwar and asked if I would give him Rs 500. I felt it to be on the higher side and so said, 'Baba, may I offer Rs 251, instead?' He refused and walked out, seeming a bit annoyed. I suddenly recalled reading in Sai Baba's biography, *Sai Satcharitra* that when Baba used to ask for a particular amount, it had to be given, as he wouldn't take anything else. I regretted my words and immediately asked Ramu to call him back. He returned within a few minutes saying that the ascetic was not to be seen anywhere. I rushed out myself to see if I could find him, but the sadhu had, indeed, disappeared.

My sister and her daughters were also with us at that time and they too had come down on hearing the commotion. She, however, told me not to dwell too much on it and Chhaya, agreed with her.

The rest of the day passed normally, but in the evening, a strange incident happened. We were in the lobby after dinner, when unexpectedly the crockery in the cupboard behind us began to tumble down, pushing the cupboard doors open. There was no reason at all for the dishes to fall and it sent a wave of shock through me, for the incident of the morning was still in my subconscious mind. I attributed this to the Baba's anger and insisted that we should go then and there to the Sai temple at Lodhi Road to offer the amount and distribute sweets to devotees. It was only after asking for forgiveness at Baba's feet that I felt a little better.

***

My visits to Narasimha Rao became more frequent as his health had begun to fail. One day, I asked him, 'Babuji, why is Sonia Gandhi still annoyed with you?' In his usual cryptic manner, he just said, 'I didn't want to be another Kesri!'

The Party had offered Sonia Gandhi the Presidentship after Rajiv Gandhi's assassination, but she had outrightly refused at that grievous moment. Consequently, Narasimha Rao had been appointed Congress President in May 1991 with her consent. It is said that an understanding had been undertaken that after sometime, he would resign from his post. A month later, when Congress came into power with the backing of a coalition, Sonia Gandhi had again been asked to become the Prime Minister, but she declined, one reason being Rahul Gandhi's refusal in allowing her to accept, as he feared for her life. Subsequently, a decision taken by the Party high command with the tacit assent of Sonia Gandhi, was to appoint Narasimha Rao as Prime Minister.

I recalled meeting Narasimha Rao after a meeting of the Parliamentary Board in April, when the tickets were being finalised. He had been in poor health and had even declined to fight the Lok Sabha elections. Rajiv Gandhi had accepted his decision, based on his health. But Destiny had its own Divine design. He became the PM, when he had not even wanted to be an MP! As soon as he became PM, overnight he became really vibrant, all health issues forgotten! Later, however, Narasimha Rao didn't give up his Party Presidentship as was expected of him, even though he had been appointed Prime Minister. That explains Sonia Gandhi's antipathy towards him. This was explained to me by Vasant Sathe. He said that if Sonia Gandhi became President of the Party, she would have wielded phenomenal power, as she had support from the whole party. She could have even forced Narasimha Rao to resign from the Prime Minister's post, like it had been done when Kesriji had been ousted from the post of Congress President.

When Shivraj Patil lost the Lok Sabha elections, I went over to sympathise with him. As I got up to leave, I reminded him about a quote which I had shared with him a while back:

Mun ka ho toh achhchha,
Mun ka na ho toh aur bhi achhchha

He didn't respond, but his expression made me realise that I had committed yet another faux pas! However, within three days, Sonia Gandhi appointed him as the Home Minister of the country! I again presented myself at his home, this time with flowers and sweets and he immediately hugged me. I said softly into his ears, 'Babuji, I was really regretting saying that to you on my last visit, but now I am truly glad for you! Now you will be in the Rajya Sabha for six years with no tension of contesting for Lok Sabha elections!' He hugged me joyfully, offering me sweets. My unthinking words had turned out to be fortunate for him!

Chapter 3

Family Matters

CHHAYA AND I were attending a religious function at her sister's home when we heard that her second brother had suffered a massive brain stroke, leaving him paralytic. We visited him in the hospital, and seeing his pathetic condition, I couldn't help but recall his past aggressive nature.

After their father had passed away, Chhaya's family had shifted to Bhiwani, where her two elder brothers had got jobs in Birla Cloth Mills. The mill owners would give books and uniforms to all children who didn't have a father. Chhaya thus became a beneficiary of the scheme. However, sometime later, an officer objected that although she didn't have a father, she lived with her brothers who were working at the mill and as such, she was not entitled to the scholarship. Subsequently, the benefit was withdrawn, causing much angst to this second brother. He was so furious that he had rushed to the book counter in the factory to demand the benefit. The in-charge had refused to comply, saying that he was just following orders from above. This incensed Chhaya's brother even more and he tried to hit the store assistant with an iron rod that was placed nearby. Fortunately, he missed the assistant as he pushed his chair backwards against the wall and the rod thus hit the table, shattering the glass top. I was shocked at his story of self-confessed violence, and asked, 'What if you had actually hit him and he had died? Didn't you even once think of all those who were totally dependent on you—your wife, your three children and your siblings?'

'One cannot think rationally in an enraged state!' he had justified.

'My father used to say that anger is never blind but very wise and shrewd! It's an intelligent force which doesn't allow you to be angry at those more powerful than you,' I had asserted strongly. He lived in a paralytic state for more than thirteen years before finally passing away in 2017.

***

While trying to register a plot, I had to run around a bit trying to put together several missing documents. I got home late at night and asked Chhaya to serve me dinner as I was hungry, but she told me to wait as she was watching a TV serial and it was just about to end. Her response made my temper shoot up. I abused her and tried to snatch the remote from her hand, simultaneously demanding my dinner. This put her in a frenzy too, and unable to retaliate in any other form, she picked up a small cane chair she had been sitting on and flung it towards me. It missed me, but hit the wall. The incident made me recall her brother's violent reaction to the factory staffer. It seemed to be an inherent family trait.

The next morning, I summoned her third brother and his wife to witness what her behaviour was putting me through. I literally burst into tears, trying to make them realise the gravity of my situation. 'In what way had I wronged you that you offloaded such an insensitive woman onto me? You knew she had an aggressive nature and even our statures didn't match, so why did you do it?' The eldest brother, putting aside his ego, had persuasively asked me to get married, even though my intuition was telling me not to do so, as I was not comfortable with the family's vibes.

Just three days after our marriage, her fifth brother's wedding had been held, for the family had been waiting for the daughter to be married first. I couldn't stop venting over past grievances. The couple tried to soothe me, and also admonished Chhaya. In retaliation, she walked out of the house, a ploy she always used to counter uncomfortable situations. I got to know that such dramas had also taken place occasionally during her adolescence, but here I was, still dealing with them. Over the years, I had to face a few uncomfortable situations where Chhaya's family was concerned. But they too have had to suffer many repercussions, for inevitably, karma comes back to haunt one. The constant strife at home would give me a sense of insecurity. It pushed me deeper into spirituality.

***

I may have removed Karan's name from the registration document of my plot, but later feeling a little guilty, I helped him to get a townhouse in the DLF area, putting the initial Rs 6 lakh deposit, myself. He was with Citibank by then, so he was able to get a loan for the remaining Rs 18 lakh. Besides, he had already got a benefit of Rs 2 lakh as the deal was done through a good friend of mine. By a stroke of luck, within eighteen months, it was sold for exactly double the amount for Rs 48 lakh; Karan thought this was a far easier way to make money than by hard work! Getting him into the real estate business at that time was a big blunder on my part. He was only twenty-four and this windfall went straight to his head. The universe had manipulated me to take a step that proved detrimental for both of us later.

***

I had always cherished Osho and once came across his younger brother, Shailendra Shekhar giving a discourse. He was shorter, but his appearance and mannerisms resembled Osho. Ecstatic, I presented my poetry book to him, introducing myself as a devoted disciple of Osho. He immediately opened my book, exclaiming within a moment, 'Oh this is really beautiful poetry! May I quote from this?'

I told him that my poetry has been possible through Osho's blessings and I was delighted to hear this.

***

I was once in a meeting with the general secretary at the Congress headquarters when the youngest of the three Aggarwal sisters called me thrice. Surprised, I called her back. Much to my shock, she started wailing loudly. I managed to calm her down and finally she said that the family had lost their case in the High Court and consequently had to vacate their beautiful South Delhi house they had been living in for three decades at a nominal rent. I consoled her that everything would turn out well as at least the family was fine, and I assured her of my help.

I seemed to have a tendency of attracting women who were facing deeply traumatic situations and were in need of solace. At another time, Ruby Singh lost her Jet Airlines job and she too called, crying at her misfortune, for her father too was seriously ill.

I gave her assurances with encouraging statements that she was capable enough to easily get another job. I promised to meet her the next day at the Sai Baba temple. It's my experience that women get deeply attached to mundane things, which cause them a lot of anguish. And somehow, what they can't share with their own family members, they prefer sharing with a friend! Later, with a little effort, the sister found a good house and Ruby too got a job, and her father recovered as well, but at that point of time, they had felt totally shattered.

***

Narasimha Rao's passing away in December was quite an unfortunate event in my life, for I regarded him as a great support. I had lost my own father at the young age of twenty-nine and since then, I had manifested a tendency of attaching myself to older people, looking for that parental support, which I seemed to be lacking in my own life. I got along well with older people and they too would bless me with their affection. When my father had passed away, Kumar Pashi fulfilled the void created by his passing, and later, Rajiv Gandhi too became a support. Kesriji became a pillar for me followed by Narasimha Rao and subsequently, Mani Shankar Aiyar. It's a fact that if great personalities shower even a little attention on you, it becomes a source of immense security, knowing one can turn to them in times of a crisis.

I had visited Narasimha Rao on Diwali, just a couple of months prior to his demise. He was in bad shape, breathing heavily. I felt a wave of compassion and while leaving, spontaneously said, 'Babuji, I will pray for your peaceful life.' It may not have been the most appropriate thing to say to an octogenarian, but I would often deliver such controversial gems! He was naturally vexed and retorted, 'No, Manzar, I don't want a peaceful life, I want a useful life!' a statement that shook my core. His words conveyed a vital life message, and his desire to be functional to his last breath touched me deeply. Its only when we are of service to others that it gives us blissful happiness, a state of mind much higher than being peaceful!

When I reached Narasimha Rao's house at 9 Motilal Nehru Marg after hearing the news, only three people were present, one near his body, and two in the lobby. A former Prime Minister, who had been the Congress President, surely deserved to be kept in state, but due to Sonia Gandhi's extreme antagonism towards him, he was not given any respect at all. Even Kesriji's body had been placed with dignity at the Congress Party office before being flown to be cremated at his hometown. I felt truly wretched at this, especially as his family was not present.

I sat down at his feet, touching them emotionally, his final statement echoing desolately in my ears, 'I want a useful life!' It was unfortunate that this philosopher king of India had not been valued by those in power, even though death is supposed to dissolve all grievances. Achievement may take one to the top, but then one stands alone there and ultimately, the end too becomes lonely! The next day, his son came to take his body back to their hometown.

After Narasimha Rao's demise, I felt low and melancholic. Mahi would often comfort me, 'Maheshji, this is all part of life! You have to face losses and move on! He was, after all, old, and besides he was not related to you. You can't keep moping. I suggest you read a page of the *Bhagavad Gita* daily before sleeping.'

I began to inculcate the habit of reading a page every night. She also said, 'Don't you repeatedly say that we must unconditionally surrender to God's will? You preach but don't practice your own philosophy,' she mocked. Life would always be full of challenges; it was how we faced them that mattered. Everything happens for a reason and was responsible for shaping our nature and future. 'If you had gained a good, supportive wife and obedient children, maybe your creative side wouldn't have bloomed. Neither would you have gone into spirituality!' Mahi echoed what Kumar Pashi would often tell me.

'I once came across a beautiful quote, 'God grant me the serenity to accept the things I cannot change, the courage to change the things I can, and the wisdom to know the difference,' Mahi said to me by way of encouragement.

'Dale Carnegie!' I interpolated excitedly. 'I read his book, *How to Stop Worrying and Start Living* in my college days and these were my favourite lines from it!

'There was another very inspiring one from the same book: 'For every ailment under the sun, there's a remedy or there is none. If there be one try to find it, if there's none, never mind it!'

Mahi laughed delightedly at the simple message. 'And Babuji always loved to say, This too shall pass,' I concluded on a happier note.

***

I organised a grand party in our basement to celebrate our silver wedding anniversary on 7 February 2005. One of the guests was the fourteen-year-old son of Karuna Chaturvedi, who gave me an unexpected, deep compliment, as he was leaving. 'Uncle, every guest of yours seems to be full of immense joy and enthusiasm!'

Indeed, the evening was steeped in a magical exuberance, with everyone participating enthusiastically. A close friend, Naresh Manaktala gave an uplifting speech. By chance, two princesses, who were close to me were in town and were there, and also a foreign couple who lived nearby. The food was sumptuous and my sons involved themselves heartily in the celebration, as at that time, they had not become entirely alienated with me. For the first time, along with their mother, they had presented me a jewelled Sai locket, which I wear even today.

***

Senior Congress leader Bhupinder Singh Hooda walked regularly in Lodhi Gardens and I would often meet him there. Once, after the 2005 Haryana elections, when Congress had gained a majority, I said to him, 'I infer that you may become the chief minister of Haryana.'

He was surprised, especially as Bhajan Lal was a strong possibility.

'It's just a thought. I feel Sonia Gandhi won't let him become CM, as he was close to Narasimha Rao. You are in a powerful position; you are a senior MP and close to Sonia Gandhi,' I added. Five days later, he invited me to his home for breakfast at 9 am. I asked, 'Some good news?'

'Just be punctual!' was all he said.

Habitually constrained, I finally reached almost fifteen minutes late, to find him at the dining table. He told me that he needed to hurry as he had been summoned to 10 Janpath, for which I congratulated him heartily. He was a heavy smoker, even smoking while walking in Lodhi Gardens. I had once ticked him off lightly, mentioning that it was counterproductive to smoke while walking. He said that he walked to fill himself up with oxygen so that he could smoke guilt-free the rest of the day.

His habit once landed him in hospital and when I visited him, his wife, Aasha, said that if I was his friend, why couldn't I stop him from smoking?

'Bhabhi, his rationalisation is such that no one can stop him.' Both had laughed. Recently, when I met him at IIC, we got talking about the old days and I reminded him of the Lodhi Garden smoking anecdote. Amused, he retorted, 'You were one of the few people who dared to allude to my habit of smoking.'

He told me that soon after that, his father, Chaudhary Ranbir Singh, had seen him smoking and threatened satyagraha, (a form of self-suffering to coerce another to change). 'It's been seventeen years. I have not touched a cigarette since.'

***

A few weeks later, my elder son brought home his girlfriend and informed us that he wanted to marry her. Rinki was from

Amritsar, a beautiful, slim and tall girl. She was living alone in Delhi and had only her aged parents for relatives. This was quite unacceptable, as ours was an extended, well-reputed family, even if relationships within the family were not all that cordial. I took her birth details and got the horoscopes matched. The astrologer opined that the marriage shouldn't take place as it wasn't conducive for my son's health. My son was adamant and also consulted another well-reputed astrologer, who also corroborated the earlier prediction. One evening, I took both my sons to India Gate and over our ice creams, I put my case forward. I was surprised that I didn't lose patience and explained things to them very lovingly. They listened attentively.

'Look son, my father held the wedding functions for his children in five-star hotels, and I want to do the same for you both. Tell me, who will come from her side? Marriage is not just about the couple; it's a union between two families! I want you to give me a year and I will look for a good match for you. If I don't, you can do as you wish. I cannot change your Destiny, for its your free will that will carry you towards it. I can only try to point you in the right direction.'

He agreed to my advice. I asked him, 'I hope you have not committed to marry her?'

'No, Papa!'

'That's very good! And if she ever tries to emotionally manipulate you that I have surrendered to you and, therefore, you should marry me, tell her that I too have surrendered to you, so what's the big deal!'

Both my sons were amazed at what seemed to be a well-researched thesis! There and then, I decided to look for a good match for him with great earnestness so that he could be weaned away from a misalliance!

About this time, Mani Shankar Aiyar gave me an honourable position as a member of the Hindi Advisory committee in the Petroleum and Natural Gas Ministry. It's a prestigious nomination, with meetings held with the minister in Parliament House with the chairmen of petroleum companies and top ministry officials. One of Chhaya's brothers was also in the committee through the offices of his son-in-law, an IAS officer and the PS of a State minister. The first meeting I attended was presided over by Mani Shankar Aiyar and he encouraged me to present my views and suggestions. It was about the use of Hindi and I said that instead of focusing on using the language extensively, we should try to speak and write it correctly, emphasising on quality more than quantity. The minister praised the points I had raised. Even Chhaya's brother lavished praise upon me, saying that I spoke the best! He even went to the extent of saying that I was finally utilising my full potential and doing a mighty fine job of it.

Meanwhile, I was often travelling to visit temples and pilgrimage spots. Neera's husband invited me to visit the Naimisharanya temple near Lucknow, along with him. The temple was connected to the marriage of Lord Vishnu with Devi Lakshmi and Devi Prithvi and was a must on the tourism map for those facing difficulty in marriage or in begetting a child. It was as if the universe was supporting to make my son's marriage possible. Neera and her husband were going with their daughter, son-in-law and a niece who was divorced, besides another friend. It was a wonderful trip and I remember chatting for hours together on the lawns of the Dharamshala we were staying in.

A month after our anniversary, I received a call from the wife of Delhi's former police commissioner, informing me that she, her sister and brother-in-law wanted to meet me. Subsequently, they came over to the house. They came straight to the point saying that they had heard that I owned a 300-sq yd plot in Ardee City in Gurgaon and wanted to purchase it. I said I didn't have plans to sell it just yet. They offered to buy it at a 65 per cent appreciation of the amount I had invested. I was not expecting such a hike! I called up my property friends and they told me that its value was more than their offer. The commissioner's wife nonchalantly offered to have me speak to her husband. I pointed out that I was being offered more on the market, but they very adroitly tried to manipulate me to accede to their offer. Finally, I acquiesced and thus sold off my plot within six months at a very good profit! Such windfalls allowed me to live generously without having to put in much physical work.

However, the situation had its own repercussions. A few days later, my younger son requested for Rs 2 lakh for a college exchange programme to Paris for a month. Two students, a boy and a girl, were usually chosen for this programme and although, it was a Diploma, it had no academic value. I protested that it was a huge amount but my son was adamant, finally making me give in, despite my reservations about his age, as he was not even twenty-two. My son had planned to go with a friend, the daughter of one of my friends. Thus, they both packed their bags and were to catch a late-night flight, which got cancelled, and then was rescheduled for the next day. Sometime later, I mentioned the incident to a friend who was a secretary of the All India Mahila Congress Committee. She suggested that I should demand for compensation from the airlines. Under her guidance, I shot off a few mails to the airline authorities, ultimately telling them that I was a politician and would file a suit against them, besides highlighting their laxity in leading newspapers.

Meantime, there was another development at home. Karan demanded that he too be given either two lakhs like his brother or sent to France. He created a terrible scene, crying pathetically. Finally, I had to agree. One good thing that happened, however, was that the complaint I had lodged against the airlines, resulted in them giving us a free ticket to compensate for the physical, mental and emotional torture caused. I gave the ticket to my elder son and sent him off too. From him we learned later that the younger fellow was enjoying himself in Paris with his friend and other foreigners, with barely any focus on studies. I could only marvel at his impudence. About a month since he had left, a strong wave of panic rose in me and I felt impelled to call him up. The moment I heard his voice, I couldn't stop my tears. He assured me that he was perfectly fine and would be back soon. Both boys returned a fortnight later, noticeably slimmer.

I was a regular at the Sai Temple on Lodhi Road and would often notice a smart lady, who too came daily. We began wishing each other, and one day, I introduced myself and found out that she worked as a director with Sycorian Matrimonial Services.

I was delighted and told her that I was looking for a match for my elder son and though I had placed ads in both the leading newspapers, we hadn't received an encouraging response. Within two months, she had introduced us to my daughter-in-law's family. Theirs was a staunch Arya Samaj family and were hesitant interacting with ours, for the combination of politics and poetry didn't appeal to them. When we had to submit the family biodata to the Matrimonial Services, I had discussed with the family whether I should mention only about my real estate investments or also about my hobbies of being a politician and a poet. Both my sons, it turned out were quite happy with my achievements, even though they didn't acknowledge them! The younger even described me as a politician who had access to top leaders and had often written Sonia Gandhi's speeches while Karan added that I had won awards from both the Hindi and Urdu Academies for my poetry.

Karan's girlfriend, Rinki, would often call for Karan who had begun to ignore her. I tried to console her, pointing out that the match wouldn't have worked out as the horoscopes were not compatible. Meanwhile, the Aggarwal family that had been matched with ours by the matrimonial services were getting us investigated and when satisfied, approached us to take things forward.

***

Around the same time, I got a call from a lady, who wanted to meet me, but refused to divulge her identity. Her voice was so melodious that I naturally couldn't refuse her. She came to my house the same evening! I was surprised to know her identity. Not only was she attractive but she was also a well-known name on the small screen. As she introduced herself, I realised that her parents were famous singers, whom I knew. Naina told me that her father had asked her to meet me, and immediately called him, then handed the phone over to me. I was delighted to speak to him, as he had been my role model for decades, but was taken aback when he requested me to counsel his daughter, as she had been through a divorce recently. I did the best I could, and we started meeting, regularly. Naina even called me once demanding that I come immediately for coffee at Khan market, saying she would kill me if I didn't! Her audacity made me laugh, but it also scared me a little and made me wonder if her overbearing attitude was the cause of her divorce! When a common friend pointed out her ex-husband to me, I was astonished by his magnetic personality, for she had given me a completely different picture! I told Naina that in my opinion, she had done a blunder in divorcing him! I was reminded of a sher I had heard earlier:

Bus ek kadam utha tha galat rahe shouq me
Manzil tamam umra mujhe dhoondhti rahi

(Only one awry step did I take in the throes of desire
Those lost horizons scoured for me lifelong)

It was a great dilemma for me: why did I attract people who were in a somewhat similar state as my own? My life was no bed of roses, yet I felt that somehow, I was giving them strength, for my challenging circumstances had filled me with compassion for one and all. Osho says that when we are permeated with love and compassion, we have the power to captivate people, drawing them towards us.

American research says that if we are filled with positive vibrations, our white blood corpuscles which are essential for energy and vitality, increase. Someone standing next to such a person also benefits greatly. And if we are negative and anyone comes into our vicinity, their bodies too register a decrease in their corpuscle count.

Naina seemed to derive that positive energy from me, for she felt uplifted in my company. Her parents were glad and appreciated my role in bringing her back to form.

Maybe Ram Babu Sharma, who had become the President of the Delhi Congress, also felt that attraction, for he was another one of my admirers. He had publicly declared that he was a votary of Bhagatji but was also Manzar Sahab's votary-in-chief, much to everyone's amusement. He would take me along with him for meetings at AICC, which elevated my position in the Party. He regularly organised events on national occasions, and was very visible on the political scene. I noticed that when I accompanied him, my vibrations would change. It gave me a sense of power, for it is a totally different feeling when one realises that people are following you. That power also inspires one to sacrifice in the interest of a cause.

After the coalition government came into power, Lalu Prasad Yadav was nominated as the Union Railway Minister. Later, when he came across Dr Karan Singh, who, was an MP and also the President of the India International Centre, he requested that he be granted membership of the prestigious IIC. Dr Karan Singh agreed instantly, but every prospective member has to be approved by a board of seven trustees. If a controversy arises, decision is taken through a count of votes. When Dr Karan Singh proposed his name, there was instant opposition, for not only was Lalu Prasad implicated in a fodder scam but he also had a habit of constantly chewing betel leaves! Votes were then cast in which four of the trustees rejected the application. Dr Karan Singh resigned immediately. When I read about it in the newspapers, it suddenly hit me that I had made a mistake in refusing the membership when it was offered to me in 2002.

After this controversial episode, membership of the IIC was opened for the public. Prof Narang suggested that I should apply now, so I filled out the form. But alas, my application was rejected. I went to meet the new President, Prof M G K Menon, a well-known scientist to let me know on what grounds my application had been rejected.

'In 2002, your chief librarian, H K Kaul had invited me to fill the form, but I didn't have time to join, and now what has happened in these three years that it is not being considered?' I asked directly.

He said he would look into it and asked me to come the following evening. It turned out that my application had been put in the wrong category and the secretary, Venugopal, regretted the confusion.

'Manzar Sahab, we will look into the matter,' he said.

A few days later, I received a call from the secretary, IIC, informing me that I had been made a temporary member, but the membership would have to be renewed every three months. I accepted with alacrity, for my point had been proved and indeed in 2008, I was offered a better option in the form of an associate temporary member, with a tenure of three years. This special category allowed a few highly deserving people to be added. Only twenty-five new members including Sachin Pilot and the Metro man, E Sreedharan, were thus made a part of the IIC under this new provision.

Chapter 4

In Search of Enlightenment

THE CONGRESS PARTY elections were to be held in 2005. Harikesh Bahadur was in-charge of Jharkhand and Bihar and had nominated me as the District Returning Officer (DRO) in Palamu, where I was welcomed warmly, despite strife between different factions of the Party. One group spread the rumour that the DRO had been kidnapped and this news also appeared in newspapers. I had already been shifted to a Rajya Sabha MP, R K Anand's house. Harikesh Bahadur called up the district President to ascertain that I was fine and had informed V George, too.

After finishing my work in Palamu, I requested the Jharkhand Congress President, Sushila Devi, to send me to Gaya, Gautama Buddha's sacred land. I sat under the Bodhi tree where Buddha had attained enlightenment, experiencing its sanctity. It is said that Lord Ram performed the *pind-daan* ritual for his parents in a river just beyond it, so I too got it done for my parents. I visited several Buddha temples and also the hill where he had stood, gazing continuously at the sky for seven days. I had a Divine experience in an ancient Vishnu temple as well, and the priest there guided me to buy a copper Sheshnag to donate to a Shivling temple in Delhi. Worshipping there would then help to relieve my troubles as well as fulfil my wishes. I followed his instructions and it proved really beneficial, for a few months later, performing a ritual there resulted in my son's marriage.

The publication of my book had opened some interesting avenues. Women, especially were getting enamoured with me. I got a call from the principal of Ramjas School on Pusa Road to judge a poetry competition for their high school students. I asked how the principal had got my reference, and she said that a 'A poet and a politician is a lethal combination!' Perhaps, Jennifer Tytler had suggested my name, but I couldn't be sure. It was a very good experience especially as I was acquainted with one of the judges, who had been one of my youthful crushes!

***

After my unexpected windfall in the real estate market, I faced a sudden slump, for I could not conclude any deals for the next five months. I was focused on my son's nuptials, considering them to be of much more importance, although I wondered whether my last sale had attracted an evil eye!

But I dismissed those thoughts as things were looking up for Karan, for we received a call from Anil Aggarwal, who had been referred by my Sai Mandir friend. A meeting was fixed and they visited us one evening. We were impressed by their persona and they too, liked our son. But we had only seen the girl, Malini in a photograph and although I had a few reservations, Karan was in favour of the match. All this happened within seven months of my visit to the Naimisharanya temple and it strengthened my belief in the power of the Divine and in the intensity of faith.

During a visit to Shirdi at Dwarkamayi, I met a sanyasi in orange robes. Just a few weeks earlier, someone had presented me with a picture of Sai Baba and this sanyasi looked a lot like the Sai Baba in that picture! He told me that his name was Vasantgiri. He reminded me of another white-robed yogi, Anandgiri, whom I had met in 2000 at the gates of the Sai temple on Lodhi Road. He too had looked very much like Sai Baba. The baba who had come to my home had been Laxman Giri and he resembled Sai Baba as well. Was there some sort of Divine coincidence that all three had names that ended with 'Giri'?

I asked him about the way one should live. He said that one should do one's karma diligently and also spoke about wisdom and integrity.

I added, 'This is what I have read in the *Gita!*'

'Baba was well-versed in the *Gita* and knew the 700 shlokas by heart. He preached love, compassion and generosity.'

'His main messages that he preached were *Sabka Maalik Ek* (everyone's master is the One) and *Shraddha-Saburi* (Faith and Patience); keep faith in the Divine! Plato too has said, 'Faith is the highest faculty.''

'Baba also said that if one is able to develop all these qualities in the self, one doesn't need anyone's recognition or respect. One reaches a space of deep contentment.'

'Something like this is in the *Sundarkand* part of the *Ramayana* as well, Baba, which I love to quote:

Jo bhajte Bhagwan ko karte par upkar
Wo nar mujhko ati priye jinhe niti se pyar

(Constantly thinking of the Divine altruistic become
Those are dear to me who righteousness love)

Baba Vasantgiri smilingly said, '*Achhchha hai.*'

'There's one more thing, Baba. Guru Nanak Dev also said:

Ek noor se sub jug upja,
kaun bhale kaun mande

We are all born from the One Divine Light, so no one is less or more. All these enlightened souls say the same thing!'

'But of course, they do! After all, son, all the Gurus have the same soul; they are not separate!'

In gratitude, I touched the Baba's feet and made some offerings to him.

***

On the home front, Lakhan, after returning from Paris, had become even more arrogant and over-confident. When I returned from one of my travels, I noticed a bruise on his forehead. Karan told me that when Lakhan had gone to drop me at the airport, he had got into a fight with the parking attendants who had roughed him up! 'Your aggressive nature will harm you a lot, son! This is not a rational way to behave. You should have thought of the consequences,' I counseled him passionately, trying to make him understand that when faced with an adverse situation, the only prudent thing to do is to step back.

On another occasion, I had to attend Chhaya's niece's wedding at Claridges, and on the way, I decided to visit the Sai temple. As I left the temple, I saw a middle-aged couple on a scooter knocked down in a hit-and-run and that the man's leg was bleeding profusely. A crowd had gathered, but no one was helping. I hastily took charge, and requesting some bystanders to move the scooter to the side, we put the victims into my car and I drove them to the emergency at AIIMS hospital. Since it was a medico-legal case, the hospital authorities informed the police, who soon came and behaved as if I must have hit them. Infuriated, I scolded them saying that this is why no one helps accident victims. I directed them to the injured gentleman's wife. She emphatically supported me, saying I had been no less than an angel for them. The doctors accepted later that if I had not rushed them to the hospital, the man might have bled to death! My clothes were soiled, so I had to go back home before reaching the wedding venue.

The couple remained in touch with me for years after that, greeting me on festivals and always thanking me for my timely help. I would say that it was all Baba's Grace for they too were his devotees.

***

On 1 January, Anil Aggarwal invited us to their home to meet Malini. Since I dabbled in numerology, I was always juggling with numbers. Number one represents the Sun, so I bought two brass Suns to invoke the Sun God's power and Grace. The power of one was four, for it was the first of January and Sun-day too, and both our house numbers were one and by buying two Suns, its power rose to six, which is numerologically auspicious.

Malini was of slight build and seemed pretty nervous. I took a backseat, allowing the other three to come to a decision. They were satisfied with the match. Malini's grandfather, who was a bit disabled, came out with a walker, apologising about his inability to participate actively.

I said to him, 'Babuji, whenever there's a mishap, we shouldn't focus on the damage, but should be thankful for what has been saved!'

'Yes, indeed a lot has been saved,' he acknowledged.

'Be thankful for that! It gives one a lot of strength in adversity.'

Malini's father led me to a different room to ask me how we wanted the wedding conducted.

'I don't expect anything as such, but in our family, functions are usually held in five-star hotels, so I would also like my son's wedding in one.'

'Yes, that's absolutely fine,' he agreed.

'And my guest list won't exceed 600,' he added.
'Ours will be maximum of 400,' I replied.
'Great! All will be easily adjusted in a five-star's banquet hall. I will host the *sagai* also in a five-star hotel.'

Then I asked him what was the total budget he was thinking of. He proposed an amount which was half of what I had expected! Later, it struck me that as I had called them up twice in two months to ask their intent, they might have felt that we were desperate for the marriage! Whatever their first impressions, they did eventually mellow down. Once our talks were final, we consulted an astrologer and decided to hold the *sagai* on 25 February with 1 March 2006 fixed as the date for the wedding. I was acquainted with the owners of the Meridien, so we were able to at least get the wedding venue fixed.

The girl's father suggested Ashoka Hotel for the Roka ceremony, and that was booked for 22 January. I was a bit tense with the sword of Damocles hanging on my head in the form of Rinki. What if she came and created a scene? So tense was I that I overlooked getting a new outfit made for myself, forgetting that as the groom's father, I too would be in the limelight. The function, however, went off well, with close relatives on both sides participating enthusiastically.

The days leading up to a wedding are usually a whirl of shopping activities, and Rinki's matter was still to be resolved. More trauma was added, when, Karan, after a heated argument walked out of the house just a few weeks before his wedding. He didn't return either that night or the whole of the next day. I also realised that I had forgotten about the invitation cards! Even though there was uncertainty about where Karan was, we went to the printers to order the cards.

Karan came back late in the night, without an apology, but I was relieved that at least he was back! I realised that he too must have been going through a lot of stress where Rinki was concerned.

Kesriji's PA, Veer Singh, who had become my associate, and Pradeep Sethi helped me in the main, gigantic task of sending invitations. Our domestic help, Ramu, also proved to be really helpful. I had wanted to give the invitation card personally to Sonia Gandhi after giving one to V George, but she sent a message to leave the card and sweets with George. George even said that she might come as the venue was pretty close, but eventually she did not.

Meantime, my elder sister, Simran, had to leave for America to join her daughter for something urgent. I was disheartened, but she promised to send her husband and her younger daughter a week before the wedding.

The hectic schedule pushed me into a state of fear and when in fear, one can only turn to the Divine. Consequently, my visits to temples intensified and along with visits to the Sai temple, I began to pray to Shiva and Hanuman at the Namdev temple, just next to the Sai temple.

I would still meet Sania, the matrimonial alliance lady at the temple and I requested her to accept her fees, but she refused, saying that Baba had directed us. Smiling, she added, 'I will definitely take them for your younger son, though!'

On another day when I was looking very disturbed, she suggested that I do the Navgraha puja as well, and directed me to a nearby South Indian Vishnu temple in which the Lord's feet had been carved in one section of the temple. Those feet had been cast in silver as well and placed on the original ones. The panditji would pick them up and touch a devotee's head with them to give blessings.

A mantra is written next to them: 'Surrender to my feet. I will take care of your deeds, worry not.' It was a Vishnu Padam Mantra given by a saint to Sant Ramanujacharya, with the warning that he shouldn't share it with anyone, or else his head would shatter. But Ramanujacharya found it very effective and felt that he should share it, reasoning that death was inevitable, so why be scared of hastening it? He stood on top of a low mound and requested the villagers to gather around and learn it for their own benefit, but not to share it. As soon as he finished intoning the mantra, Lord Vishnu appeared and told him that he was very happy with his gesture. 'You are truly a saint and your love for your brethren is great! Only those who can sacrifice themselves for others can be called a Saint.' Ramanujacharya could only bow and say, 'My Lord, I am truly blessed!'

Henceforth, I became a frequent visitor at this temple as well. The strength from all my worshipping helped me cope with the stressful days leading up to the wedding!

From the Ramanujacharya story, I understood that what one has must be shared with everyone else. The Divine who came to bless Ramanujacharya also stated that he was being tested to see if he would share. Indeed, whether it's knowledge or wealth or power, it should be shared with all. The thought reminded me of Amir Qazalbash's popular sher:

Badal ho toh barso kisi be aab zami per
Khushbu ho toh har ore bikhar kyun nahi jate

(If a cloud, rain on barren lands
If a fragrance, disseminate all over)

Chapter 5

Wedding Bells

DUE TO TIME constraints, we could only get bookings at the Grand Hyatt Hotel in Vasant Kunj for the *sagai* ceremony. Some of the guests thus couldn't make it to the function as it was not a centrally located venue. Karan received a gift of eleven golden guineas while we parents were given four each, with two for my younger son; all this was far beyond my expectations! Many senior Congress leaders graced the function along with the DPCC President, Ram Babu Sharma and area MP, Sajjan Kumar. Wanting to do something special for them as they both had uplifted me in some way or the other, I got Anil Aggarwal to present my share of the guineas to both, much to their surprise. A few days after the function, Sajjan Kumar called me expressing his astonishment that the guineas were pure gold!

Lakhan and his friends stole the show with a vibrant dance performance to conclude the sangeet evening. He dressed up as Aishwarya Rai, much to everyone's amazement, especially as none of us could guess his identity till almost the end! Two of his girlfriends dressed up as Amitabh and Abhishek Bachchan and all danced amazingly well to the popular song, *Kajraare*. It enhanced the tempo of the evening, encouraging many to take to the dance floor.

Sajjan Kumar was there till late into the evening, enjoying

every moment of the festivities. With my usual thoughtlessness, I remarked, 'Bhaisahab, don't you have any meetings today?'

'Manzar Sahab, do you want me to leave?'

I apologised hastily, thanking him for staying and enjoying the party. Chhaya's brothers were stunned at my temerity. Indeed, even our scriptures say that one should speak only when essential or only if one can add some value. And when we do speak, our words should be both *shreyskar* and *priyeskar* (good and lovable ones). Words should be used judiciously for they have tremendous power and convey not only our thoughts, but also showcase our nature and behaviour.

Two days before the main wedding, the Meridien Hotel informed me that as the American President, George Bush, was visiting India, his staff and dogs were expected to stay at the hotel, and due to security reasons, the hotel management had to cancel our programme on the premises. It was as if I had received a punch on my chest. I almost fell down in a swoon, sure that either my head or my heart would burst with the shock! The house was full of relatives gathered for one of the pre-wedding rituals. Everyone was naturally stunned with the news, as finding a venue this late was an almost impossible task.

My brother-in-law, Simran's husband, exclaimed, '*Waah*!' I stared at him open-mouthed. 'Are you happy with this development,' I asked belligerently, making him immediately check himself. I had taken his help in drafting an invitation letter for Sonia Gandhi and I could feel that the scale of the wedding celebrations were causing some envious reactions.

I reached the hotel early the next morning, along with a few close relatives. The hotel management did offer to make arrangements elsewhere, taking responsibility for redirecting all guests, but I knew very well that my VIP guests would not take kindly to that and perhaps would not proceed to the new venue. I moved heaven and earth till noon, trying to tell them to let the programme remain, as the banquet was in a totally different section of the hotel and definitely posed no threat for the VIP foreign guests. Finally, I appealed to Mani Shankar Aiyar to help find a way out. He called the owners immediately, telling them that the host was like his younger brother and was now in a great panic, which could prove detrimental to his health. Besides, the US President was staying at Maurya Sheraton, so security was not much of an issue. Thankfully, they acceded to his request and the traumatic situation was resolved.

On the wedding day, I reached Meridien Hotel with the bridegroom at around 6.30 pm and was pleasantly surprised to see a number of guests already in the banquet hall. Most of them were, of course, from the bride's family, but senior Congress leaders like Bhishma Narain Singh, Prof K K Tiwari, Harikesh Bahadur, Tariq Anwar, Ram Babu Sharma, two Delhi Cabinet ministers, along with former director of CBI, Sd. Joginder Singh, who told me that he had come at 6 pm as he had to leave for another function at 7, made me feel exuberant. Soon after we reached, Union Cabinet Minister, Mani Shankar Aiyar came with his wife, Suneet Aiyar followed by the then governor of Sikkim, B P Singh who arrived with his complete retinue. The bride's uncle who was the chairman of a private university, also came with his contingent of eight SPG type, safari suit-clad security guards, his personal protection force. Chhaya's brother felt a bit offended, commenting that even the Union Minister and governor had left their security outside, but he had got them inside.

There was a raised dias for the rituals just outside the main hall, with comfortable seating all around. The ceremony was over by 8 pm, which was the time I had given for the reception. Thereafter, along with the bride and groom, I was on the stage to greet the guests, as they streamed in to bless the newlyweds.

My guests were not only from political and literary circles, but included the elite layer of the judiciary, the media, the bureaucracy and the legislature. Besides them, there were also prominent classical dancers, senior doctors, along with relatives and friends from both sides.

My family was surprised to see so many VIP guests gracing the occasion, even bringing precious gifts. Unexpectedly, Jagdish Tytler had also come, for Jennifer was not well. All my lady friends from the political, literary and social world, including Mahi, Hema and two of my princess friends graced the occasion with enthusiasm bearing beautiful gifts. Sheila Dikshit, the Delhi CM enthusiastically hugged my wife to wish her, blessing the new couple warmly. Both she and Mani Shankar Aiyar presented precious silver gifts to the newlyweds. Former Chief Justice of India, Ranganath Mishra attended the function with his family.

The evening was truly magical, as if God Almighty was showering His choicest blessings on that enchanting evening. At one point during the evening, I surveyed the scene with gratitude; there were more than 700 guests who had a lavish dinner. I recalled a moment when I had once thought whether my son's wedding would be as grand as Jagdish Tytler's daughter's wedding in 1998? That evening, my energy was phenomenal; it was as if I had been Divinely charged! I would come down from the stage to greet my VIP guests and then see them off before getting back up the stage again. Anil Aggarwal even asked me wonderingly, 'Where are you getting so much energy from?' Around midnight, Sahib Singh Verma arrived, and that's when I finally got off the stage to greet him. Ahmad Patel, Sonia Gandhi's political secretary had also been one of my distinguished guests. He presented monetary blessings to the couple and stayed for quite long, enjoying the evening.

The evening had been a magnificent success, and it was a memorable wedding. It's all Divine grace, I said to myself. As soon as everything was over, I made my way to the Sai temple and lit lamps to my beloved Sai and to the other deities to offer my deep gratitude. The fear that my son's ex-girlfriend could have caused a scene, was now finally gone. When I happened to mention my concern to Karan the next day, he admitted that he had the same fear. It was over now, thanks to Divine grace!

Chapter 6

Dark Depths of Depression

I HAD USED up so much of my energy that just three days later, I collapsed. I had lost all sense of food or sleep, and was following an erratic routine. Besides, Rinki's grief would haunt me. Finally, all of it took a toll on me, making me feel as if my heart was sinking. I was taken directly to the chief physician at RML Hospital on 6 March. I explained to the doctor that it had been a continuous couple of months of intense stress. He exclaimed, 'So it was anxiety and not energy that was keeping you in a high state on the wedding day!' He prescribed a tablet for fifteen days before sleeping.

I did not get much relief, and a few days later, I asked Dr Jayprakash, Kesriji's personal doctor, about the medicine I had been asked to take. He said it was a tranquilliser and could become addictive. He advised me to meditate to release my stress. He meant well, but at that time, I needed that medicine and stopping it, made me feel much worse. Consequently, I returned to Dr R S Tonk after about a month and he immediately concluded that I had probably not taken the medicine for the prescribed time. He now strictly advised me to take it for a month. I again took it for about a fortnight, and then asked Dr Sanjiv Zutshi if I should continue for a full month. And so again with Dr Sanjiv's encouragement, I again stopped taking my medication. It became a case of private versus government doctors as each tends to be critical of the other's treatment.

Over the next two to three months, my condition worsened, and I began having frequent anxiety attacks which would leave me in a state of restless confusion. On 30 May, I had a severe attack and was rushed back to RML hospital. Dr Tonk was not available, so the medical superintendent, Dr C P Singh, who was very well known to me, sent me to Dr Smita Deshpande, head of the psychiatry department.

She asked me if anyone in my family had been a depression patient.

'Yes, my mother,' I told her.

'Anyone else?'

'Yes, my eldest sister, too.'

I recalled that my maternal grandfather too had been a patient. She prescribed a high dosage of a strong mood stabiliser often given to depression patients, saying that I would have to take it regularly. However, as was my nature, I once again met Dr Tonk who pointed out to Dr Smita that I was not in depression, but in a state of high anxiety. She apologised, saying that she had prescribed the mood stabilisers due to my family history.

***

Malini was an ideal daughter-in-law, respectful towards all and adept in household chores. She was working, but she would still help out in the kitchen in the mornings and evenings. Even then, Chhaya would find fault with her, often cribbing about minor things to me. This was adding to my tension.

I would often feel uncomfortable about being at home all the time with Malini around, so I would make it a point to visit the temple or go somewhere when she came back in the evening. Chhaya would taunt me, saying that if I had done something tangible instead of just drifting around, I wouldn't need to hide my face from my daughter-in-law. Her taunts undermined me so much that I began to wonder if I had ever done any good in my life. Everything I had achieved in my life so far, my poetry, crores made through property, my goodwill with senior leaders, my innumerable political, poetical and social interactions, all got reduced to zilch! Both my sons and Chhaya also had a grouse against me telling me that I couldn't even get a petrol pump allotted in my name and had only wasted my time getting pictures clicked with senior leaders.

Around this time, in one of my lucid, better intervals, I decided to invest again in real estate, especially since I had not earned any profits for months. I booked five plots in a resettlement area in Badarpur, investing Rs 2 lakh, with the hope of good returns. However, when nothing moved for almost four months, I demanded my money back, but that took another three months.

In July, Chhaya's youngest brother called in great panic, saying his daughter, who was unhappy in her married life, had been poisoned by her husband's family. Chhaya and I rushed to the hospital to find the boy's family gathered together in full force, while Chhaya's brother and his wife were the only ones there. It was now a police case, since allegations were being made on the husband's family, which they belligerently denied, claiming that she had taken the poison, herself. I had to use all my conciliatory skills to calm them down, for the situation could have easily escalated.

My niece had inadvertently drunk some phenyl on her own, but fortunately doctors had been able to flush it out of her stomach. After almost six or seven hours, two of Chhaya's brothers finally strolled in with their wives. I showed my displeasure at their lack of support to their brother who was in a deep crisis, even though they lived in the vicinity, while we had rushed from the other side of town!

Besides I was not well, and was being treated from RML hospital. And yet I had to face the brunt of the situation alone, for even the girl's father was avoiding his son-in-law's family.

***

In August, Mani Shankar Aiyar wanted me to attend an important meeting of the Ministry of Panchayati Raj. Though I was not well, I reached the venue on time. The meeting was presided over by the minister with the secretary, two additional secretaries and four joint secretaries being present. Outsiders usually did not attend such ministerial meetings. It was only Mani Shankar Aiyar's affection that made it possible for me to participate. Detailed reports of all programmes undertaken by the Ministry from 2004 to 2006 had to be compiled in three volumes which had to be presented in Parliament. Mani Shankar Aiyar wanted me to supervise the translation work. I felt a deep sense of inadequacy, for I knew I wouldn't be able to cope with this huge project, but I quietly acceded. Maniji requested Mr Srivastava, one of the additional secretaries, to coordinate with me. Later, I got a call from Mr Srivastava, for he had understood the state of my health.

'Manzar Sahab, I don't think you're feeling well,' he said.

'Yes, Srivastavaji, I am undergoing treatment from RML Hospital for anxiety.'

'Manzar Sahab, don't worry. We will arrange HRD Ministry's official team of translators to assist you in the work!'

'Then, I will be really happy to do the work!' I said, feeling relieved and grateful for his astuteness. It was truly the magnanimity of the minister, Mani Shankar Aiyar, who acknowledged my name in the official presentation.

About this time, my younger son got a job in a multinational company in Mumbai, after his MBA studies. But within a month, he started cribbing about the travel conditions and demanded that he be given a car. So, I sent him the down payment for a small car and asked him to manage the EMIs.

He encouraged me to visit him in Mumbai, for a change of scene. Towards the end of August, Chhaya and I visited Mumbai. But I was once again feeling restless and so consulted another doctor, who once again changed my dosage. The dosage made me a little absent-minded and once during the Ganesh Chaturthi immersions, I just began to walk deeper into the waters, totally unaware of my actions. Chhaya and Lakhan had to pull me back. The incident shook Lakhan, for he was more sensitive than Chhaya, and he seemed really bewildered at my unusual behaviour.

Within a week, we returned to Delhi, for I was feeling uncomfortable in Mumbai. On 16 September, I experienced a shooting pain in my head, which made me cry out loud. I called Dr Tonk who advised me to go directly to VIMHANS. Feeling inadequate and vulnerable, I called up my brother to cross-check Dr Tonk's recommendation, and he too encouraged me to go. Karan and Chhaya took me there at once and we found a very good psychiatrist, Dr Anandi Lal, who correctly diagnosed my malady. He was astonished at the number of doctors I had already consulted, since I had all my prescriptions with me. He emphasised the need to take my medicines regularly and not to keep consulting different doctors. The treatment there finally helped to put me back on my feet.

So far, I hadn't got much sympathy from my family, as none of them realised the gravity of what I was going through. On the contrary, they had even accused me of putting on an act. Even my brother, a doctor, had not come to visit me even though he was well aware of my health and situation.

On my sixth visit to VIMHANS, Dr Anandi Lal expressed surprise that no one from my family was accompanying me on my visits to him. He said that my wife or son should have been accompanying me for quite often, he needed inputs from the family about my condition. I simply told him that she didn't want to come. I guessed he realised that my relationships might be the reason for many of my issues. In his efforts to understand the root cause of my malady, he asked me my routine just before my son's wedding.

'I have never had any kind of routine,' I said to him.

'But I used to have regular interactions with a few of my women friends, which I curtailed after the wedding.'

Malini was from a very religious family and she would touch my feet in the morning and also before going to sleep. That somehow made me reluctant to continue my liaisons outside the house.

The doctor then asked whether I had my 'own chair and table' at the Congress office?

When I denied this, he took a serious view, saying that while the real estate business was my bread and butter, my friends and politics were my medicine. They were essential for me to get back into form.

Almost all my friends were desirous of talking to me, some even offering support to help me come out of my anxiety, but somehow, I didn't feel like talking to them at all. It was strange, but I seemed to have developed antipathy towards women.

Early in 2007, I spoke to V George about my dilemma. He helped me out once again, and got me not only a table and chair, but an entire room. He gave me Ajit Jogi's room who had earlier been the chairman of the SC/ST department, but was now the CM of Chhattisgarh. It was indeed a great help and I enthusiastically began going there daily, often taking my lunch along. But I was still not feeling well from deep inside. The fact of the matter is that when one's heart and mind are restless, even heaven can become hell.

Some of my acquaintances would stop by to enquire about my well-being, some showing pity, others giving unwanted advice, a few showing derision at finding me sitting in Ajit Jogi's chair, all of which began to affect me. Consequently, I stopped going there, feeling it unethical.

Lakhan came back to Delhi in March, after only a few months as he didn't like the work culture in Mumbai. He became more aggressive as he now began to feel frustrated as well. We requested Chhaya's brother to help him find a good job, and about a month later, he recommended him to the multinational, Ernst and Young. After a rigorous hiring process, he was hired as an executive consultant at a good package.

When Lakhan turned twenty-four, I thought that since I had purchased a flat for Karan when he was the same age, I should now do something similar for him. I did not want him to hold it against me if something happened to me, especially since I was not at all well in those days. So, I decided to buy a flat for him in Vaishali, in a project belonging to my friend, B L Gaur, a real estate developer. I took Lakhan to meet him and when the conversation turned towards work, I requested B L Gaur to put me in touch with some business opportunities, as I was at a low point, workwise.

Lakhan was embarrassed at this and let me know about his displeasure on the way home. I retaliated, telling him instead that I was talking to a friend and that he should be thankful that I was getting a flat for him. I was investing Rs 10 lakhs in it, and he would immediately start receiving rent. Neither of my sons volunteered to give us financial assistance, even though they knew that I had not earned anything for a year and half. Instead, all three, including Chhaya had become more critical of me. I could only pray more intensely to the Divine to help me come out of my health and financial crisis. My working capital had become less than half of what I usually had, therefore, insecurity gripped me, breaking my confidence.

Karan had promised to give us Rs 20,000 on behalf of himself and Malini, but he never did, adding further to my feelings of insecurity. Lakhan's behaviour too had been deteriorating daily, as he began to think that I would be incapable of conducting a grand wedding for him, like I had done for Karan. Both brothers even got into physical fights a couple of times and had to be separated, forcibly. Chhaya seemed fed up with my continuous illness. My only support at home was Chikoo, our dog. Animals have a way of sensing when someone is not well, so he would often sit close to me or plonk himself on my lap, and this would make me feel better.

The year was not a good one. My doctor brother suffered a heart attack. Another one of Chhaya's brothers, her fourth, had a massive brainstroke. Her second brother was already ill and this was stressing her out, since she was very attached to them. All this was creating a highly negative environment at home.

This became another reason for the constant strife at home for Chhaya wanted me to accompany her on her hospital visits to see her brother. To make matters worse, both sons got fractures in their legs at different times. A couple of months later, Karan slipped into depression, making him behave irrationally. Malini was traumatised by his constant chatter and had once come running downstairs to seek our help. We rushed him to our family doctor, and I called his father-in-law to join us. He was prescribed anti-depressants and fortunately became better after a few months. But these incidents were creating a negative atmosphere at home.

Dr Anandi Lal diagnosed later that I was indeed in depression, and put me on stronger medication. This broke me further and I even appealed to Baba to call me back from this present life. As I was coming out of Lodhi Road temple that day, I met a baba on crutches. His aura was so strong that I couldn't stop myself from touching his feet and asking his name. He had come from Ujjain and his name was Shambhu

Giri. I was really astonished to hear his name. I asked him if I would ever come out of my present condition. He blessed me smilingly and said, 'Sure!' I felt it was Baba, himself, who had come to bless me and help me out. Baba's benevolence always filled me with gratitude, encouraging me to visit Shirdi every year in December. I would converse with Baba, and ask him why he was 'playing with me'? 'You energise me only when it's time to visit you!' I cried to him, one day.

As usual, Baba responded! A flat that I had booked in 1982, had got embroiled in legal issues, but somehow the case had finally come to the High court, and there was a hope that the case would soon be resolved. Mahatma Buddha said that we are all pure souls, and not made up of any elements. This thought would deeply inspire me, making me realise that I too was a soul, and had no connection to the sufferings of the body and mind. It reminded me of the words of the tenth century Sufi poet, Mansur Al Hallaj:

Ana-al-Haqq or 'I am truth,' 'I am God.'

The words had got Al Hallaj into a lot of trouble with the orthodox community in Baghdad, and the King had ordered him to be dismembered and put to death. While each part of his body was being riven, he chanted, 'This is not me, *Ana-al-Haqq*.' It is said that even when his head was being cut off, his words echoed in the air. He had been deeply influenced by an Indian yogi and followed a philosophy of Advaita.

Personally, I prefer the Dvaita philosophy, which considers that man is a part of the Divine, made in His image and will merge back into Him once he leaves this world. During the days I was suffering from anxiety, both Buddha's and Mansur's words would give me solace, and helped me detach myself from my body, mind and surroundings. A meaningful *shloka*, *Brahm Satyam Jagat Mithya* portrays the eternal Sanatan philosophy, that 'God is the only truth and this entire creation is an illusion'. It made me realise that I had been living in the illusion that my life and relationships were real when actually, we needed to learn to live in detachment.

Mirza Ghalib's couplet helped me strengthen my detachment from life and reconcile to the thought of death:

> *Na tha kuchh toh khuda tha*
> *Kuchh na hota toh khuda hota*
> *Duboya mujhko hone ne*
> *Na hota mai toh kya hota*

> (When there was nothing, there was God
> And if there's nothing, God is still there
> My very existence destroyed me
> If I didn't exist, what difference would it make?)

The couplet made me realise that death was not something to be feared. On the contrary, it was our friend, allowing us to unite with the Divine, our ultimate love.

***

When I had felt a little better, Mahi suggested that I should start practising Pranayama and going to Lodhi Garden once again, for walking and meeting friends. She assured me that this would put me in a better frame of mind. However, in my enthusiasm, I overdid it, and it became counterproductive. Finally, I reduced my pranayama practice to fifteen minutes, giving three minutes to each kind of pranayama. There was now some definite improvement and Mahi felt it was time to take me to the Yogoda Dhyan Kendra in Gol Market area to start on more serious meditation.

Around mid-2007, Ram Babu Sharma, the DPCC President called: 'Mahesh ji, where are you? I haven't seen you for so many months.' I tried to explain my condition, saying that I was on strong medication that made me sleep for long hours.

'But now you have to manage somehow to come!' was his next statement. 'Elections for the Delhi Municipal corporation have been declared and I need your wholehearted support!'

I tried to make excuses, but he was insistent. 'Even if I have to set up a bed for you in the Congress office, you have to come. Just your presence gives me strength,' he said.

I felt deeply honoured by his regard. He continued, 'You should think of the Congress party as your mother and she needs you now!' It made me feel intensely emotional. But despite his impassioned requests, I didn't have the strength to either go or personally apologise.

***

In the beginning of 2008, an old friend resurfaced from the United States. She was a gynaecologist, but now was also an MD in psychiatry. I was surprised to learn this and informed her that she was Godsent for me! I explained my condition to her and she asked me to visit her at Pant hospital. She said that she would arrange a consultation for me with the head of the department. She insisted that I should come with my wife and commented, 'Maheshji, to me, you don't sound really depressed!'

I suddenly realised that this was actually so! Talking to her had animated me to such an extent that I was almost feeling my normal self.

The next day, I went to Pant hospital with my younger son, as Chhaya was unable to go. I had to give my case history all over again and when the professor enquired about any particular stressful event, I told her about my elder son's misalliance with Rinki, and also about my strained relationship with my family. I could tell that Lakhan was getting upset.

The Professor encouraged me to continue with some of Dr Anandi Lal's medication and suggested a few more.

On our way home, Lakhan castigated me for holding the family responsible for my illness and failures. I tried to explain that they were unaware of the pressures they had heaped onto me, but it was of no use and he continued to rage. My family was certainly partly responsible for my condition, but they didn't want to accept that. The eldest did feel a bit guilty, since he realised that his past relationship had given a lot of stress to me.

Meanwhile, the society flat court case was also progressing, and when the dates for the court hearing came up, I would get positively charged. My doctor friend commented that during certain periods, I seemed completely fine, but I did have bouts of deep anxiety and those were definitely a cause of worry.

I had lost my appetite and my weight was down to 54 kg. Chhaya would try to blame our daughter-in-law, saying that things had deteriorated after she came into our family. I would admonish her, telling her that she should be happy that our son had bonded well with his wife, unlike us who were always at loggerheads.

On Karwa Chauth, Chhaya got upset with Malini's father, because instead of coming personally, he had sent sweets through a messenger. She thought this was an insult and also found several faults with the *mithai* that had been sent. So, she went and dumped the sweet box outside Karan and Malini's room. The couple came out of their room and were stunned to find the sweets on the floor. Chhaya then began abusing Malini. This naturally upset Karan and we had to restrain him from acts of violence. The children wanted to leave the house immediately, but I assured them that I would set up their separate kitchen on the first floor, so that they could live independently, upstairs. As it is, Chhaya was very critical of Malini's presence in the kitchen. I think she was a bit envious of the bonding between the couple. On the other hand, I was thankful that we had got such a sensible daughter-in-law who was able to handle our very difficult son, who, could, at times, be even more eccentric than me!

***

A few days later, Shiv Pande, the Ujjain city Congress President called to say that he was in town and wanted to meet me. I invited him home, as I was still not well and he came with a few of his office bearers and was impressed with my warmhearted hospitality. He was quite concerned about my illness and invited me to Ujjain, saying I should get a special ritual performed at Mahakaal as I could be a victim of the 'evil eye'. I also needed to perform a special puja there for Karan, as he had a Kaalsarp (a dosha) configuration in his birth chart. Karan and I embarked for Ujjain in May. Shiv Pande had arranged a welcoming reception for us at the station by his executive committee who garlanded us, then drove us to the government guest house. They had made arrangements for our visits to the temple and for the rituals to be performed. They even took me to a tantrik to get the 'evil eye' removed.

The time was perhaps the worst for me, since I had developed physical ailments, another repercussion of depression. I also needed an eye operation. To add to my woes, I received an income tax notice about some transactions involving Rs 20 lakh during my hectic real estate dealings in 2004. Everything had piled up, making me physically, mentally, financially and emotionally broke. I needed Divine energies around me to tide over this crisis.

Other than my eldest sister, no one in my family was giving me any kind of support. Ironically, a few close friends, including Mahi were constantly encouraging and bolstering my morale. Fortunately, despite the negativity around me, the thought of taking my own life never ever entered my head. Dr Anandi Lal had asked me if I had ever entertained any such thought! I believe I was able to retain some element of sanity because of my spiritual inclinations and my friends.

Chhaya was now often avoiding going out with me to her family functions for one of her cousins had commented that she seemed to be gaining weight at the cost of my weight! Subsequently, she began going with one of our sons, making me feel left out.

Chapter 7

Climbing Back

MY INITIATIVE IN gaining the IIC membership under a new category had made me well-known in the Centre. Bhishma Narain Singh would come almost daily and now he began to invite me often to join him. He had his own coterie—of B P Singh, G V G Krishnamurty and Pran Nath Khanna.

I had established a set routine. I would leave the house after lunch and first visit the Sai temple for a few hours. I would then drive across to the Yogoda Dhyan Kendra for some relaxing meditation. From there, I would head for the IIC to join my friends every evening. Just being with them was like balm to my deeply hurt soul. By this time, I had also begun on ayurvedic and homeopathic medicines, on the insistence of Dr Jai Prakash, Parliament's chief medical officer. Veer Singh would often say that Kesriji found alternative medicine helpful.

During this bleak time, Pawan Chaudhary, a builder friend, was also very supportive. He would take me on pilgrimages and suggested that I read the *Bhagavad Gita*, daily. 'That will help you to not come under anyone's impression or go into depression further,' he had said, emphatically.

Another devotee friend, Praveen, suggested that I read the *Sai Satcharitra* regularly. I adopted both suggestions and they made a difference!

The other uplifting news at this time was that we won the Society case in the court. I had taken on the role of an arbitrator between the society's builder and the executive committee and finally brought about a compromise. I was then able to sell the flat, profiting seven times more than my investment. It was the first concrete step towards my recovery, for the thought of not having earned anything over the past few years had been gnawing at my mind. However, the family again showed no appreciation at my windfall, and even said that it was their destiny that brought the money into our lives!

The society had almost two hundred flats and a temple within its premises. Much later in 2008, I gifted and installed Baba's statue at this very temple to express my gratitude. After my book release, I had wanted to install Baba's statue, but could not find the right temple for it. I was finally able to do this; I thus fulfilled my long-cherished desire, and derived great spiritual satisfaction from it.

***

In mid-2006, Murli Deora was nominated as the Petroleum Minister and held his first advisory committee meeting at Parliament House, which I attended. Some members were complaining about the arrangements, and one was even upset that no official vehicle had been detailed for him. When it was my turn to speak, I said, 'Honourable minister, I beg my learned fellow members' pardon but we are a part of an advisory committee and here I feel more as if this is a grievances committee!' I said that instead we should focus on something more useful.

Murli Deora appreciated my thoughts and when the meeting concluded, he asked me to lead for the high tea, a great honour. I hastily said that I couldn't do this in his presence and he took my hand and lead me towards the tea area. But some of the members were annoyed with me and later a couple even accosted me, with Chhaya's brother being part of the pack.

The Petroleum Ministry held an annual poetry symposium at Siri Fort and I received an invitation for it in January 2007. It was presided over by Gopaldas Neeraj, a veteran poet who happened to be my Hindi ghazal guru. Murali Deora was the chief guest. I managed to shine that evening, accumulating accolades, especially from Neeraj! My family attended the event, too, but, as usual, they weren't all that appreciative.

Soon after, on the night of 3 January 2009, I was restless because of Chhaya's uncaring attitude towards my illness. That night, I was unable to sleep, so I took two more heavy pills. When I finally slept, I had a scary dream! I dreamt that I was at the Sai temple, standing in front of the huge statue of Baba. I was backing away from the statue, but had miscalculated the distance to the steps. As I was teetering dangerously on the top step, I felt as if Baba swiftly stepped forward and catching hold of my hand, pulled me to safety. I woke up to find myself soaked in sweat. I felt that I had faced death but, in that moment, Baba himself had rescued me! That night proved to be a turning point, for thereafter I began to improve. A thought began to take root—that it was not yet time for me to go as Baba wanted something more to be done through me.

In the morning, I called up Dr Anandi Lal and told him about the double dose I had taken. He wanted to see me, so I drove across, but unfortunately, as I was not in my complete senses, I dashed my car against another. The doctor was aghast at my condition, even more so at the fact that my family had allowed me to drive alone. He immediately prescribed an antidote which made me feel better.

Later, when I was telling Mahi about this, she was overcome with emotions and said with anguish, 'What can I do to help you come out of this mess?' I assured her that just her presence was enough to alleviate my woes. She insisted that I reduce my medication, as I seemed to be taking too many tablets. Thereafter, I stopped going to Dr Anandi Lal, recalling that psychiatrists had a tendency of holding onto their patients. I gave up all my medication, retaining only my sleeping pill. In the long run, it proved beneficial. I also returned to my family doctor, Sanjiv Zutshi, who diagnosed the cause of my malady as my weakened nervous system.

***

I was acquainted with Malti Subramanian, the principal of Daulat Ram College, and once when I was sitting forlornly on the lawns of the IIC, she enquired about my health. She suggested that I should just be aware and kill my negative thoughts just as soon as they come! 'Only your mind can uplift you!' she added.

'Maltiji, there's a quote about it: Our life is what our thoughts make it! But unfortunately, I have no control over my thoughts.'

'Use your will power,' she encouraged me.

Bhishma Narain Singh and his group too would uplift me, showering their love and affection on me. G V G Krishnamurty, who dabbled a bit in astrology, commented, 'Maheshji, until your karmic period ends, you will continue to suffer and once that is over, simply consuming the Baba's *bhabhuti* will heal you completely.' Back in 2002, another astrologer friend had mentioned that the placement of the Moon and Ketu in my birth chart would uplift me for a period of five years, but later also give me problems for an equal length of time.

My friend in the temple, Praveen, too had gone into depression in the latter half of 2009 and had offered to take me to his homeopath, Dr Abha Majumdar. She put me on strong dosages which gave me a feel-good factor and put me back on my feet by the end of the year. Dr Abha Majumdar soon left India, but referred me to Dr G S Johal, who turned out to be Mani Shankar Aiyar's family doctor as well. He reduced my dosages as such strong potency was not beneficial in the long run. He brought me quickly back to normalcy, so much so that when Malini's grandfather passed away in 2010 and her father requested me to speak a few words in his memory at his prayer meeting, I was able to do so eloquently. The appreciation greatly enhanced my confidence.

Karan and Malini had set up their kitchen on the first floor but had still not made any move to contribute towards household expenses. One day, I persuaded Chhaya to accompany me to their rooms upstairs, but they refused point blank. I offered to get the second floor built for him at a cost of Rs 10 lakh, with separate electricity and water meters, but Malini didn't agree. When Lakhan learned of Karan's refusal to contribute, he began giving Rs 10,000 to his mother every month. I was glad that he had begun to realise his duty towards his parents. Once, he had declared, 'There's no doubt that our father has given us a princely life!'

***

At the Dhyan Kendra, I met Pratima Sethi, a tall, gracious widow, and we became friends. Both her daughter and son were almost thirty, but neither was married. We met occasionally for tea and would sometimes visit each other's home on festivals. Her friendship became instrumental in reviving my interest in the fairer sex!

Meanwhile, at home I was still trying to persuade Karan to construct the top floor. A few months later, he asked me to instead give him the money I planned to spend on the construction. He also demanded that I write my will, which again I refused, saying that I wasn't going to die anytime soon.

One day, we were again arguing in the lobby. Hearing our raised voices, Lakhan came downstairs and since we were standing close in an aggressive pose, pushed us both apart, forcefully. Chhaya had just thrown soapy water on the floor for cleaning, and everything was slippery. I slipped, hitting my head against the edge of a glass table. I was deeply hurt, and blood started oozing from my head. I became unconscious and the next thing I knew was that Dr Sanjiv Zutshi was putting stitches on my head. He recommended that I should immediately be taken to the neurological department at Apollo hospital, where an MRI showed a clot in my brain. I was admitted into the ICU for observation and the neurologist said that I had been in a very serious state and a delay of even half an hour could have cost me my life, or caused an epileptic or paralytic attack. Thankfully, I had access to the best doctors who saved me, although I now had to take neurological medication for a few years.

Astrologically, it had been foretold that after 18 November, Mars would play a prominent role in my life for the next seven years in four aspects: it would increase strife in my life; I would need surgery; I would get into an argument with a lady; but I would also be blessed with name and fame. And amazingly, all things came true!

By the beginning of the next year, I began to look urgently for a match for Lakhan, who was now keen to get married. On Chhaya's suggestion, I had placed a matrimonial ad for him in 2008, but nothing had clicked, not even through Sania, my friend from the matrimonial services agency. I was now feeling confident and capable enough of handling things on my own, once again.

My eldest sister, then introduced me to a matchmaker. It was through her that we met Sanvi's family and the match clicked. It was pretty surprising because the proposal had come six months earlier too, but I had refused on the grounds that the girl had lost her father! Things worked out soon and on 22 May, a lavish ceremony was held to celebrate Lakhan and Sanvi's Roka at Claridges hotel. A few days before that, Sanvi's mother, Malti, had begun speaking to me late into the night. Her concerns were of managing everything on her own, especially as she learnt about my political connections. I reassured her that all we were asking for was dinner at a five-star hotel. I told her that she didn't need to worry about anything else and even offered to help her with arrangements. After that, she took to calling me regularly and would have long conversations about arrangements for the wedding. Lakhan did not approve, for according to him, she was a social 'butterfly'. When I mentioned this to Malti, she shrugged it off with a nonchalant, 'Maheshji, let them bark!' Another time, she demanded to know what jewellery would we be giving to her daughter. I had retorted that since we were not asking for anything from them, she had no right to ask me!

Lakhan was smitten with Sanvi, so much so that he even kept the Karwa Chauth fast, usually kept by wives for the long life of their husbands, even though they were still not married. He said that Sanvi, too, was observing it. Meanwhile, Malini and Karan had moved out, much to my relief, for I had been wondering how two daughters-in-law would adjust with my rather difficult wife. Lakhan had got the first-floor rooms renovated luxuriously, wanting to give the best to Sanvi, and had begun demanding money rather aggressively.

On 10 November, the engagement ceremony was hosted at the Meridien Hotel, another grand occasion, graced by friends, relatives and a few senior politicians. The lavish affair was followed by the wedding three days later at Park Royale.

It, however, was not as magnificent an affair as my elder son's wedding, since I had been out of touch with politics for almost four years. Mani Shankar Aiyar was out of town, and while Sheila Dikshit had assured me of her presence, she was unable to come at the last moment, even though her PA along with her security staff had reached the venue.

Ahmad Patel did come, that too well before time as he had to go for a CWC meeting. I was still on the way when I received his call asking about my whereabouts, and he promised to come once again when his meeting was over. Fortunately, Sanvi's uncle had recognised and welcomed him, and he had handed over his monetary blessings to him and left before my arrival. My friends from IIC, Bhishma Narain Singh and his group were able to attend. It was not as glittering an evening as my elder son's marriage, so, Malti, Lakhan and myself were feeling a bit disappointed!

A few days later at IIC, I met my old friends, all photo journalists with the *Times of India*, who had made a short movie on Karan's wedding. I apologised for not inviting them to my younger son's wedding, letting them know that my depression had made me forgetful. I asked them who was in charge of the Page 3 section of the newspaper. One of them, Madanlal, told me that his good friend, Dinesh Sharma looked after Page 3, so I requested him to arrange a dinner meeting at IIC. I was hoping that if a small news item appeared on Page 3, it would help alleviate the situation. Obligingly, Madanlal arranged an initial meeting, which led to a deep friendship with Dinesh Sharma. Subsequently, a seven-column spread, along with six pictures, was published in the coveted Page 3 section on 8 December, much to our delight.

Malini's uncle, the chairman of a private university called and was astonished at how I had got such extensive coverage! He informed me that in his annual budget of Rs 4 crore for advertisements in the *Times of India*, all he could ever get published was two pictures with a one-column write-up!

***

Soon after, in January 2012, I met Sriprakash Jaiswal, the

Union Coal Minister at the gates of the Sai temple. After the customary pleasantries, I presented my book to him, and he ended up inviting me to his home on Teen Murti Marg, the next day. During my association with Kesriji, he would occasionally visit him and that's how we had got acquainted. Now he not only began to invite me often to his home, but also visited mine for dinner a few times.

As Sriprakash Jaiswal was the chairman of the campaign committee for the Uttar Pradesh Elections, he handed over the responsibility of campaigning in several districts of UP for the Congress Assembly candidates soon after. He said I was a good orator and an Urdu poet, and could, therefore, influence both the minorities and the Vaishya community votes.

Just days before, I had lost my eldest sister on 12 February. She had been suffering from depression for many years, and her condition had worsened with time. Unable to bear her sufferings, she had begged me to pray to Baba to release her from her misery. I, therefore, had appealed to him, asking for solace for her, and amazingly, she passed away just three days later.

I took the opportunity to perform my sister's *pind-daan* at our ancestral place at Garh Ganga while on the UP campaign trail, on my way.

While visiting a number of cities in UP, I sometimes got the chance to speak at public meetings which received media coverage. This opened new avenues for me as I became quite friendly with Pankaj Trivedi from News X. He later gave me the opportunity to be a panelist for several political debates with senior politicians and bureaucrats. I wasn't so comfortable conversing in English, initially, but nevertheless, I began appearing on News X news shows. Cameras and lights were set up in my drawing room, much to my family's wonderment! The shows allowed me to interact closely with a number of prominent figures, including Venkaiah Naidu, Joginder Singh, former Director CBI, and Justice Markandey Katju, speaking on various topics in a surprisingly confident manner!

There are always some repercussions when someone climbs a few steps up the ladder of success and I wasn't spared, either. As I began to get footage on electronic media in television debates, the chairman of the media department of AICC, Prof Janardan Dwivedi asked me to meet him at his office. He commented rather sarcastically, 'Manzar Sahab, you seem to have become a self-proclaimed spokesman of AICC! In what capacity are you speaking on behalf of the Party?'

I retorted: 'I am speaking on behalf of the Party as a committed worker! For about four decades, I have been associated with Congress and have I not recently spoken on its behalf for the UP campaign? And you know that I worked with you and Mani Shankar Aiyar in drafting Sonia Gandhi's speeches.'

'But you should have sought the Congress Committee's permission to appear in such debates,' he reiterated.

I said that I was well aware of the Congress ideology and had not spoken against the interest of the Party, ever. Nevertheless, he instructed me to discontinue speaking on behalf of the Party, promising that he would look into appointing me as an official spokesperson, but nothing ever came of it and my stint as a television debater thus came to an abrupt end after only seven debates.

Chapter 8

Life Around IIC

IN JULY, CHHAYA and I travelled to Kashmir, fulfilling my long-cherished desire of revisiting it. I wanted to visit Amarnath Caves, being Lord Shiva's devotee, and we went there by helicopter. On the short flight, I became friends with the parents of a Brigadier, through whom we were able to go right inside the temple's inner sanctum. During the evening *aarti*, my tears flowed freely, as if I was pouring out all my angst at the Lord's feet, asking for mercy in my life. The divinity of that moment stayed with me for a long time. It was an adventurous seven-day trip in which we participated in rafting, skiing, going right up to the Pakistan border and also staying in a houseboat. The owner of the houseboat was fond of *shayari* and he shared one of his favourite couplets, which I can recall even today:

> *Sadiyon ka raijaga meri raaton me aa gaya*
> *Mai ek haseen shakhs ki baton me aa gaya*
>
> *(I have experienced many sleepless nights*
> *Ever since I have fallen for the words of a beautiful lady)*

After returning from the trip, a pleasant surprise awaited me. When I visited the Dhyan Kendra on Guru Purnima day on

3 July, my attention had been caught by a serene-faced lady, dressed in a simple cotton saree. Her divine look mesmerised me and I went over to meet her, and handed over my visiting card. Almost a month later, she had got in touch, apologising for the delay. That's when I learnt her name, Meenu Minocha.

Meanwhile, things were turbulent at home for Sanvi was not as amenable as Malini. Chhaya would often crib about her, criticising her way of doing things around the house. Sanvi was also working, and was always in a rush in the mornings and would leave without even making their bed, which became a sore point with Chhaya. I told her that there was absolutely no need for her to go upstairs. Did she want to chase them away like she had done with the elder daughter-in-law, I asked Chhaya bluntly. But it had no effect on her and one morning, she scolded Sanvi, causing her to burst into tears.

Just like Karan had done earlier, Lakhan, too began to aggressively defend his wife, forcing me also to take a stand, thus leading to a lot of unnecessary conflict. Malti was aghast. 'Which mother-in-law checks out her daughter-in-law's room?' she asked. I told her that I had already ticked off Chhaya and added that Sanvi too, was over sensitive. However, I was upset at Malti's censorious way of talking, and so told her off as well. I was so put off by this phone conversation that I boycotted her and since then, have never stepped into her house. I counselled the family to live amicably, thereby creating a temporary truce in the house.

In early September, communication expert, counsellor and past life therapist, Meenu Minocha invited me to a gathering at her home, introducing me to her family. I was received warmly by all, and jelled well with all of them. Over the next few days, we spoke a couple of times and I found myself completely awed by her communication skills that were laced with both wisdom and spirituality. Her grasp of the English language seemed superb, and she already knew many of the profound quotes which I would often share with my intellectual friends! She was a language instructor with a reputed institute, and I thought that perhaps she was just the right person to translate my Urdu poetry.

Professor Narang had suggested that I should think of getting my poetry translated into English, since its universal significance deserved to reach a wider audience. I spoke to Prof Anamika, who taught in Delhi University and Makhmoor Sayeedi, and both encouraged me to go ahead. The next year, I had presented my book to an IIC friend, Jahanara, an Oxford English scholar, and she, too, was very appreciative of my poems, emphasising that they deserved to be translated. Jahanara had even introduced me to a poetry translator, Madhubala, who seemed more interested in conditions for the work than in translating!

While talking to Meenu, I mentioned a line of one of Madhubala's translated poems, where she had used the term, 'his heart beat.' Meenu said that the word 'throb' would be a better one. She had understood the exact connotation the word portrayed and I enthusiastically requested her to try working on my translation.

'Maheshji, I am neither an Urdu scholar nor a Hindi poet! Definitely not my line of work!' she said emphatically. But the thought stuck in my mind, for my intuition was telling me that she was meant to do it. I finally persuaded her to try translating a couple of my poems, promising to explain the meaning of the Urdu couplets. Rather reluctantly, she agreed and on 13 October presented the first draft of her work to me. It only strengthened my belief that she would do full justice to my poems. Subsequently, she took on the work and most of it was done through emails and phone conversations, since it was essential to understand the subtle nuances of the background and the state of mind that had birthed each couplet.

The translation work gave my life a new meaning and goal

and completely brought me out from my depressive state of mind. I was fascinated by Meenu Minocha's spiritual mien and magnetic aura. Over time, she became deeply involved with my poetry, immersing her heart and soul into translating the poems!

When I had been nominated as a member of the Coal Consumer Council in the Coal Ministry, I shared the news with Meenu, and was delighted with her response, 'Rise and shine!' It was the first time that I had received such simple and profound encouragement! A while later, I was invited to Kolkata for the first meeting of the Coal Consumer Council in Burdwan and was given a five-star welcome, which made me feel really good. When I voiced a desire to see the coal mines, the chairman personally showed me around, even descending about 2,500 feet below the surface of the earth. It was a rare and unique experience for me.

In 2013, I decided to create a trust for social service, the Sai Shanti Bhagwat Foundation. I involved fifteen of my close friends and it took me about ten months to coordinate and formulate the guiding principles for the trust with the help of lawyers. I wanted it to be a completely non-profit organisation run with my own funds. When bhakti or devotion evolves, one encounters two of its offshoots, wisdom and detachment. And when one gets closer to the Divine, one is able to detach from life. In the autumn of one's life, I thought it appropriate to spend some part of my savings on philanthropic activities. I had married off my children, had a three-storey house and a settled income for my advancing years, so it made sense to fulfil my obligations towards humanity. But by the time I was ready for the registration of the Trust Deed, I realised that many of the members had financial expectations from the whole setup. This upset me and I dropped the whole project completely!

On 30 March 2013, my first granddaughter was born. My daughter-in-law had to be admitted two days prior to the delivery, so I would spend time with Sanvi, reading the *Bhagavad Gita* to her, for I had heard that it has a spiritual effect on the unborn child. Maybe that's why I share a special bond with my granddaughter! Sanvi's mother had arranged a helper for the baby and for all the foods essential for the new mother. Chhaya was not happy with this, as it was making her feel redundant. Consequently, when Sanvi went to visit her mother's house for a week with the baby in the beginning of June, Chhaya set up the kitchen on the first floor without consulting any of us. Relations naturally deteriorated even further and once I was forced to call the neighbours, who somehow brought about a compromise. However, my younger son, too, decided to shift out within a week!

Chhaya couldn't bear the thought of the imminent separation and was sobbing her heart out. Unable to bear her emotional turmoil, I told her to tell them not to leave, for I too had become attached to my granddaughter.

***

Jawahar Uniyal, who ran a couple of NGOs, was also associated with Bhishma Narain Singh's group at IIC and one day, he visited my home on some work. I had met him earlier, but he had not given much credence to me. But when he came to my house, he was impressed by both my lifestyle and picture gallery! Much impressed, Jawahar asked Bhishma Narain Singh's opinion about making me an advisor in his NGO, the Indian Economic Development and Research Association. Bhishma Narain Singh enthusiastically endorsed the idea.

Subsequently, Jawahar Uniyal organised a national conference at the India Habitat Centre and invited me to be a part of the inaugural ceremony, lighting the lamp and giving the opening speech.

About this time, Bhishma Narain Singh's eldest son passed

away and a prayer meeting was held. Pran Nath Khanna suggested that I conduct the proceedings as a number of dignitaries were present. Bhishma Narain Singh asked me to pay homage to the departed soul on behalf of the whole gathering. I had had an emotional connect with the deceased and was thus able to speak eloquently about him. Syed Sibte Razi jocularly nominated me to speak his condolence speech as well, saying that I had the knack of bringing the dead back to life!

***

I happened to meet Bejan Daruwala, a renowned astrologer at IIC in September and requested him to interpret my chart. He spontaneously commented, 'You are a unique human, Mahesh!'

I countered, 'But isn't every person unique in his own right?'

'I am eighty-three years old and so know what I am saying! Nobody can be like you in the cosmos.'

He then gave me two pieces of advice, the first being that I should 'talk less' and second, that I needed to market myself, better. He also told me that 2014 and 2017 would be remarkable for me. Astrology is a truly deep science and can give accurate insights about an individual, for both years did prove to be fortunate for me. We became good friends after that, with Bejan Daruwala inviting me daily for tea at IIC, where he was staying for three days, even calling to tell me to join him quickly.

Later, when I was telling Meenu about my conversation with Bejan Daruwala, she wasn't surprised. 'But of course, you're unique! You're no less an ocean of passion and compassion!'

I was overwhelmed. None of my friends had ever given me such a charming compliment. Excitedly, I exclaimed, 'And you're a Divine gift of God to me!'

***

Sriprakash Jaiswal would take me along on his tours to different states in his own car. I noticed that the moment I sat in the car, he would request his driver to switch off the car radio. He explained that he listened to FM, when he was alone. 'But when you are present, what need do I have for FM? You're more knowledgeable and entertaining than any such channel!' he added. When I shared this with Chhaya, she said, sarcastically: 'People regard you as a comedian and use you for entertainment.'

'What's wrong in that? Making someone laugh is a Divine virtue! At least, they're using me and not misusing me like you!' was my instant rejoinder. She would often point out that all my political friends only used me and didn't have any real value or regard for me and I would retort that if the top echelons found me entertaining, it was well worth it!

On one such tour with Sriprakash Jaiswal, he was accompanied by MLA Bansi Pahadia. When we stopped for tea, we couldn't help laughing uncontrollably at some of the MLA's misinterpretations. One of the MLA's jovial, rather sarcastic home truths was that a congressman ascended his chair with a shroud, as Congress leaders didn't ever like to vacate their positions till death! He called them 'international beggars.'

The minister, Jaiswalji, himself had an interesting observation about me and proposed that I dress up as a baba in saffron robes and preach on TV. He was even willing to be the sponsor of this show. I did not take up the offer.

SEVENTH DECADE
SPIRITUAL SIXTIES

Chapter 1

High on Translations

INDIA INTERNATIONAL CENTRE had opened its permanent membership category in the beginning of 2014, and I promptly applied for it. Soli Sorabjee, the President of IIC, assured me that I would have no trouble in becoming permanent, and instructed his PS and the secretary of the IIC, accordingly. All trustees, including Kavita Sharma the director, were supportive, though once she had commented lightly that getting Rajya Sabha membership was easier! Mani Shankar Aiyar proposed my name; it was seconded by Uma Vasudeva, and so things became easier, giving me a lot of relief.

In 2014, my poetry translations were finished, and I approached Mani Shankar Aiyar to write a foreword. He did so readily, that too within five minutes. It was very well-written, one that gives me much joy to read, even today. I requested Dr Karan Singh for an endorsement, and he too obliged. Meenu had expressed a desire for an endorsement from Khushwant Singh so I approached him, as well. I had presented my book to him in 2002 itself and once later when I had gone to meet him, I learnt that he wasn't well, so I had left some fruit for him. Despite his ill health, he wrote a thoughtful postcard to me, showing his appreciation for my humble gesture, a letter which I treasure till today! He enthusiastically accepted my request, even though he was not well and sadly passed away about a month later. His son, Rahul Singh, informed me of his demise and I raced back from Gurgaon just in time to be the last person to pay homage to Khushwant Singh, before helping Rahul slide his body into the electric crematorium. Later, Rahul Singh told me that the endorsement for my book was the last handwritten note his father had done.

I approached a few more of my literary and political mentors, including Soli Sorabjee, the former attorney-general of India, for endorsements. All obliged. Bhishma Narain Singh and his friends had been discussing the translations of my poems, and had been quite impressed by them. Jawahar Uniyal suggested that I should get my book released by either the President or Vice-President. I immediately began to figure out how this could be done. Recalling that Bhishma Narain Singh was close to Hamid Ansari, I requested him to check if the Vice-President would release the book. But Bhishma Narain Singh later told me that he had not been successful in arranging a meeting. I bumped into Venu Rajamony at IIC, the press secretary to the President, and when I asked about the possibility of the President releasing the book, he expressed some reservations, saying that it had already been released and this was only a translated version. I, therefore, once again turned my attention towards the Vice-President, M Hamid Ansari, who was Mani Shankar Aiyar's friend and whom I had met at a three-day conference in Bhopal. However, the Vice-President's PS also raised the same objection. That left me with no option but to solicit Mani Shankar Aiyar's help in the matter.

Makhmoor Sayeedi suggested that I visit Nizamuddin Dargah to offer a *chadar* as it helped to resolve issues. I, therefore, went to seek His Grace, the Pir Nizami assuring me that my desire would be fulfilled. Indeed, on 7 May, when I received an initial set of books from the publisher, I was able to lay the first copy of my book at Sai's feet, the second at Hazrat Nizamuddin. With a feeling of deep love and appreciation for her work, I then eagerly went to present the third copy to Meenu Minocha. Her family was thrilled to see her name and picture in the book. The book presented a really vibrant impression, for Imroz, who had designed my earlier book covers had created an eye-catching painting on a white background, giving it a distinctive look.

It was Mani Shankar Aiyar who gave the idea of presenting rather than getting the book released. And thus, with his blessings, things were arranged for me to present the book to the Vice-President on 9 June 2014, even getting media coverage for the event. Permission was given for eleven members to be there, including my beloved, fourteen-month-old granddaughter, Tara, who behaved angelically throughout the proceedings, besides Meenu Minocha and her husband. Chhaya presented a bouquet to the Vice-President, while I presented a shawl and the book to him, besides reading out an introduction to my works. I followed this up with reciting my favourite divine prayers before I read out one of my ghazals. Mani Shankar Aiyar then invited Meenu Minocha to read out its English translation. On the whole, it was a very dignified evening, with the Vice-President showing appreciation for my poetry and prayers.

The presentation was telecast on the Rajya Sabha channel the same day, but as it is not a popular channel, the Doordarshan director general, S M Khan, a good friend, released a news clip on national television. It was re-telecast on the ten 'o' clock news a few days later!

The translation of my book and its release by the Vice-President brought me a lot of prestige. A week or so after it, I found Prof Jyoti Nagpal's visiting card among my papers. She was a French scholar while her husband was chairman on the Board of a private university. When I called her, she told me that she had just returned from a visit to France. I presented her with a copy a few days later. When Bejan Daruwala had checked my chart, he had told me that my book may be published in seven languages. With that thought in mind, I asked her if she would like to translate it into French. She was hesitant at first, but later agreed to take up the project after reading my poetry. This time it was much easier, as the English translation had already been done by Meenu.

A few weeks later, I held a dinner in Mani Shankar Aiyar's honour, inviting Balram Jakhar and some of the others who had written endorsements for my book. Mani Shankar Aiyar's wife, Suneet, had also come, but Chhaya refused to attend the party. She had once even excused herself from attending a dinner I had hosted for my brothers and their wives, making my eldest brother comment that the hostess was conspicuous by her absence. I was really embarrassed!

Mahi was very happy with the event, delighting in the way Meenu Minocha had added real value to my life. I had invited her for the celebratory dinner I had hosted for both my translators, Meenu Minocha and Prof Jyoti Nagpal and their husbands. Dr Kavita Sharma, director IIC was another esteemed guest. Chhaya had refused to attend even that party. Her argument was that she was usually left out of the conversation and would just be sitting quietly in one corner, so what was the point of her going!

Some days after the release of my book, I met an old friend, Arif Mohammed Khan at IIC after almost a decade and presented my book to him. He congratulated me heartily and later called up to appreciate my poetry. He subsequently invited me to a dinner at IIC, which he was hosting for a few bureaucrats including a senior IAS officer from the Prime Minister's secretariat. Thereafter, we became close friends, having frequent long phone calls as well. I would also occasionally invite Mani Shankar Aiyar, Arif Mohammad Khan and other senior leaders for luncheons or dinners at IIC while Arif Mohammad Khan would often entertain me at the Gymkhana Club.

A meeting on 20 August at IIC was held to mark Rajiv Gandhi's birth anniversary and I was invited to read out the ghazal I had written in his homage. It was very well received and after the event, a tall, handsome Congress functionary from Outer Delhi area, Dr Ram Bir Singh, showed his appreciation for it with a discussion on Rajiv Gandhi. I invited Ram Bir and his friend for coffee at the IIC lounge. He was charmed by my hospitality and as we parted, he assured me that I could call on him anytime as he had extensive contacts in many places, especially in the UP belt. It so happened that a builder in Agra was not returning an amount of Rs 6 lakh and I had almost written it off. This was seven years ago. I asked him if he could help. He enthusiastically invited me to go to Agra with him the very next day to meet the superintendent of police, and when we did, she readily agreed to help. Within two days, the builder returned the whole amount in three installments, with Rs 1.5 lakh as interest. It made me wonder how Rajiv Gandhi's memory was still blessing me even after twenty-three years!

***

My eldest granddaughter loved to have breakfast with me. When I peeled a banana for her, she would affectionately reciprocate by peeling one for me and would try to feed me. Once, when she was hardly two and a half years old, she asked her grandmother why Dada didn't go to office when both her mother and father did! Her innocent query was very amusing, but it was also embarrassing for me that even a tiny tot was questioning my inactive lifestyle! Thereafter, I took pains to show her my poetry books and tell her about my property deals, but this was of course beyond her comprehension. Little did everyone know back then that I was already practising the concept of 'work from home.'

Once she began school, she was quite active and was even given the mike to speak on stage on Independence Day! When she was about four years old, she would love to look at a picture of herself in my English poetry book, and saw a few pictures of me speaking on the mike. She wanted to know how someone had given me a mike! In her eyes, I didn't deserve to speak on the mike! This became a standing joke amongst my family and friends as well.

My elder son had moved to Noida, but he would occasionally come and stay overnight at our home. Perhaps some relative had encouraged him to do so, with the intention of safeguarding his share in the property. On 2 October, 2015, their twin daughters were born after more than eight years and both Malini and Chhaya got busy in taking care of them. We didn't have a separate guest room, so they started sleeping in the drawing room, but Karan objected strongly. I got the lobby area on the first floor converted into a makeshift room and they moved there. However, Lakhan wasn't happy with this development and demanded that he be given space in the basement. Karan also wanted more space for himself for his commercial venture. He was now working with my nephew, Manish, as his manager.

Manish travelled regularly, and he had wanted Karan to assist him in dealing with labour issues at his production units. Karan was working with him on a monthly remuneration of Rs 2 lakh. The two rooms in the basement were cutting into the open space in which I often held my gatherings, but since Congress had not returned to power in 2014, my political activities were greatly curtailed.

***

Once Mani Shankar Aiyar had asked me: 'Mahesh Bhai, in your opinion, what are the causes of our defeat?'

'I feel there are two main reasons, rampant corruption and humongous arrogance!' I strongly felt that the intoxication of power had made the Party lose direction. Mani Shankar Aiyar didn't respond, going into thoughtful silence.

***

In October, Jawahar Uniyal invited me to Thailand, where he was holding an awards event, at the 7th International Summit on 'Generating Global Partnerships' at Bangkok. He couldn't find any senior leader to grace the occasion and since he was well acquainted with my presentation skills on stage, he requested me to come along. He was so insistent that I had to leave a property deal midway! I handed it over to my elder son. I lit the inaugural lamp along with the deputy prime minister of Thailand. My speech went down well with the audience, as I added a touch of spirituality at the end, so much so that one of the award winners touched my feet! It was an enjoyable five-day trip, giving me an opportunity to explore a foreign country for the first time.

Chapter 2

IIC Diplomacy Vs Home Wars

ARUN JAITLEY, WHO was in charge of Defence and Finance ministries, would often come to IIC. Once when he arrived at the lounge with a couple of friends, he found it full. I happened to be drinking tea with a friend and we both got up and invited him to our table. He appreciated my gesture so much that he would sometimes invite me to his table, which was magnanimous on his part since we were from different parties. I told him that he had been my role model forty-four years earlier, when he was on the English debate team from Sri Ram College while I was on the Hindi team from Ramjas College. By 2015, I had become good friends with all the three who had inspired me during my college days—Arif Mohammad Khan, Harikesh Bahadur and now Arun Jaitley.

On one occasion, when Arun Jaitley invited me to join him, he had asked me what I used to do and I thoughtlessly answered, '*Mohabbat* (love)!' He didn't take kindly to my flippant comment and subsequently withdrew his camaraderie! I had alienated Ashok Gehlot similarly in 2004, when I had given a similar response to his query. We had been on good terms before that. Indeed, many a times, my wayward attitude has been detrimental for me and my relationships!

On Diwali, Lakhan wanted to hold a card party in the basement, as he did every year. However, on the eve of the party, Karan set up an exhibition of quilts and bedcovers with the intention of taking advantage of the guests invited. The younger one was furious and demanded that Karan remove all the stuff. The situation blew up into a full-fledged fight between the two. I had never before seen such aggression among brothers in my own family. Subsequently, both brothers began to demand that I sell the house, with the tacit support of the ladies. Their argument was that the area was not safe for women, especially the young daughters of the house. Conditions deteriorated further, especially as Karan, without informing me, actually placed an ad for its sale!

I had shared this with Balram Jakhar who consoled me by saying that such arguments were pretty common and were currently happening in a very senior politician's home, which had been declared as a memorial, yet every member of his family was laying claim on it! Aren't most disputes in society due to three causes: wealth, woman and land?

***

I once visited Prof Anamika's home at her invitation and met her family. I presented my book to her and we spent an enjoyable evening together. About a month later, she called up saying, 'I am so glad to see that Meenu has been able to understand the essence of your poetry.' She expressed her amazement at the 'range' in my life! I asked her what she meant by that. 'I was aware of your poetic acumen but was definitely not acquainted with your charisma! From Rajiv Gandhi to Rajesh Khanna, from Khushwant Singh to Dr Karan Singh! What a range! You must write your bio-novel!' she replied.

'Why are you making fun of me?' I demanded. She assured me that she was serious. I laughed it off but the thought took root in my mind. I asked Meenu Minocha for her opinion, but she was noncommittal. Then, I asked Mani Shankar

Aiyar, 'Bhaisahab, a Professor friend suggested that I write my bio-novel. You know me well; do you think I should do so? Will anyone like to read about my life for I am neither a leader nor a celebrity?'

'Do only leaders or celebrities write their biographies? Have you not heard of Nirad C Chaudhuri, *An Autobiography of an Unknown Indian?* Definitely, you can write your life story!' was Mani Shankar Aiyar's encouraging response.

That gave me the impetus I needed and I started thinking how I should go about it. A few days later, I got a flash about the title and called up Mani Shankar Aiyar, 'Bhaisahab, how does *Love Infinite* sound for the title?' He heartily approved and I began to look around for someone to help compose my story in a literary format. I wanted Meenu Minocha to help since she had done the translations well, but she was hesitant.

The translation of my poems into French was in full swing and I would often spent hours at Prof Jyoti's house, explaining the couplets. She felt that translating them directly from the Hindi-Urdu version would help retain their essence better. Her husband, Dr Ajit Nagpal, cooperated wholeheartedly.

About this time, Mani Shankar Aiyar brought out a book on the current political scenario, *Achhe Din? Ha! Ha!!* tabulating fifty-two lapses over fifty-two weeks of the new government's tenure. He challenged anyone from the BJP Cabinet to come and counter them in an all-party panel discussion, but not a single minister came forward!

Through Venu Rajamony, press secretary to the President, I attended the 2016 'At Home' gathering on 26 January at Rashtrapati Bhawan, hosting distinguished personalities from all over India. Accompanied by Venu Rajamony, the President, Pranab Mukherjee, personally greeted the guests. It was a very enriching experience!

I had got my eleven 'prayers' printed on small placards and would present them to all whom I met as my visiting card. It helped strike up conversations with people at large, who appreciated how I was promoting spirituality! About this time, I had also come across *Ashtavakra Geeta*, which Osho regarded as being higher than even the *Bhagavad Gita*, and it too influenced my spiritual inclinations. Ashtavakra was deformed at eight parts of his body, and once when he entered Raja Janak's court to participate in a spiritual debate, many among the gathering laughed at him. He demanded of the king, 'Your Majesty, is this a gathering of learned people or of 'skin traders' (those who work with the skins of dead animals)?' The King asked why he was saying this, and he had replied, 'For they are giving more importance to my skin rather than my wisdom! How can they see the Divine if they can't even see my soul?' His response effectively silenced the court and the subsequent wisdom that the twelve-year-old boy displayed in the debate was so phenomenal that the King accepted him as his Guru, bowing at his feet!

A major event in the country around this time was the government's decision on Demonetisation, an economic blunder initiated by Narendra Modi. At 8 pm on 8 November 2016, the PM had suddenly appeared on television to announce to the nation that post-midnight, currency notes in the denomination of Rs 500 and Rs 1,000 would become redundant with immediate effect. The drastic step plunged the nation into utter chaos for a great scramble ensued to change currency at the banks before the deadline of 31 December. I had Rs 3 lakh in cash at home, while Chhaya had saved Rs 6 lakh. Unfortunately, I forgot completely about the Rs 5 lakh that I had placed in a locker!

The unprecedented move destabilised the entire economy and hampered business in all sectors. The unorganised and cottage industries sector suffered a major setback from which they have still not fully recovered. Not only the entire Finance Ministry but even the Reserve Bank of India were in a state of panic as the rules and by-laws were changed about forty times in fifty days! Parliamentary debates conveyed serious doubts whether the Prime Minister had even taken into confidence his own Finance Minister, for it was categorised as a top-secret mission. Opposition leaders claimed that even the Governor of the Reserve Bank had not favoured this. It was also alleged that only the BJP President, Amit Shah, was in the know apart from the Prime Minister.

The reasons given for the sudden Demonetisation scheme, were that it was being done to eradicate black money, printing of counterfeit currency and to check terrorist activities. None of the three were checked. Rather, the nation had to print even more currency notes than were in circulation before since the well off, managed to convert their money with the help of CAs and bank officials! Economists even raised doubts over how the printing of Rs 2,000 notes in place of the banned notes of Rs 500 and Rs 1,000 could eradicate or curb black money in the country's parallel economy. Indeed, duplicate Rs 2,000 notes came into the market in November itself. Later, the economists were proved right when within seven years, Rs 2,000 notes, too had to be withdrawn from circulation. Our former Prime Minister Dr Manmohan Singh proved absolutely right when he declared in the Parliament that this step of Demonetisation will reduce India's GDP by minimum 2 per cent.

The Prime Minister accepted Demonetisation to be a mistake, declaring that he was ready to face any kind of repercussion, 'even hang me at the crossroads,' he had said. His dialogue still resounds in my ears, including his words, 'I am a *fakir* and will ever remain one! Whenever my countrymen desire it, I will pack my bag and depart.' Our country has seen and tolerated many such political gimmicks, and this time too, the gullible people of India showed great patience and let it pass. The Congress leadership called it a great scandal, but failed to convince people how it was so. Narendra Modi is a master in converting every adversity into an opportunity and Destiny helps him to sail through!

***

On 16 July, 2016, I lost one of my great support systems with the demise of my dear friend Hema. Her children decided that I should pay homage to her departed soul on behalf of the gathering. I had first met her on 28 June 1995 and without hesitation, I will say that she was the best lady in my life! She was better than me in all respects and yet never argued with me on anything. We conversed daily in the evening for almost seven years, with her daughter even commenting that her mother's face would light up when my call came! We would sometimes meet for lunch and then go for a drive, and at times, she would invite me to her home for lunch. Ours was a wonderful bonding and only once, did I ever raise my voice with her and her only reaction was a single tear, making me regret my words. She was not only my friend, but also my reformer and her passing left a great void in my life. Yet, despite spending so much time together, I failed to understand her psyche. A few months after her death, one of her close friends said to me, 'You did a great injustice to Hema.' The comment was totally unexpected.

'She waited a long time for you to initiate a closer friendship,' added the friend.

I was speechless at her insinuation. 'How could you have expected her to accede at the initial stage itself! Her daughter was still unmarried, then. Why didn't you approach her later?'

'It never occurred to me after her initial denial! I was content to just be with her! Sometimes, somebody's presence is enough in your life!'

It made me realise a very deep truth about relationships

that a woman wants a man to woo her in different ways before she capitulates!

***

Meera Mehra, a tall, gracious lady in her early forties and a Director in an IT company, would occasionally visit Delhi from Shimla. I met her in September at IIC, where she too was a member. We messaged occasionally, though we lost touch for a while when she went abroad. She has understood me very well, sympathising with the many situations in my life. With her coming into my life after Hema's demise, it seemed that God has always compensated me for any losses I might have incurred, for she filled the vacuum left behind by Hema to some extent. She makes me feel truly valued and actually gave me a hundred and five points out of hundred, when I asked her to evaluate my personality! Three decades earlier, Jennifer had given me an overwhelming hundred points to the same question, but Meera was a step ahead. She has been too generous in her thoughts and words calling me a 'magnetic mentor' and a 'clear-headed companion'! She is a wonderful woman and an amazing conversationalist. For me she is a dear, distant friend who has given me joy and energy with her regular interactions. She too feels uplifted and motivated after talking to me.

***

The Aam Aadmi Party saw a phenomenal rise under the leadership of Kejriwal, but at the cost of sacrificing all values and principles. He even went back on his own promises and commitments, alienating his mentor Anna Hazare as well, for he had specifically advised his protege not to create a political party as his was a social movement. Anna Hazare had a long-standing link with the RSS and is on record to have said that both RSS and BJP used him to gain victory in 2014. This has been justified in Pranab Mukherjee's biography, brought out by his daughter, Sharmistha Mukherjee.

Anna Hazare formulated a committee with members like Shanti Bhushan, Prashant Bhushan, Arvind Kejriwal, Yogendra Yadav, and Kiran Bedi to pressurise the government to pass the Jan Lokpal Bill, appointing Ombudsmen to oversee activities of senior leaders including Chief Ministers and even the Prime Minister. Kejriwal, who was with the IRS, ran an anti-corruption NGO and had won the Magsaysay award. His resilience and courage helped him formulate the AAP, and in Delhi, he was able to overthrow the Congress party.

It was said that a strategy of the BJP and RSS was behind his unprecedented rise. Arvind Kejriwal became the Chief Minister of Delhi thrice, as his policy of giving free resources earned him a huge following from among the masses. It is believed that Yogendra Yadav gave him the idea of doling out free electricity and water, attracting the poorer sections of society while his blatant antipathy towards the ruling party, BJP, earned him the support of the minority community. However, a spectacular rise also has a tendency to fall sooner or later and that's exactly what has happened to AAP. The very agenda that had helped them to rise became a bane for the party, resulting in the top leaders coming under the radar of the corruption department and landing in prison. According to media reports, the one politician who had declared that he didn't even want an official car or even security was accused of having spent a whopping Rs 50 crore in renovating the government accommodation allotted to him! BJP had manipulated Kejriwal's rise to finish off Congress in Delhi, but ultimately, they had to strategise to bring his party down.

Chapter 3

Blessed at Mt Kailash

HARIKESH BAHADUR HAD written 'Poet at a Glance' for my English translation book on my request, but now for my French translation, I requested Arif Mohammad Khan to do so. He was a knowledgeable scholar, and also a linguist, being familiar with Farsi and Arabic. He had studied the philosophies of different religions, and could quote *aayaaten* from the *Quran* and *shlokas* from *Santana* scriptures. When I approached him, he was delighted and enthusiastically agreed. He exclaimed, 'Manzar Sahab, you have your own distinct outlook! We have to read up before speaking, but you speak directly from your heart. A poet is an original creator, in line with Mother Earth and a woman, and your words are really impactful!'

'You are so magnanimous, Bhaisahab!'

'Your persona is above any post or position and you don't even need them. You have always lived in your integrity and never compromised anything, unlike us who have to, being in the system and adjust our integrity according to the different ideologies that we need to uphold. You use politics as a social platform! Indeed, it will be my pleasure to write for your book.'

I had become quite close to Arif Mohammad Khan, talking for long hours with him on the telephone. Often, he would call me while he was travelling and one day we spoke for almost three hours! When he informed me that he had reached his destination, his wife, who was accompanying him, took the phone from him and said to me, 'Manzar Sahab, in all my thirty-eight years of marriage, I have never seen my husband talk so extensively to anyone! And what a range of topics you have covered!'

Arif Mohammad Khan had said once, 'I invariably learn something new from you each time we talk! Your only drawback is that you sometimes become a bit acerbic!' Churchill, too had said something similar to his associate, 'Though your tongue occasionally becomes acidic, you always add something to my knowledge whenever you speak!'

'That's large-hearted of you, Bhaisahab, rather I learn much more from you for you are truly well-read!' Our talks ranged from philosophical to spiritual.

***

2017 saw the release of the French translation of my Hindi-Urdu poetry book, which was a landmark in itself. An even greater event was that it was released by the Honourable President of India at Rashtrapati Bhawan, perhaps unprecedented in the history of literature! When I had spoken to Venu Rajamony for the possibility, he had advised me to involve Mani Shankar Aiyar, since he was close to the President. He readily obliged and we immediately got a date for the presentation, 29 March. Unfortunately, Prof Jyoti and her husband were abroad at that time, so they couldn't accompany us. So, it was only Chhaya, me and Mani Shankar Aiyar. I presented the shawl and the book to the President, while Chhaya felicitated him with a bouquet of flowers. I was carrying the English translation of my book, and Pranab Mukherjee noticed that and asked, 'English and now French also?' I thanked him and added, 'I have been your devotee since 1982.'

'But I became a Minister only in 1973!' the President commented with a smile.

'I got a picture clicked with you in 1982!' I quickly flipped through the French poetry book and showed it to him, deepening his amusement at my obvious attempt to please!

The launch of the French translation raised my graph further in my circles. The former Chief Election Commissioner, G V G Krishnamurty was the first to congratulate me heartily and even invited me home for lunch. He said to me, 'Mahesh ji, I didn't realise the depth of your thoughts! I am impressed by the abstract form of your poetry! I would love to review it.'

He presented me a shawl and a beautiful pen, making me feel really venerated. Later, when I had once used the pen in Sheila Dikshit's presence, she admired it so much that I presented it to her!

Prof Jyoti was a renowned impressionist painter since childhood and had created a beautiful painting for the book's cover. However, a friend, Ramotar, who had visited Kailash Mansarovar had sent me an amazing picture of the sun rising above the sacred mountain. Since I have a deep connect with both Shiva and the Sun, I requested Prof Jyoti to paint that picture for the cover and she readily agreed, saying it would have a greater impact. When Ramotar saw the painting, he remarked, 'Mahesh ji, "Kailash" seems to be inviting you!' That roused an intense desire in my heart to visit the holy abode of Shiva Parvati! I went on my own with a trip organised by my friend, Sudhir Gulati. The journey was considered to be risky and so before leaving, I wrote my will and even got it registered. Though I had a wonderful experience at the sacred mountain, right from the beginning, things were somehow mismanaged due to my overexcited state. First, I forgot to collect my suitcases at Lucknow airport and was already on my way to Nepalgunj, when an official from the airlines called me up about my suitcase, and I had to go right back. At another point while waiting near the helipad in Simikot on the mountain side, my wallet, complete with all my credit cards and money, fell from my pocket. I wrote it off as lost, but thought of checking where I had been sitting, and miraculously found it lying there! Despite the many glitches, the Divine Himself was ensuring that my journey should be hassle and sickness free, even though I am susceptible to the cold. I connected well with my fellow travellers thanks to my gregarious nature. I was the seniormost among them and had taken both my books along and shared the pictures in my mobile with others in the group, making them marvel at my reach.

From Nepalgunj, we were to be transferred by a small plane to Simikot and from there by helicopter to Hilsa and then onwards to China. But bad weather had us stuck in Nepalgunj, itself for three days. Because of rain, we could not spend two nights at the next stop, an essential process of acclimatisation to the rarefied atmosphere. Every day, we would head towards the airport and return disappointed after waiting long hours, wondering whether we would be even able to complete the journey. We barely slept for a couple of hours daily as many of us would stay up late at night chatting. Finally, on the fourth day we went to Simikot where we stayed only for one night, followed by another night at Hilsa, whereas, it is essential to spend two nights at one place for getting acclimatised. By the time we reached Kailash on the seventh day, it was late evening and we were all hungry and tired. We were directed by our guide to purchase a can to store the holy lake water. The beautiful salesgirl there was having a mango and I couldn't resist complimenting her. 'And that's an equally beautiful fruit you're having.' Much amused, she offered a mango to me and I accepted it as if it was a Divine gift from my revered Shiva Himself!

While being transported by bus from the hotel in China to Kailash Mansarovar, I took a nap and had a vision of Sai Baba. In my dream, I saw the woman sitting in front of me holding something covered in her lap. When I asked her what it was, she unveiled a small statue of Sai Baba! Many regard Baba to be a manifestation of Shiva and I was amazed that he was showing me his presence there as if to prove that they were connected.

We were soon at Mansarovar, perhaps the most beautiful and spiritual lake on Planet Earth, with deep clear waters that glistened like glass. At a height of about 15,000 feet, its huge size is indeed a wonder of Nature! NASA research has shown that Kailash Parvat can be regarded as being at the centre of the earth, while the longest rivers of Asia are sourced from here. We were told to take a dip for only a minute or so as the waters are freezing, but I remained in the lake for almost five minutes. Kailash Parvat was visible and I couldn't stop gazing at its towering Divinity. Suddenly, I could see a black outline of the images of Shiv and Parvati on the snowy slopes, which made me ecstatic. I excitedly called out to my fellow travellers if they could see it, but none of them could, laughing that I must be hallucinating! To this day, I believe that I was indeed blessed by their glimpse! Beautiful, ethereal swans flock the lake and I couldn't resist taking out a variety of the foodstuff I was carrying with me and offering it to them. They happily flapped around me, accepting the titbits. The rest of the group had by now gone to have their meal. One of our co-passengers, in his forties, suffered a heart attack and had to be rushed back to the hotel. Sudhir Gulati suggested that I too should go back with him and not risk the journey around the mountain. Submitting to his advice, I went back with the patient in an ambulance and had a long, sound sleep after many days.

The group faced many tough situations during the rest of the journey, and by sending me back, it seemed that Lord Shiva had protected me! While I was there, I got the news of the birth of my fourth granddaughter. That was another auspicious omen.

Chapter 4

A Spiritual High and a New Low

AFTER MY RETURN, in July, I had a serious confrontation with my elder son and banned him from the house. It was the bane of my life that my sons were constantly creating dissension for me. People beget sons to have a stable support in their old age but I seemed to be caught in strife with them all the time. Often, I agonised why I had not been blessed with a daughter. My friend's words echoed in my ears, 'A son is a son till he gets a wife, while a daughter is a daughter all her life!' One of my advocate friends and a senior police officer, whom I would meet at IIC, advised me to sell the house and I finally decided to initiate the process of selling. When Arif Mohammad Khan got to know of this, he actually visited my home to request my family to live peacefully together in the house, considering it to be both well-built and well-located!

Mahfooz Ali, my neighbour, was instantly interested in buying it, since he had an extensive family. 'Manzar Sahab, after all neighbours should be given first priority!' he told me.

A couple of months later, while on a visit to Shirdi, I caught a chest infection and eventually, I had to be admitted to Moolchand hospital where I had to stay for six days before being discharged. I was once again feeling very low and felt as if I would slip back into depression, but thankfully my illness made my family a bit sympathetic towards me, which comforted me a little. I had also taken up yoga and pranayam at the Yoga center on Ashok Road and that helped me to remain balanced.

Around the time when I had released my book of poetry in French, G V G Krishnamurty had thought of suggesting my name for a Padma Shri award, and in the next two months, we put in a lot of effort meeting distinguished veterans for recommendations. Mani Shankar Aiyar supported my cause, wholeheartedly. Arif Mohammad Khan, who was a member of the Nodal committee guided me about the process, though he frankly stated that he was not very hopeful about my chances. By December, the list of the awardees was submitted to the Home Ministry for final approval, before being sent to the PMO. Bhishma Narain Singh had a familial connection with the then Home Minister, Rajnath Singh, and vociferously advocated my nomination, and subsequently, Rajnath Singh invited me to meet him in his office. Kharag Singh, his senior PA was a good friend of mine and he too put in a recommendation for me. When I entered the Home Minister's office, he stood up to welcome me and invited me to sit next to him on the sofa. There couldn't have been a greater honour! However, he stated his inability to help me, even though he knew that I deserved it, as it was the prerogative of the Prime Minister.

Although a number of senior leaders, including Dr Karan Singh, had supported my candidature for the award, my political activism and difference of ideology did not go in my favour. Well, at least, I had the satisfaction of my name reaching the highest level!

In February 2018, our drains got blocked because of construction in Mahfooz Ali's house. Even though the MCD were on the job, Chhaya complained non-stop, berating me for not ticking off the neighbour. Karan happened to have come and took his mother's side. He had once again lost his job and while both were arguing with me, Lakhan joined us downstairs and showed his support for me. The family was now divided into two warring factions leading to disputes daily. It felt so oppressive that I was now more determined than ever to sell the house. Another senior Muslim leader was ready to give me my asking price, but for several personal reasons, I wanted my neighbour to have it.

Around this time, one of my close relatives got nominated as an MP in Rajya Sabha, allegedly by paying a hefty amount of money.

Meanwhile, the house deal was finalised and I told Lakhan about it. I also informed him that I had decided to divorce his mother and would give her 40 per cent of the sale amount along with other assets, and that I would settle the balance 15 per cent between the two brothers, while keeping 45 per cent for myself. Lakhan was supportive and even offered to live with me paying me regular monthly rent to ensure an income for me. He shared these plans with his uncle, who objected, asking where Chhaya would go. I was disappointed by his attitude. On the one hand, he would acknowledge that I was the one to set him on the path towards political ascendancy, yet he could be very churlish towards me if ever I achieved anything! Now he supported his sister's stand of not giving me a divorce, yet demanded the transfer of the house amount in her name. Chhaya even threatened me that one of her close relatives would lodge a complaint against me in the IT department if I didn't do so. Politics in families and society is considerably much more than what goes on in actual political circles!

I did not want to involve myself in any sort of litigation, so I had to accept her unfair demand.

Some friends, including Arif Mohammed Khan, also advised me against initiating divorce proceedings. Mahi and Uma, another close friend of mine from Ahmedabad, did not favour it. Ramotar Gupta also pointed out the folly of staying with my son, since he was aware of the various untoward incidents happening in my home. He vehemently insisted that I should stay with my wife, separately from my sons and their families. He said that I had once told him that my sons were worse than her. He, himself had lost his wife and was living a lonely life with his sons settled abroad. He told me that it was indeed a very difficult situation to be in.

Thinking it over, I too realised that it was better to stay with my wife for if I were to create a balance sheet, she did have many points in her favour, the topmost being that she was a very good housewife! If she was not an ideal wife, I don't think I was good husband material either! Besides, I had seen the attitude of quite a few of my lady friends and Chhaya scored over most of them! I recalled the time of my marriage when she had thanked me profusely for approving of the match for her weight had been a minus point. Her brothers had pressurised me so much that I had actually rejected another proposal where they were ready to spend Rs 3 lakh on the wedding while Chhaya's family had offered only a third of that amount. I had thought that since she didn't have a father, she would be malleable, but the actual reality turned out to be totally opposite to my expectations.

Chapter 5

Domestic Upheaval and an MOU

A RAY OF light shone through these stressful times of selling and buying and visits to the lawyers. Uma, my Facebook friend from Ahmedabad called on my birthday. We had been in touch since August 2017, and now she was in town, and wanted to meet personally. I invited her to a club for I had to meet my lawyer nearby. Her pictures didn't do justice to her vibrant beauty or correctly portray her sensuality. Uma was in her mid-forties and told me that I, too, looked far younger and more energetic than my age. She was tired after her journey, so, I got her a room at the Club to rest while I went for my meeting. Later, we spent an intimate, blissful and memorable evening together. I told her that she had come at a very crucial time of my life, since I had just sold my home. She was shocked but then consoled me, 'My father considers me to be his lucky daughter! You will soon be in a better position! It will be a blessing in disguise.'

Thereafter, I set things in motion to buy a separate house in Defence Colony for us both, while my sons were to get their own homes. Over the next few days, I checked out more than thirty residences, finally settling on one I had liked best. In times of need, God endows me with phenomenal strength, for I did the shifting and setting up of the house singlehandedly, since Chhaya had gone to stay with Karan.

Uma's words had proved prophetic for I purchased my new house just five days later on February 21, and it was definitely much better than my previous one!

Moreover, I had been able to release my stress completely, transporting me to a completely different world. Our relationship continued later on too as she would often come to Delhi, while I went twice to Ahmedabad.

At about this time, a former Union minister of the BJP approached me with a request to help him join the Congress party. He had been bypassed for the position of Cabinet minister. I felt euphoric as he would be a great asset for our Party. I approached Dikshit, but she was reluctant to request Sonia Gandhi as she felt she wouldn't agree. I then went to Mani Shankar Aiyar, but he didn't really acknowledge my request. I, finally went to 10, Janpath to meet V George and when I requested him, he got quite excited and immediately asked me to write a letter to Sonia Gandhi for an appointment. But Sonia Gandhi, too, rejected my request, justifying Dikshit's doubt. Much later, he got a good post in Narendra Modi's cabinet.

***

Though the registry of our Nizamuddin house was to be done in June, we shifted to our new Defence Colony home in May itself. It was a unique experience living on the first floor with other people in the same building. The top two floors were occupied by single women officials of the Embassies of USA, Japan and Belgium while Colonel Vinay Mullick, son of late Brigadier Mullick, lived on the floor below us. We hit it off well and he began to regard me as an elder brother. The three foreigners were a bit reserved and kept to themselves, and only occasionally, would our paths cross. I met the US representative, Margaret, for the first time in the lift, and she asked me on which floor I lived. I then asked her floor and when she replied that it was the third floor, I commented 'You're living nearer to God than any of us!' making her laugh out loud. She was the friendliest amongst the three, and even visited us a couple of times.

I arranged a small house warming party for only a few relatives soon after shifting and all were quite appreciative of our new home. I then held a get together for my mentors on 7 August, inviting Mani Shankar Aiyar and his wife, Suneet, Sheila Dikshit, Arif Mohammad Khan, Sri Prakash Jaiswal, H K Dua, Subhash Kashyap and B P Singh. Sheila Dikshit was unwell, but sent three beautiful gifts and a letter through her PA. It was an enjoyable evening, with everyone in a very relaxed space for almost four hours. I had invited Colonel Vinay Mullick as well and he later expressed his amazement that such senior leaders were treating me at par! His observation made me feel delighted and I said, 'It's their humility that makes them great! They really shower a lot of love and affection on me!'

***

'How do you become so friendly with people so quickly?' Arif Mohammad Khan had once asked.

'Bhaisahab, I am sure you know that each individual has mind, intellect, consciousness and ego. We just need to pamper the ego; that's the most important factor for any individual. That can easily be done by giving genuine love and respect to the other!'

'Well said, Manzar Sahab!'

'But I have a problem also and the problem is that the friendships dissolve as mercurially as they form!' He found this amusing and added, 'That reminds me of what Maulana Abul Kalam Azad once said that many Muslims fervently come to me for advice but as hastily back off, finding my secular views, unpalatable!'

I got introduced to the personal secretary of Sri Sri Ravi Shankar by one of his devotees and we became quite friendly. He was quite impressed by my books and profile, and in September 2018, I was invited to Sri Sri Ravi Shankar's ashram in Bangalore as he agreed to relaunch my books in front of his very extensive congregation, which included many foreigners. I was called onto the stage to address that huge gathering. I started by admiring Sri Sri Ravi Shankar, saying that he was a true living Guru and a truly enlightened saint of the present times, who had impressed, influenced and inspired me and millions more! This evoked a huge round of applause from the audience. I stated that Sri Sri Ravi Shankar had been an important part of my evolvement for it was after learning the Sudarshana Kriya back in 2000 that I was able to truly evolve. It was a wonderful experience being in his presence and living in the Ashram. I had met Uma and her family at the Ashram and a few months later, she along with her husband came to Delhi to visit Barsana and Vrindavan.

***

In November, Sriprakash Jaiswal's granddaughter was getting married in Ashoka hotel and I was in charge of welcoming the guests, as I was well acquainted with the VIP guests. I had a similar responsibility at his elder granddaughter's wedding earlier. I met both Ahmad Patel and Anand Sharma and the former hugged me quite warmly, as we were meeting after almost two years. He asked me to come and meet him soon, making me wonder what could be the reason. Another senior politician enlightened me that my name was again up for discussion as a candidate for the upcoming general elections. Sheila Dikshit had become the President of the Delhi Congress and soon after, she asked me to submit my biodata, marking it as important. However, a win for our Party was doubtful as Narendra Modi had scored by getting a surgical strike conducted on a terrorist camp in Balakot, in retaliation to the suspicious killing of forty security personnel by Pakistani terrorists at Pulwama. It had been stated in some media reports that the strike had the tacit support of the American President, Donald Trump. It seemed amazing that a country that had banned Narendra Modi's entry for almost twelve years after the Godhra incident, was now supporting him, and even inviting him to visit the United States of America.

It just goes to show that the country matters much more than an individual! Narendra Modi had even declared at a public meeting in USA, *'Ab ki baar, Trump Sarkar!'* which was a faux pas.

Coincidentally, he didn't win, for it was Joe Biden who soon came into power.

Also, our intellectual Congress leader, Rahul Gandhi had voiced a derogatory slogan against the Prime Minister, accusing him of being a thief without any evidence, which only harmed the image of the Party. I had even requested Sheila Dikshit to talk about this to Sonia Gandhi! I brought up the topic with Ahmad Patel, but he only laughed it off. In the eyes of the public, there was absolutely no comparison between Rahul Gandhi and Narendra Modi, who had been in power since 2001, CM for thirteen years and now PM for five years. Rahul Gandhi, on the other hand, had never even accepted any office, though Manmohan Singh kept offering him ministerial posts. Ultimately, I didn't get the ticket for undefined reasons and moreover, we lost the elections heavily!

***

A new dispute raised its head in my household. Chhaya's brother had made us sign a Memorandum of Understanding, considering it a better option than divorce, through which

I had made over an ample amount to her name and even registered the house in both names. We had decided not to interfere in each other's life along with other terms and conditions. It was like a treaty, through which I had bought my peace and freedom! Yet though I had purchased peace, I never actually experienced it! Chhaya began to negate me, bickering most of the time. Her favourite dialogue was that no one would even endure me even for a few days, while she had done so for so many decades.

Once the MOU had been formalised, she had begun neglecting her household duties and would even cut corners in preparing my meals. I was not even getting fresh food daily and that began to tell on my health. She would hoard eatables, especially those coming from her family. Most of our disputes arose from the topic of food. She was a glutton for taste and stashed away even her favourite savouries, not giving them to anyone, other than her children. She would blame me for spying on her for I would often go through her cupboards for the stuff she hid away, when I was only trying to rescue them before they got spoilt! I once asked her why she was so adamant about food. Did she not get enough as a child? That's when she shared that since her father passed away before her birth, she had lived with her brothers' wives and their children in Sonepat while the brothers worked in Bhiwani, on a modest salary. The elder sister-in-law would keep a tight control on food, and if treats came from her husband, her five children had them all, making Chhaya feel deprived. Besides, the sister-in-law would make her work for her food. It was quite an emotional tale and gave insights into the lack she had faced while growing up. Her story also highlighted the importance of having a father to maintain balance in the family. I regretted not having tried to understand her psyche much earlier in our relationship. I tried to compensate by bringing her favourite foods, but sometimes she wouldn't have them. Perhaps, she felt guilty for not contributing towards the household expenses as had been stipulated in our MOU. Subsequently, I had to make a peace pact with her, by giving her a monthly allowance for her daily sweet and fruit expenses!

We had our own portions in the house and this began to give me a sense of detachment from everything else, even from my own sons. However, I was very attached to my four granddaughters. The youngest, Lara, would toddle into my room when she was barely a year old. The older ones loved to talk and would make very relevant observations. Five-year-old Moni once demanded to know why I was bending forward in my portrait, and why couldn't I stand straight? Her twin, Noni, would take me to task if I wasn't paying attention to her. Once while talking to her, I got distracted by the television, and she asked petulantly, 'Are you talking to me or the television?' They would often have breakfast with me and loved to talk about their activities as well. We would sometimes play cards and other games.

As there was no interference in each other's lives, I began going on pilgrimages regularly. It is an undeniable fact that only when faced with extreme degradation, does one struggle to raise oneself. That was my situation in my own home, for no opportunity was missed by my family to pull me down, reminding me of Jean Paul Sartre's quote, 'The other is Hell!'. When we are alone, we are actually with the Divine, able to rise to a blissful consciousness. Osho's words too made sense that being alone is our Destiny, for we have come alone into this world and that's how we will leave it. My search for spirituality thus deepened, since only that gave me solace. In June, I went on the Chardham yatra again with Sudhir Gulati, visiting Yamnotri, Gangotri, Kedarnath and Badrinath. They were all one-day trips as we went by a six-seater helicopter to each place starting from the base camp at Dehradun. I was again the oldest amongst them and yet I was the only devotee to take a dip in the freezing waters of Gangotri! At Kedarnath, we had VIP entry and when I shared mine and my family's names with a priest there, he advised me to get *Rudrabhishek* performed. I did the *Rudrabhishek* with my own hands, making me feel as if I had been specially blessed by Shiva. At Badrinath, I met a Mahamandaleshwar who gave religious discourses on television. He guided me to get a *pind daan* done for all my departed ones, a three-hour long ritual on the banks of the Alaknanda, naming all my departed family members, in-laws and friends, including Kumar Pashi and Rajiv Gandhi, a total of twenty-eight names! As soon as we finished, it started to rain, as if the Heavens had been waiting for us to complete the *pind daan*!

2019 strengthened my desire to write my bio-novel. Prof Anamika encouraged me to note down main incidents of my life and said that she would guide me to compile them. Dr Kavita Sharma occasionally went through my work. I had begun this task on my birthday that year in Shirdi, creating a format for how I wanted to go about it. The earliest memory I had was the birth of my brother on 18th September 1956 and that became the starting point of my story. I decided to do it in chronological order, dividing my life into seven decades, cataloging important events of each decade. Mani Shankar Aiyar agreed to give his general supervision to the work, which encouraged me immensely. I showed Prof Anamika my first decade draft a year later in 2020, making her exclaim that it could turn out to be an amazingly wonderful story!

***

It has been one of my great misfortunes that those of my family, friends and mentors whom I loved and who were also attached to me, showering me with their unconditional love and affection, left this world at the peak of our emotional bonding! My father, next only to the Divine, left in 1983 when I was twenty-nine years old. My mother, followed him a few years later. Srikant Verma passed away in 1985, at an unlikely age, while Rajiv Gandhi left at barely forty-seven years in 1991. Another great support, my poetry Guru, Kumar Pashi left me in 1992 when he was only fifty-seven. Sitaram Kesri had become my backbone, but he moved on in 2000, leaving me quite distraught, followed by Narasimha Rao in 2004. Vasant Sathe, too, had become quite close after my book release, but passed away in 2011. 2013 brought another loss, for my first political Guru, Vidya Charan Shukla was assassinated. In an unfortunate incident, my great emotional support, Balram Jakhar, had a hip fracture, which rendered him helpless, finding release in 2016. Bhishma Narain Singh was seriously ill towards the end and was on a ventilator, before he expired in August 2018. A high-profile prayer meeting was held at IIC, where many senior leaders were present including Dr Manmohan Singh and Rajnath Singh. I got emotional while paying tribute to his magnanimous personality. My words touched many, with Nikhil Kumar, the former Delhi Police Chief Commissioner telling me later, 'Manzar Sahab, you were supreme!' I could only respond humbly, 'Your greatness, Bhaisahab!'

I had met Sheila Dikshit on her eighty-second birthday in March, presenting her with a saree. She exclaimed, 'What a beautiful saree! You spoil me, Mahesh ji!' Despite her age and four heart surgeries, she had been given a ticket by Sonia Gandhi and Rahul Gandhi for contesting as an MP in the upcoming Lok Sabha elections. One evening, her secretary, Akhilesh Tripathi, called, requesting me to persuade her not to take up the nomination. Her family were concerned about her delicate state of health, but to no avail. Her family thought that I might be able to influence her. I immediately called her, insisting that she should consider her health and not accept this responsibility especially when summer was at its peak. She joked, saying, 'But Mahesh ji, you told me not to panic when I was leaving for France for my heart surgery! You were the one to encourage me not to lose my battle before even beginning.'

'Very true, madam! Battles are first fought in the mind and then in the battlefield!'

'That's a very philosophical statement!' she exclaimed. 'And you also said that the time and place of death are predestined, Maheshji! How should we 'go' then, sitting dispiritedly at home or in harness?' 'Madam, you're right! Even in the *Bhagavad Gita*, Krishna advised Arjuna that one must die while performing one's duty!'

'Besides, you know how indebted I am to our Party, having been associated with it for almost four decades!' She passed away after contesting elections in July 2019.

On 9 November 2019, the Supreme Court ruled in favour of the Ramjanambhoomi, causing much elation among the Hindus. I mentioned to Mani Shankar Aiyar that I felt the judgement to be contradictory. 'Mahesh, this is only a judgement, not justice!' he commented. I marvelled at his perspicacity.

Uma's mother wanted to visit Ayodhya, so I accompanied the two of them at the end of November, thus getting the opportunity to take a dip in the holy Saryu river. I felt so blissful that I decided to revisit once the temple was actually built!

Arif Mohammad Khan became the Governor of Kerala in 2019 and invited me for a state visit in January the next year. His wife called up Chhaya and insisted that she accompany me. Thus, we enjoyed their hospitality for a week, staying in the Governor's house itself and also visited Kanyakumari, Rameshwaram and Madurai, visiting all the famous temples there, including the Meenakshi temple. We even visited the mysterious Padmanabhan temple in Trivandrum, where it is said that if a particular gate is opened, it would flood the entire state. Therefore, it is permanently locked on orders of the Supreme Court. The temple houses an amazing statue of Lord Vishnu reclining on a giant Naag, with a lotus upholding Brahma emerging from its navel. Goddess Laxmi is seated at its feet. We were given VIP treatment when we visited.

Chapter 6

The Pandemic Years

MARCH 2020 WITNESSED an unprecedented and devastating event with the advent of a pandemic, bringing life to a complete standstill. A lockdown was initiated in the whole country on 25 March, closing down every activity for an indefinite period. On that day, while I was going to the Sai temple, I happened to see a banner at the Arya Samaj temple, offering food to any destitute in the evening. They also appealed for donations. Once I was back home, I wrote a cheque for Rs 5,100 for the Arya Samaj temple. The organiser appreciated my gesture, saying that I was the first to contribute. Thereafter, I undertook more such philanthropic tasks since they began to give me inner peace. I would also go daily to the temple and distribute food among the poor living in nearby slums. After some time, a few young men were inspired and voluntarily joined me, creating a systematic distribution process, complete with social distancing. I also helped out some friends who mentioned they were facing financial problems. The destitution around me affected me so much that I gave up my afternoon meal, taking only breakfast and dinner. No help was available for household chores, so I began to wash my own utensils and helped out at home. I found the tasks so satisfying that I have continued washing my own utensils to date.

My daily temple visits didn't find favour with my family for the sons were concerned that I could carry the infection back home, especially since I didn't like wearing a mask. I felt it to be a genuine concern, so distanced myself even more from Chhaya. An ACP on his regular rounds once stopped me near the temple demanding why I was not wearing a mask. 'Sir, I will die of wearing a mask before I die of corona!' I replied. He smiled and moved on, giving me up as a hopeless case, for I took the opportunity to present him with my poetry book. Ultimately, he became a good friend. My reasoning was that life had no allure for me, so better to die doing something worthwhile. I wasn't afraid of death but feared becoming bedridden, as I had no hope of anyone caring for me. The pandemic was providing an opportunity to leave the world in a quick, effortless manner.

Indeed, it is life that kills us, not death! Many saints gave up their lives in the service of humanity. I had once said to Sheila Dikshit, too: 'Death is certain, time of death is certain, place of death is certain and even the reason of death is certain!' After all, '*Dar ke aage jeet hai*' (victory ensues subsequent to conquering fear)! Some 95 per cent of our fears are unfounded, so why fear the infection floating around! I had also noticed that the poor in the slums were not following any of the norms set, neither of wearing masks or keeping distance, nor of washing hands, yet none of them were getting Covid. It just went to show that humans have an inbuilt immunity. Similarly, our body is capable of withstanding heat and cold, but we have weakened ourselves by exposure to comfort!

During the pandemic days, Narendra Modi encouraged citizens to light lamps, bang *thalis* or clap hands at a set time in an effort to bring in an element of unity. A foreign ambassador remarked sarcastically, 'It seems the Prime Minister of India is seeking Divine intervention to fight corona!'

I asked a very senior BJP leader what was happening

in the country. He said that Modi knew how to engage the public and had the power to attract, influence, inspire and impress the public, moulding them according to his desires. He added, 'Mahesh Sahab, when a politician becomes a leader of the masses, they follow him blindly. When such a leader even misrepresents the truth, they are ready to believe him. A leader of classes, on the other hand, even those of only a section, can't leave an impression even with the truth! That's the magic of Narendra Modi!'

'But he got only 37 per cent of the votes in 2019, and 63 per cent were against him!'

'But those sixty-three were not united. Unless there's unity among them, nothing can be gained.'

Another time, I asked Mani Shankar Aiyar, 'Bhaisahab, in a democracy, don't you think ten donkeys are better than nine horses? I think it's purely a numbers game!'

He agreed with me, adding, 'Even Winston Churchill commented that though Democracy is not flawless, it is still the best form of government.'

At the peak of the Covid wave, Chhaya had a bad toothache and couldn't stop crying. In those pandemic days, no dentist was available, so we we panicked, wondering what to do. The sons were not willing to take the risk of venturing out. She appealed to her MP brother, but he didn't help either. Finally, I called the MS of RML Hospital and he said that the head of the dental department would be available for us. That was the first time I wore a mask, as he insisted, and took Chhaya to the hospital where literally not even a bird could be seen on the premises. She was finally treated for her pain, but only after our third visit. Often people outside the family circle can prove to be a strong support system! Moreover, at the end of the day, a husband and wife have to support each other, for she too was there for me when I slipped in the bathroom at 2 am, a few months later. I was bleeding profusely, so, she called up our younger son, then both took me to the hospital. The next day, Col Vinay Mullick too said, that we could have woken him up and he would have taken us to the hospital. It's always good to maintain friendly relations with neighbours. A devotee had once asked Hazrat Mohammad how we would know if the Lord was happy with us. He had replied that if your neighbour was happy with you, understand that the Lord is happy with you!

In September, a joint secretary of the Home Ministry, called me up about an opportunity to visit Leh in Ladakh as part of a twenty-member delegation. It was to attend a programme in the first week of October, organised by them and co-sponsored by the RSS-VHP to worship the holy River Sindhu. Senior leaders were reluctant to go because of the pandemic, but I had no such reservations, so, I had a wonderful trip into the scenic mountains. I later travelled to Shirdi in November. There were hardly any devotees, making me feel that God becomes more benevolent towards those who take the initiative for a larger cause.

I would often wonder what karma was responsible for the strife surrounding me inside my home while those outside showered me with such unconditional love, affection and gratitude. I realised the import of the words I had prophetically composed decades ago:

> *Apne jo the wo humse bahut tang aa gaye*
> *Kya baat humme thi ki jo gairon ko bha gaye*
>
> (*Those who were my own with me were peeved*
> *Yet some facet in me to strangers appealed*)

My wife and sons were usually disruptive, interested only in the wealth and assets I had. Even my brothers had not only done me out of my rightful inheritance, but I heard later, they had even planned to take my life. Chhaya's brothers were equally acrimonious towards me. It made me consult astrologers who said that my horoscope indicated adverse situations, so I should accept it as my Destiny. I would wonder that if everything happened according to God's will, why would He want a husband, a father or a brother to be insulted. Islam and Christianity propagate that the Devil overpowers the Divine and allows negative impacts, but I didn't accept this theory, for how could the Devil become more powerful than the Divine? Finally, I got the actual answer from Osho, who quoted Krishna's words presented by Maharishi Vyas in the *Bhagavad Gita*, that it is not the Devil who makes you do wrong nor is it the Divine who pushes you to do good. God is just an energy, Omnipresent in Nature with its three aspects, *sattvic, rajasic* and *tamasic; sattvic* is spiritual, rajasic is connected to royalty and luxury, while tamasic is evil. These three traits are present in human beings and sometimes one or the other is predominant. We behave according to our dominant trait, becoming enlightened and saintly when our sattvic quotient is strong, rajasic when we seek luxury and comfort, while tamasic traits cause our aggressive faculties to come to the forefront. The best part is that though we are dominated by these traits, we also have the power to balance out these qualities, toning down the negatives to make the positives rise. I found Osho's explanation very scientific for even the atom has three components, electron, neutron and proton.

By now, I realised that we are living in an entirely illusory world, which our scriptures have described as Maya. So, I always emphasise, that we can't come out of this 'Maya' since it is the creation of God Almighty. And we the living beings, '*Jeev*' are part of God's created 'Maya.'

I would also often wonder about my status: was I married, unmarried or divorced? I finally decided that I was 33 per cent of all three! One of my poet friends, Talib Rampuri once commented that you seem to have given *Mehr* without even getting divorced. I added, 'That too when my father got us married without taking any dowry!'

Even as the pandemic raged on, I continued working on my bio-novel, and with Dr Kavita Sharma's cooperation formulated the second decade, sending the final draft to Mani Shankar Aiyar for his perusal. I would also send drafts of my story to a few other esteemed friends, among them, Arif Mohammad Khan, Prof K K Tiwari, H K Dua, Dr Kavita Sharma and Prof Anamika and each liked the way my story was unfolding. H K Dua called me to say that if Mani Shankar Aiyar was checking my work, I didn't need to send it to anyone else, for his knowledge of English and politics was much deeper than anyone else's. Mani Shankar Aiyar appreciated my story, remarking that it was a 'Wonderful recitation of your transition into adulthood!' He considered it to be a very frank and true rendition of my life's story, giving me immense happiness and a lot of encouragement, and of course boosting my enthusiasm to write further. I drafted my story chronologically, delineating, retracting, reworking on the manuscripts several times, while labouring on each and every word.

While Dr Kavita Sharma was helping me with my story, I too was helping her translate her book, *Queens of Mahabharata*. Her delineation about the history of controversial queens had attracted a lot of publicity, and her publisher had requested her to bring it out in Hindi as well. She had roped me in for frequent consultations and the book was brought out under the title, *Mahabharat ki Maharaniyan*.

In early August, Arif Mohammad Khan, Kerala Governor visited my home, along with his two sons. I had made arrangements at home for dinner for ten of my important guests and served dinner to his twenty security personnel as well in the parking area. I had also invited Venu Rajamony and his wife Saroj, Dr Kavita Sharma, and Subha Rajan. My younger son declined to come while Chhaya refused to cook, saying she was not well. I finally ordered meals for everyone from well-known food outlets. Fortunately, Karan and Malini were there to help me as the hosts. It was the first time in my life that a get together organised by me had not been so perfect, causing me regret. My sons would visit their mother occasionally, and their visits often instigated strife between us. Chhaya would also remind me that one of the clauses in our MOU had been that I would set up an office somewhere and so be out of the house for a few hours, regularly. I would retaliate that she seemed least bothered in upholding any of her clauses, while I still had fulfilled many. Despite giving such a huge amount to Chhaya, whom I considered as a 10 per cent wife, she would occasionally get into an argument with me on something trivial, then would lock herself in her room, forcing me to fend for myself for my brunch. She used to wake up before me and have an early breakfast and sometimes serve me the same breakfast on consecutive days. I made out a menu for all seven days and handed it over to her. As it is, I was having only two meals a day, brunch and dinner! My lawyer and ACP friend encouraged me to find a place, considering it to be good idea, also saying that I couldn't stop my children from visiting their mother. I finally rented a one-room apartment in south Delhi in October. Initially, I would leave the house when the children visited, but now, I remain in my own room, for I love the company of my lovely granddaughters and they seek me out, too. I often take them for an outing to the IIC along with my elder daughter-in-law and their maid, which we all relish enormously. Some of the IIC staff showed their appreciation, saying that out of the more than 10,000 members, I was the first they had seen hosting his grand-daughters so lovingly!

When we spend with a philanthropic bent of mind, the

universe compensates us in more ways than one! In March 2022, my very close relative called to wish me for Holi, and apologised for some of his lapses. But I refused to relent, saying that his breaking of my trust had hit me very hard. I told him I could never forgive him. I continued to say to him, 'Your brother once told me that the elders in your village felt worried about you that you were the least capable of all your brothers and yet you are the one who has reached great heights beyond imagination. You took it as a challenge and put in phenomenal efforts to rise so high! I am happy that I was able to sow the seeds of your political career, but now I don't want to have any interaction with you for you are no longer bothered about what means you use to attain your ends. You are selfish, using and misusing people for your own objectives! I have yet to see a more conniving man than you, one who has more colours than a rainbow!' He has never called me again.

My family had never supported or encouraged me in any way. Neither had they ever displayed any pleasure at my triumphs, monetary, literary, political or social. Even when I was felicitated by Sri Sri Ravi Shankar, Lakhan had said rather petulantly, 'Yet another attainment!'

Chapter 7

Stuck in the Status Quo

I HAD NOW begun to go on pilgrimages almost ten to twelve days every month. The rest of the time, I remained involved in my story, with Mani Shankar Aiyar often giving excellent remarks to some excerpts, endorsing and encouraging me to a great extent. Much to my delight, he called it an insider's story since I was portraying many political interactions with some of the top Indian political leaders, including Prime Ministers and Congress Presidents, frankly and truthfully. 'I don't add any angle to my narrative, else it wouldn't be an authentic representation,' I told him. I shared my friend, Krishna Bihari Noor's popular couplet with him:

Sach ghate ya badhe sach na rahe
Jhoot ki koi inteha hi nahi

(Truth remains not truth if lessened or added to
Untruths can have no limits.)

Even Prof Anamika admired me for my candour and narrative skills.

Mani Shankar Aiyar received a few copies of his autobiography on 9 August 2023, from his publisher and he gave me one of the first prints, asking me to write a review on it, which made me feel really honoured. He gave me the biggest compliment ever, writing in my copy, that he 'had ridden on my support for over two decades'. I was overwhelmed! Mani Shankar Aiyar's book, *Memoirs of a Maverick* was launched on 23 August at IIC. Prior to the launch, I had told him that 'that was the exact time of our Chandrayan's landing on the moon! It is a historical moment for our country!' That had put him in a quandary and I had assured him that my intuition was telling me that all would go very well. And that is exactly what happened. The auditorium was jam-packed on the day of the launch, despite the exciting event in the skies! When I reached the venue, there was no seat available and even some distinguished guests were being forced to stand at the back. I immediately garneted a few chairs from the IIC staff, setting up another row and seated them all.

Mani Shankar Aiyar also gave me a letter of recommendation for a popular publisher friend of his, referring to me as a personal and political colleague who had written his autobiography. I was delighted that he had elevated my Bio-novel to the position of Autobiography! Mani Shankar Aiyar has since published another part of his autobiography, *The Rajiv I Knew*, and a third is due, *A Maverick in Politics*, covering the period, 1991 to 2016. He suggested that I call my Autobiography, *A Life of Love Infinite*, instead of *Love Infinite*. He has been my political mentor and now I regard him as my literary Guru, and the fourth greatest man in my life after my beloved father, my poetry Guru Shankar Dutt 'Kumar Pashi' and beloved leader Rajiv Gandhi, all who added real value to my life in a big way.

Meanwhile, a series of unprecedented activities were happening in the country, questioning the very credibility of the government. Looking at the unfolding events, a senior journalist remarked, 'If Congress was evil, BJP has proved itself to be a greater evil while the Kejriwal factor has shown itself to be the greatest evil.' I agreed with him, for even Darwin's theory of evolution believes in concepts such as 'Survival of the fittest' and 'Struggle for existence.' Politics is *Rajneeti*, a word made by combining *Raj* (rule of law) with *neeti* (righteousness) but over the years, if anyone now wants to survive in the political field, they have to abandon dignity and integrity and resort to mainly money and muscle power. The law of the land has changed completely to one of underhand tactics for there is neither transparency nor accountability in the Government's machinery. Kejriwal had shamelessly called himself *kattar imandaar* (a 'thoroughly upright person') but the person next to him in command was in prison, as also his right- and left-hand men. They had been denied bail for months, and eventually, Kejriwal too was arrested.

In one of his appearances on electronic media, he had declared that he and his party members would be arrested as the Modi government was out to get them, but he had also assured senior workers of the Party that they would all get released as some court or the other would definitely grant them bail! And that is exactly what happened. In my fifty years of association with politics, I have never seen politicians like Modi and Kejriwal, for both made a mockery of the political system, distributing freebies in the form of free electricity and free grains. Kejriwal also got rid of many senior, erudite politicians from his party, giving credence to the words of Abraham Lincoln, 'The first-rate leader prefers first rate workers but a second-grade leader prefers a third-rate worker' as he was, perhaps, full of insecurities.

When Narendra Modi got the support of three hundred and three MPs in 2019, I recalled the old saying that 'Power corrupts and absolute power corrupts absolutely'. At least Rahul Gandhi doesn't resort to white lies and subterfuge, but unfortunately, he still has a long way to go before he can leave an impact on the masses. After the Congress party's ignominious defeat in 2019, our tally had gone down to about fifty MPs, forcing Sheila Dikshit to observe that the oldest party seemed to be at its lowest ebb ever! I commented that even BJP once had only two MPs so there was always a possibility of a comeback. 'You have a higher track record than even Modi for you have three consecutive tenures to your credit! There's nothing to worry about, we will rise again!' Indeed, at that point of time the party had become quite weak, so much so that even I once had to face the ire of a disgruntled BJP businessman, leading to a heated argument when he used foul worlds for our leaders. When a party weakens, its workers too lose strength!

BJP is at the helm once again and the country appears to be in the throes of a virtual democracy rather than in a real one, for the ruling Party is in control of all aspects, beginning with print and electronic media which has earned the epithet of 'Godi media.' It also has all the state agencies which have statutory powers under their thumb, such as the CBI, Income tax and ED. Even the Supreme Court sometimes seems greatly influenced by the Government of India. Justice A N Grover had once prophesied that the Supreme Court wouldn't be totally independent and this was in 1978, when I met him for the first time. Back in 1973, three judges of the Supreme Court, including himself, had been superseded in a controversial move by the then government. A retired IAS officer now said to me that back then, Indira Gandhi had declared Emergency, but now the country was in the space of an undeclared Emergency. It is a matter of fact that Narendra Modi has not even fulfilled any of his promises in his 2014 Manifesto, including the promise of creating two crore jobs every year, and presently, the country faces the highest rate of unemployment.

Modi is still giving free rations to some eighty crore people, courtesy Indira Gandhi's Green Revolution, even though the pandemic has long ended, looting the exchequer and turning the country into beggars in the process. Corruption seems to have been legalised since the gullible Labharthi beneficiaries openly promise to vote forever for the BJP!

The infrastructure of the country was laid under the regimes of Pandit Nehru, Indira Gandhi, Rajiv Gandhi and Narasimha Rao, and the present government is just reaping the benefits, while cursing the ones long gone. BJP seems to have forgotten that Pandit Nehru took over the leadership of the country in the most challenging circumstances, when it was emerging from centuries of bondage under the British and Mughals. Even in the Babri Masjid incident of 1986, it was Arun Nehru who got the doors unlocked. *Shilanyas* was done by Rajiv Gandhi while the Masjid itself was brought down during the time of Narasimha Rao, yet Modi has cleverly stolen the limelight by getting the Supreme Court judgement to build the temple and then went on to perform the actual consecration ceremony himself to establish the idols in February 2024.

The four Shankaracharyas, considered to be the supreme Sanatana authority in India were not in favour of inaugurating the temple as it was inauspicious to perform consecration of idols in an incomplete temple. The temple was still incomplete and a part of the temple complex was still being constructed. But Narendra Modi, had his eyes on the forthcoming General elections, and was, therefore in a tearing hurry to open the temple's precincts. BJP has been using and misusing the name of Lord Ram since 1987 to further their own ends. Religion shouldn't be an issue to be fought over. A political leader's endeavour should be to bring righteousness into politics rather than politicising religion!

I had met Omar Abdullah once while travelling by air and he was very friendly. Narendra Modi had revoked Article 370 on 6 August 2019 and made Jammu and Kashmir, a full-fledged state into a Union Territory, something that is unconstitutional in my eyes. This is like raising a child to be a man, and then reducing the man to a child again! When I asked Omar Abdullah why they had accepted this, he gave a melancholic response saying that they were helpless as a Supreme Court ruling had been given in favour of the Central Government. He too regarded the revoking of Article 370 to be a failure.

***

I wished to set up Lord Hanuman's statue at the Devi temple in Shirdi and the Chairman of the Trust happily agreed. It was to be installed on 29 November 2022, but just one day before, he sent his regrets for being unable to fulfill the commitment. I was highly disappointed. A friend assured me that if the statue had come, it would find its own niche, making me feel relieved. By an amazing turn of events, the idol finally got consecrated with complete rituals conducted by two pundits in my home temple, exactly three months later.

I had set up a Trust in the name of Sai and my late parents, the 'Sai Shanti Bhagwat Foundation' in April 2023, for philanthropic activities and for the setting up of an old age home with an orphanage and a section for destitute widows and the handicapped. In June, I called the first meeting of all trustees at IIC to discuss how to achieve the aims of the Trust. With the consent of all seven trustees, Col Anil Sachdeva was nominated as Vice-President, Dr Sanjiv Zutshi as general secretary, Manish Gupta as treasurer and I as President. I intended to plan the utilisation of the funds. I had also committed to plant a thousand trees in areas with less vegetation and requested each member to plant the same number each on behalf of the Foundation. We decided to meet every month. My family was not in favour of the Trust and threatened my nephew, Manish Gupta, our treasurer and accused him of coveting my money. I immediately told him to back out, for I didn't want him to run into trouble. Subsequently, I continued to set up idols in different temples, something which I had been doing since 1998. Dr Karan Singh had established a grand temple at Lodhi Road about fifty years ago, and I would often go there. Its priest requested me to contribute something there as well from my Trust. Looking around the temple, I noticed that there was a very small idol of Goddess Saraswati in a side room and decided to set up a larger one in the main area. I had been praying to her for about four decades since a sadhu had given me Her mantra

Aem Namo Bhagwati Vad Vagdevi Swaha

I called Dr Karan Singh for permission which he happily gave and even came with me at ninety-three years of age, to select a beautiful brass idol from the Tamil Nadu Emporium. It was consecrated ritualistically on 15 August 2023. I obtained his approval to set up the Navagraha idols along with the idol of the Sun in October, followed by Shiv Parvati. I had been worshipping Shiv-Parvati for the past fifty-five years! The auspicious idols came to my home from Jaipur on 20 January 2024 and were consecrated by Dr Karan Singh at the temple on 22 January, at exactly the same time that the idol of Ram was consecrated at Ayodhya! Dr Karan Singh called a week later, overwhelmed at the way the idols had been set up. He too had created a trust in the names of his parents, 'Hari Tara Trust' and said to me, 'I have known you for about forty years and never realised your depth! We even share the same reverence for our parents, creating trusts for them!'

'It's all the Divine grace of God, Babuji!' I said.

He told me that he had set up about 200 temples from Kashmir to Kerala through that Trust but never had anyone offered to do anything for them. God is truly happy with you. I name you *Rangeela Bhakt,*' Dr Karan Singh added with a smile.

Chapter 8

A Journey of Love Infinite

MY LIFE HAS been a journey of love infinite, encompassing the innumerable hues of love. Love gives birth to prayer! If we pray with intensity, we get closely connected to the Divine bringing spiritual miracles into one's life. My prayers have mostly been answered in some way or the other, the biggest example being my experiences with the Sun God. However cloudy it maybe, when I offer water to the Sun God with love, devotion and reverence, it will show a glimpse of itself through the clouds! This has happened hundreds of times in my thirty years of Sun worship. I had posed this question to Dr Karan Singh, saying, 'When I offer water to the Sun God, how do my vibrations cover the millions of miles in between and reach it? It usually bestows a glimpse to me, despite heavy clouds! And my earth family is unable to recognise my vibrations!'

'Mahesh, true vibes of love can even go beyond the Universe! It depends on the intensity of your feelings. Besides the Sun is a very powerful receiver while people here are not!' was his enlightening response.

Lord Shiva has also helped me experience miracles. I have been able to visit all his twelve Jyotirlingas all over India. I even visited Pashupatinath temple in Kathmandu in 1993 and holy Kailash Mansoravar in China. It was at Mount Kailash that I had a mystical experience of going into a trance. I felt I wasn't on Planet Earth, an ecstatic moment. I feel so connected to the Divine and I feel I can pour all my issues at His feet. I feel deeply connected to Lord Hanuman too and have worshipped him for the past twenty years and that's why he came into my home too! It has been my greatest fortune that I have set up the idols of all the five Divine Deities—Shiva, Sai, Surya, Saraswati and Sankatmochan (Hanuman) whom I revered the most.

In Sanatan Dharma, we either worship the *Nirakaar*, the formless or the *Sakaar*, where form is given in the shape of idols. Jagadguru Shri Kripaluji Maharaj explains it very simply that we are not just worshipping the idols, but are actually worshipping the Divine through the idols. It's difficult to connect to the formless form of God, for that's the path of meditation which everyone cannot follow. The idol form makes worshipping the Divine easier. Once Osho had pointed out some controversial characteristics of Avatars, and Jagadguru Kripalu Acharya had responded that when Gods incarnate on Earth, they do so for a purpose, that is incomprehensible to ordinary mortals.

I had learnt the Art of Living with Sri Sri Ravi Shankar, but during Covid, I was introduced to the Art of Dying! Osho says this is a necessary learning. Both Gurus emphasised the importance of love, service and surrender. Be ready to serve everyone with love and affection and surrender all our thoughts, words and deeds at the Divine's feet and ask Him for strength to follow His directives. A life well lived is a life spent in service, not just for the self.

J Krishnamurty states that people are not only fearful of dying, but also of living! They are filled with unfounded fears their whole life, and this stops them from living fully.

The time of the pandemic gave birth to many testing situations. The one endeavour that granted me some solace was this resolve to get my autobiography going. I owe my gratitude to Prof Anamika, whom I had met at a seminar through a well-known Hindi writer, Kamleshwar, back in 2000. She was the first to suggest that writing would grant me my desired equanimity. 'A poet among politicians is like the poet Edmund Spenser and Rahim, exposed to the many ironies of life and if he takes a vow not to budge from the truth, he can create a masterpiece', she had said. But it was Mani Shankar Aiyar's categorical encouragement that finally prodded me to initiate the project a few years later. From then on, I would spend hours formulating my story, sustained by a spiritual and emotional support proffered by many well-wishers including Uma, who would encourage me to focus on it rather than on her health. My writing had become a way of channelising my pent-up energy and emotions, for my post-depression years had boosted my vitality, when normally people lose it! When someone has been chosen for a Divine purpose, the universe itself conspires to get the ground ready for him.

Over the years, I lost many of my close women friends—one moved on to the next world, one to the United States, another to greener pastures, while Uma developed serious health issues. Consequently, I didn't have any close woman friend and often felt the lack of a feminine touch. I am a worshipper of Devi, and I would often appeal to my Ishta Devtas to either bless me with a compatible companion or to cleanse out the craving for one from my being! I am reminded of Pandit Jawaharlal Nehru's words in *Discovery of India*, written during his sojourn in jail: 'Except for the soft touch of a woman, I have everything I need!' It cannot be denied that ultimately it was my spirituality, my Divine Blessings and my creative work which became lifelines to keep me afloat. I would derive a deep feeling of gratification in service to others, finding intense satisfaction in feeding birds, animals and the needy. It gave me an opportunity to be of service to the poorest of the poor and bringing a spark of happiness into their lives became the central motivation of my life. I would also derive immense pleasure in watching birds gather around my home, including an occasional peahen for the seeds I would scatter for them to eat.

The celebration of my seventy years is a fitting culmination to this saga of my life! February has always been my special month with my birthday on the 16. I wanted to make it truly spiritual, so decided to visit Radha's birthplace, Barsana and then go onto Govardhan and Vrindavan from 6th to 9th February. I had started my spiritual journey from Barsana in 1997 and wanted to reconnect to those moments now. At Govardhan, while the priest was conducting a ritual to pray to Lord Hanuman, I noticed that he completed it in front of a pillar with a calendar picture of Lord Rama. I was surprised that there was no idol of Lord Rama in that temple. I immediately sought the management's permission to set it up and they happily agreed. I felt truly blessed that I was being given the opportunity to bring in the Lord's statue.

After my return from Vrindavan, I left for Shirdi on 14 February to celebrate my seventieth birth anniversary with my beloved Baba.

Once there, I sought permission from the CEO of Sai Sansthan to construct an old age home of 10,000 to 15,000 square feet for orphans, handicapped and destitute women. The Sansthan will provide the land and I will construct the facility which they will run. Over the past few years, I have made it a point to be out of the city during any celebratory event, festivals or birthdays, preferring to spend it with strangers, a few who thereafter become my lifelong friends. At Shirdi, on my birthday, I lighted seventy oil lamps in the temple precincts while my beloved friends, Madeena Mir and her husband, Riyaz Mir, who were miles away in Kashmir, gave me the most magnificent present of my life! They arranged a surprise celebration at the hotel in collaboration with the

A divine moment at the Shirdi Saibaba Samajik Mandir, 2022.

Presenting English and French translated book to Sri Sri Ravishankar at his Bengaluru Ashram on 18 September, 2018.

Meeting Dr Karan Singh on his 92nd Birthday at his residence on 9 March, 2023, Mansarovar, New Delhi.

Presenting poetry book and later addressing the gathering.

At Kailash Mansarovar, June 2017.

Meditating in front of the Kedarnath Temple.

Enjoying the serene view.

Holy Badrinath Temple, June 2019.

Praying at the Sindhu River, 2020.

Standing in front of the Somnath Temple.

14 January, 1980, at the first National Mushaira, 'Zindagi' at Gwalior.

Standing in front of the Indian Flag near Sindhu River.

My elder son presenting flowers to Mani Shankar Aiyar on his first visit to our house in 1992.

Author felicitating the wife of Union Minister Mani Shankar Aiyar.

The author felicitating the Union Minister for Petroleum and Natural Gas at his home, in the benign presence of senior leader V C Shukla and Dr B N Singh.

The author with his mentor, Mani Shankar Aiyar.

Author at his home introducing guests Mrs Suneet Aiyar, Dr Namwar Singh, Kamleshwar, and other distinguished guests to his first political mentor, V C Shukla.

The Times of India's coverage of the wedding of the author's son on 8 December 2011.

The poet with President Shankar Dayal Sharma.

From the left: The author, J P Aggarwal, Prof K K Tiwari, Sundar Marathi Naval Prabhakar, my younger son, and Sheila Dikshit, former Chief Minister of Delhi.

Author with Sheila Dikshit.

Author felicitating Sheila Dikshit as the Chief Minister of Delhi.

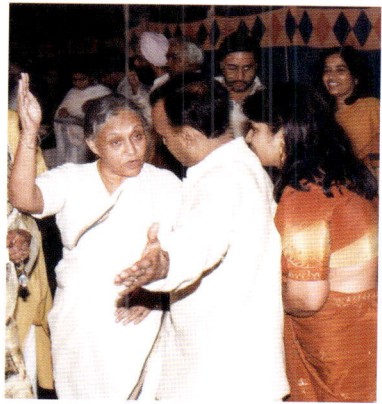
The author with CM Sheila Dikshit and his wife.

Author with Mrs Jennifer Tytler at his son's birthday at his residence in Nizamuddin.

Pawan Khera, Chairman, Media and Publicity, standing behind Sheila Dikshit.

Author with two of his very good friends.

Author with two of his good friends at a function hosted by the author at his home.

Author presenting the signed copy of his poetry book to Uma Vasudev and Aruna Vasudev in 2002.

Author's friends.

Author interacting with his friends.

Author with his good lady friend.

Author with Dr Kavita Sharma, Principal of Hindu College, Prof Harish Naval, Hindu college.

Author with his friend.

Author with the late senior Congress leader, Dr Arjun Singh, at the Congress Plenary Session in Tirupati, 1992.

Author with his colleague.

Author with his lady friend.

Author's wife greeting his lady friend.

Author's wife interacting with his friends.

Author presenting his poetry book to Laura, who came from Germany to learn Hindi and Urdu.

Author with his friends from the French Embassy at his son's birthday.

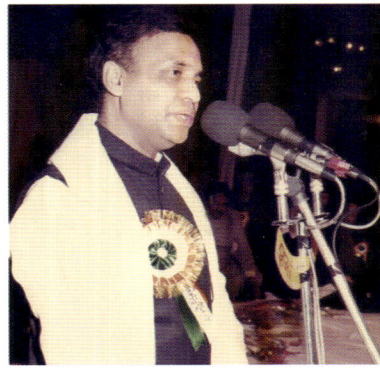

Author reciting his ghazal at the prestigious Mushaira on the eve of Republic Day at Lal Quila in 1999.

Author's good lady friend.

Author at the age of 12, at the post-wedding ceremony of his sister.

Author with his poetry guru, Shankar Dutt Kumar Pashi.

Poet with the dancer & the singer before the launch.

Padma Bhushan Uma Sharma Dancing on my Ghazals on 21 July 1985 at FICCI Auditorium.

Poet presenting his poetry to his school Principal. Dr Gulshan Kanwal after the launch.

Poet presenting his poetry to Karuna Goenka.

Author presenting a poetic tribute to the late Rajiv Gandhi by reciting a ghazal dedicated to his memory at the All India Kavi Sammelan and Mushaira, organised by the All India Congress Committee on Rajiv Gandhi's first birth anniversary after his martyrdom (21 May 1991), on 28 August 1991.

Author presenting flowers to Mrs Suneet Aiyar, with Mohd. Arif Khan seated on the sofa behind her.

On 7 August 2018, the author hosted a housewarming party, with his mentor Mani Shankar Aiyar and his wife as the chief guests. The invitees included Arif Mohd. Khan, Shri Prakash Jaiswal, H K Dua, and Subhash Kashyap.

Mani Shankar Aiyar having dinner with his wife at the author's house on his son's birthday.

Author having a conversation with Mani Shankar Aiyar.

Author with senior Congress leader V C Shukla and Dr B N Singh.

Author ushering in Dr Manmohan Singh at the prayer meeting.

Author paying tribute to Dr Bhishma Narain Singh on 18 August 2018 at IIC.

Condolence meeting at IIC.

Congress President Sitaram Kesri having lunch at the author's home on 28 February 1998.

The author with the former President of India Mr R Venkatraman at a political function, October 1996.

The author being conferred with an award by the Union Cabinet Minister of Law Sh Hans Raj Bharadwaj in New Delhi on 23 November 1992.

Author with Former Prime Minister P V Narasimha Rao and Mani Shankar Aiyar in May 1995.

Author with Former Prime Minister of India, Inder Kumar Gujral.

Author with Union Cabinet Minister, Pranab Mukherjee.

The author is lighting the lamp to inaugurate the 7th International Achievers Summit-2015 on 'Generation Global Partnerships' at Bangkok, Thailand with the Hon. Deputy Prime Minister of Thailand.

Author speaking at an international seminar in Bangkok.

A lady felicitating the author at a national seminar in New Delhi.

Author lighting the lamp at the National Congress in the presence of Dr Iqbal Singh, Shivraj Patil, Major Ved Prakash, and Chief Justice of J&K High Court, Justice Khan.

The author being felicitated with a shawl & Shield-Mohabbat Award by Sh K Satyanarayan Raju (Former Union Cabinet Minister) in New Delhi, on January 1, 2007.

The author sharing the stage with his mentor, Mani Shankar Aiyar, and other dignitaries.

Author's wife felicitating the Union Coal Minister, Shri Prakash Jaiswal.

The author lighting the lamp.

Standing at the extreme right is the author with his two elder brothers, Bhabhi, and sister, with his father and Jeejaji on the left.

Author's eldest sister.

Author's elder Jija ji

Author with his four granddaughters.

Author with his wife (left) and elder sister (right).

The author felicitating former Chief Justice of India, R N Mishra.

Congress President Sonia Gandhi's newly nominated Political Secretariat, Ahmed Patel felicitated by the author at his home in June 2003.

Wife Smt Gauri Aggarwal felicitated the author at the launch ceremony of Hindi & Urdu edition of *Manzar Dar Manzar* in New Delhi on 20 Jan 2002.

The author with Hon'ble Prime Minister of India Sh Rajiv Gandhi & Dr Balram Jakhar (Speaker Lok Sabha) at a political function at PM House on 10 May 1989.

The author with the Hon'ble former President of India, Shankar Dayal Sharma, and former Union Cabinet Minister, Mohsina Kidwai.

Author organised a national function at FICCI Auditorium, New Delhi, on July 21, 1985.

The author among senior leaders of Congress at a demonstration against the BJP government in 1994.

Letters of appreciation for the poet and his poetry from senior leaders.

Sheila Dikshit

I have known Mahesh ji for more than twenty years now, so am well-acquainted with his cultured mannerisms, without which his endearing persona would be incomplete! He presented me with "The Essence of my spirit" the English translation of his much admired Hindi-Urdu composition, "Manzar Dar Manzar", which he had unveiled to the world in 2002. Then, I had the opportunity to bless the release, enthralling the literary world with his profound insights of romanticism and philosophy.

This time around, I was pleasantly surprised with his courage in challenging the stalwarts of the literary world by putting his renowned work into the hands of, Ms. Meenu Minocha. Mahesh ji's acumen has definitely paid off and the resultant effort has been well received! I'm delighted at the popularity of his work and i wish him well in all his future endeavors!

Sheila Dikshit

DR. GVG. KRISHNAMURTY
(DOCTOR OF LAWS, JHANSI & LONDON, HON CAUSA)
FORMER ELECTION COMMISSION OF INDIA

1402, MALAYAGIRI, KAUSHAMBI
OPP. DELHI ANANDVIHAR, ISBT,
GHAZIABAD, U.P.201010 MOB. 9810130711
TELS: 0120-2773056 & 4117026

15.9.2015

ALL OVER THE WORLD, IN EVERY CIVILISATION, THINKERS, WRITERS, AUTHORS AND POETS CONTINUE TO OCCUPY A HIGLY HONOURED PLACE. BEING IGNITERS OF IDEAS AND DISSEMINATORS OF VALUES. WRITING POETRY, PARTICULARLY IN STIRRING UP EMOTIONS IS DIFFICULT AND SOMETIMES IS A CHALLENGE TO CURRENT CONCEPTS AND BELIEFS. IN OUR COUNTRY FROM VALMIKI TO GHALIB IT IS A PERENNIAL RIVER OF NEW FOMULATIONS OF THOUGHTS ELEVATING HUMAN MINDS TO GREATER ECHEOLONS OF MULTIPLE PLEASURES FROM GENERATION TO GENERTION.

SHRI MAHESH MANZAR IS A WELL KNOWN POET IN URDU AND HINDI IN MODERN INDIA WITH SPECIALISATION IN GHAZALS AND NAZMS. TRANSLATIONS INTO OTHER LANGUAGES IS ALWAYS MORE DIFFICULT PARTICULARLY IN POETRY. PROJECTING THE EMOTIONS AND INTENTS OF THE POET.

IT IS REFRESHING TO NOTE THAT A REVISED NEW EDITION OF HIS BOOK " MANZAR DAR MANZAR, THE ESSENCE OF MY SPIRIT " IS COMING OUT, CONTAINING ENGLISH TRANSLATION OF HIS MULTI-DEXTROUS INNOVATING POETRY IN URDU AND HINDI.

TO CITE A PIECE - EVERY MOMENT OF LIFE GIVES A DEEP COUNSEL, ALL I NEED IS TO MAKE EACH INSTANT SEGATIOUS " MAKES YOU THINK, THINK AND THINK. I AM HAPPY TO HEARTILY COMPLIMENT THE POET SHRI MAHESH MANZAR FOR BRINGING OUT A NEW EDITION OF HIS INSPIRING POETRY TO THE DELIGHT OF READERS WITH ALL BEST WISHES

(DR. GVG. KRISHNAMURTY)

SHRI MAHESH MANZAR
D-13, NIZAMUDDIN WEST
NEW DELHI

B-2, Nizamuddin East, New Delhi-110013, India
Tel. : 011-24356941, Mobile : 9971283487

ARIF MOHAMMED KHAN
GOVERNOR OF KERALA

RAJ BHAVAN
THIRUVANANTHAPURAM-695 099

20 March 2020

I have great pleasure to pen the following lines for the English translation of the poetry of Mr. Mahesh Manzar, titled "MANZAR DAR MANZAR" in English the book is named as "The essence of my spirit".

I have known Sri Mahesh Manzar for last more than two decades. Basically, his poetry is a celebration of love and romance. But he also has the sensitivity to feel the pain of every injured soul and the rare ability to express this pain in the most empathetic words. Another distinction of Mr. Mahesh Manzar is that he can be rated as an accomplished AHLE ZUBAN, the real Urdowala, despite the fact that he had no formal education in Urdu.

It is by its art and literature that a society is judged at the bar of history. They are the reflection of the vitality of a race. They decline when people suffer from spiritual exhaustion. It is generally said that art is an expression of a higher order which supersedes the natural activities of man. If happiness is like the bloom on the cheeks of youth, if grace is the perfection of nature, poetry manifests the deeper impulses residing in the hearts of men.

These manifestations appear only when man has the courage to be lonely in his mind, and free in his thought. We can only imagine what Mr Manzar must have gone through while giving birth to his soulful poetry which can stimulate and inspire many people.

An Italian proverb says that the translators are traitors, but Ms. Meenu Minocha has done the translation with such finesse that the truth of the proverb becomes questionable.

With very best wishes for Mahesh Manzar Sahab and the translator of this English edition, Ms. Meenu Minocha.

[Arif Mohammed Khan]

Mahesh Manzar's Manzar Dar Manzar

Dr. Subhash C. Kashyap
62, Sainik Farms,
New Delhi - 110060

I am hardly competent to comment on the poetic effulience of Janab Manzar's work. But I have been an ardent lover of Urdu poetry. Manzar is a very accomplished poet. As a student of philosophy, I am particularly impressed by the metaphysical and spiritual content of his poems. Some of these remind me of Allama Iqbal's Asrar-e-Khudi and of Jalaluddin Rumi's and Al Gazzali's Sufi Falsifa.

As a language, Urdu is a very powerful medium of expression. It was born and nurtured in India It is ours and occupies a very eminent place in our thought, literature and culture. Authors like Mahesh Manzar render yeomen service to our ethos and emotional quotient through their pen.

First, Manzar's works were published - printed and reprinted - in Urdu and Hindi. Later, Minocha did a remarkable job and rendered a singular service by very faithfully and with exceptional competence translating Manzar into English and making him available internationally.

Thousands of years earlier, at the very dawn of human thought, civilisation and culture, our forefathers asked the question, 'Who am I, Where did I come from, Why am I here, What is the aim of life?' Manzar is asking the same eternal philosophical question when he queries "Kaun hun main Kahan se aya" (Who am I and what my antecedents?).

As for Manzar's philosophy of life, his social thought and humanism, I cannot resist quoting him when he says :

Where everyone is of value for the other
Such a class is what we need to foster.

Subhash C. Kashyap

21 September, 2015.